Borders and Border Regions in Europe and North America

Borders and Border Regions in Europe and North America

EDITED BY

paul ganster
alan sweedler
james scott
wolf dieter-eberwein

institute for regional
irsc
studies of the californias

S D S U
DO NOT ENTER
PRESS

1997

Table of Contents

IV. Transboundary Cooperation Issues in North and Central America / 235

List of Maps

Preface

In June of 1994, a group of scholars from Europe and North and Central America congregated in Berlin in order to attend a three-day conference on issues related to international border regions and transboundary cooperation. The conference, titled "Borders and Border Regions: New Roles in a Changing Global Context," was organized jointly by the Institute for International Security and Conflict Resolution and the Institute for Regional Studies of the Californias (both at San Diego State University); the Institute of Regional Development and Structural Planning (IRS) in Erkner (by Berlin), Germany; the Science Center for Social Research (WZB) in Berlin; and the Institut des Études Politiques (IEP) in Paris. Economists, political scientists, historians, geographers, conflict resolution experts, and sociologists, among others, were in attendance.

The purpose of this scientific encounter was to encourage a genuine internationalization of research on transboundary cooperation. In order to do this, it was felt that discussion should be kept as broad as possible, allowing for a treatment of economic, cultural, political, environmental, and security components of transboundary regionalism. As is evident from the international literature, a bewildering array of concepts are being circulated and popularized in an attempt to give meaning to a post-Cold War world. We are offered attractive and exciting new concepts of political geography, such as *regions states* and *local foreign diplomacy* while the environmental imperative, the paradigm of *bioregionalism*, is forming the basis of local attempts at transboundary problem solving.

We have attempted here to put these new (and/or seemingly new) concepts into a clearer perspective with regard to international border regions and transboundary cooperation. The essays included in this book have been elaborated and expanded upon since the June 1994 venue. The topics addressed, the manner in which border related issues have been examined, and even the basic tenors of the individual contributions are varied, making for a multifaceted approach to the study of transboundary cooperation issues. This is indicative of the fact that the study of transboundary cooperation dynamics requires both focused interdisciplinary coordination and careful generalization. Thus, this book attempts to address a research deficit—the fact that much local-level and microregional study of transboundary cooperation within international border regions has been overly reductionist and has generally not considered the more global economic and political contexts of interstate interaction nor invited analytical reflection of the complexity of the factors that condition transboundary relationships. This is, indeed, unfortunate as such patient and cautious reflection, informed by cross-cultural knowledge, provides the only basis for bridging theory, research, and day-to-day practice.

Despite the thematic and geographical diversity of this book, the essays contained herein are united by a comparative approach that emphasizes change in the functional roles of actual political boundaries and the dynamics of transboundary interaction as characterized by a constant tension between factors promoting cooperation and those engendering or nurturing conflict. We thus hope that this book will encourage continuing comparative study of border regions and the development of transboundary regionalism—in part by reaching as wide a readership as possible. To this end, the Institute of Regional Development and Structural Planning in Germany has published an edition of this book with chapter abstracts in German for European distribution.

Finally, the cooperating institutes and scholars involved here have decided to publish this volume not only for purposes of basic research but also for practical reasons. The experiment of Polish-German Euroregions—an attempt at new forms of bilateral cooperation that transcends the boundaries of the European Union and the great cultural, political, and economic differences between both countries—is unfolding at an ever-intensifying pace. The same directions of development are clearly present in the U.S.-Mexican and other international border regions. Researchers and practitioners with a vital interest in promoting and supporting this cooperation in any border region would do well to analyze and to try to learn from the experiences of other international border regions.

The Editors

Acknowledgments

A number of individuals deserve special recognition for their assistance with the development and production of this volume. Bertha Hernández, of the Institute for Regional Studies of the Californias at San Diego State University, carried out the copy editing of the manuscript. Ulla Sweedler provided aid with the copy editing, especially the European bibliographic materials. Lori Palmer, of the Graphics Department at San Diego State University, revised and produced the final versions of the illustrations. Harry Polkinhorn, Editor of the San Diego State University Press, read the entire manuscript and made many helpful suggestions. Guillermo Nericcio, of the Department of English and Comparative Literature at San Diego State University and Memographics, and Lorenzo Antonio Nericcio, of Memographics, designed the cover. Finally, the publication of this volume was made possible through a generous grant from the Fred J. Hansen Institute for World Peace and support from the William and Flora Hewlett Foundation.

I
Introduction

Dynamics of Transboundary Interaction in Comparative Perspective

James Scott
Alan Sweedler
Paul Ganster
Wolf-Dieter Eberwein

1. Introduction

This volume is a collection of essays on issues affecting the political, economic, social, and cultural significance of international borders. It is an undertaking that is particularly timely due to global events that are rapidly changing our understanding of international relations. The contributors to this book share basic research and practical interests in broadening discussion of border region related problems and deepening understanding of the multifarious—and often contradictory—processes that condition human interaction across national borders.

Such collaborative attempts—exceedingly rare up to now—are not only necessary from a research standpoint but also from a practical, problem-solving perspective. Although borderlands research has intensified in recent years, it has, to an extent, remained parochial, concentrating on a small number of geographical regions of the European and North American continents and devoting little attention to developments elsewhere. While it is understandable that U.S. and Mexican scholars focus primarily on problems along their mutual border and that European borderlands experts deal almost exclusively with transboundary cooperation in specific regions of Europe, it is surprising that only a handful of comparative border-region studies have been carried out (e.g., Martínez 1986; ARL 1992). This dearth of comparative analysis is particularly unfortunate in view of the important practical role borderlands research could play in the development of transboundary cooperation.

This essay begins at the macro level, where borders and border regions are discussed in terms of their changing economic, political, security, and cultural roles within an increasingly global society. From there, the focus shifts to a more detailed discussion of the functional roles of borders and transboundary cooperation. These first two sections set the stage for a set of essays on transboundary cooperation issues and attempts at local and regional cooperation in Western and Eastern Europe, North and Central America, and Scandinavia.

With reference to specific regional situations, the essays provide insights into the following aspects of transboundary interaction: (1) the determinants of transboundary conflict and cooperation in different political, economic, and social settings; (2) the effects of new geoeconomic blocs, in particular NAFTA and the EU, on border-related issues; (3) changes in national security concerns and their effects on interstate and interregional cooperation; and (4) the evolution of local transboundary action and the role of formal and informal networks in solving local problems.

Consequently, a major objective of this collaborative effort is to establish a framework for future interdisciplinary and international research on borders, border regions, and transboundary cooperation. Despite the great differences among border regions—differences that manifest themselves in the history, politics, and culture as well as socio-economic, geographic, and demographic characteristics of individual border areas—the contributors believe there also exist basic similarities that allow comparative analysis both from a theoretical and practical point of view. For this reason, specific topics and case studies have been chosen that exemplify cooperation and conflict and provide certain common denominators for future comparative study.

2. Borders and Border Regions in a Globalizing Society: Some General Considerations

Until relatively recently, international diplomacy was an exclusive and jealously guarded function of the nation-state. Issues dealing with (among other things) military and political security, the demarcation and protection of international borders, extradition treaties, the protection of citizens in foreign countries, as well as important macroeconomic questions, have been, and still are, the prerogatives of national governments. In these days of rapid economic and political change on a global scale, however, subnational actors, such as states, provinces, regions, and cities, are playing an increasingly vital role in international relations—a trend that shows every indication of continuing and, indeed, accelerating. Simultaneously, border regions permeate the sovereignty of the nation-state as they respond to the exigencies of transboundary problem-solving—largely through informal cooperation and tacit agreements among local authorities. Understandably, much discussion has taken place about the increasing importance of subnational diplomacy and border regions in the international system.

Paraphrasing the observations of Keohane and Nye, Ivo Duchacek (1990: 2) has reminded us that

> today, in contrast to previous eras of international relations, trade, investment, technology and energy transfers, environmental and social issues, cultural exchanges, migratory and commuting labor, and transfrontier drug trafficking and epidemics have forced their way on to the foreign policy agenda, usually below, but sometimes parallel with, the great issues of national security, military balance and diplomatic status. This expansion of the field of foreign policy into nonmilitary and non-diplomatic areas ... has now become a characteristic feature of global and regional interdependence.

The internationalization of domestic affairs is perhaps the most immediately perceptible effect of globalization. It has affected traditional hierarchical relations between centers of power and the local level and modified perceptions of the concept of territorial sovereignty. Globalization is a phenomenon that also manifests itself in increasing transnational investment flows and the rapid development of international communications networks. Consequently, as the pressure of international economic competition has increased on states, regions, local communities, and other subnational governments, subnational initiatives aimed at attracting foreign investment have also multiplied rapidly. Globalization is intrusive. Whether we desire to accept it or not, international events are increasingly affecting local communities and influencing many aspects of everyday life. At the same time, local events have a significant impact upon global developments. This element is significant in that it implies a process of decentralization and fragmentation of political structures and policy-making. The state, once guarantor of sovereignty, cultural identity, social stability, and national economic interests, has seen its authority undercut by international processes beyond its control.

Due to their greater flexibility and capacity to react rapidly to new economic circumstances, considerable importance is being attached to regions and cities as innovators and catalysts of economic development. Similarly, one could conclude that globalization is creating conditions under which international border regions will be able to transcend the limitations placed upon them by national boundaries. Border regions, once perceived as political and economic peripheries in a hierarchical world of nation-states, might thus be developing into zones of potential international cooperation and synergy. The process of integration within the European Union (EU) involves not only the development of a unitary market but, more importantly, the pooling of national sovereignty and the diffusion of security concerns. This, along with the creation of new economic blocs such as the North American Free Trade Area (as established by NAFTA) and the South American Common Market (MERCOSUR), denotes a shift of power from national to supranational institutions. Within these larger zones of cooperation, the stage could be set for more comprehensive coordination and, ultimately, integration of national policies.

These optimistic scenarios, however, are only part of the global picture. The dramatic events that have seen the collapse of the Soviet Union, the reunification of Germany, Sino-Russian reconciliation, and a rapid decline in defense spending by the major powers, have signaled the end of the confrontational but stable geopolitical order of the postwar world. At the present moment, with so much change occurring in the international system, no new, clearly definable world order seems to have materialized. Deterritorializing events, such as the deconstruction of nation-state authority and geopolitical certainties, coincide with the reterritorialization of regional and ethnic identities and ideologically informed attempts to imbue geopolitical and geoeconomic realities with new meaning (Ò Tuathail and Luke 1994: 382–83). One unhappy consequence of this has been the resurgence of nationalism and violent ethnic conflict, particularly in countries of the former Soviet bloc. Deterritorialization has also robbed many of a sense of national destiny and pride, often provoking a reterritorialization that results in protectionist and even chauvinistic responses. Thus, in some parts of the world, borders have lost much of their relevance as delimitations of territorial power, whereas in others, there is a move back to territorial politics, nationalism, and violent contest between nations.

Even in North America and Western Europe, ambiguities remain with regard to shifts in national-security policy that could counteract positive effects of the opening of borders. National military security has, indeed, retreated into the background. This has allowed a greater degree of interstate trust and a refocusing of security concerns on truly global problems, such as the environment and management of the seas. At the same time, with the opening of borders and the lack of direct military threat, immigration, minority-rights issues, and the possible repercussions of regional conflicts on nation-states could provide incentives to act restrictively on individual freedoms—and, in some specific cases, to intensify border controls.

These considerations indicate that in this emerging global society, conflict and cooperation will coexist much as they have in the past. While it is self-evident that many of the trends associated with globalization are contradictory and difficult to categorize, those with an interest in the economic, political, and cultural dynamics of border regions must nevertheless ask themselves what consequences these contradictory processes might have for transboundary cooperation and border areas in general.[1]

Subnational Foreign Policy

The point of departure for this comparative study of border regions is the transformation of a world order based on nation-states and competing military blocs. With the deemphasis of security as a strategic component of international relations, it appears that regions are emerging from the paternalistic control of the state, defining their own policy interests and, more and more, engaging in their own form of foreign policy by establishing transboundary problem-solving dialogues. Thus, Björn Hettne (1994) has expressed the notion that an organic, self-defining regionalism is slowly superseding the imposed and statist regionalism defined by national-security interests. This new regionalism is seen to be a logical development in a world gravitating toward a decentralized and multipolar order.

In his essay in on interregional cooperation in this book, Pertti Joenniemi offers a provocative reading of the evolving new regionalism, arguing that it, unlike nationally or ethnically defined policies, promotes an international-relations outlook that allows unity, tolerance, and diversity. The political promise held out by self-defined and spontaneous regionalism is particularly relevant to the future role of border regions and transboundary cooperation in Europe, North America, and elsewhere. Indeed, outwardly oriented and inclusionary border regions (as opposed to defensive and exclusionary ones) could play a major role in easing ethnic tensions and establishing lasting forms of peaceful cooperation between nations. With the gradual decline of nation-states as insular and defensive entities, the exclusionary role of borders has diminished as well. Subnational paradiplomacy, the generally informal avenues through which regions articulate and promote their interests internationally, has thus begun to take root in transboundary situations (Duchacek 1986). This allows border regions not only to establish an international local-government dialogue but also to promote transboundary problem-solving mechanisms that serve basic regional needs. Furthermore, as Hall and Castells (1994) observe, regions and other subnational units have begun to assume not only a policy-making but also a vital economic function, both nationally and internationally.

Possible Economic Futures for Border Regions

In the past, border regions have been generally classified as inherently peripheral and backward areas within nation-states. Economically speaking, this idea has been supported by classical theories of economic geography, which accept the nation-state as the most important reference unit of market space. Lösch (1940) maintained that political boundaries create high transboundary transaction costs. As boundaries delimit the jurisdictions of nation-states in competition with one another, these additional costs are due, in great measure, to trade barriers, disjointed and nationally-oriented infrastructures, and different value systems. Christaller's (1932) influential model of the development of settlements as market areas cemented, in the minds of planners and practitioners alike, the notion that border regions were characterized by stunted central places with truncated economic spheres of influence.

Niles Hansen (1981: 21–34), among others, has challenged this view, demonstrating that, at least in the case of North America and Europe, many border regions are among the most dynamic and prosperous of any within their respective nations. Similarly, the globalization paradigm suggests that the internationalization of economic and, to a certain extent, political life, will eliminate the very barriers Lösch and Christaller referred to. In place of prohibitive transboundary transaction costs, border regions will offer complementarities not available elsewhere. Viewed in this light, border regions can be best understood as areas of synergistic collaboration within the context of increasing international competition.

In the global economy, national industrial policies are more and more difficult to formulate and execute in the face of international financial markets and decisions taken by globally minded firms to transfer productive activities to low-cost countries. As structural unemployment intensifies (partly as a result of new geographic divisions of labor), the capacity of national labor policies to protect domestic jobs diminishes commensurately. In his contribution to this book, Norris Clement enumerates several policy implications of a possible paradigm shift as nationally oriented economic thought gives way to more globally minded concepts. Clement argues that border regions are best understood as areas of mutually beneficial collaboration within the framework of increasing international competition. Indeed, within the global economic environment, regions seem to be displacing the nation-state as the primary actor in the economic arena. As competition between regions on a global scale intensifies, border regions will be forced to emphasize transboundary cooperation and complementary as comparative advantages in their attempts to maintain or enhance economic viability.

The Paradox of State Power

At a more theoretical level, an international-relations continuum might be conceptualized, based on economic interdependence and locally driven regionalism where the development from conflict to cooperation characterizes a maturation process of transboundary interaction. Research conducted in transnational settings, such as the U.S.-Mexican borderlands, suggests that, over time, transboundary relations evolve from initial periods of alienation and hostility to situations of more or less peaceful coexistence. Then, as transboundary interaction intensifies, these relations transform into interdependence and finally to a stage of transboundary integration where the border basically ceases to be a dividing line in the classical sense (Martínez 1992). Consequently, it is argued here that, as interaction becomes more intense, border regions become bridges between nations and help eliminate both physical and psychological barriers to wider bilateral or multilateral international cooperation.[2]

While locally driven transboundary and interregional cooperation can help nations link up, the supporting role of central governments in facilitating such cooperation should not be underestimated. This, at the same time, represents a basic contradiction: nation-states have, as yet, not been able to devise administrative and legal mechanisms for dealing with subnational foreign policy. Oftentimes, central governments seek to minimize or otherwise hinder such activities, despite arguments that global ecological sustainability and international competitiveness are less and less determined at the level of the nation-state. Many observers have even pondered the demise of nation-states as relevant actors in international relations, focusing on the inflexibility of national governments and their limited ability to react rapidly to changing global economic environments (Bell 1977; Latouche 1990).

Such predictions of nation-state irrelevance are, without doubt, gross exaggerations of reality. Most sovereign states, regional disharmonies notwithstanding, seem quite robust and stable indeed. In Malcolm Anderson's sobering estimation, even the basic and ever increasing necessity to cooperate across borders will not necessarily further the cause of transboundary regionalism within the European Union because this would at some point require "special jurisdictions or even an interpenetration of jurisdiction on a scale not seen in Europe since the abolition of feudal rights" (Anderson 1982: 11). Furthermore, one cannot overlook the fact that citizens often expect direct action from governments in satisfying their individual demands. As global economic competition increases, local and regional interests will demand from their respective national governments redoubled efforts in representing and supporting their interests internationally.

Didier Bigo discusses the evolution of the defensive role of borders and border regions within the context of globalization. He agrees as well that globalization is undermining the capacity of nation-states to maintain discrete political, cultural, and economic space within clearly defined administrative boundaries. Bigo points out, however, that the globalization process is being partially counteracted by the creation of larger supranational zones of cooperation and new forms of territorial control. As borders lose their function to prevent "undesirable" population flows, drug trafficking, crime, terrorism, and other dangers perceived as emanating from foreign countries, internal controls increase, often singling out ethnic minorities.

The control function of the nation-state thus abandons the border, its geographical home, and turns to groups that popular opinion might consider as constituting a risk. Such policies of internal checkpoints could have severe implications for race relations in the multiethnic societies of North America and Europe, perhaps neutralizing many of the positive effects of the opening of physical borders. Therefore, in extending this argument, Bigo suggests that potential economic benefits of free trade could be offset by the national and international tensions created by attempts to control population flows.

The apparent contradiction between intensifying subnational paradiplomacy and the persistence of national authority—a paradox of state power—is central to the issue of transboundary cooperation. No viable alternatives to the nation-state as an organizer of political, social, and economic life exist. What is required, then, is a reconciliation of national-sovereignty concerns and national-policy prerogatives with the desire and need of subnational governments to conduct their own brand of foreign policy. For this reason, utilitarian concepts, based on arguments of administrative efficiency, environmental protection, and the promotion of citizens' welfare have frequently been employed to legitimize attempts to institutionalize transboundary cooperation (Anderson 1982; Herzog 1990; Stoddard 1984).

These arguments for subnational foreign policy are attractive precisely because they are—at least from a policy standpoint—rational and emphasize the mutual benefits of transboundary cooperation. Thus, in supporting interregional interaction, the nation-state can realize tangible economic benefits and important regional development goals without compromising national sovereignty. As James Scott explains, these are precisely the arguments that have been used to promote the Dutch-German EUREGIO, a transboundary association touted as a model of subnational paradiplomacy in Europe. Furthermore, Scott argues that a new European border-region policy based on principles of synergy and the negotiated pooling of national sovereignty is gradually evolving. However, as several other studies in this volume indicate, the solution of many intractable international conflicts—which, in turn, threaten the development of transboundary cooperation—will require a cooperative spirit that transcends even the integrationist logic of the European Union or the cooperation philosophy of NAFTA.

3. Case Studies

Based on the various studies presented here, it would appear that geoeconomic and supranational tendencies play a decisive role in determining the progress of international border-region integration. Thus, the U.S.-Mexican and U.S.-Canadian cases might be characterized as transboundary situations influenced by the limited-cooperation logic of NAFTA. This logic recognizes, for example, the fact of functional interdependence of Mexican and U.S. border cities but does not envisage actual integration—at least within the foreseeable future. Instead, NAFTA's primary goal is to remove barriers to trade and the flow of investment capital. As such, the present NAFTA context does not include the creation of a unitary labor market or of supranational political institutions (with the notable exceptions of the North American Development Bank, the Border Environment Cooperation Commission, and the trilateral Commission on Environmental Cooperation) that might coordinate national policies. Despite some positive developments in transnational cooperation, pervasive socio-economic asymmetries and the issue of illegal immigration will therefore make it unlikely that border-region policy will be reformulated to promote border-region integration.

By contrast, in Western Europe, the dynamic of the European Union with its increasingly powerful institutions indicates that border region issues have largely been depoliticized. As the EU is based on national-sovereignty guarantees for individual member states, as well as on a general consensus as to the redistribution of wealth, subnational diplomacy has lost much of its controversial character.

This supports the view that, within the Union, border-region integration is a realistic scenario. This, however, raises questions about the future role of the EU's external boundaries and whether an integrationist logic will be politically viable with respect to Poland, Hungary, and other former COMECON states. Even more seriously, many of the new international borders reestablished after the Soviet Union's demise can scarcely be classified as zones of cooperation. Here, it is conceivable that regional conflicts will continue and even widen if ethnic, territorial, religious, and, as a result, economic disputes continue unresolved.

Nevertheless, in the case of Scandinavia and the Baltic Rim, new and promising forms of transboundary cooperation appear to be evolving. The Baltic Sea Regional Council of States, established in 1992 and representing 12 states as well as the EU, is the most prominent institutional manifestation of this burgeoning regional dialogue and seeks to promote economic development, cooperation in social policy, human rights, and environmental protection. At the more local level, numerous informal transboundary networks are being established, much in the way that they have developed in North America and Western Europe. Municipal governments in Finland and Russian Karelia, for example, are in the process of defining joint economic-development strategies in order to remove the stigma of peripherality that has characterized this part of Europe for generations.

These regional case studies underline the fact that conflict and cooperation are simultaneous events, determined by the overlying logic of international relations and the propensity of local and regional actors to engage in transboundary-cooperation dialogues.

North and Central America

Historian and borderlands expert Oscar Martínez claims that interaction on the U.S.-Mexican border has gradually evolved with the development of interdependent urban realms far from the centers of national power in Washington, D.C., and Mexico City. A basically conflictual boundary—one synonymous with territorial disputes, ethnic tensions, and the historical animosities between Anglos and Hispanics—has been transformed into one of peaceful cooperation. Indeed, progress toward transborder integration has been taking place in a number of areas. These include economic integration, the emergence of a border culture, cooperation by federal and state government agencies on transborder issues, local government cooperation on transborder issues and planning, cooperation among groups of artists and intellectuals, transborder collaborative efforts of higher-education institutions, and the development of binational agendas of nongovernmental organizations and charities. As such, Martínez suggests that the U.S.-Mexican borderlands might serve as a model for cross-cultural understanding and accommodation.

Similarly, Paul Ganster describes how increasing interaction and interdependence between communities on the U.S.-Mexican border are strengthening efforts at local-level transboundary problem-solving. Moreover, this progress in transboundary regionalism is being achieved despite the vast socio-economic asymmetries that characterize the U.S.-Mexican borderlands and political and economic crises that have periodically affected Mexico. The borderlands can thus be seen as an *interface* between two very different neighbors who, out of necessity, must cooperate with each other. Within the context of NAFTA, which has institutionally strengthened the process of transboundary cooperation, Ganster sees the U.S.-Mexican borderlands as eventually developing into a zone of integration.

Samuel Schmidt, however, points out that persistent cultural stereotypes still affect how Mexicans and Americans interact in transboundary situations. Americans often perceive Mexico as being seen as *culturally* undependable, mercurial, inefficient, and weak. Mexicans, in turn, harbor images of an aggressive, arrogant, and devious United States. Schmidt illustrates how these stereotypes, along with basic differences in administrative priorities, encumber joint planning efforts along the common border. More disturbingly, Randy Willoughby warns that the issue of internal security is especially volatile in the context of U.S.-Mexican relations. Here, resentment of illegal immigrants and undocumented workers is creating a political atmosphere that engenders intolerance and draconian legislation (such as California's Proposition 187). Willoughby concludes that popular perceptions of a loss of sovereignty, born out of fear of *uncontrollable* population flows, could have political consequences that extend far beyond the borderlands, threatening civil society itself. Thus, despite decidedly positive elements of U.S.-Mexican transboundary regionalism, political and cultural barriers to more forceful and comprehensive transboundary problem-solving remain considerable.

In his discussion of transborder conservation initiatives, Pascal Girot describes how the Central American isthmus has recurrently alternated between periods of heightened interest in regional integration and periods of *Balkanization*. Girot's analysis of these collaborative efforts reinforces the notion that integration has had widely differing impacts among and within these countries. Border regions have played, and continue playing, a key role in Central American integration, despite the fact that most economic and political-integration efforts have focused on the nation-state, its capitals, and the economic elite. The 1990s are bringing about dramatic changes after a decade of war in Guatemala, El Salvador, and Nicaragua. Legitimate elections have been held in most of Central America's seven countries over the past few years. Within the context of present political circumstances and under the influence of NAFTA on regional integration, the emphasis of Central American cooperation has shifted to environmental issues and economic integration. This relationship between the structural adjustment and the stringent monetary policies implemented since 1990, the new emerging social actors, and innovative environmental-integration initiatives will be addressed, particularly in light of transboundary conservation and commercial initiatives such as SIPAZ, and the La Amistad projects among Panama, Costa Rica, and Nicaragua. Finally, the role border regions in Central America will be required to play in what is being called the new decade of integration will be critically examined.

The Canadian-U.S. case presents us with an altogether different situation. Interestingly enough, despite identical standards of living and the lack of overwhelming cultural differences or political conflict, the Canadian-U.S. border is one of relatively little interaction and of only tentative transboundary cooperation. As Roger Gibbins points out, it also cannot be classified as a borderlands culture along the lines of the U.S.-Mexican experience. Nonetheless, Gibbins reminds us that it does present a fascinating and perhaps unique case of transboundary interaction. Unlike many border regions of the Americas, the Canadian-U.S. border is not characterized by socio-economic asymmetries nor (if the special case of Québec is disregarded) by great differences in language and culture. Furthermore, Canada and the United States are both federations where the provinces and states respectively enjoy wide decision-making authority and where local autonomy is hypothetically sacrosanct.

However, a much more subtle asymmetry comes into play here, one that cannot be defined as a border-region issue as such. It is a question of vast differences in population, geographical size, of Canadian identity in the face of American economic and cultural predominance, and of the realities of Canada's geography. Gibbins (1989) has described Canada as a borderlands society, a vast country in which 90 percent of the population live within a thin strip along its common border with the United States. Intensely sensitive to events in the United States, Canada strives to maintain control of its own cultural destiny. Whereas American policymakers are often not aware of issues concerning Canada, the Canadian provinces and federal government remain preoccupied with the United States. It is the one-sidedness of this relationship that often makes the solution of disputes over natural resources and environmental issues difficult (Sadler 1986).

Therefore, despite the North American Free Trade Agreement and the friendly relations between both countries, transboundary cooperation along the Canadian-U.S. border remains low-key. The only (and admittedly advisory) institution of binational environmental-policy coordination, the International Joint Commission was created in 1911. Since then, little has materialized that might indicate the development of a truly binational and transboundary perspective toward the use of natural resources, the most important issue along the Canadian-U.S. border.

Transboundary Conflict and Cooperation
in Western and Eastern Europe

The process of political and economic integration has, without doubt, been the single most important factor in the development of transboundary cooperation in Western Europe. Overcoming a violent history characterized by national rivalries and religious intolerance, the member states of the European Union no longer seem primordially obsessed with territorial and cultural sovereignty—despite the often heated debates over federalism and centralism in the EU. This has allowed the establishment of a vast network of formal and informal transboundary arrangements that have served to improve international dialogue and cooperation among national, regional, and local governments (Scott 1989: 1993). At present, over sixty border region associations operate on the EU's internal and external borders, bringing together representatives of various levels of government as well as business people, academics, and motivated citizens.

Local governments on the border between Germany and Holland have been especially successful in building up long-term, transboundary working relationships. James Scott focuses on the EUREGIO, located in the central portion of the Dutch-German border and one of the few border-region associations to have established its own transboundary parliament, the Council of the EUREGIO. Largely advisory, the Council is a permanent body in which representatives of municipalities, special districts, and councils of government, as well as senior government observers, debate issues of mutual interest to EUREGIO citizens. For this reason, the EUREGIO has been identified by the EU as a model border-region association, enabling it to assume a pioneering role in the institutionalization of transboundary cooperation. Furthermore, the experiences of transboundary cooperation along the Dutch-German border, combined with the more general momentum of European integration, have helped construct a *de facto* European border-region policy, based on synergistic economic cooperation and a negotiated suspension of national sovereignty.

The apparent successes of the EUREGIO model automatically raise the question of its transferability to other border-region situations. Scott emphasizes that the establishment of the unitary European market and European institutions, as well as aspects particular to the Dutch-German border, are largely responsible for this success. Indeed, the binational political and cultural context in this corner of Europe is characterized by a lack of socio-economic, structural, and administrative asymmetries along with commonalities of economic, social, and environmental problems. At any rate, the precedents set here have encouraged supporters of transboundary cooperation in the Baltic region, on the Finnish-Russian border, as well as on other external boundaries of the European Union, to promote their own form of subnational diplomacy. As Veikko Tikkanen argues, the experience of the twin cities of Kuhmo-Kostamuksha demonstrates that a transboundary dialogue can indeed flourish even on the economic and political periphery of Europe.

Unfortunately, circumstances for the development of transboundary cooperation in Europe are not always favorable. Socio-economic asymmetries, such as those between East and West, are a problem. However, a potentially more serious and long-lasting barrier to cooperation is that of *asynchronous* development. In post-Cold War Europe, advanced industrial nations and civil societies coexist with unstable and often autocratic regimes that preside over fragile economies. In Central and Eastern Europe, territorial nationalism and ethnic-minority conflicts have again come to the fore while, at the same time, Western Europe edges toward integration and a new definition of citizenship.

In his essay, Kristian Gerner describes how the ideological vacuum of post-socialism has recreated old conflictual situations in the former Soviet Union. Despite the political and economic liberalization that has taken place, Russia appears to be distancing itself from Western norms of civil society and constitutionality. Provocatively evoking the civilizational and religious schism between the Western and Eastern Roman empires, Gerner suggests that nationalism, populism, and xenophobia could create a new East-West divide that might well affect international relations for years to come. Whether or not one accepts this view in its entirety, one need only reflect on the development of conflict in Armenia, Azerbaidjan, Georgia, Moldavia, Chechenia, and the Crimea to see how differently Europe is evolving. Here, prospects for transboundary dialogue are bleak due to ethnic and territorial conflicts that have escalated—or could potentially escalate—into full-fledged military confrontation.

Central Europe is another case of asynchronous societal development. In Hungary, border-related issues are a national obsession. As Zoltán Hajdú's study indicates, the loss of two-thirds of its territory in 1919 and the subsequent minority status of millions of Hungarians in Romania, Slovakia, Serbia, and the Ukraine have effectively converted Hungary into a "borderlands society." Precisely because of preoccupations with the fate of their national minorities in neighboring states, accusations of irredentism and hidden political agendas have been leveled frequently at Hungarian governments. However, it is Hungary, having perhaps learned more from the past than its neighbors, that has championed a *spiritualization* of frontiers in which the ethnic and cultural significance of international boundaries would diminish, replaced by a basic desire to coexist and cooperate. Resistance toward transboundary cooperation in this part of Central Europe stems from Romanian, Serbian, and Slovakian fears, regardless of how irrational, of Hungarian nationalism and irredentism. In this perspective, the movement to establish Central European Euroregions, such as the Carpathian-Tisza association, acquires a special significance.

In addition, the redrawing of Eastern Europe's geopolitical map has eliminated old political borders (the *socialist iron curtain*) and created new ones of greater subtlety. What in effect has taken place is a division of Eastern Europe according to levels of systemic modernization and economic development. The four so-called Višegrad states of Czechlands, Hungary, Poland, and Slovakia are associate members of the European Union and will at some future date be eligible for membership. The same only tentatively applies to the Baltic states of Estonia, Latvia, and Lithuania, and to Slovenia. Still struggling to restructure their economies, often embroiled in regional conflicts, are Ukraine, Russia, Bulgaria, Romania, Georgia, and several of the new Asian republics of the former Soviet Union.

The Western border regions of the Višegrad Four thus represent relatively successful regions that, due to their proximity to the European Union and affluent countries such as Austria, are experiencing a growth in services, trade, and direct foreign investment. Here, transboundary cooperation has been developing both within a framework of local projects and the interregional Alps-Adriatic association of which Austrian, Hungarian, and Slovenian regions are members. The eastern borders, basically rural and peripheral to begin with, generally present a much different picture.[3] Transboundary cooperation attempts such as those pursued by Poland, Hungary, Slovakia, and Ukraine (Euroregion Carpathia), have, for example, made little progress due to ethnic tensions. Furthermore, the economic-emergency situation experienced by Belarus, Ukraine, and Lithuania, as well as the presence of over 400,000 Russian troops in the Kaliningrad exclave, serve to cloud future prospects for economic cooperation and general regional development. With regard to the special situation of Kaliningrad, the former East Prussian Königsberg, Lyndelle Fairlie criticizes the *Maginot Line* mentality of Russia in which the strategic position of the exclave is interpreted in terms of international threats and not in terms of the possible opportunities that increased interregional cooperation might bring. These strategic disadvantages not only impede economic cooperation within Eastern Europe but could also threaten to create a future barrier to European integration.

To paraphrase Hajdú, the tendencies of cooperation and integration along the western borders of Hungary and the other Višegrad countries coexist with tendencies of conflict and disintegration along their eastern frontiers. Meanwhile, in the former Yugoslavia, ethnic and territorial conflict seems to be on the agenda for quite some time to come. For this reason, as Bohdan Gruchman and Franz Walk point out, despite oftentimes difficult circumstances, the newly established Polish-German Euroregions hold out the promise of pioneering East-West cooperation. Alongside Czech-German and Austrian-Hungarian examples, the Polish-German Euroregions are among the few Central and East European transboundary experiments whose activities demonstrate a short- to mid-term promise of obtaining political and economic results.

4. Interdisciplinary and Comparative Research on Borders and Border Regions: An Attempt at Generalization

Borderlands research is an intrinsically multidisciplinary exercise that requires a broad cross-cultural and comparative scope in order to flourish. As the cases illustrated here show, each border region is unique in its own way, having developed under a specific set of circumstances. This uniqueness does not make the task of comparative research any easier and, in fact, may motivate some to doubt the practical utility of such research. However, it is argued here that there are many more similarities among border regions than meet the eye. This becomes especially evident when border-region research is approached from a functional perspective that concentrates on the dynamics of transboundary interaction and is informed by recent economic and international-relations developments.

As the case studies have indicated, there are numerous factors that influence transboundary cooperation, either positively or negatively. Cooperation can result out of necessity or be blocked by national pride and racism. The ability to cooperate, given that a desire to do so exists, will, in turn, be influenced by the ability of transboundary actors to understand one another's motives, by individual freedom of movement, and a cultural capacity to reciprocate. In almost any given transboundary situation, elements that promote cooperation as well as conflict will coexist.

In our view, the quality and intensity of border-region interaction is determined by at least four major factors that, depending on the specific border region context, will not always be of equal importance, nor will they be concurrent. These factors are:

1. Motivations based on economic and environmental-security considerations to interact across borders. Equally as important is the imperative to deal with negative externalities that transcend jurisdictional boundaries but have large-scale international impacts. Transboundary cooperation is thus fueled by a natural drive for economic gain, a desire for peace, and motivations to solve mutual political, economic, and environmental problems in a transboundary context. However, the intensity of cooperation will often depend on the existence of a political and business elite willing to invest time, effort, and, to an extent, money in promoting the development of transboundary networks.

2. The issue of symmetry and asymmetry—that of similarities and differences between nations—is a ubiquitous and decisive factor in the development of transboundary cooperation. Degrees of symmetry and asymmetry can be defined through several variables, some of which can be measured quantitatively, others of which must be described qualitatively. Among the most important

indicators of symmetry/asymmetry are: *(a)* standards of living, wage scales, and other basic socio-economic indicators; *(b)* demography, population size, and population dynamics; *(c)* financial resources available to local and senior governments; *(d)* sectoral development and the degree of industrialization; *(e)* the issue of local power and the degree of political decentralization; *(f)* similarities and differences in political culture and legal traditions; and *(g)* degrees of cultural and linguistic affinities across national borders.

3. Similarly, the aspect of asynchronous economic, systemic, and societal change can greatly affect transboundary interaction, particularly in the context of post-socialist transformation.

4. Closely related to the aforementioned factors is the basic international and supranational context of conflict and cooperation. Serious conflict in a regional setting does not allow for the development of long-term transboundary relationships based on trust and a perception of mutual interest. Similarly, in situations where nations strive for regional integration, border regions may develop into interdependent and functional units with decision-making powers that transcend the traditional jurisdictional competencies of the nation-state.

These factors by no means constitute an exhaustive list. They represent only some of the major generalizations ventured by this study. However, at the same time we attempt to generalize, we cannot simply ignore history, language, culturally defined perceptions of borders and border regions, and other elements that create specific (and partially unique) contexts for transboundary cooperation. Information on specific border situations must be circulated in order to promote a more global understanding of border regions as zones of contact between nations and peoples. For this reason, more—not fewer—detailed case studies are required. The greater our knowledge of local situations, the better our capacity to synthesize information and, as a result, generalize.

5. Conclusion: Possible Policy Consequences

It goes without saying that the significance of international state boundaries must be deemphasized in order that transboundary regions of the nation-states can acquire and develop a dynamic of their own and alleviate minority problems in border areas. However, the political and economic destinies of border regions will be largely determined by their ability to develop their own specific identity beyond national or ethnic categories. As Kristian Gerner and others argue, this can only be achieved if the possibility of multiple identities and allegiances (in the sense of a spiritualization of the border) is eventually recognized and accepted.

It can be assumed that regional and local interests are more likely to coalesce at national borders in situations where economic and political integration are at an advanced stage and where national concerns over sovereignty issues have accordingly diminished. Similarly, the propensity to cooperate is largely determined by an environment of mutual understanding and trust. This could mean that under such circumstances where both conditions coincide, international and interregional competition are not limiting factors of transboundary cooperation and that unique synergy effects can be achieved here through a cross-border pooling of resources. This, however, is a very optimistic view of things, influenced by the West European experience and one which may not provide much practical assistance for regions where ethnic and/or political conflict, illegal immigration, income differentials, and other problems limit cooperation.

In the case of the U.S.-Mexican borderlands, it is conceivable that free trade might provide an opportunity for strengthening transboundary cooperation, particularly if special border-region programs are created and funded within the North American Free Trade Agreement (NAFTA) framework. European experience has shown that transboundary project management in economic development, infrastructural planning, and other areas has solidified working relationships and promoted institutional forms of cooperation. Local-federal as well as international partnerships in administering such programs would also work toward establishing a new transboundary policy framework. However, Mexican mistrust of the United States intentions and American fears of mass immigration from Mexico will continue to persist as long as the border between both countries separates rich from poor. This, as well as a host of other problems, including different philosophies regarding the role of the state and economic asymmetries, has hindered the creation of supranational institutions that might provide a framework for integration.

By the same token, European border regions, particularly those on the EU's external border, might profit from the experiences of the U.S.-Mexican border, where synergistic urban economies have developed thanks to the *maquiladora* (assembly industry) program and the United States' willingness to allow the duty-free importation of products assembled at low cost in Mexican factories. A maquiladora complex on the Polish-German border, for example, could bring just the sort of economic growth and technological-development benefits that advocates of transboundary cooperation are struggling to achieve. Furthermore, the dangers of environmental degradation could be avoided through careful binational planning and supervision.

However, there are wider and politically more sensitive implications to the concept of creating maquiladora-like regional synergies on the Germany's eastern border. A transboundary exploitation of the locational advantages of German infrastructure and technology, coupled with inexpensive but skilled Polish labor, may seem progressive and mutually beneficial from a German perspective, but also as presumptuous, perhaps even neo-imperialist, from a Polish one. It is also very unlikely that the EU will tolerate the creation of highly competitive free-trade zones on its eastern borders, particularly with aid from its regional-development fund. At the same time, many local-government actors involved in German-Polish transboundary cooperation are seeking alternatives to outright emulation of cooperation models such as the German-Dutch EUREGIO, noting the unique features of the region and the special situation on the external boundaries of the European Union.

These considerations, brief as they are, indicate that it is very difficult to construct policy models of transboundary cooperation due to the fact that overlying socio-economic, political, and cultural imbalances and/or differences have direct repercussions on national policy—most notably on internal security. The alternative to a priori models of transboundary cooperation, including those based on very real practical experiences, is a distillation of lessons learned by actors involved in transboundary interaction. In this way, we might be able to isolate the most important components of border-region cooperation and possibly determine what potential activities can either promote or be counterproductive to transboundary cooperation. Based on the various border-region experiences discussed in this book, we can provide a synopsis of forms of interaction that might prove helpful in general terms.

Notes

1. The concept of reterritorialization is also indicative of attempts to establish a new, comprehensive understanding—new mental maps, as it were—of the post-Cold War world. Indeed, a host of modern world views appear to be vying for recognition and acceptance, many of which still see the world in statist and centralist terms (Ò Tuathail and Luke 1994: 386–94). Among the more questionable are those that see global affairs in terms of a clash between Western civilization and its Judeo-Christian traditions and those parts of the globe associated with Islam, Eastern Orthodoxy, and other major religions. Others see the world developing within the context of more or less peaceful competition between economic teams—nations or groups of nations forced to develop and exploit comparative advantages through strategic policies and their ability to organize economic life efficiently (Lester Thurow 1992; Michael J. Porter 1993). Still others take a decidedly more globalist and decentralized view of things. Kenichi Ohmae (1990; 1993) states, for example, that in the coming borderless world, regions will be the determining agents of growth, replacing resource-based and other economic nationalisms. Finally, the geoecological world view should be mentioned, particularly because it stresses the irrelevance of national borders and the need to establish a truly global dialogue on economic and social issues in order to save the planet from environmental catastrophe.

2. This evolutionary concept at the level of border regions is reminiscent of developmental models of international relations proposed by Durand, Lévy, and Retaillé (1993). These models

operate from the assumption that interdependence and globalization are powerful forces transforming a world system based on nation-states through the gradual evolution of a multicentered world society. Integration within a world society would imply the substitution of national (and hence, parochial) policy-making by supranational institutions taking decisions on economic, environmental, social, and security policy. At the micro level of border regions, it would allow the creation of transboundary governments and agencies that could formulate and execute coordinated regional-development strategies and have the means to solve local problems.

3. This polarization of development on the western and eastern borders of the Višegrad states has been documented for Poland by Gorzelac (1993), for Hungary by the Hungarian Ministry for Spatial Development and the Environment (1992), for Czechlands by a team of geographers led by Martin Hampl (1993), and, in the case of Slovakia, by unpublished statistical and cartographic documents prepared in 1993 by the Center for Strategic Studies, Bratislava.

References

Akademie für Raumforschung und Landesplanung, eds. 1992. *Grenzübergreifende Raumplanung. Erfahrungen und Perspektiven der Zusammenarbeit mit den Nachbarstaaten Deutschlands.* Hannover: Verlag der ARL.

Anderson, Malcolm. 1982. "The Political Problems of Frontier Regions." *West European Politics* 5 (4).

Bell, Daniel. 1977. "The Future World Disorder." *Foreign Policy* (Summer).

Christaller, Walter. 1933. *Die zentralen Orte in Süddeutschland* (Central Places in South Germany). Jena: Gustav Fischer Verlag.

Council of Europe/European Conference of Ministers Responsible for Regional Planning (CEMAT). 1994. Resolutions Adopted at the 10th Session of CEMAT, 6–7 September. Oslo.

Duchacek, Ivo. 1986. "International Competence of Subnational Governments: Borderlands and Beyond." In *Across Boundaries. Transborder Interaction in Comparative Perspective*, Oscar J. Martínez, ed. El Paso: Texas Western Press.

Duchacek, Ivo. 1990. "Perforated Sovereignties: Towards a Typology of New Actors in International Relations." In *Federalism and International Relations. The Role of Subnational Units*, Hans J. Michelmann and Panayotis Soldatos, eds. Oxford: Oxford University Press.

Durand, Marie-Françoise, Jacques Lévy, and Denis Retaillé. 1993. "Introduction: Espaces-monde, mode d'emploi." In *Le Monde Espaces et Systèmes*, Marie-Françoise Durand, Jacques Lévy, and Denis Retaillé, eds. Paris: Presses de la Fondation Nationale des Sciences Politiques & Dalloz.

Gibbins, Roger. 1989. *Canada as a Borderlands Society.* Borderlands Monograph Series #2. Orono: The Canadian-American Center, The University of Maine.

Gorzelak, Grzegorz. 1993. *Poland 2005: The Scenario of Regional Development.* Warsaw: Euroreg/University of Warsaw.

Hall, Peter, and Manuel Castells. 1994. *Technopoles of the World.* London and New York: Routledge.

Hampl, Martin, ed. 1993. *Problémy regionálního rozvoje v Ceské republice: Potenciál, subjekty, mechanizmy* (Regional Development Problems in the Czech Republic: Potentials, Frames of Reference and Mechanisms). Prague: Faculty of Social Geography and Regional Development of the Charles University.

Hansen, Niles. 1981. *The Border Economy: Regional Development in the Southwest*. Austin: University of Texas Press.

Herzog, Lawrence. 1990. *Where North Meets South*. Austin: University of Texas Press.

Hettne, Björn. 1994. *The New Regionalism. Implications for Global Development and International Security*. Helsinki: UNU World Institute for Development Economics Research.

Ilner, Michal, and Alois Anderle. 1994. "The Regional Aspect of Post-Communist Transformation in the Czech Republic." *Czech Sociological Review* 2 (1).

Környezetvédelmi és Területfejlesztési Minisztérium (Hungarian Ministry of Spatial Development and the Environment). 1992. *Jelentés a Területi Folyamatokról 1992* (Spatial Development Report, 1992). Budapest: Ministry of Spatial Development and the Environment.

Latouche, Daniel. 1990. "State Building and Foreign Policy at the Subnational Level." In *Perforated Sovereignties and International Relations: Trans-Sovereign Contacts of Subnational Governments*, Ivo Duchacek, Daniel Latouche, and Garth Stevenson, eds. New York: Greenwood Press.

Lösch, August. 1940. *Die räumliche Ordnung der Wirtschaft* (The Spatial Organization of the Economy). Jena: Gustav Fischer Verlag.

Martínez, Oscar J., ed. 1986. *Across Boundaries. Transborder Interaction in Comparative Perspective*. El Paso: Texas Western Press.

Martínez, Oscar J. 1992. "Borderlands Entering New Stage." *Mexico Policy News* (Fall): 22.

Ohmae, Kenichi. 1990. *The Borderless World. Management Lessons in the New Logic of the Global Marketplace*. New York: Harper.

Ohmae, Kenichi. 1993. "The Rise of the Region-State." *Foreign Affairs*, 72 (2).

Ò Tuathail, Gearóid, and Timothy W. Luke. 1994. "Present at the (Dis)integration: Deterritorialization and Reterritorialization in the New Wor(l)d Order." *Annals of the Association of American Geographers* 84 (3).

Porter, Michael J. 1993. *The Competitive Advantage of Nations*. New York: The Free Press.

Rajcak, Milan. 1994. "Districts and Socio-Economic Regions of the Slovak Republic and Their Adaptability to New Socio-Economic Conditions." Paper presented at the International Conference on Development Issues of the Regions of the Višegrad Four Countries in the Context of their Integration with the European Union, Smolenice (Slovakia). November.

Sadler, Barry. 1986. "The Management of Canada-U.S. Boundary Waters: Retrospect and Prospect." *Natural Resources Journal* (Spring).

Scott, James. 1989. "Transborder Cooperation, Regional Initiatives, and Sovereignty Conflict in the Upper Rhine Valley." *Publius: The Journal of Federalism* 19 (1).

Scott, James. 1993. "The Institutionalization of Transboundary Cooperation in Europe: Recent Developments on the Dutch-German Border." *Journal of Borderlands Studies* 8 (1).

Stoddard, Ellwyn R. 1984. "Northern Mexican Migration and the US/Mexican Border Region." *New Scholar* 9 (1–2).

II

Borders and Border Regions
in the Global Context

The Political Science of Frontiers

Malcolm Anderson

1. Introduction

The general role of frontiers in contemporary political life is seldom explicitly analyzed by political scientists. This is partly because boundary effects on the behavior and values of the populations enclosed by them are almost impossible to assess, let alone measure. Indeed, attempts to measure them seem shallow and produce obvious results which derive directly from the assumptions on which they are based.[1] More significantly, there are basic differences of view about frontiers in the historical and political science literature that are seldom made explicit.

Some historians and political scientists regard the characteristics and functions of frontiers and borders as dependent on the internal organization of societies, and the way in which political power is exercised in the core regions of states. Debates among realist, pluralist, Marxist, and interdependence theorists in international relations arise out of different views about the nature of the state; frontiers are regarded as epiphenomena whose role and function are dependent on the core characteristics of the state. For others (including most political geographers), the characteristics of the frontier are fundamental influences on the way a society develops and on the political options open to it. The vast literature specifically on frontiers—the historical classics of Turner and Prescott Webb, geographical treatises, borderland studies, and a very diverse literature on border disputes—gives little guidance for the examination of the great changes now occurring as states are easing frontier controls or finding that they cannot use frontier controls to police and control their territory.

2. Definition of the International Frontier

Any attempt at a general political analysis of frontiers must have a clear point of departure. The starting point here is that frontiers can be analyzed (and, in normative political theory, criticized) in the same way as other political institutions and processes. Frontiers are not simply lines on maps, the unproblematic givens of political life, where one jurisdiction ends and another begins. In the contemporary world, frontiers between states may be regarded as important institutions and processes. As institutions, they are established by political decisions and regulated by legal texts. The frontier is the *basic* political institution: no rule-bound economic, social, or political life in advanced societies could be organized without them. This primordial character of frontiers is embodied in public international law by the 1978 Vienna Convention on State Succession. When a state collapses, the agreements concerning its frontiers remain in force; frontiers are therefore regarded as prior to the reconstitution of a state and are recognized to be a prerequisite of this reconstitution. Also, frontiers and borders define, in a legal sense, the identity of individuals because the conditions for claims to nationality and exercise of rights of citizenship are delimited by them.

Within its frontiers the state is a sovereign jurisdiction, and the Weberian doctrine of the monopoly of the legitimate use of force on its territory is still almost universally recognized. The doctrine of sovereignty remains a central part of thinking about states and relations among them. The doctrine implies that states have absolute control over their territories and can impose this control at their frontiers. The claim of the modern state to be "the sole, exclusive fount of all powers and prerogatives of rule" (Poggi 1978: 92) could only be realized if its frontiers were made impermeable to unwanted external influences. But this view of the frontier of the sovereign state is not part of an immutable, natural order. Different conceptions of the frontier as an institution existed before the modern sovereign state, and other kinds will emerge after its demise. In this regard, there are now signs of seismic political change.

Frontiers are part of political processes with four defining dimensions. First, frontiers are instruments of state policy because governments attempt to change, to their own advantage, the location or the functions of frontiers. Although there is no simple relationship between frontiers and inequalities of wealth and power, government policy on frontiers is intended to protect and to promote interests. Second, the policies and practices of the state are constrained by the degree of *de facto* control that the government exercises over the state frontier. The incapacity of governments in the contemporary world to control much of the traffic of persons, goods, and information across their frontiers is changing the nature of both states and frontiers. Third, frontiers are basic markers of identity, in the twentieth century usually national identity, but political identities may be larger or smaller than the nation-state. Frontiers, in this sense, are part of political beliefs and myths about the unity of the people, and sometimes myths about the natural unity of the territory. These "imagined communities," to use Benedict Anderson's (1991) phrase concerning nations, are now a universal phenomenon and often have profound historical roots. They are linked to the most powerful form of ideological bonding in the modern world—nationalism. Imagined communities may transcend the confines of the state, and myths of regional, continental, and hemispheric unity have also marked boundaries between friend and foe (Connor 1969). But *myths* of unity can be created or transformed with remarkable rapidity during wars, revolutions, and political upheavals.

Lastly, frontier is a term of discourse. Meanings are given both to frontiers in general and to particular frontiers, and these meanings change from time to time. Frontier is a term of discourse in law, diplomacy, and politics, and its meaning varies depending on the context in which it is used. In the scholarly languages of anthropology, economics, history, political science, public international law, and sociology, it has different meanings according to the theoretical approach used. Sometimes scholarship is the servant of political power when frontiers are in dispute,[2] while at other times, it is part of the scarcely heard disquisition of the classroom. People who live in frontier regions, or those whose daily life is directly affected by frontiers as obstacles to communication and contact, have a richer form of discourse. For them, the term frontier is associated with the (often irksome) rules imposed by frontiers as institutions, and is also suffused with popular symbolism based on how the frontier is perceived, as either barrier or junction (Strassoldo 1970). The layers of discourse—political, scholarly, popular—always overlap but never coincide. Divergent mental images of frontiers are an integral part of frontiers as processes.

What frontiers are, and what they represent, is constantly reconstituted by human beings who are regulated, influenced, and limited by them. But these reconstructions are influenced by political change and the often unpredictable outcome of great conflicts, against a background of technological change. The military technology developed in the closing stages of the Second World War altered the strategic significance of control of territory; the military independence of many sovereign states was drastically reduced, and the frontiers of these states became indefensible. Now, with instantaneous communication of information, *information sovereignty* has been lost; the development of mass, rapid, and inexpensive systems of transport has resulted in all developed countries and frontier crossings by individuals annually number more than the total population. New territorial questions have consequently emerged on the political agenda.

3. New Frontiers

The most interesting questions—because they put frontier disputes into a radically different perspective—concern boundary-making, and the related attempt to establish international regimes, in uninhabited spaces. The thinking about these spaces has the potential to effect major revisions in concepts and perceptions of the frontiers between states. Uninhabited spaces, and the activities that take place in them, are having effects upon the politics of territory and on thinking about frontiers in inhabited regions.

Clearly, some empty spaces are so vast and so inhospitable that no serious attempt has been made to establish sovereignty rights within them. But boundaries are drawn in some spaces that are not normally inhabited or are occupied only on a temporary basis. Consequently, conflicts arise about many uninhabited zones. The large number of international treaties, conventions, understandings, and case law concerning them indicate serious potential for conflict as states attempt to establish various kinds of positions in them. Empty spaces are an increasingly important domain of public international law. International regimes are sometimes considered necessary because spaces that belong to no one or for which no one feels responsible offer temptations to plunder, exploit, or misuse, without regard to the interests of others or to the longer-term consequences of activities.

The public international law developed for empty space departs from the traditional focus of acquisition of territory and conflicts over frontiers. New concepts have been developed. Some derive from ordinary language, such as "the common heritage of mankind"; others have analogies with the concepts of private-law notions of property rather than with territorial dominion implied by the doctrine of sovereignty. According to one influential view, private property is a complex bundle of relationships among people involving rights, duties, and obligations (Honoré 1961). This may also describe the legal regime for uninhabited spaces in that much of it (the major exception is airspace where absolute "territorial" sovereignty has generally prevailed) concerns rights, duties, and obligations established between states rather than absolute territorial dominion.

Unfortunately, this observation does not go very far in the quest for understanding boundaries in uninhabited spaces and the ways in which they may be similar or dissimilar to the frontiers between human groups. As Jeremy Waldron (1988: 28) has written about private property, "If that were all, there would be no problem about definition if [the bundle of rights] remained constant for all or most cases that we want to describe as private property, the bundle as a whole could be defined by its contents. The problem is, of course, it does not remain constant, and that is where the difficulties begin." This is *a fortiori* true of the regime for uninhabited spaces. The regime for each category of empty space is specific to it. No regime, with the exception of aspects of maritime law, remains stable for long periods. Although concepts associated with environmental protection are forming a link between them, no rights and obligations common to all uninhabited spaces are even hypothetically suggested. However, the argument here is that states attempt, as far as they are able, to acquire property rights in order to facilitate exploitation or use of the resources of these spaces. Mutual recognition of other states' rights is often, although by no means always, necessary to achieve this end.

4. Categories of Empty Spaces

Boundary questions concerning uninhabited land, seas and oceans, airspace, and outer space have therefore the potential to transform perceptions and rules concerning frontiers between states. From the eighteenth to the twentieth centuries, land areas regarded as uninhabited gradually diminished in number and importance. Claims to territory based on discovery (and even effective occupation) have disappeared. The Empty Quarter of Arabia, the great deserts of Africa, Asia, Australia, and the smaller deserts of North and South America are now regarded as under the effective occupation and control of states. Even the vast, sparsely populated Arctic tundra, with its scattering of perhaps forty indigenous peoples across Europe, Asia, and North America, who are now often outnumbered locally by colonizers from the south, is under the effective sovereign control of the states (Malaurie 1992). The single great wilderness remaining is Antarctica, where no claim to state sovereignty is yet recognized by the international community. Instead, an unusual treaty regime, based on a compromise between claimants and other interested parties, has regulated the territory's use; increasingly, its stability is in question.

The Antarctic continent, like oceans, seas, and estuaries, is uninhabited in the conventional meaning of the term—all inhabitants are temporary residents. A few hundred people stay in the various scientific stations throughout the winter. In the summer months, several thousand arrive, supplemented by a few tourists. The international interest in Antarctica has been the belief that it contains mineral reserves of very considerable value;[3] it is also a focus of scientific interest as the last great wilderness and a unique natural environment, rich in research possibilities. Among the many factors that will determine whether or not Antarctica is exploited are discovery of new resources elsewhere, commodity prices, technological progress, and the political regime agreed for the continent.[4]

The remoteness and the inhospitable nature of the climate and the terrain of the continent make the traditional bases of claims to territory—discovery, occupation, historical rights, proximity, and geographical contiguity—in international law virtually inapplicable. A situation has arisen in which "Antarctica is unique—an entire continent of disputed territory" (Auburn 1982). No established rules of international law exist that allow states to successfully uphold claims to sovereignty in it.[5] Seven states have formal claims to territory (Argentina, Australia, Chile, France, New Zealand, Norway, and the United Kingdom), with about one-sixth of the continent remaining unclaimed. With the exception of Norway, no states have considered unilaterally renouncing their claim. States with an interest in Antarctica scrupulously avoid any action that might implicitly involve the recognition of the claims of others. This evasion of the issue of sovereignty was a second-best solution for claimant states. As Peterson writes, "The compromise on sovereignty, forming the basis of the Antarctic regime, was not the first choice of most participants. The claimants would have preferred acceptance of their claims" (Peterson 1988).

The 1959 Antarctic Treaty System (ATS) was signed by 12 states, including the USSR and the United States, as well as those with territorial claims.[6] The 13 original consultative parties were subsequently joined by other states as participants or observers until, by 1991, a total of 41 states were associated with the system. The signatory states all had active scientific programs in Antarctica and accepted responsibility for the continent. They reached no conclusion about the basis of territorial sovereignty in the continent, but they specifically excluded the presence of military bases and military forces. Flowing from this basic treaty, four other agreements have been negotiated—Agreed Measures for the Conservation of Antarctic Flora and Fauna (1964), Convention for the Protection of Antarctic Seals (1972), Convention for the Conservation of Antarctic Marine Living Resources (1980), and the Protocol on Environmental Protection (1990).

Difficulties arose over the agreement for a conditional ban on exploitation of resources, reached in the 1988 Convention for the Regulation of Antarctic Mineral Resources Activities (CRAMRA). Australia and France refused to ratify it, instead jointly proposing an international natural park, preserved in perpetuity. The idea of the Antarctic as the common heritage of mankind goes back to the 1950s, and was championed by the World Conference on National Parks in 1972 and by Greenpeace (using the phrase "global commons"). The increasing national and international importance of the ecological movement was a cause of tension in the ATS. France and Australia jointly proposed the negotiation of a comprehensive environmental-protection convention. Nongovernmental organizations and vocal Third World countries at the UN alleged that the ATS was a secretive club. Signatories to environmental protection agreements have been accused of ignoring their spirit, and some of them were suspected of preparing the ground for exploitation of mineral deposits (Charney 1991).

Traditional international law does not provide any precedents that could help to design a regime for the continent. There is general agreement among its members that the ATS should be improved, but there is little prospect of a new regime until a new factor emerges (such as a rogue state engaging in mining). The continuation of the present regime remains the second-best choice of most states and the majority of all interested parties, but it can only be replaced by another international regime and not by a reversion to the principle of territorial sovereignty.

Parallel developments have been taking place over oceanic international waters and the deep-sea bed. In the last 30 years the basis for delimiting maritime boundaries has been highly controversial, but it is now agreed on in broad principle.[7] There are many current sea-boundary disputes both because large resources are at stake, because the technical problems of drawing boundaries in coastal waters can be intractable, and because sea boundaries may be part of a series of interlocking disputes between neighboring states. According to one recent estimate (Johnstone 1989), there are 300 bilateral delimitation issues outstanding, and other estimates put the potential figure even higher. The extension of the territorial rights of states beyond the old three-mile limit and the concept of the Exclusive Economic Zone have been sources of new disputes. These new disputes have sometimes stimulated creative solutions. An agreed delimitation is not the only possibility—joint development or management zones that cross hypothetical boundaries have, in some cases, been adopted.

Although prior to the 1960s there had been attempts to extend territorial waters to protect resources (particularly fisheries), the great impetus for renewed interest in maritime boundaries was the discovery and exploitation of offshore oil and natural gas reserves after 1945. In the United States, offshore exploitation in the Gulf of Mexico led to the Truman Declaration that expressed a claim to the continental shelf as the natural extension of national territory for the purposes of exploiting resources. The precedent was followed in the Persian Gulf, in the North Sea, and in the Mediterranean where, sometimes with difficulty, the continental shelf was partitioned by the riverine states. The stakes in maritime boundary-drawing are high because their impact could change global balances in the next century, if, as seems certain, competition for mineral resources becomes intense.

The legal issues are complex and subject to fine legal analysis.[8] The third United Nations Conference on the Law of the Sea (UNCLOS III) successfully negotiated the 1982 Convention, which entered into force in November 1994. The Convention established three maritime zones to which states could lay claim—the territorial sea (up to 12 nautical miles), the contiguous zone (another 12 miles), and the Exclusive Economic Zone (200 nautical miles), all distances measured from the low-water mark. In addition, states may, according to the Convention, claim jurisdiction over the continental shelf, which varies in extent and often has to be partitioned between neighboring states. The implications of claims to the continental shelf and to the EEZ vary from one region of the world to another, some of which have been intensively studied.[9] On the deep-sea bed, the less developed countries at the United Nations have taken the view that the rich countries should not exploit sea-bed resources to their own exclusive advantage. The 1982 Convention embodies the principle that the high-sea and the deep-sea bed form part of the common heritage of mankind.

In terms of damage to the marine environment, a particular focus has been on dumping of nuclear waste and other noxious materials. Before the 1980s, most nations that had nuclear-power stations and nuclear weapons routinely dumped at sea. In response to pressure, a convention was signed by the nuclear powers in London in 1983 for a ten-year moratorium on dumping. The facts were, however, hard to establish. There were suspicions, but little evidence, about Russia's dumping activities until 1993. When the countries involved in the 1983 Convention reassembled in London ten years later, Russia revealed extensive and potentially dangerous dumping north of the Arctic Circle and in the Sea of Japan. The making permanent of the ban on dumping showed that the rich countries were prepared to support an international regime for the protection of the high seas, but any agreement is virtually impossible to monitor. Moreover, the problem of dumping at sea is much wider than that of radioactive materials. It also includes the dumping of munitions, dredged material—often heavily contaminated—from rivers and estuaries, and chemical wastes. Although regional attempts have been made to place curbs on these other forms of dumping, they remain a major hazard. The issue, however, has been placed firmly on the international agenda.

Airspace boundaries are normally regarded as coextensive with land boundaries, although there is some technical dispute about exactly what that means. A line drawn vertically from the outer territorial limits of the state, extending to the limits of the atmosphere, has been regarded as within the sovereign jurisdiction of the state. At what altitude airspace ceases is uncertain and has never been defined in an international treaty. The conventional limit is the so-called von Karman line where aerodynamic flight becomes impossible.[10] Sovereignty over airspace, in the twentieth century, has been important for two main reasons. The first is military; any armed intrusion into airspace is regarded with almost the same seriousness as terrestrial intrusions. During times of international tension, approaching and infringing on the airspace of opposing states has been regarded as a method of showing determination to pursue a quarrel. The principle that countries may respond forcibly to intrusions is universally recognized although overreaction, such as the 1983 shooting down of the South Korean airliner in the Soviet Far East, is the subject of considerable international outcry.[11]

The second reason for the importance of sovereignty over airspace is commercial. With the associated, but distinct, right to control landing rights, it has been used as a powerful means of protection of national airlines. The ability to restrict overflying rights and landing rights for foreign airlines has allowed national airlines to benefit from a monopoly rent and to enter into cartel agreements with other national carriers to share lucrative routes. However, three pressures are making inroads into sovereignty over airspace. The first is deregulation of the market for air travel, which has been spreading in the highly industrialized world; the logic of this deregulation is an open-skies policy. The second is concern about atmospheric pollution (part of more general issues of environmental protection discussed below). The third is the technical requirements of air-traffic control in places where airspace became congested across international frontiers.

To illustrate the last of these pressures—all states are bound by air-traffic control arrangements, negotiated through the International Civil Aviation Organization (ICAO), from which they can only withdraw at the cost of damaging their own interests. Even when they disapprove of the principles on which these arrangements are based, state protests are either verbal, or the states temporarily withdraw from the arrangements. The ICAO acts as an arbitrator and does not, in principle, infringe upon state sovereignty. But an agreement for European airspace—Eurocontrol, established in 1961—contained elements of supranationality. Although members of Eurocontrol became dissatisfied and diminished its supranational aspects by a revised convention in 1981, supranational practice is necessary in very busy airspace in order to achieve the necessary coordination of air traffic (Weber 1983). Although the principle of sovereignty over airspace is not denied,[12] the large number of aircraft on international routes has effectively removed, in all but the most unusual circumstances, the options of closing airspace or modifying international air-traffic agreements.

In outer space, five significant agreements have been reached.[13] Issues relating to outer space, with the exceptions of satellite broadcasting and observation satellites, have been pushed down the international political agenda. The real fear in the 1980s, of the progressive militarization of space, was prompted by the development of antisatellite and antimissile technology.[14] According to the 1967 Treaty, although defensive action was permissible,[15] nuclear and other offensive weapons were banned. The Strategic Arms Limitation Agreements (SALT) of 1972 and 1979 and the Anti-Ballistic Missile Treaty of 1972 banned interference by the Soviet Union and the United States with each other's satellites engaged in the monitoring of these agreements. In 1983, the Strategic Defense Initiative (SDI) was launched by President Reagan, who defended this Star Wars initiative as defensive—incoming Soviet missiles would be destroyed by lasers in space. Whether the laser-beam weapons stationed in space function effectively remains an unanswered question, but the United States partially abandoned the program as a result of arms-limitation agreements with the Russians and the virtual disappearance of a direct Russian military threat.

Very difficult problems of outer space, with military implications, remain. The most obvious is development of high resolution observation satellites for commercial purposes by a French-Belgian-Swedish consortium. In 1986 SPOT 1 (Satellite Pour l'Observation de la Terre) and in 1990 SPOT 2 broke the super-power monopoly on this technology that, although developed for ostensibly civil surveying, became available for military purposes (Krepon et al. 1990). Whether the spread of this technology will affect the stability of the international system is a matter of speculation, but it is certain that more states will be able to see more clearly what is occurring in other states' territory, further eroding the sanctuary provided by territorial sovereignty. Another potentially important issue is the pollution of outer space by the debris of space vehicles which can endanger the safety of satellites (Reijnen 1989). The responsibility for clean-up costs of debris from satellites that damage private property on reentry to the atmosphere or to another state's territory is a practical legal issue (regulated in principle by the 1972 Convention on International Liability for Damage Caused by Space Objects) and will increase in importance if schemes for hundreds of low-level satellites for multimedia communications come to fruition.

A basic problem of extra-atmospheric space is similar to the problem in Antarctica, although in a very different physical context—how to establish a regime where states exercise rights to conduct nonharmful activities, where territorial sovereignty and boundary making are inappropriate. The 1967 Treaty governing the activities of states in exploration and utilization of extra-atmospheric space, including the moon and other celestial bodies (which by 1990 had been ratified by 92 states) recognized that territorial rivalries could not be transferred from the earth to outer space. Article I subsection 1 established a new principle, that the exploration and utilization of space was the "province of all mankind," and thus it was made equivalent to the principle adopted by the United Nations Conference on the Law of the Sea, which accepted that the seas were "the common heritage of all mankind," a notion that sharply contrasts with sovereignty.[16] The Bogotá Declaration, contesting this, has been ignored by all states with satellite launching capabilities.[17]

The 1967 Treaty also affirmed the principle that states bear international responsibility for their activities in outer space. The absence of a doctrine of sovereignty raises interesting legal issues of jurisdiction, civil responsibility, intellectual property rights for technical and scientific discoveries, and copyright.[18] It is difficult to envisage how these problems can be solved to the satisfaction of all without the establishment of a genuine international jurisdiction. Without this, the states that have technological superiority will have an overwhelming practical advantage in any disputes that arise.

5. Empty Spaces and the Frontiers of States

There are now intrusions across frontiers that have the potential to cause radical change in the way large numbers of people, particularly in the rich countries, perceive the territory of their states and the significance of their frontiers. One has already been discussed—the availability to a significant minority of states (and private corporations) of high-resolution observation satellites makes it impossible for states to hide any major activity, even in remote and inaccessible locations. A second kind of intrusion is transfrontier pollution and the harmful, potentially disastrous effects of some forms of economic activity. A third is the cultural and political impact of international telecommunications, an impact that commenced in a minor way during the First World War and reached its culmination with the introduction of direct satellite broadcasting of television in the late 1980s. Frontiers and sovereign control of territory provide, at best, very limited defenses against the impact of these phenomena.

The protection of the environment has become a major political issue although scientific knowledge of the environment is still limited and there is no definitive answer yet to the basic question of why the biosphere should be protected. There is, however, agreement that much of the effort of environmental protection must be based on international cooperation. A core difficulty is that any measure of environmental protection inevitably promotes some interests and harms others.[19] The first recognition of a common interest in environmental protection dates from the beginning of the twentieth century (Lyster 1985). After the Second World War, the United Nations and its specialized agencies took a leading role.[20] The UN was flanked by others—the World Meteorological Organization, the International Maritime Organization, the International Civil Aviation Organization,[21] and the International Atomic Energy Agency. Regional organizations—the Organization for Economic Cooperation and Development,[22] the European Community/Union,[23] and the Council of Europe[24]—have given an increasing place to environmental issues in their deliberations and decisions. Nongovernmental organizations, such as the International Union for the Conservation of Nature and its Resources (established in 1948) and its better known progeny, the International Wildlife Fund (1961), have mobilized nonofficial groups and interests. The Worldwatch Institute, with its widely noticed reports and studies and, above all, Greenpeace, with its spectacular direct action, have helped to effect changes in international environmental matters. Nongovernmental organizations with international membership and outlook have been influential actors in establishing international environmental regimes.

There are certain key dates and events in the development of international environmental regulation that include a mixture of environmental catastrophes that have popularized certain ideas or concepts. The 1967 wreck of the oil tanker *Torrey Canyon* on the Scilly Isles had great impact because it affected two countries, Britain and France, simultaneously, and because the areas of spillage were tourist destinations and sites of great natural beauty. More than thirty major spills have taken place since the *Torrey Canyon,* but perhaps only the 1989 *Exxon-Valdez* spill in the ecologically fragile Alaskan fjords has made a comparably great impact, because of massive U.S. and international media coverage. Another catastrophe, the 1984 explosion of the Union Carbide plant at Bhopal in India, stimulated debate on two major issues—the export of toxic-waste materials and the relocation of dangerous manufacturing processes in countries with minimal environmental regulation.[25] The most recent landmark catastrophe was the explosion in April 1986 of one of the four Soviet (now Ukrainian) nuclear reactors at Chernobyl, 120 kilometers north of Kiev. The catastrophic consequences illustrated dramatically that state frontiers afford no protection against a major incident and that international cooperation of a systematic kind is necessary to control and remedy the consequences. The environmental, financial, and international regulatory consequences of Chernobyl have not yet been fully resolved.

Among influential developments that introduced or popularized concepts are the 1970 UNESCO report *Man and the Biosphere*, the 1972 UN Convention on the Protection of the Global Cultural and Natural Patrimony, and the UN Program for the Environment. These UN initiatives made the idea of the interdependence of environmental issues familiar, which in turn promoted the ideas of the common heritage of mankind and global stewardship.[26] The term "common heritage of mankind" entered common usage in international proposals and legal texts by UNESCO. The new discourse on the environment modified the traditional discourse about frontiers.

Despite all the problems of defining the general objective of environmental protection and of designing internationally enforceable regimes, some progress has been made. International organizations (such as the International Atomic Energy Authority) have assumed responsibilities for research, exchange of information, regulation, control of the application of rules, and even management of natural resources. Institutions and arrangements have been set up at global, regional, subregional, multilateral, and bilateral levels, depending on the nature of the problems. Some problems are truly global, such as the protection of whales and the ozone layer. Others are local, such as the purity of water, which is a matter for cooperation between neighboring states. For example, some relatively old bilateral agreements infringed the territorial principle, such as the 1944 International Boundary and Water Commission between Mexico and the United States, which gives diplomatic immunity and freedom of movement to officials of both nationalities to inspect water shortage and pollution problems.[27] But when disputes about the trade-off between economic development and environmental protection occur across international frontiers, the disagreements tend to remain unresolved.

The regional level of international organization has assumed a major role in environmental protection, especially in Europe. Between 1967 and 1991, the EC adopted no fewer than eighty directives containing measures of environmental protection directly applicable in the member states. The EU member states of the EC take the collective view that common environmental rules are essential in the construction of a unified market.[28] Regional environmental problems, such as pollution of the Mediterranean,[29] sometimes have to be tackled without the help of a pre-existing regional organization that groups all the interested states. However, the general system of international arrangements for environmental protection is emerging as a real constraint on the exercise of state sovereignty. Influential international nongovernmental organizations and transfrontier political coalitions have been established, which apply pressure on both governments and international organizations. Perceptions of territorial sovereignty are changing because, in environmental matters, states no longer appear to have the right to sanction activities within their frontiers.

International broadcasting is a different kind of intrusion into state territory, but its potential impact on mentalities and cultural identities may be greater than issues of environmental protection. International radio broadcasting has been a powerful instrument for pursuing military, political, and economic objectives during most of the twentieth century (Wasburn 1992). But the Cold War use of radio and the dominance of Western, mainly American, media were in due course subject to vigorous criticism from left-wing critics and from Third World governments. Noam Chomsky (1982) was a late but distinguished critic of the Cold War broadcast propaganda. The influence of the Western media in the poor countries has been variously described as electronic colonialism, cultural domination, and media imperialism.[30] These phrases were invented by left-wing scholars, advancing one form or another of dependency theory. They represented the poorer countries as pawns in the hands of advanced capitalist countries, often held in thrall by their own belief systems that had been deliberately manipulated by Western capitalist interests. Demands were formulated for a new world-information order. Proposals were put forward in the UNESCO Report (1979) of the International Commission for the Study of Communication, which suggested a number of radical ways of reducing Western media dominance. These were almost entirely disregarded.

The appearance of direct television broadcasting by satellite provided potentially an even more powerful instrument of transfrontier influence than radio, particularly in the case of broadcasting services devoted to news and information (CNN is currently the only truly global satellite news service). A specific image of global relations can be projected along with selective factual, linguistic, political, and social propaganda, which, though unlikely to affect decisively the outcome of particular crises, can, through cumulative long-term effects, powerfully influence perceptions of the issues at stake in global competition. The ending of the Cold War does not presage the termination of international conflict over such matters as the environment, access to scarce and valuable resources, economic competition, and movement of people. In the future, control of information and powerful means of communication are likely to be more, rather than less, important.

There have been few attempts to create an international regime for regulating direct television broadcasting. A UN General Assembly resolution of 1982 on principles governing utilization by states of artificial satellites was hostile toward direct television broadcasting, because Third World governments were concerned about the political implications of unrestricted reception of these broadcasts in their territories. This resolution attracted a large majority but was not supported by the industrialized countries that had access or could easily acquire access to the necessary technology. There is little that Third World countries can do to control the effects of direct satellite broadcasting, except for the extreme of banning the discs and aerials necessary for reception of the broadcasts (a step that Iran took in April 1994). Other moves have been limited to Europe and, far from being restrictive, have been concerned to guarantee free communication of information, unless it conflicts with views of public morality.[31] The European Community was also concerned about arriving at a common European approach to satellite broadcasting so that it could negotiate as a bloc with the United States and Japan.

6. Conclusion

International negotiations about uninhabited spaces have become more intensive in the last twenty years; the trend is likely to continue. States attempt to extend their "reach" into empty spaces to gain benefits, to establish rights, and to prevent other states from establishing positions that, at some time in the future, may be to their strategic advantage. Activities in these spaces, made possible by new technologies, have raised fundamental questions about frontiers and sovereignty. However, arrangements have been established that encourage states to cooperate within recognized forums rather than engage in unrestrained competition, even though the medium-term stability of these arrangements is uncertain. Uninhabited spaces have already been the focus of attempts to create global, comprehensive, and enforceable regimes. International regimes, which may be defined as "collective action by states, based on shared principles, norms, rules, and decision-making procedures which constrain the behavior of individual states" (List and Rittberger 1992: 86), are essential to the management of the problems raised. The degree to which decisions are enforced depends on the assimilation of international agreements into the domestic law of states. This varies because of the uneven ratification procedures of states. Progress on creating global regimes is, and will continue to be, one measure of the extent to which sovereign states, in principle having complete dominion over their territories, are constrained by cooperative and regulatory arrangements. Global regimes will make the concept of sovereignty obsolescent and alter the nature of the international frontier as a political institution. Frontiers will take on some of the character of boundaries between states in a federal system.

In general, the technologies of telecommunications, transportation, surveillance from space, and mineral extraction have altered the significance of the control of territory and of the frontiers between state territories. The ease of crossing frontiers, of communication across frontiers, of establishing transfrontier economic and social relationships, and of utilizing empty spaces in pursuit of interests has altered perceptions of frontiers as effective barriers to human activity. These altered perceptions influence all the political processes that occur at or across frontiers. Developed states are no longer greatly concerned about changing the location of frontiers to their advantage, but they are intensely concerned with the functions of frontiers and the purposes they serve. Since states are now unable to control most transfrontier transactions, a much more complex search for comparative advantage over competitor states has become apparent. Moreover, states are now operating in a changing cultural environment. In cultural terms, frontiers have lost some of their sharp-edged quality. Participation in transfrontier and sometimes global cultures affects political identities and political institutions within states. An allusion to these themes is sufficient indication of the complexity of frontier processes and that much work remains to be done in the political science of frontiers.

Notes

1. For example, J. R. MacKay (1969). But when statistical analyses of boundary effects are firmly embedded in historical accounts of the development of boundary relations, a much enriched account may result. See Z. Rykiel (1985).

2. The relationship between the Nazi regime and an academic discipline (*Ostforschung*—research on the East) is a chilling example. See M. Burleigh (1988).

3. There have been a number of estimates of doubtful reliability. See J. F. Splettstoesser and G. M. Dreschhoff, (1990).

4. See discussions in J. F. Lovering and J. R. V. Prescott (1979) and more recently G. D. Triggs (1987); there are also three useful contributions in C. H. Schofield (1994).

5. *Antarctic Treaty System Handbook,* 6th edition 1989: viii.

6. For the text of the Treaty and all other relevant legal instruments relating to Antarctic see W. M. Bush (1982–1988).

7. For an excellent up-to-date survey of this complex field see W. C. Gilmore (1994).

8. See especially P. Weil (1989).

9. See, for example, J. P. Craven, J. Schneider, and C. Stimson,(1989); more generally see G. H. Blake (1987), F. Earney (1990), and B. Kwiatkowska (1989).

10. J. R. V. Prescott (1987); V. Enscalada (1979); P. J. Martin et al. (1985).

11. It was also subject to radically different interpretations. See M. Parenti (1986).

12. The right of overflight of international straits lying within territorial waters, even for military flights, is, however, included in the 1982 Law of the Sea Convention and according to some authorities already was part of customary international law.

13. For the texts of these, see T. L. Zwann (1988); for a review of all the treaties and agreements on outer space or having implications for space travel and exploration see G. H. Reynolds and R. P. Merges (1989), especially chapters 3–8

14. There was no treaty ban on antisatellite technology, and it was relatively easy to develop. See J. S. Nye and J. A. Schear (1987).

15. Some, however, argue that the effects of Articles I and IV of the Treaty are to ban all military activity.

16. A. Cocca (1986); N. M. Matte (1987).

17. The 1976 Bogotá Declaration of eight equatorial states (Brazil, Columbia, Congo, Ecuador, Indonesia, Kenya, Uganda, and Zaire) claimed sovereign rights over that part of the geostationary orbit above their territory—the rest, they admitted, was "the common heritage of mankind." They based their claim on two propositions: first, that the 1967 Treaty did not define outer space; second, that they were not provided with the relevant technical knowledge when the 1967 Treaty was being negotiated. A basic weakness of this claim was the difficulty, in practice, of asserting sovereign rights at the altitude of the geostationary orbit (35,800 kilometers). Also the 1969 and 1979 conventions on outer space ban the appropriation of outer space, the moon, and other celestial bodies.

18. For a review of these, see P. M. Martin (1992).

19. However, Ambassador R. E. Benedick argues strongly the case for some states proceeding more quickly than others in environmental standards in order to raise the standards of global stewardship; Benedick (1991).

20. See P. S. Thacher (1992). This collection is a basic source on the philosophical, legal, political, and institutional issues of international environmental protection.

21. Ships and aircraft have been regarded as major international polluters and, as a consequence, the IMO has adopted rules (exceptionally difficult to enforce) against cleaning out of bilges, and the ICAO has made rules against noise and gas emissions.

22. In 1970, the OECD established a committee for the environment that produced a series of studies, declarations of principle, and recommendations particularly *Problems of Transfrontier Pollution* (1974), *Legal Aspects of Transfrontier Pollution (1976)*, and *OECD and the Environment* (1978).

23. The EC has played the most important role in terms of enforceable directives that apply to its member states. Its first major project was the First Action Program on the Environment (1974–1976).

24. Notably, the 1968 European Convention for Water, the 1972 European Convention for Soils, and the 1970 Declaration on the Environment.

25. For examples of both on the U.S.-Mexican border, see C. R. Bath (1992).

26. These ideas were an essential intellectual basis for the banning of CFC gases by the 1985 Vienna Convention for the Protection of the Ozone Layer, the 1987 Montreal Protocol, and the 1990 London Revisions of the Montreal Protocol.

27. S. Weintraub (1990). In February 1992, after much criticism of the often U.S.-generated pollution of the Mexican frontier region, the two countries adopted in 1992 an action plan for the environment of the Mexican-United States border region. This plan, although lacking adequate financial support, is a model of flexible cooperation.

28. The interconnection of environmental and economic matters goes back to the origins of the ecologist movement from the protagonists of zero growth in the early 1970s (Dennis Meadows and his associates at MIT), the Club of Rome, and the Greenpeace movement. The phasing out of the use of CFC was explicit in international agreements such as the 1987 Montreal Protocol, and in influential reports such as the 1987 Bruntland Report. However, it is only in the context of the EC that there is a direct link between environmental and economic regulation

29. See P. M. Haas (1990).

30. See, for example, T. L. McPhail (1981).

31. Where stations are broadcasting pornography for profit by selling decoders, it is possible to ban the marketing of these devices. The station Red Hot Dutch had its revenues withheld in this way by a British government decision in 1993.

References

Anderson, B. 1991. *Imagined Communities. An Enquiry into the Origins and Spread of Nationalism* (revised edition). New York: Verso.

Antarctic Treaty System Handbook, 6th edition. 1989. Cambridge.

Auburn, F. M. 1982. *Antarctic Law and Politics*. London: Hurst.

Bath, C. R. 1992. "The Emerging Environmental Crisis along the United States-Mexico Boundary." In *The Changing Boundaries in the Americas. New Perspectives on the U.S.-Mexican, Central American and South American Borders*, Lawrence A. Herzog, ed. San Diego: Center for U.S.-Mexican Studies, University of California at San Diego.

Benedick, R. E. 1991. *Ozone Diplomacy: New Directions in Safeguarding the Planet.* Cambridge: Harvard University Press.

Blake, G. H., ed. 1987. *Maritime Boundaries and Ocean Resources.* London: Croom Helm.

Burleigh, M. 1988. *Germany Turns Eastwards. A Study of Ostforschung in the Third Reich.* Cambridge: Cambridge University Press.

Bush, W. M. 1982–1988. *Antarctica and International Law: A Collection of Inter-State and National Documents.* 4 vols. Dobbs Ferry, NY: Oceana Publications.

Charney, J. I., ed. 1982. *The New Nationalism and the Use of Common Space: Issues in Marine Pollution and the Exploitation of Antarctica.* Totowa, NJ: Allanheld, Osmun.

Chomsky, N. 1982. *Towards a New Cold War.* New York: Pantheon.

Cocca, A. 1986. "The Common Heritage of Mankind: Doctrine and Principle of Space Law." *Proceedings of the International Institute of Space Law* 17–24.

Connor, W. 1969. "Myths of Hemispheric, Continental, Regional, and State Unity." *Political Science Quarterly* 84 (4).

Craven, J. P., J. Schneider, and C. Stimson, eds. 1989. *The International Implications of Extended Maritime Jurisdiction in the Pacific.* University of Hawaii, Law of the Sea Institute.

Earney, F. 1990. *Marine Mineral Resources.* London: Routledge.

Enscalada, V. 1979. *Air Law.* Alphen aan den Rijn: Sijthoff and Nordhoof.

Gilmore, W. C. 1994. "Sea and Continental Shelf." *Stair Encyclopedia of Scots Law.* Vol. 21. London: Butterworths.

Haas, P. M. 1990. *Saving the Mediterranean: The Politics of International Environmental Co-operation.* New York: Columbia University Press.

Honoré, A. M. 1961. "Ownership." In *Oxford Essays in Jurisprudence*, A. G. Guest, ed. Oxford: Oxford University Press.

Johnstone, D. M. 1989. *The Theory and History of Ocean Boundary Making.* Kingston: McGill-Queens University Press.

Krepon, M. et al. 1990. *Commercial Observation Satellites and International Security.* New York: MacMillan and the Carnegie Foundation for International Peace.

Kwiatkowska, B. 1989. *The 200 Mile Exclusive Economic Zone in the New Law of the Sea.* Dordrecht: Nijhoff.

List, M., and V. Rittberger. 1992. "Regime Theory and International Environmental Management." In *The International Politics of the Environment*, A. Hurrell and B. Kingsbury, eds. Oxford: Clarendon Press.

Lovering, J. F., and J. R. V. Prescott. 1979. *Last of Lands: Antarctica.* Melbourne: Melbourne University Press.

Lyster, S. 1985. *International Wildlife Law.* Cambridge: Grotius.

MacKay, J. R. 1969. "The Interactive Hypothesis and Boundaries in Canada: A Preliminary Study." In *Spatial Analysis: A Reader in Statistical Geography*, B. J. L. Berry and D. F. Marble, eds. Englewood Cliffs: Prentice-Hall.

Malaurie, J. 1989. *Les Derniers Rois de Thulé. Avec les Esquimaux polaires face à leur destin.* Paris: Pion.

Malaurie, J. 1992. "L'Arctique soviétique, face aux miroirs brisés de l'occident." *Hérodote* 64 (January-March).

Martin P. J. et al. 1977. *Shawcross and Beaumont: Air Law.* London: Butterworths.

Martin, P. M. 1992. *Droit des activités spatiales.* Paris: Masson.

Matte, N.M. 1987. "The Common Heritage of Mankind Principle in Outer Space." *Annals of Air and Space Law.*

McPhail, T. L. 1981. *Electronic Colonialism: The Future of International Broadcasting.* London: Sage.

Nye, J. S., and J. A. Schear, eds. 1987. *Seeking Stability in Space: Anti-Satellite Weapons and the Evolving Space Race.* New York: University Press of America.

OECD. 1974. *Problems of Transfrontier Pollution*. Paris: OECD.

OECD. 1976. *Legal Aspects of Transfrontier Pollution*. Paris: OECD.

OECD. 1978. *OECD and the Environment*. Paris: OECD.

Parenti, M. 1986. *Inventing Reality. The Politics of the Mass Media*. New York: St. Martin's Press.

Peterson, M. J. 1988. *Managing the Frozen South*. Berkeley: University of California Press.

Poggi, G. 1978. *The Development of the Modern State*. London: Hutchinson.

Prescott, J. R. V. 1987. *Political Frontiers and Boundaries*. London: Allen and Unwin.

Reijnen, G. C. M., and W. de Graff. 1989. *The Pollution of Outer Space, in Particular of the Geostationary Orbit; Scientific, Policy and Legal Aspects*. Dordrecht: Nijhoff.

Reynolds, G. H., and R. P. Merges. 1989. *Outer Space: Problems of Law and Policy*. Boulder: Westview Press.

Rykiel, Z. 1985. "Regional Integration and Boundary Effect in the Katowice Region." In *Proceedings of the 7th British-Polish Geographical Seminar, 23-30 May 1983*, J. B. Goddard and Z. Taylor, eds. Warsaw: Polish Scientific Publishers.

Schofield, C. H., ed. 1994. *Global Boundaries*. London: Routledge.

Splettstoesser, J. F., and G. M. Dreschhoff, eds. 1990. *Mineral Resources Potential of Antarctica*. Washington D. C.: American Geophysical Union.

Strassoldo, R. 1970. *From Barrier to Junction: Towards a Sociological Theory of Borders*. Gorizia: ISIG.

Triggs, G. D., ed. 1987. *The Atlantic Treaty Regime. Law, Environment and Resources*. Cambridge: Cambridge University Press.

Waldron, J. 1988. *The Right to Private Property*. Oxford: Clarendon Press.

Wasburn, P. C. 1992. *Broadcasting Propaganda. International Radio Broadcasting and the Construction of Political Reality*. London: Praeger.

Weber, L. 1983. "European Organization for the Safety of Air Navigation (Eurocontrol)." *Encyclopedia of Public International Law*. Vol. 6. Amsterdam: North Holland.

Weil, P. 1989. *The Law of Maritime Delimitation—Reflections*. Cambridge: Grotius.

Weintraub, S. 1990. *A Marriage of Convenience. Relations between Mexico and the United States*. New York: Oxford University Press.

Zwann, T. L., ed. 1988. *Space Law: Views of the Future*. London: Kluwer.

The Changing Economics of International Borders and Border Regions

Norris C. Clement

1. Introduction and Overview

Recent changes in the structure of global economic and strategic relationships are dramatically transforming the functions of international borders and presenting new challenges and opportunities for cities-regions located near them.[1] This essay attempts to synthesize the major themes that have emerged in this context and refers to experiences in both Europe and North America. The general argument that will be developed here can best be synthesized as follows:

1. Historically, the economic function of international borders has largely been derivative of the political, economic, and strategic functions of the nation-state. That is, borders were regarded primarily as symbols of and instruments for maintaining national sovereignty and carrying out national policies. As such, borders were utilized to regulate the entry (and sometimes the exit) of goods and services (things and people) in accordance with the policies of the nation state, independent of the needs of border communities. Consequently, economists tended to treat borders primarily as barriers to international commerce, cutting them off from their natural hinterland, thereby limiting the development of those cities-regions[2] located adjacent to them.

2. Recently, however, a new political-economic environment has emerged from the growing acceptance of free-market policies—including global *freer trade* and regional trade blocs—and the end of the Cold War. This new *borderless* global economic environment is now eroding the historic functions of international borders and opening up new options for the development of *border regions*. Nevertheless, development under these new conditions is not guaranteed. In this context, *transborder collaboration*—co-existing with *transborder competi-*

tion—appears to be an important condition for development as regions displace the nation state as the relevant economic unit for formulating and implementing development policies.

In the first section of this paper the changing economic function of borders is explored. The second section synthesizes the main elements of recent thinking in the area of regional development generally in the context of the increasingly internationalized economic environment and the implications for the development of border regions specifically. The third section develops the implications of this analysis for public policy in border regions and discusses some of the responses that have already been implemented in response to these changing global economic conditions. The scope of the analysis is limited to Europe and North America.

2. The Changing Economic Functions of International Borders

> During this phase (WWII–1969), the border was conceptualized as a political line of demarcation between two autonomous nations or systems, a barrier to each through which the flow of people, goods, and services was monitored and controlled. The people and institutions which reflected these two cultures lying in juxtaposition to each other along the bi-national border were peripheral elements of each national system. Any form of cooperation or "leakage" which was not controlled by the central authority of each nation-state was seen as a dysfunctional element to both national systems. Solutions to these border problems were available only through the paternalistic action of federal diplomatic engagements (Stoddard 1986).

Stoddard's description of scholars' conceptualization of the border, based on the dominant international-relations paradigm of that period, still represents the basic position of most central governments today and has heavily influenced the concept of borders in other academic disciplines.

In economics, despite the lack of any general theory of borders,[3] international boundaries are usually associated with barriers to trade, including tariffs and quotas as well as qualitative restrictions. Such barriers tend to reduce the volume and value of trade and its associated benefits (i.e., production efficiencies and higher living standards). Additionally, to the extent that they are temporary or politically unstable, borders are associated with higher levels of risk and therefore tend to discourage investment and (legal) economic activity in adjacent regions.[4]

Of course, borders are not absolute barriers to trade but serve mainly as screening agents (permeable membranes) regarding what can *legally* flow from one political jurisdiction (country) to another and under what conditions. Commodities (and persons) that cannot legally pass through the ports of exit/entry are either excluded from international trade (or passage) or are compelled to utilize illegal means if they are to get to the other side. Thus, informal/illegal markets develop for smuggling items of high value (low-volume items such as drugs, exotic animals, and persons), while crossing costs vary according to the degree of risk and the severity of penalties, which, in turn, depend mainly on the strength and effectiveness of the two countries' law enforcement capabilities.

Historically, the quantity and quality of restrictions imposed on the flows of commodities and persons at their borders varied significantly between countries in accordance with national political, economic, and cultural norms and policies. In many cases, it was (and still is) these differences between national norms and policies that create(d) many of the opportunities for international trade and investment flows (e.g., U.S. direct foreign investment in Mexico during the period of industrial protectionism) and border transactions (i.e., prohibition of alcoholic beverages in the United States as an important factor in the development of Mexican border cities during the period from 1920 to 1933).

In summary, in market-based economies, goods and services (both inputs and outputs), technology, and people flow across borders in response to a constellation of market and nonmarket (i.e., social/cultural) conditions.[5] Clearly, the opportunities for generating profits presented by differences in price, quality, and availability of goods and services between countries is a powerful force for generating transborder flows of goods, services, finances, technology, and people.[6] However, in order for international sales/purchases to be realized, all commodities (and persons) must somehow pass *the border* (i.e., through ports of exit/entry). At that stage they are scrutinized according to the regimens of both countries. That is, importing countries allow goods, services, and people to enter only upon payment of required fees, presentation of necessary documentation, and compliance with elaborate sets of regulations, all of which are usually formulated at the national level in accordance with national interests.

Now, the question is, how does this view of the border square with today's conditions? In the last decade, due to the changing economic, political, and strategic factors indicated in note 1 at the end of this essay, Western European and North American borders have become less significant, *as economic barriers*, than at any time since the Great Depression of the 1930s, when tariffs were at their highest during this century. Tariff rates have been reduced significantly while quotas and qualitative restrictions are being phased out, largely due to negotiations carried out in the context of the General Agreement on Tariffs and Trade (GATT) and regional trade blocs (i.e., the European Union [EU] and the North American Free Trade Agreement [NAFTA]).[7]

In Western Europe, where the process of regional economic integration has proceeded the longest and the deepest, restrictions on the mobility of goods/services, capital, and labor have been dramatically reduced within the EU creating two significantly different types of borders: *internal* (between EU member states) and *external* (between EU member and nonmember states).

Looking at Europe as a whole, the disintegration of the Soviet Union and the reduction of Cold War hostilities resulted in spectacular changes between nations that were previously on different sides of the Iron Curtain. Paradoxically, however, this has not resulted in a uniform easing of restrictions. In many places, as old regimes suddenly disintegrated, more openness on borders prompted an urgent need for new mechanisms to facilitate flows of persons and products across international borders,[8] but in others (e.g., between the states of the former Soviet Union) these changes resulted in less openness.

In North America, where the process of regional integration is still viewed as rather limited (i.e., movement to a free trade area as opposed to "economic union" as in Europe), even in the long term, it will be some years yet before the concept of internal and external borders becomes operational.[9]

Nevertheless, for internal borders the traditional economic functions are changing significantly while for external borders they are still relevant, but decreasingly so, due to the expanding influence and coverage of the GATT and the International Monetary Fund (IMF) in the entire world economy. Thus, except where borders are still being contested (e.g., between some of the republics of the former Soviet Union) or are still relatively closed for national-security reasons (e.g., between Estonia and Russia), the volume of (trans)border crossings of both goods (i.e., exports, imports, and border transactions) and people seems to be increasing. Similarly, interaction between people and governments formerly separated by international borders is increasing as they attempt to improve living standards and resolve the many local transborder economic, social, political, and environmental problems that cannot be prevented from spilling over international borders.

Additionally, the economic development-prospects of border regions are also changing dramatically. Residents of localities adjacent to international borders, that formerly were isolated and/or underpopulated and usually poor (i.e., probably located on a European external border), are now actively searching for development policies that often include collaboration with localities on the other side. However, these localities frequently differ greatly in "geographical size, population density, their economic characteristics and problems and degree of development as well as cultural-linguistic characteristics" (Martinos and Caspari 1990: 3) and therefore often have difficulty in actually achieving collaboration.

On the other end of the scale are localities that formerly benefited from "the development of trading activity at the border, the storage of goods and earnings derived from the collection of duties ..." (i.e., probably located on a European internal border with a high volume of dutiable trading) (Hansen 1981: 25). Now, however, with the virtual disappearance of barriers to goods and people between member nations, the economic activities associated with the border (perhaps a large part of the region's economic base) have also dwindled or, in some cases, disappeared.

In both of these special cases, the economic fortunes of border regions are changing due to the changing economic functions of their particular border, factors outside the control of the regions themselves. There is, however, a much more general case that, hopefully, will enable the identification of variables that are in the power of the region to control, at least partially, thereby enabling them to formulate strategies for economic development.

3. The Dynamics of Globalization

This section attempts to synthesize the main intellectual components of a paradigm shift regarding the new role of cities-regions in today's increasingly globalized economic environment. From this general synthesis, some implications can be derived regarding the prospects for the economic development of border regions-cities in the next section.

Figures 1 through 4 illustrate four levels of change, moving from technological change (1) to the effects on economic structures (2), which in turn affect the changing spatial distribution of industry (3) and changing government structures and functions (4).

In Figure 1, the main motor of change is identified as technological change, primarily in the transportation and communications sectors, but also in the information/computer sectors. Not only have these key services become more inexpensive, but they also have become faster and more widely available throughout the world. Thus, many firms are now freer to go international (geographi-

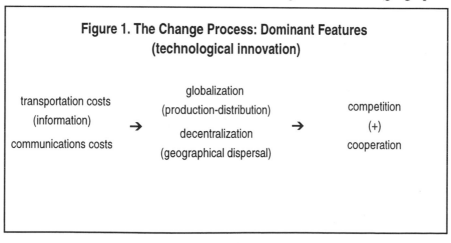

**Figure 1. The Change Process: Dominant Features
(technological innovation)**

transportation costs
(information)   globalization
                                    (production-distribution)   competition
          →   →   (+)
communications costs   decentralization   cooperation
                                    (geographical dispersal)

cally), to locate any or all phases of production wherever costs are lowest or conditions most appropriate to the firm's overall strategy.

Smart firms are now able to devise global strategies, decentralizing and/or dispersing their operations and managing them from afar through fax, voice, and data transmission, while shipping components and products via transportation systems which each day become more economical and offer more options.[10] The resulting spatial redeployment of production, along with the tendency toward trade liberalization carried out under the auspices of multilateral institutions such as GATT and the formation of regional trade blocs such as the EU and the NAFTA, as well as the emergence of many Third World countries as major manufacturing powers, have dramatically increased global competition. But as demonstrated below, the accelerated pace and cost of technological innovation has stimulated firms to increase their cooperation with other firms as well as with governments and universities.

Figure 2 outlines the main changes in economic structure in recent decades. What is well known is the transformation of production in all developed economies, although in varying degrees, from the real goods sectors (agriculture and

---

Figure 2. Economic Structures (how firms organize and do business)

OLD/TRADITIONAL	→	NEW/ EMERGING
agriculture/manufacturing	→	more service activities (information, financial, and tourism)
large firms: economies of scale	→	smaller firms: economies of scope (flexible production systems)
national market perspective (inputs and outputs)	→	international perspective offshore sourcing (inputs) production phases dispersed global marketing (outputs)
centralization of functions (everything in-house)	→	decentralization of functions (outside specialists and blurring of manufacturing-service sectors)
stable, full-time work force (high pay, full benefits)	→	more temporary, part-time workers (fewer benefits)
hierarchical organization	→	work rules more flexible
competitive activities (exclusively)	→	new strategies require cooperation, complex alliances, and networks (firms-governments-universities)

manufacturing) to service and information-based economies. The shift from large- to small- and medium-sized firms as the main source of new jobs is also well documented, as is the shift from a regional/national perspective to an international one (i.e., sourcing input—both component parts and human services—offshore and marketing outputs globally).

What is not so well known, however, are the enormous changes taking place within firms, especially high-tech companies, changes that include:

- The emergence of computer-aided technologies that permit manufacturing firms to efficiently produce small quantities of custom-made products. Such flexible production systems respond to economies of scope instead of the economies of scale associated with traditional, large manufacturing firms.
- The gradual demise of traditional assembly lines and hierarchical organizational structures.
- More use of outside technical and business services (outsourcing), together with increased use of subcontractors, blurring the traditional distinction between manufacturing and services while creating new kinds of industrial clusters.

While these new practices often result in lower costs and an enhanced ability to respond to new market opportunities, employees' work roles and traditional notions of job security are changing considerably, increasing the need for worker retraining, counseling, and relocation services usually provided by various levels of government.

Finally, note that firms no longer are exclusively competitive. The need to innovate rapidly and the enormous costs of developing new products and tech-

---

Figure 3. Regional Structure (reflects changing location determinants)

OLD/TRADITIONAL	→	NEW/EMERGING
core-periphery: dynamic industries in core	→	old core (restructured, diverse) new core (smaller, niche markets) periphery (most other regions)
location factors (costs; proximity to resources, markets, and suppliers)	→	congestion costs in core rise mature industries → low wage areas new industries → climate, quality of life, labor force, research facilities
border regions in periphery	→	new core (?): new opportunities available, but not guaranteed

niques have pushed firms into cooperative networks and alliances with competing firms, governments, and university research centers (Reich 1990).

Figure 3 summarizes the effects of these changes on the regional (geographical) structure, or location of industry: the spatial dimension of the story. Traditionally, regional structures were viewed in a dichotomous framework of *core-periphery*. Traditional core areas—formed on the basis of proximity to resources, suppliers, and markets—were characterized mainly by large-scale manufacturing firms involved in the production of producer goods and consumer durables, as well as large financial firms. Meanwhile, activities like agriculture, forestry, fishing, mining, and small-scale manufacturing were located in the periphery.

Now, however, it is clear that since industrial restructuring began in both the United States and Europe in the 1970s, traditional core areas have been transformed in terms of both production techniques and product types (i.e., most mature products have either been automated or moved to lower-cost regions) and a *new core* has emerged, mainly in southern states. Simplistically, the firms of the new core areas generally possess the main characteristics of the modern firm, as portrayed in the previous frame. What is important here is that these firms seek different location characteristics that, within some limits, emphasize qualitative aspects (e.g., climate and environment) over quantitative cost factors. And, in the new scheme of things—disappearing economic borders—the cul-de-sac quality of border cities diminishes, presenting many new opportunities if they are able to negotiate collaborative relationships with their neighbors "on the other side" in order to fashion development strategies for the transborder region.

Figure 4 outlines the major changes in governmental structures and functions that have come mainly in response to changes already presented in Figures 1–3.

- At the national level, stabilization measures and monetary and fiscal policies, traditionally used to combat the extremes of the business cycle, have become less effective in the 1990s due to: *(a)* increased globalization resulting in fewer degrees of freedom, *(b)* large budget deficits that make stimulatory policies politically unacceptable, and *(c)* a growing awareness that economic problems in the United States and Europe are structural not cyclical.
- Growing dissatisfaction with statist policies has resulted in a shift to the traditional conservative tendencies of less reliance on and more selective uses of government.[11]
- Restructuring frequently is good for the economy, while bad for the people, at least in the short run, resulting in growing demand for govern-

ment services and/or transfer payments. The attack on welfare has also meant scapegoating immigrants in many countries.[12]

- As national governments attempt to reinvent government, new forms are tried, beginning with decentralization and expanding to strategic urban networks, especially in the EU.
- With new emphasis on high tech, high value-added activity, and rising income gaps between regions, smart (subnational) governments devise strategies better to play the new economic game by improving or maintaining the quality of life. These include increased investment in physical and social infrastructure and the development of new relations between private, public, and academic institutions in order to improve productivity and what is sometimes called the *innovative milieu*.

Figure 4. Governmental Structures and Functions
(responses to the above)

OLD/TRADITIONAL	→	NEW/EMERGING
stabilization policies: (national level)	→	less national autonomy due to globalization, budget deficits
industrial policies (national level)	→	[in U.S.] now expanding at national and regional levels [in EU] subordinated to regional policies shaped in Brussels
social welfare system	→	under attack everywhere as unemployment and welfare costs grow (immigrant role here important)
large, centralized (national level)	→	decentralized → local/regional (reinvent roles/structures) EU: internal borders disappear, transnational government emerges, and strategic urban networks form
universities: national governments support education and basic research	→	R & D/training functions at regional level increase as do alliances with firms/governments (private-public-academic partnerships)

4. Implications for the Economic Development of Border Regions

Before examining the implications of this analysis for public policy in border regions, it might be helpful to restate it in summary form, especially as it relates to border regions.[13] First, it is clear that the traditional economic functions of borders—as barriers to international commerce—are rapidly eroding as a consequence of a constellation of technological, economic, and political-strategic factors. Second, as a consequence of some of these same factors, economic enterprises are not only conducting business differently but are doing it in different places, resulting in changing regional structures between and within nation states, new roles and structures for governments at all levels, and expanded options for border regions located in the traditional periphery.

In brief, the main implication of section 2 of this paper, "The Changing Economic Functions of International Borders," is that continued erosion of the traditional functions of borders will, *ceteris paribus,* stimulate the following changes—in varying magnitudes and over time—in the affected countries and their border regions:

- increased (transborder) flows of trade[14] (i.e., both traditional exports/imports and border transactions), investment, and labor (if permitted under the new regime)
- changes in both the level and the structure of trade, investment, output, consumption, and employment[15]
- changes in the location of many economic activities[16]

These changes occur in response to the changing structure of prices that now confronts producers and resource owners, both within and outside of the area, who will respond to new profit- and income-maximizing opportunities. In the traditional economics literature, the gains from trade, which incidentally are not necessarily evenly distributed geographically or sectorally, emanate from comparative advantage, economies of scale, and more competitive—and hence more efficient—domestic markets.[17]

The major implication of section 3, "The Dynamics of Globalization," is that many border regions traditionally relegated to the periphery of economic activity may now be able to attract new industries and/or stimulate the expansion of existing ones. This, in turn, could lead to new forms of economic development in the region.[18]

It would be incorrect, however, to conclude that, because of these new conditions, economic development for border regions is now assured. On the contrary, economic development in the post-Cold War era may be even more difficult to achieve than before, precisely because of the new, more competitive environment that now exists. Thus, many border regions are likely to continue to remain in the periphery, both geographically and economically.

Equally important is the fact that economic expansion in most countries of North America and Europe in recent years has occurred without significant (positive) employment effects. Therefore, we have, in many instances, situations where "the economy is doing quite well, but the people are not."

What, then, differentiates cities-regions that will prosper in the new economy from those that will stagnate or deteriorate? There is no one factor that can be identified; clearly, location is important, as are a diverse economic base, a well-trained work force, links with research institutions, modern telecommunications and transport facilities, a high quality of life and the institutional capacity to design and implement future-oriented development strategies (Commission of the European Communities 1992: 22). However, in the case of border regions there is yet another factor that is important: a functioning system of transborder cooperation.

As previously noted, border regions vary a great deal with respect to population density and economic development, but most tend to suffer from certain handicaps including lower incomes and higher unemployment rates in their own national context, a peripheral position with respect to national economic and political decision making, a multitude of problems imposed by the propinquity of different legal and administrative systems, poor cross-border communications, and a lack of coordination in public services as well as differences in culture and language.

The challenge, then, is economically, administratively, and culturally to unite the regions that were previously divided by the international border. Alternatively, it can be said that not only must border regions do everything that other regions must do in terms of increasing their competitiveness, but they must also do it *in collaboration with* the region(s) on the other side. This not only increases the number of decision makers but also increases the heterogeneity of the decision-making body and complexity of the decision-making process.

Nevertheless, transborder cooperation of some kind is absolutely necessary due to the presence of economies of scale associated with the creation of physical-infrastructure facilities as well as the many positive and negative externalities involved in the economic-development process. That is, the construction of bridges, highways, and port facilities is frequently only feasible if financed by all parties deriving benefits from them. Even if only one side was able to finance the construction of, say, a regional airport, some of the benefits would accrue automatically to the other side. The same can be said for the provision of social infrastructure (i.e., educational and health services and police and fire protection). Similarly, regional efforts to promote the region's exports and transborder tourism, as well as to extol the region's virtues as a retirement haven or good place to invest and do business, can frequently be done cheaper and more effectively in concert. Lobbying efforts in the two nations' capitals or before international and/or regional governments (e.g., the EU in Brussels) can frequently be much more effective if done collaboratively.

Thus, formal and/or informal transborder consultation-coordination mechanisms must be formed in order to formulate and implement the various phases inherent in a strategic plan for increasing the region's international competitiveness. The existence of such mechanisms does not imply anything a priori about the nature of the transborder relationship, which can range from peaceful coexistence to partners in development. Additionally, it must be noted that in many areas (e.g., attracting new firms to the region or business for convention centers) there will be a strong element of competition between the two regions.[19]

The question of how to form collaborative mechanisms is a complicated one, and most transborder communities begin from ground zero to fashion their own home-grown response. However, where there is little history of local cooperation to build on, communities in Europe can now learn from the experiences of others via an EU pilot project, Linkage Assistance and Cooperation for the European Border Regions (LACE) (Association of European Border Communities 1991). This project, a component of a relatively large EU network of border regions, attempts to disseminate *know-how* on a wide variety of border issues among European border communities.[20] Of course, this type of organized, multilateral effort is important, and outside agencies can provide needed expertise and guidance. Nevertheless, establishing positive, local, transborder synergies is an essential element of the socio-economic development process. This process, in turn, depends on the commitment and skills of local leaders on both sides of the border and the willingness of their national governments to allow such processes to occur, possibly at the cost of eroding their own power.

Along the U.S.-Mexican border no such network exists, at least in any formal sense. Each twin-city seems to struggle to make do with an *ad hoc* blend of informal and formal mechanisms. At the same time, the annual meeting of the ten border governors (four from the United States and six from Mexico) provides a slim thread of coordination between the otherwise disparate state governmental efforts in transborder collaboration along the 3,000-kilometer boundary. Additionally, a private lobbying group, the Border Trade Alliance, focuses on border issues of special interest to private firms (e.g., border crossings, bridges, and toxic-waste disposal sites). Perhaps a binational network organization like the League of U.S. Border Cities and Counties that existed briefly in the late 1970s should be formed both to lobby for the border region's interests in Washington, D.C., and Mexico City and to exchange *best practice* experiences on building transborder collaboration. Such an effort could unite private, public, and academic efforts in this area and could even be linked, via Internet, to similar efforts in other parts of the world.

5. Conclusions

Much remains to be said regarding the process of planning for transborder regional development. However, planning processes lie outside of the scope of this paper and have been discussed extensively elsewhere (Clement 1994; Kresl 1992). There are two issues, however, that should be addressed in this final section.

First, it is important to clarify that the mainstream approach utilized in this analysis embraces the perspective that border regions must adopt a strategy of cross-border cooperation in order to become more effective competitors in an increasingly globalized economy. Implicit in the argument is the assumption that, if transborder communities are successful at formulating and implementing a strategic plan for improving their competitive position, the region's exports will increase and firms will be attracted to the region. Thus, jobs—hopefully, high-paying jobs—and a larger tax base will be generated that can be utilized to improve the region's physical and social infrastructure, attracting capital into the area, creating a virtuous cycle of development (Reich 1992).

What the analysis neglects to say, however, is that thousands of other communities in North America and Europe are competing with one another to find their niche in the global economy and, at the same time, attract those high-tech corporations that represent the pot of gold at the end of the rainbow. Clearly, not all regions will succeed. This is partly because they have not been able to mobilize their resources in such a way as to become competitive with comparable regions, and partly because some regions in Eastern Europe and the developing countries are able to offer many of the same resources at a fraction of the cost. Thus, transnational corporations, being highly mobile and relatively responsive to favorable cost conditions, will, when strategically convenient, locate in low-cost areas where human and environmental conditions are abysmal, leaving previously developed regions in demise.

The question that begs to be answered is the following: Is there an alternative development strategy, one that is not so dependent on the vicissitudes of the market, or, perhaps more appropriately, is there an alternative to the type of development that regions now are so actively seeking? The concept of sustainable development at the regional level, while still somewhat undefined, deserves more attention by both academics and practitioners.[21]

The final issue to be addressed here is the importance of comparative research in all of these areas. The basic premise is that, despite their many differences, border regions throughout the world exhibit many similarities. Thus, there would seem to be many benefits to virtually all kinds of research that, when coupled with the expertise of practitioners and networking organizations, could contribute a wealth of information to both new and old transborder regions.

Notes

1. The major changes are well known, but are perhaps worthwhile noting here. First and foremost is the long-term tendency toward increased internationalization of the economy throughout the post-World War II period that was fomented by the United States and by the two main multilateral economic institutions that came into existence after WWII: the General Agreement on Tariffs and Trade (GATT) and the International Monetary Fund (IMF). This tendency was reinforced since the 1980s by the formation and/or deepening of regional trade blocs in both Europe and North America. Second is the dissolution of the Soviet Union in the early 1990s, which has had most effect on Europe but, of course, has affected the entire world. Finally, the emergence of supply-side economics in the United States and Mexico's debt crisis in the early 1980s not only influenced North American economic policies but provided added impetus to market-oriented, liberalization, and privatization policies throughout the globe.

2. Notes on terminology: (1) Throughout this paper the terms city and region will be used interchangeably. It is understood that in each region, however defined, there is usually a leading city and a hinterland as well as smaller cities. The identity of the region, however, is usually defined by the use of the leading city's name. (2) The terms *border* and *frontier* will not usually be used interchangeably, although they can be. Border will simply refer to a boundary dividing two political entities or jurisdictions, while frontier has the connotation of a zone of undeveloped or unsettled territory.

3. Chapter 2 of Niles Hansen's book on the U.S. border region with Mexico (1981) provides an accessible summary of the relevant theoretical work in economics on borders and border regions.

4. In the orthodox economics literature, barriers to trade are generally regarded as barriers to economic development; however, economic history is replete with examples of how protectionism was used to stimulate national development. Indeed, it can be argued that import substitution industrialization, which usually provides for high degrees of protection, has been an important phase in most countries' development, from Japan and the United States to the NICs (newly industrialized countries) of the post-World War II era.

5. A recent study of border crossers at San Diego-Tijuana ports of entry (San Diego Dialogue 1994) resulted in the following classification of *primary purpose* (listed in order of declining importance): shopping, social visits, work, tourism, and other (including attendance at cultural and sporting events).

6. Some data on these flows are available to border communities in the United States and Mexico (e.g., exports, imports, border crossings, and international tourism). However, one important category, local transborder shopping expenditures and purchases (border transactions), usually goes unreported. Mexico's central bank regularly conducts surveys of these *transacciones fronterizas* and reports them on a periodic basis in its national Balance of

Payments statement for the border region as a whole, but not for each individual set of twin-cities (e.g., San Diego-Tijuana).

7. From the orthodox perspective, regional-integration efforts are regarded as second best to multilateral (i.e., GATT) initiatives for at least two reasons: (*a*) lowering trade barriers only between member countries can result in costs (i.e., trade diversion, switching import purchases from lower-cost nonmember countries to higher-cost member countries), as well as benefits (i.e., trade creation switching purchases from higher cost domestic producers to lower cost member countries); and (*b*) external barriers to trade from nonmember countries can be raised to protect member countries from international competition, thereby creating a fortress with respect to the rest of the world.

8. Border crossings between Western European and Soviet-bloc countries were strictly regulated during the Cold War. With the sudden disintegration and/or liberalization of the old order came sudden and unanticipated border traffic of people as well as goods. Anecdotal evidence suggests that most local governments were not prepared for such events, and a great deal of chaos and improvisation occurred.

9. A free-trade area provides for the elimination (over a specified period of years) of trade barriers between member countries on a specified group of goods (or all goods), with each country determining its own level of external tariffs against nonmembers. The next higher level of integration, a customs union, provides for free trade and a common external tariff, while a common market adds free movement of labor and capital. Finally, an economic union includes factors such as group-determined policies (e.g., macroeconomic stabilization policies), harmonization of standards, and eventually a common currency.

10. The dramatic decline of (real) oil prices since the early 1980s has probably accelerated many of these trends as well.

11. Clearly, the growing interdependency of capital markets limits national autonomy in this sense, as changes in interest rates frequently result in changes in exchange rates—if they are flexible—as short-term capital moves to take advantage of the differentials.

12. The high (over 10 percent) rates of unemployment in most European countries are often blamed on overgenerous welfare benefits, overregulation, and inefficient state-owned industries; however, there is considerable opposition to dismantling these policies. In the United States, anti-statist sentiment is also high; however, the Clinton administration openly supports the expansion of certain policies (e.g., expanded health care and training programs) that could expand the government's role in certain sectors of the economy.

13. The methodological question of what constitutes a region will not be addressed here. It is sufficient to say that this question frequently is answered simply by defining the border region in terms of administrative units (i.e., those municipalities/counties adjacent to the international boundary). Other approaches define border regions in more conceptual terms, utilizing the concepts of internationality and/or of intensity and extension of border relations (Hansen 1981; Bustamante 1989).

14. This will occur for a variety of reasons, including the decline of transactions costs associated with the elimination of borders.

15. Changes in exchange rates can also affect these variables by changing the relative prices that border shoppers and exporting/importing firms face on a daily basis. Additionally, exchange-rate instability can influence investment in border regions.

16. Under most forms of regional economic integration, incentives and/or subsidies for firms locating in border regions, which frequently are poorer than regions located in core areas,

must be phased out over a specified period of time. The absence of subsidies then provides a level playing field for firms from both sides of the international boundary. A good example of this is the duty free zone of Baja California and neighboring states on the Mexican-U.S. border, which will be phased out under NAFTA.

17. Wonnacott 1991, p. 10. Traditional economics does not systematically treat the costs of trade (i.e., the increases in unemployment and bankruptcies that can lead to the demise of entire communities as a result of increased competition), since the models indicate that, in economic terms and under certain assumptions, gains outweigh losses.

18. The phrase "new forms of economic development" can be interpreted in two ways. In traditional or mainstream economics this would refer to changes in the structure of output of a region as it moved from reliance on the primary-sector activities (i.e., agriculture, forestry and mining, which traditionally have characterized resource-based, underdeveloped economies) to the secondary- and tertiary-sector activities (i.e., manufacturing and construction, as well as commerce and information-related services). These structural changes would, in the traditional theory, result in increases in efficiency that would, in turn, result in changes in certain economic indicators (e.g., GDP per capita and higher urban/rural ratios) that reflect development.

An alternative model of development, "sustainable development," holds that traditional structural changes and concomitant changes in economic indicators might lead to short-term gains in output and consumption, however, at the expense of both the carrying capacity of the physical environment and the quality of life usually associated with stable human communities. While the author is very sympathetic to the sustainable development model, the analysis of this paper will be confined to the traditional/mainstream analysis.

19. Some competition can be minimized if complementarities can be identified and made operational. For example, currently in the San Diego-Tijuana region on the U.S.-Mexican border, a study is being carried out to explore the feasibility of a cross-border industrial strategy. Such a strategy, based on the comparative advantages of each region could increase economic activity on both sides of the border by attracting reverse investment and substituting imported components with components manufactured in the region (San Diego Dialogue 1994).

20. Specifically, LACE provides the following services: technical assistance to border regions; the establishment of a database; the promotion of networking between border regions; and dissemination and publicity (Association of European Border Regions 1991). Note also that the Inter-American Development Bank has created an Institute for the Integration of Latin America (INTAL) that developed special programs in relation to "the border as factor of integration" (Pérez Castillo 1992).

21. A common definition of sustainability is ensuring that the use of resources and the environment today does not damage the prospect of their use by future generations (International Centre for Sustainable Cities 1994: 6).

References

Association of European Border Regions. 1991. "Information Brochure: Linkage Assistance and Cooperation for the European Border Regions." Gronau, Germany: EUREGIO.

Bustamante, J. A. 1989. "Frontera México-Estados Unidos: reflexiones para un marco teórico." *Frontera Norte* 1.

Clement, Norris C. 1994. "Local Responses to Globalization: New Opportunities for the San Diego-Tijuana Region." In *North American Cities and the Global Economy: Challenges and Opportunities*, E. Fry and P. Kresl, eds. Forthcoming.

Commission of the European Communities: Directorate-General for Regional Policy. 1992. *Regional Development Studies: Urbanization and the Functions of Cities in the European Community*. Brussels.

Hansen, Niles. 1981. *The Border Economy: Regional Development in the Southwest*. Austin: University of Texas Press.

International Centre for Sustainable Cities. 1994. *Opportunities for Achieving Sustainability in Cascadia*. Vancouver and Seattle: The Cascadia Institute and Discovery Institute.

Kresl, P. 1992. *The Urban Economy and Regional Trade Liberalization*. New York: Praeger.

Martinos, H., and A. Caspari. 1990. *Cooperation Between Border Regions for Local and Regional Development*. Brussels: Commission of the European Communities, Directorate-General XVI.

Pérez Castillo, Juan Pablo. 1992. "Free Trade, the Border, and Integration." In *The Mexican-U.S. Border Region and the Free Trade Agreement*, Paul Ganster and Eugenio Valenciano, eds. San Diego: Institute for Regional Studies of the Californias, San Diego State University.

Reich, R. B. 1992. *The Work of Nations*. New York: Vintage Books.

San Diego Dialogue. 1994. *Who Crosses the Border: A View of the San Diego/Tijuana Metropolitan Region*. San Diego: University of California at San Diego (UCSD Extension).

Stoddard, E. R. 1986. "Border Studies as an Emergent Field of Scientific Inquiry: Scholarly Contributions of U.S.-Mexico Borderland Studies." *Journal of Borderlands Studies* 1.

Wonnacott, R. J. 1991. *The Economics of Overlapping Free Trade Areas and the Mexican Challenge*. Toronto and Washington, D.C.: Canadian-American Committee, C.D. Howe Institute, and National Planning Institute.

Interregional Cooperation and a New Regionalist Paradigm

Pertti Joenniemi

1. Introductory Remarks

In discussing the global phenomenon of transboundary and interregional cooperation we must also address the capacity of subnational units—in this case, of regions themselves—to initiate and develop such cooperation. We are being forced, it would seem, to readjust our geopolitical mental maps and reevaluate the roles that international organizations, nation-states, regions, subregions, cities, and nongovernmental organizations play in international affairs. The evolution of an international economy, as well as changes in geopolitical configurations in many parts of the world, is providing regions with the means to redefine international relations in their own best interests. The key to increased subnational paradiplomacy lies in a supranational context where issues of security are no longer narrowly or strictly nationally defined.

This paper attempts to expand upon new paradigms of international relations theory by stressing the role of self-defined regional identities in establishing patterns of transboundary and interregional cooperation. In Europe and elsewhere, the resurgence of regions that once enjoyed considerable autonomy, as well as the strengthening of new regional identities, is contributing to the increasing complexity of relationships between nation-states.

Old regions have a place within a certain theoretical and conceptual context whereas *new* ones defy traditional definitions. The very talk about new regions implies that they are increasingly recognized as conscious and purposeful agents with considerable capacity for action. A change in emphases seems to be taking place in the sense that the effective power wielded by new regional formations and regional actors has increased; they are no longer subthemes or side aspects of *Realpolitik*, nor can they be treated separately from concepts such as sovereignty and the centralization of state power. Regions are increasingly referred to in reverent terms, indicating a stronger ontological status; they are provided with symbolic significance, acquire formal names, and, in many cases, are creating their own institutions.

As an emerging phenomenon, self-defined regional formations are the focus of considerable attention as well as debate in the social sciences. It often starts with the very definition of what regions are. In a recent pilot study on what he calls the *new regionalism*, Hettne (1994: 4) writes: "We cannot define regions because they define themselves by evolving from objective, but dormant, to subjective, active existence." Hettne thinks of regionalism as something previously subsumed within the confrontational Cold War logic, representing an imposed type of regionalism, a tool of statist policies and control if not a form of subimperialism. However, this kind of regionalism, integral to previous policies and structures, is in retreat as a result of hegemonic decline. Instead of the former *malign* forms we now have posthegemonic and *benign* forms of regionalism.

To talk of a new regionalism—as opposed to some supposedly old forms—represents a bold discursive move. It endows regionalism with attributes and properties only key actors in international politics are assumed to have, thereby challenging traditional concepts of identity, authority, and order, as well as transforming international relations theory itself. The new regionalism is taking shape within the context of a more multipolar world order and is particularly flourishing in Europe. The relative success of regional cooperation here gives reason to imitate and copy the formula in other parts of the world. It represents something qualitatively new; no longer created from the outside and "from above," the new regionalism has developed "from below," driven by a spontaneous process from within (Hettne 1994: 2–4).

2. The Baltic Sea Region

With the demise of previous rigidities and the end of the divisive order of the Cold War years, regionalism is also a new force around the Baltic Rim. Geographically speaking—and going from East to West—we are dealing with Norway, Denmark, Germany, Sweden, Poland, Belarus, Kaliningrad (Russia), Lithuania, Latvia, Estonia, Finland and the Karelian area, and Russia (St. Petersburg and Karelian districts). As it happens, there has been considerable preparedness on the part of regions along the Baltic Rim to make use of the opportunities that have opened up with the fading away of the old order. The winds of change that have produced an increasingly multipolar and pluralist Europe also inspired a vigorous debate on the challenges and prospects regarding Northern Europe. A process of new thinking, social mobilization, and internal restructuring is now underway, and interregional cooperation, previously limited to narrow environmental issues and fishing rights, has developed apace.

Interest in greater interregional cooperation has been expressed at different levels, embracing a wide variety of issues. The net effect has been that previous notions of the Baltic Sea as a defensive and divisive geographical boundary have lost most of their relevance. While obstacles still remain, such as differences in democratic practices, economic systems, and levels of economic development, these appear not to have played a decisive role, and in some cases they have even fueled cooperation. Regional perceptions of conflict between opposing systems have given way to philosophies that interpret the Baltic Sea's role as that of a bridge—a linking and unifying element. This discourse has both symbolic and pragmatic effects, changing the nature of the Baltic Sea region in terms of political space. Agendas have been altered, and issues of cooperation, growth, environmental problems, and, more generally, centralism versus regionalism, have gained importance.

It is justifiable to speak of regionalism in the sense that the Baltic Sea has established itself as a frame of reference, as something of common value and importance and as a symbolic expression of political renewal. Various projects have emerged with names and labels that differ markedly from those in the past (Petersen 1993). An awareness of the problems and challenges that loom large, and also of the needs and potentials, has been fostered.

The Baltic Sea is, furthermore, a joint platform for rather different actors, such as states, international organizations, parliamentarians, provinces, firms, cities, nongovernmental organizations, and people. It appears that also around the Baltic Rim, regionalism allows and invites very different actors to meet across a broad set of issues. Such pluralism lies at the heart of the very understanding of the essence of regionalism—a concept that cannot be narrowed down to a tidy and specific definition, but instead retains an openness that accommodates a variety of ideas, paradigms, and images (Joenniemi and Waever 1992). The delineations are not very strict geographically or otherwise; there is room for activities and endeavors that do not necessarily pertain in any strict sense to the Baltic Rim. Norway, rather far from the Baltic Sea, has often been invited to participate as well.

The foreign ministers of the countries located around the Baltic Rim came together in Copenhagen in March 1992 to establish a Baltic Sea Region Council of States. The Council is undoubtedly the most important, although not the only, institutional embodiment of regionalism in the Baltic Sea area and serves to strengthen the state-centric aspects of the dialogue. The Council has been assigned the task of assisting new democratic institutions, but its agenda also includes economic and technological cooperation, humanitarian matters and health care; cooperation in the fields of culture, education, tourism, and information; as well as transport and communication. Security was deliberately excluded from the agenda, but this has not prevented some of the members—primarily the Baltic republics—from raising security-oriented issues. The concept applied has been one of functional international cooperation with an emphasis on democracy, human rights, and the market economy. In addition to Finland, Denmark, Norway, Sweden, Germany, Poland, Russia, Estonia, Lithuania, and Latvia, the European Union is also a member of the Council.

For a number of reasons, the regional cooperation developing around the Baltic Rim can be seen within the New Regionalist context. It is not a continuation of the old regionalism that was formed in a bipolar Cold War context, but has been taking shape within a more multipolar world order and a more cooperative Europe. The regional arrangements are of a transboundary nature, and they have not been created from the outside and from above but have grown out of initiatives within the region and often from below. Certainly the impact and influence of the European Union is considerable, and Baltic Sea regionalism can be seen as a strategy of linking the European Union closer together with its eastern neighbors. While important, however, this European connection cannot, in itself, explain the emergence and growth of regionalism in the Baltic Sea area.

The obvious importance of the Baltic Sea Region Council of States notwithstanding, the region consists essentially of various networks from which it derives its potential strength. Political institutions can be seen primarily as a supportive architecture that allows different regions, cities, groups, and/or individuals to establish links and connections across borders and across the sea. It is also to be noted that regionalism around the Baltic Rim forms a comprehensive, multidimensional process, and is not specific with regard to objectives, as has been the case with the old regionalism (Hettne 1994: 1–2).

3. Regional Arrangements Gain Ground

The emergence of interregional cooperation in the Baltic Sea region seems to be one indication among many that there are profound changes underway in the formation of political space. In the ongoing rearticulation of political space, the constitutive power of regional formations has increased, indicating that a regionalist momentum has become too strong to be arrested by the standard repertoire of politics and international relations. Regions, in their new forms, are no longer as peripheral, marginal or oppositional as they used to be, nor are they mere side aspects or reflections of real politics, void of any life of their own. On the contrary, they contest the unchallenged and undivided power vested in the sovereign states, thus challenging the basic principle of structuring political space and time. They defy established hierarchies inside states and transcend boundaries—the ultimate demarcation of society, community, and political life in any true sense of the word. They also maintain considerable capacity of action as a sign of power and real existence, although this attribute does not appear to be as important in determining their overall impact.

The linkage to the post-Cold War period and other factors seems to imply that these trends are particularly conspicuous in Europe. The Baltic Sea region is hence part of a larger pattern. The fall of the fascist regimes in Southern Europe in the 1970s, the self-assertion of the Atlantic partners in Europe in the early 1980s, and the downfall of the Communist regimes in East and Central Europe, are events that brought with them considerable homogeneity, and one might say homogeneity in areas traditionally characterized by heterogeneity. As the Cold War overlay evaporated, there has been a Europeanization of Europe, further strengthening homogeneity in the form of market principles, democracy, and respect for human rights, but also bringing out the cultural diversity that has long been suppressed by the uniformity characteristic of the nation-states.

The consequent decline of the inside/outside metaphor, essential for statist identities, providing for similarity inside and difference at the outside, gives rise to many changes. For example, it becomes difficult to pinpoint *the other* and to argue that the security dilemmas that originate with otherness are placed on the outside, that is, in the sphere of international relations, a field that is qualitatively different from the domain of domestic issues.

4. An Indirect Challenge

In post-Cold War integrated Europe, regionalism is part and parcel of a more general development that seems to be displacing sovereignty, security, and other concerns of the nation-state. Such a deemphasis on security is a truly forceful move with a number of consequences. The gist is provided by G. M. Dillon as follows:

> For one of the principle dogmas of the political discourses of modernity, carried in particular but not exclusively in international relations and strategic studies, maintains that security is the primary goal of political subjects, their condition of possibility; indeed, the raison d'etat [raison d'état] for the modern political actor, the state, without which it is further argued there can be no politics and therefore no other legitimate forms of political agency (like citizenship) (1988: 101).

Regionalist formations seem to follow a very different form of understanding, less constrained by the modernist script. In the best of cases, regions, as regional complexes or systems, might have some capacity for conflict resolution. However, the chief concern is generally to prevent ecological degradation, achieve economic growth, generate new human contacts, and, above all, to provide identity; the preservation of sovereignty and the guarding of strict territorial control are of secondary importance. Many transregional formations were submerged by the Cold War overlay, which sought to arrange all relations in correspondence with the overarching bipolar order and the prevailing binary modes of thinking with clear-cut distinctions of inside and outside. In that superpower arrangement any alternative constellations, particularly if they contained seeds of ambiguity, were confined by lines drawn by the security structure. Thus, with the reappearance of Europe, there also begin to emerge several smaller patterns. They often have very little to do with security, except the nonconcern itself, but they are made possible by the removal of the security overlay.

It seems likely that the new European order will facilitate the development of smaller subregional identities and in this way at least indirectly raise the question of the basic organizing unit and the constituting principles of the emerging system. If Europe were to be divided again in a more traditional multipolar sense, with a return to power-balancing, the politics of containment, and an emphasis on *negative otherness* beyond the borders of the state, then regional cooperation might again be restricted or suppressed (Waever 1993). This is because states would have to arrange themselves primarily according to the requirements of the modernist political script, stressing the primacy of security concerns, defining political space in exclusivist terms, and limiting their contacts with certain other states. The new rivalry in Europe would force states to seek alliances and bring about a movement toward exclusive groups instead of multiple and overlapping cooperation.

However, the most likely scenario for European security is one where mutual fears and power-balancing among the major powers of Western Europe are kept in check by the European Union, which will be large enough to serve as security anchor of the entire continent. In this kind of Europe, traditional security problems will mainly be located in the periphery and will not be significant enough to function as a constitutive factor for the system as a whole. Instead of interstate wars there are civil wars and civil strife. There is violence, but violence of a kind that is hard to confront and contain with ordinary political means and institutions; it is violence rarely motivated by achievement-oriented action and aspirations and frightening because it tends to take on forms that are unexpected and haphazard.

War and violence hence tend to be ontological issues, at least as much as security challenges are in a traditional sense. Violence appears at unexpected places and assumes forms that are difficult to grasp and control, but it only constitutes a serious threat to those who are within its direct sphere of influence. There are good reasons to assume that war, as such, is marginalized, both as a potential major war and in the forms of ongoing minor wars. They no longer seem to constitute the same basic horizon for the conduct of international politics. In an integrating Europe, security divisions will not be cutting across the continent, or parts of it, in the way they used to. They do not appear as a threat of large-scale, interstate violence, and, accordingly, they will not stand in the way of cooperation or the emergence of new principles of organizing political space.

To the extent that security problems remain—and they certainly do—these tend more to have a uniting function, calling for concerted action such as humanitarian interventions, peace keeping, or peace enforcement in troubled areas. They do not divide and undermine transboundary relationships to the same degree as before. There are, in other words, both positive and negative reasons for the emergence of a more cooperative, flexible, and less security-geared Europe. Under such conditions, the concept of *defining in* becomes more important than *defining out* in the delineation of political space. Furthermore, the integration scenario of one relatively soft center is more likely to open up space for shifting and overlapping patterns of cooperation.

From a security perspective, it is also worth noting that transborder regions have a potentially stabilizing function, especially in Eastern Europe. The German researcher Bernard von Plate (1991) argues that through them it could be insured that "the reawakening of the ethnic groups leads neither to mediaeval *Kleinstaaterei*, nor to the violent change of interstate borders." In other words, unlike ethnicity or nationalism, regionalism allows for both unity and diversity. It is built on the preeminence of particularity, thereby providing the distinction and the criteria for identity, but it does so smoothly and flexibly. The definition of who *we* are is not given in advance and based on binary oppositions. It does not originate with the ever-present danger of war that provides for a language and system with exclusive nation-states as principal sites for politics and political subjectivity. Identity and meaning are not preordained, but are to be constituted and confirmed by joint action and experiences.

This change in the relationship among culture, politics, and identity, as reflected in new regionalism, seems to be rather important in indicating the entry of high modernity in the European arena (Paasi 1996; Cappellin and Nijkamp 1990). Under these new conditions, regionalism combines unity with diversity. It enables the consideration of community and social exchange without suppressing either aspect. There is high demand for such conceptualizations and organizing principles in the constitution of new political space if one wants to avoid the security dilemmas inherent in other, often competing conceptualizations that aspire to the same effect but do this by linking the state, nation, and ethnicity in a rather closed and rigid fashion.

In its new forms, regionalism tends to lead to considerations of politics without the standard recognition of the primacy of states and without preoccupations with questions of fear, power, control, and violence. Agendas are narrower, and they do not raise identity and presence over difference and absence in the same rigid way as the ordinary, modernist discourse on international politics has been doing (Ruggie 1993: 151). More generally, regionalism allows for identities that are essentially different from the traditional closed identities construed in terms of statist security and in the form of a narrow, territorially defined and fixed self. It breaks with the basic rule of the realist discourse on international politics by aspiring to find community and to construe political subjectivity beyond the limits imposed by the binary metaphysics favored by realist conceptualizations. By separating security in the sense of general human welfare from state/military security, regionalism provides a clear rationale for constructive interaction between peoples across boundaries. Such a new discourse, based on mutual interest and broad definitions of security, makes it difficult to interpret the security function in pre-established, exclusionist terms as tends to be the case with ethnicity and nationalism.

5. Regions and the Broken Modernist Script

The unanticipated effects of new regionalism cut deep in a historical sense as well. This is perhaps best illuminated by an analogy applied by Paul Puig i Scotoni (1993), an historian and advisor to the Catalonian regional government in Spain. He asks whether the territorial entities corresponding to what once consisted of empires, kingdoms, and principalities are really able to coexist without running—as they once did—into profound and antagonistic conflicts. From a negative perspective, the increasing preeminence of regions might be seen as once again preparing the ground for major clashes by distorting communication, by blurring the basic horizons of clear-cut, territorially fixed political order or aspirations toward sovereignty, and by interfering more generally in the way disorder, chaos, and war have been conceptualized and relegated to the margins of modernity. From a more optimistic point of view, however, regional resurgence could signal a major breakthrough by finally legitimating the existence of multiple allegiances and territorial identities within one and the same political order. Is a formula now emerging that tolerates a high degree of plurality and plasticity but that at the same time produces sufficient stability and allows for a considerable amount of alterations without leading more or less inevitably to a clash of interests and conflicts that in the long run can only be settled by resorting to war and violent conflicts?

Puig i Scotoni argues that European regionalism is now stronger than ever and that this implies transcending previous historical experiences. Configurations in many ways similar to those once doomed and buried by history—or in the best of cases pushed to the sidelines—have now reappeared. More precisely, Puig i Scotoni relates current developments to the execution of Girondists by the Jacobins in 1793, seeing this as an important event in the evolution of European nation-states and as a crucial aspect of modernity. Instead of opting for a firmly centralized nation-state, the Girondists suggested an alternative principle of organization, and aimed at a federalist arrangement with liberty and democracy not only extended to individuals but also to some territorial entities below the level of the central state. Their approach, stressing diversity and the coexistence of different geographical expressions of power within the same order, and this without a fixed territorial base, was rejected by the Jacobins as something essentially premodern; it was interpreted as particularist tradition and regressive and seen as incompatible with the pure form of the nation-state. Thus, the Girondists' concept was suppressed and doomed to practical nonexistence (Puig i Scotoni 1993).

The perspective introduced by Puig i Scotoni suggests that in order to make sense of the current regional configurations one has to step beyond the dominant modernist script. One has to apply different constructions of time and space than those embodied in that script. To be reminiscent of the premodern—and some potential roads that modernist understandings left aside at an early stage to heal the incongruence between *de jure* and *de facto* power—seems to provide essential clues for placing the increased preeminence of regionalism and its ability to cut across essential divides, conceptual or practical, in perspective (Ullmann 1949).

Interpretations that remain within the modernist script tend to result in containment, in efforts to play down and control ambiguity, and thereby to restore normality and order. Regionalism is herein depicted as something authentic and genuinely different, which, in the final analysis, is a problem. It is viewed as a phenomenon that detracts from the orderly conduct of public affairs as guided by the more statist logic; it contributes to the destabilization of nation-states as major containers of politics, and this without being conducive to the next logical step in modernist thinking, i.e., the emergence of a unionist Europe or distinct world order permeated by similarity and controlled difference.

Seen in this modernist light, the formation of regions is thus thought to promote divisiveness and intransigence and to be harmful rather than helpful in the organization of political space. In challenging key aspects of the modernist script, it is interpreted to distort peaceful change by delivering false promises.

Region-formation, as a form of ambiguity, constitutes something quite unwarranted and malevolent, and should therefore not be allowed to grow in significance and guide the course of international politics.

The pursuit of *regionness*—to use Björn Hettne's expression—challenges the primacy of state politics, statist spatialization, and the understanding of state boundaries as the ultimate demarcations of society, community, and political life (Hettne 1993). Unlike clear-cut statist demarcations, regionness leans on unbundled territoriality, builds community across essential divides, and operates in terms of change, interaction, and acceleration, i.e., predominant themes of the late-modern period.

Insofar as regionalism assumes the form of political and social initiatives (which indeed it has increasingly been doing), there is quite a lot that speaks in its favor. It has various favorable effects and seems to be conducive to security, at least in the more general sense of assuring particular arrangements in the future, thereby providing meaning as well as visions and a horizon needed for change. As regionalism leans on inclusion rather than exclusion, there is a promise that the changes introduced—despite their inherently radical nature and contradictory elements contained in that process—remain basically peaceful. Regionalism seems mostly to contribute to the devaluation of historical and territorial quarrels, and functions constructively in appeasing and creating an outlet for discontent. Instead of polarizing too far, it also draws—in its current forms—attention to common experiences, real or imagined, and contributes thereby to the communicative capacities of the societies in question. It is in this sense a far more flexible and progressive theme than nationality and ethnicity. Both of these contain much stronger and absolute claims of exclusion, that is, moves based on authenticity and difference argued to be quite real and profound.

6. A Variety of Voices

There are, however, several influential voices warning that optimistic conclusions are as yet unwarranted. They do not share the view that regionalism holds promises of increased flexibility and tolerance. On the contrary, they argue that it evokes memories of pirates, roving bandits, and other forms of social disintegration and degeneration. Ralf Dahrendorf (1991) is one of these critics who thinks of regionalism as archaic and deeply problematic. There is the danger, in his view, that the new Europe will evolve—instead of a harmonious, heterogeneous community—into a rather different constellation. It may split into linguistically, culturally, and ethnically smaller, homogeneous regions that revolt and demand their independence. He maintains that regionalism is tantamount to fragmentation, anarchy, chaos, and increased insecurity. He believes it distorts the orderly conduct of public policies and threatens to take us back to the premodern. Dahrendorf fears that the strength of region formation will be conducive to a confederate Europe with far less distinct features and characteristics and with a rather weak horizon. National communality, the most valuable achievement of Western civilization, might cave in under the pressure caused by the return of the tribes.

On this scale, regionalism is obviously a threat, signaling ethnic confusion by blurring the distinction between what is *international* and what is *external*. It endangers the centrality of the sovereign state as the core and anchor of politics as well as international relations. The spread of regionalism is, hence, for understandable reasons, a cause for concern and a source of insecurity. It is understood to violate the ordinary fusion of self and other and tolerance; rather, it evokes memories of Medieval plights or the fight between the pope and the kaiser for power within one and the same political order, the split into *de jure* and *de facto* within one and the same setting. It is interpreted as representing a reversal of development and seen as a flux of political space without a concomitant, territorially defined political order. The ambiguity goes beyond the essentially contested character of all political concepts. The lack of cognitive clarity, evidenced by the difficulty of classifying regionalism, produces behavioral uncertainty. As such, it becomes too much to handle and is thereby seen as representing at worst a new domain of danger.

It is, hence, quite understandable that regionalism is taken to constitute a return of something primitive and segmented. Regionalism is seen to be out of tune with the modern project as it contains, if taken far, assumptions about the end of territoriality and the end of the nation-state. It breaks the existing coherence and reintroduces differences that were thought to be resolved and left behind in the process of development.

For Dahrendorf, regionalism seems to be, above all, an epistemological issue. It threatens, by introducing ungovernable diversity, the modern dream of undisturbed communication, clarity, and geometry and the consequent conceptualizations of political space which correspond to the requirements of regularity, hierarchy, and a clear horizon. It represents the erasure of certainty, brought about by an irruption of contingency. If nation-states—as privileged sites of politics and anchoring points for analyses of politics and international relations—decline in importance, then the next step should be world order, not the return of divisive regionness with connotations of decentralization, encapsulation, shielding, and protectionism. Dahrendorf, in treating it as a very real and uncontrollable form of difference, is obviously opposed to purporting regionalism as the next step of modern—understood as linear and natural—development, superior to the previous stage and therefore in tune with current challenges, or to conceptualizing it as a remedy to the crises of modernity. His strategy is one of rejecting regionalism and pushing it back into the darkness of history. His project is about preserving the centrality of the nation-state and having borders to serve the clear-cut function of indicating a division between the inside and the outside, between political order and anarchy.

One might, however, try to provide a different reading of the regionalist scenario. Dahrendorf's interpretation is based on positions determined and governed by the modernist script and, therefore, runs the risk of going astray more or less in the same way as some of the arguments that have been presented in favor of regionalism as the next logical and straightforward phase of modernity. The increased constitutive power of regional formations should not be interpreted as something revanchist, a backlash in a struggle where the modernist script with the centralized nation-state as one of its main embodiments is now showing some signs of weakness. Rather, it seems that the modernist script has already lost much of its relevance, and the field is not only wide open to other scripts; there is indeed a certain urgency about the situation.

New approaches are needed to fill in the void that has followed from the decreased power of the modernist one. There is a globalization of contingency, as suggested by a modernist reading, but at the same time increased tendencies toward ambiguity, indeterminacy, and uncertainty on our horizon; or to put it differently, the more evident our common needs become, the more brutal is the insistence on the claims of difference (Campbell 1990; Conolly 1991, Ignatieff; 1984). All traditional containers are rendered problematic, opening up the possibility of and creating an urgent need for alternative categorizations, such as regionalism.

This erasure of certainty brought about by the irruption of contingency implies that the Girondists do not once again challenge (and this time successfully) the Jacobins in articulating and organizing political space. Rather, they enter or occupy parts of an arena where the Jacobins—and their exclusive way of delineating political space—are increasingly just a memory. The perception that the new is somehow competing and struggling to surpass the old, thereby seriously endangering modern international relations at large, might be misleading. New time-space constructs—some resembling configurations that have occurred in historical struggles—have become possible and are needed, thus refuting much of the debate based on a modernist, oppositional reading of their interrelation. The new constructs are not due to anything self-generating. They are deliberately produced to lean on the primacy of difference, that is, difference that is relative from the very beginning, and does not present claims of exclusivity as a modernist reading leads to think.

In a sense, a Girondist argumentation and understanding appears to reassert itself and develop further once the statist, Jacobin project shows signs of fatigue. Some authors, among them Falk and Mendlowith (1973), speak of the *black hole* originating with the decline of the nation-state and inviting regionalism and other such formations to enter the political sphere. It is not a solution in any idealist sense, but nevertheless it is an option that seems to convey a certain sense of order in an increasingly complex scenery. This implies that in the arena of international politics the diffuse, paradoxical, contradictory—and perhaps, to some, uto-pian—aspects of regionalism often appear as assets, particularly if compared to other options such as nationalism and ethnic chauvinism. They tend to be seen as signs of strength rather than of weakness, whereas concepts based on modernist interpretations fail to serve as a reliable point of reference.

7. Concluding Remarks

Modernism and its linear and evolutionist interpretations emphasizing gen-eralization and uniformity, whether these explanations are used to argue against or for regionalism, have run into difficulty. There is much that indicates that the past becomes the future, and the past embraces elements that are depicted as parts of the future. The old and the new come together in combinations that appear unnatural and impossible if judged on the basis of the modernist script and the ordinary reading of international relations. They transcend the distinction be-tween the original and the fabricated. Formations appear that lean on the past as a reply to enquiries concerning origin. They do so to appear wild, undisciplined, and to show themselves as politically genuine but unmediated; all this is neces-sary to build firm regional identities (Qvortrup 1992).

Another way to put it would be to say that the relationship between physical density and dense sociability is no longer what it used to be "with aliens appearing inside the confines of the life-world and refusing to go away" (Bauman 1990: 152). The power to reclassify strangers—such as regionalism—into one of the two oppositional categories of friends and enemies, self and other, inside and outside, has weakened. There is a greater inclination today to accept the perma-nence of differentiation, and what remains is to struggle and to get along with the confused status that the presence of these previous strangers invokes. More generally, there seems to be a move toward increased tolerance, implying, among other things, that chaos is no longer the negativity that immediately appears once order is being challenged.

On the whole, this seems rather crucial. Such a trend might indicate that international politics are—in line with politics in general—increasingly turning into something that could be described as a play with signs. This change allows situations and formations out of the ordinary—such as regionalism—to emerge. The declining heterophobia associated with boundary-drawing now provides space for such many-sided configurations to occupy a relatively central position, and to do so without automatically running into outright conflict with other conceptualizations and previous configurations. The growth of regionalism neither signals the end of territory nor the withering away of the state. Due to their flexibility and qualities that have historically not been possible to combine without producing antagonism, these new configurations might be able to offer some insight into how to deal with problems traditionally associated with change. It must also be considered, though, that the challenges might be so heavy that they exceed what regionalism in its new forms has to offer. Whatever the result, it is clear that the competence of modern international relations, both as theory and practice, stands challenged. There is an acute need, but also a chance to open up, move away from, and dismiss various barriers imposed by a modernist understanding, among them the distinction of international politics as a field qualitatively different from other forms of political life.

References

Bauman, Zygmunt. 1990. "Modernity and Ambivalence." In *Global Culture, Nationalism, Globalization and Modernity*, Mike Featherstone, ed. London: Sage Publications.

Campbell, David. 1990. "Security, Order, and Identity in Europe: A Commentary." In *Beyond the Blocs. Current Research on Peace and Violence*, Pertti Joenniemi, ed. No. 3.

Cappellin, Riccardo, and Peter Nijkamp, eds. 1990. *The Spatial Context of Technological Development*. Aldershot, Hants, England: Avebury.

Conolly, William. 1991. *Identity and Difference: Democratic Negotiations of Political Paradox*. Ithaca: Cornell University Press.

Dahrendorf, Ralf. 1991. "Stammerne vender tilbage (The Tribes are Back)." *Weekendavisen* (Copenhagen), 13–19 September edition.

Der Derian, James. 1992. *Anti-Diplomacy: Spies, Terror, Speed and War*. Oxford: Basil Blackwell.

Dillon, G. M., ed. 1988. *Defence Policy Making: A Comparative Analysis*. Leicester: Leicester University Press.

Falk, Richard, and Saul Mendlowith, eds. 1975. *Regional Politics and World Order*. San Francisco: W. H. Freemann.

Hassner, Pierre. 1993. "Beyond Nationalism and Internationalism: Ethnicity and World Order." *Survival*. Vol. 35, no. 2 (Summer): 49.

Hettne, Björn. 1993. "Neo-Mercantilism: The Pursuit of Regionness." *Cooperation and Conflict*. No. 3.

Hettne, Björn. 1994. *The New Regionalism. Implications for Global Development and International Security*. Helsinki: UNU World Institute for Development Economics Research (UNU/WIDER).

Hueglin, Thomas, O. 1986. "Regionalism in Western Europe." *Comparative Politics*, 4 (July).

Ignatieff, Michael. 1984. *The Needs of Strangers*. London: Chatto and Windus.

Joenniemi, Pertti, and Waever Ole. 1992. *Regionalization around the Baltic Rim. Notions on Baltic Sea Politics and Co-operation in the Baltic Sea Area.* Report from the Second Parliamentary Conference at the Storting. Oslo NORD 24 (22–24 April).

Petersen, Nikolaj. 1993. "Regional Cooperation and Regimes Around the Baltic Rim." In *Cooperation in the Baltic Sea Region*, Pertti Joenniemi, ed. Washington: Taylor and Francis.

Pieterse, Jan Nedersen. 1993. *Globalization as Hybridization.* Working Papers Series, no. 152, Institute of Social Sciences. The Hague. The Netherlands (June).

Plate, Bernhard V. 1991. "Subregionalismus: Eine Zwischenebene in einer gesamteuropäischen Ordnung." *Europa-Archiv* (October).

Puig i Scotoni, Paul. 1993. *Girondisterna har kommit tillbaka* (The Girondists are Back). Dagens Nyheter (16 June).

Qvortrup, Lars 1992. "Modernitet og derefter" (Modernity and Thereafter). In *Kulturens spaendetroeje*, Peter Duelund, ed. NordREFO: 1x.

Ruggie, John, G. 1993. "Territoriality and Beyond: Problematizing Modernity in International Relations." *International Organizations* (Winter).

Ullmann, W. 1949. "The Development of the Medieval Idea of Sovereignty." *English Historical Review* 64 (250).

Waever, Ole et al. 1993. *Identity, Migration, and the New Security Agenda in Europe.* New York: St. Martin's Press.

Walker, R. B. J. 1992. *Inside/Outside.* Cambridge: Cambridge University Press.

Security, Borders, and the State

Didier Bigo

1. Border Controls: New Stakes

State security has always been a question of the control of people. As such, it has involved the control of frontiers against external enemies and the control of frontiers in order to impose state rule on domestic populations. Dealing as we are with effects of globalization on border regions and transboundary cooperation, we must, however, ask ourselves what occurs when the state and its agents are no longer able to control, filter, or otherwise block the flow of population that crosses borders daily. What new relationships develop between borders, the state, and policies dealing with state security? Previously, the claim of the modern state to be the sole fount of all power could only be maintained if its frontiers were, for all intents and purposes, impenetrable. Today, the control of land border crossings runs counter to commercial exchange, economic growth, and the concept of open markets espoused by Western democracies. If the principle of territorial sovereignty is to be upheld in the future—at least rhetorically—then border-security policy will have to change in response to the process of redefining allegiances between nation-states and their citizens. This point was made by Rosenau (1990) in describing the bifurcation of the world into a state-centered realm and a transnational one.

Border controls are becoming increasingly symbolic. They continue to signal control, but do not fulfill the functions of physical protection and encagement of the population as they did before (Mann 1993). Western democracies are obliged to remain open for economic and often ideological reasons. In discussing, for example, the removal of border controls within the European Union (EU), we are not simply dealing with problems of a technical or an organizational nature with regard to the transferral of border controls from internal to external borders of the Community (the Shengen Agreement and Maastricht Title VI). Rather, we are dealing with a profound change in the structure of allegiances between states and individuals and with a security process that merges internal and external concerns. The last point can be explained by two phenomena: first, by the legitimization process of the constitution of the EU, especially after the Single Act of 1985, and second, by a new perception of threat that has been transformed from an external one (the Soviet Union) to an internal one (fears concerning drug trafficking, terrorism, transborder crime, illegal immigrants, and bogus asylum-seekers). This perception of threat is manifested by the struggle between different state agencies to impose their own definitions and solutions on the security problems presently being faced.

This paper will examine the consequences transnationalization has had regarding the nature of controls that states can implement at their frontiers and inside their territories. The classical views of security issues will be challenged. Also, this paper will show that if the analysis of changing border issues with a neorealist, neoliberal, or neoculturalist view continues, as American political science tends to do, a self-fulfilling prophecy with regard to the so-called threat from the South will be created. It will also create scapegoats out of immigrants and others who could become the new post-Cold War enemy. If these visions of the *new world disorder* are deconstructed, analyzing where they come from and why, and if an alternative vision based on an understanding of new relationships among people, fears, and states is proposed, then there is a chance to avoid such a solution. Insecurity and fears need not be created in order to legitimate the role of security agencies. Instead, the real meanings of collective security in the new world must be understood. In the first part, there will be a discussion of the new dimensions of border controls and the transformations that affect them, especially in the European Union and other Western democracies. In the second part, the discussion will focus on what ways new relationships among citizens, the state, and the control of borders are affecting concepts of security.

2. Control Devices

It is argued here that in response to globalization and increasing transboundary flows of population, states change the form in which such flows are controlled.[1] To respond to the transnationalization of the world and the augmentation of flows of people across borders, is it not true that states change the nature of control by linking their own agencies (military and police cooperation), sending their agents beyond the borders, and changing the location of the control no longer along the physical frontier, but depending on an ethnic bias? To be more precise, the hypothesis is raised that if control mechanisms or devices are no longer closely tied to territoriality but rather to ethnicity, then this represents a break with the secular management of the state that must be assessed immediately.

What are the concrete changes in the forms of border control? How can the deterritorialization or the delocalization that affects them be explained? One can speak of a deterritorialization of the border because there is a delinking of the relationship between borders and the control of borders. Hence, borders acquire a symbolic quality, existing in the minds of people but not as real entities, whereas the techniques of control are more and more related to surveillance (electronic checks, data collection, intelligence against some minorities, policing at a distance, proactive actions in the countries of origins, and so forth). This explains, in part, that *de facto* citizenship becomes less important than the homogeneity of the way of life or skin color. There needs to be a knowledge of what images people have now of the immigrants, of the others, and what daily practices continue to be implemented at the decision-making level regarding public security. How are daily controls implemented by agents and what are their implications? The reforms of customs and immigration services, border police, and so on, in various European countries all go in the same direction. Hence, the question: Is control becoming selective, more or less arbitrary, based on ethnic and racial characteristics? Are *white* Europeans exempt while *the others*, the darker or black faces, are controlled (including French citizens from overseas departments and territories)? Indeed, the control of the alien look at the so-called internal borders necessarily leads to the identification of distinctive physical features and/or culture and calls on the social imagery of each country to decide who is the foreigner to be controlled, and who is potentially dangerous. Control is no longer individualized nor egalitarian; it is the control of potentially dangerous groups. What kind of changes are then involved within the notion of freedom of movement inside the European Union? Why has this notion of freedom been linked with the notion of a security deficit at the external borders and with its converse, the notion of an internal security deficit at the European level?

Research is presently being conducted in order to analyze the strategic interaction of different agencies (police forces, military police, and customs) and to understand how they perceive aliens and how they justify their procedures with reference to legal rationality or custom.[2] In each case, it will be necessary to study the concrete collaboration between police officers or, more generally, between security agencies, their institutional status, and the effects they have on the hierarchical relations maintained between those engaged in transboundary collaboration and the management sphere in the administrations at the political level. Within the scope of this paper, the concentration will be on the theoretical relationship among states, borders, identity, security, and globalization. The political rhetoric of those who espouse stricter controls—based on a perception of new threats to national integrity—will be examined in terms of the reality of these new threats. This implies a rejection of functionalist-sociological concepts of organization, which take existing discourses of state power for granted.

One of the principal questions that must be asked is, what links concepts such as *borders, security, identity, state,* and *transnational*? How should they be analyzed within the changing framework of present-day world politics? What problems do they actually present? What are the implications of the new relations among them? It would seem that the relations between the state and security concerns are restructured owing to the type of control the state can have over population as a result of the deterritorialization or at least delocalization of borders. This is especially the case within the European Union, but also with NAFTA in the United States. In fact, a global restructuring of the relations between police and aliens, both at the border and inside the territory controlled by the sovereign state, is taking place. European police forces, which dealt with immigration only marginally, have become the official bodies around which all questions concerning immigration tend to polarize. It would seem immigration and its economic and social dimensions have become security issues on a grand European scale. The same development might be seen in the United States if the NAFTA treaty evolves toward a common market.

3. A Post-Hobbesian State in a Transnational World

In classical political science—whether in its realist, behaviorist, or systemic manifestation—the terms *border, state,* and *security* pose no problem; the relationships are clear. The state controls the population within its borders and assures its protection in exchange for an abandonment of individual sovereignty. To assure the protection of the population, the state has two major means of coercion: one, to prevent the risk of outside aggression—the army; the other, to protect the population against crime and theft, and to let it live in peace and order—the police. The border indicates in an intangible manner the limits to sovereignty and, in Weber's formulation, the extent to which the state can claim its monopoly of legitimate violence. There is an absolute distinction between the internal—where the sovereign state disposes of the means to impose social order with an impressive show of force, theoretically legitimated by an initial general agreement and the inherent risk of returning to a state of generalized warfare—and the external—where the state conceives its duty as being prepared for (interstate) war in order to ensure peace.[3] There is a clear distinction between the police for security and public order, on the one, hand and the army for external security, on the other, which is evident to everyone, uncontested and materialized by the state's border. There appears to be no conceivable reason for any overlapping of functions (in the words of Raymond Aron, war or armed conflict between states is neither terrorism nor assassination, let alone maintenance of order).

Viewed historically, obvious distinctions between internal and external order are blurred. The creation of European states appears as the involuntary result of a combination of means of coercion and of capital in which the army constantly assumed internal tasks.[4] Police forces and armies are therefore not as clearly structured and defined with regard to the border as realist views would lead to believe. They are two poles in a continuum of agencies dealing with security. More essentially, however, elements of realist intellectual tradition that sanctify the state are rejected, as they prevent the understanding of present-day developments, and in particular the transnational dimension.

Transnational Movements and State Action

Economic globalization and new means of communication and travel have created new social relationships where individuals are increasingly becoming international actors.[5] We have seen the results of voting with feet, or exit options, and the implosion of authority structures that had unanimously been judged indestructible by so-called experts only very recently. But it is not only the collapse of Eastern regimes that is at issue. The contemporary state, including the democratic one, is ill-equipped to deal with cross-border flows that have grown to an extent where total control, shutting the gate, as it were, becomes illusory. Government rhetoric and administrative practice, nevertheless, lead to coercive measures (strengthening of controls on the so-called outer borders, maintenance of controls over foreign populations resident within the European Union, multiplication of identity checks to expel illegal immigrants, restriction of rights to asylum, including constitutional changes, and the consideration of militarizing frontier posts to prevent infiltration). Immigration is increasingly viewed exclusively from the point of view of security (internal, external, police, and military), and less from an economic, social, or cultural angle; it tends to be seen as a source of many current problems (unemployment, drugs, terrorism, crime, religious fundamentalism, and so forth), and its control would thus settle all these problems in one fell swoop.[6] This concept inevitably leads toward a process of blaming and *scapegoating* transnational migrants for a variety of problems. The present policy of the French government is one of supporting Schengen while maintaining the central control of the nation-state; a Europe-wide comparison would undoubtedly show that this is not an isolated instance.

One should not exaggerate European uniqueness. Schengen, by moving border controls outward, merely accelerates a trend toward *derealization* of borders that is general in all developed societies. It clarifies that borders can no longer be seen as barriers or sluice gates at a fixed geographical point. State borders are in fact passable because economic and social structures require open communication. The fact that there was a will to transfer control proves to some extent that control no longer really existed at national borders. Its transfer does not raise so much the question of the trustworthiness of neighboring police forces as it does the very question of effectiveness. Thus, the envisaged solution is to apply controls ubiquitously, if necessary. Control abandons the border, its geographical home, focusing on groups that are perceived to constitute a risk.

Toward New Forms of Control?

At present, there are no longer rigorous controls for persons crossing borders at particular terrestrial points (except perhaps in the United Kingdom), although occasional spot checks continue to be administered. With the coming into force of the Schengen agreements, controls tend more to be carried out at any given point and targeted at specific groups (such as Third World groups, even minorities within Third World countries). Hence, control becomes deterritorialized. This *delinking* of territory and control generates very significant practical and symbolic alterations that affect concepts of sovereignty, power, and its day-to-day exercise. The reforms of customs and immigration services, border police, and so forth, in various European countries all go in the same direction: control is no longer individualized or egalitarian, it is the *control of potentially dangerous groups*.

This is the logical, though unspoken, consequence of the Schengen agreements, as long as they are interpreted in a narrow sense and not as a step toward European political integration. If Schengen is seen as a forerunner, a laboratory, of a future European political community, it can be hoped (with blameable optimism) that the free movement of persons will promote integration and will make nationalism obsolescent, at least in its more outspoken forms. However, there is a refusal to believe in a potential European citizenship, which would play the role of a melting pot of all those living in the territory of the Union, and if the residents hold on to the nation-state, then the controls instituted by these states will inevitably end up in ethnic control. This will profoundly alter the democratic relationships which these residents are used to.[7] The classical differentiation between internal and external around a border is disturbed, and the difference between alien and citizen is restructured on other than territorial/citizenship lines (rise of communitarianism, religious affinities, increase of xenophobia). These new identity controls disturb the ideology of equality (especially in France where ever since 1793 minorities and communities have been disavowed), but they are the inevitable consequence of the *absence of practical guidelines and the discomfort of the majority* in its identity structures, unable as it is to determine whether it can marginally admit population groups that do not share the same modes of socialization and of living.

Prosperous societies everywhere (United States, Canada, Switzerland, among others) that currently experience recession encounter the same contradictions.[8] On the one hand, they desire free movement of capital and, to an extent, labor, but, on the other hand, they want to restrain migration movements that they encourage elsewhere by the dissemination of their life style. Their policies are therefore often chaotic because they attempt to meet opposing requirements (immigration policy versus foreign and commercial policy). However, these policies are virtually channeled by the precept that control is essential and has to be strengthened in view of world disorder, when practical studies show that real border control is an illusion.[9] Instead of exploring ways of control without violating human rights—a true challenge for the future—politicians in various countries compete in the strengthening of traditional controls, or they surreptitiously introduce undemocratic ones. In each case, a partial, truncated view of the real transnational phenomenon induces solutions with a view to the next elections. But the simultaneous nature of their behavior makes them believe that they are acting wisely, thus creating what Giddens calls the "conjuncture of circumstance."[10]

The reasons for this conjuncture, and the social construct of reality that underpins it, must be submitted for deeper analysis. The time must be taken to reflect, to measure the scope of the problem and its underlying issues, to assess its implications and the short-, medium-, and long-term effects of these alterations in the relationships among the state, the border, security, and population.

The Transnational Dimension: New Approaches to Borders

The globalization of the capitalist economy, with its infinite cross-border links among economic agents, has opened to question the ability of states to conduct autonomous, not to mention opposing, economic policies. Economic space does not coincide with the political space of the nation-state. Wealth is more or less detached from nations; it exists in transborder networks (at the level of production, finance, speculation, and so forth) and largely depends on multiple and autonomous actors who do not seek sovereign power, but rather seek the most efficient alliance of the moment. Transnationalization is thus the result of many factors, and not, as many American authors assume too readily, the simple consequence of the globalization of the economy and of the new communication technology. As the leaders of Eastern Bloc countries discovered, transnationalization uses ideology to prevent a single state from assuming its own legitimate discourse. It also uses the fact that the images of different cultures interpenetrate one another daily,[11] it uses ideas and the displacement of expert knowledge in both directions and the lasting implantation of different cultural behavior within the same territory.[12]

It is this latter innovation in the global movement of populations that undoubtedly most frightens those in power. External security has always been more or less affected by domestic considerations. Yet, until now the worlds of crime and war were of a clearly separate nature and called on totally different spheres of expertise. The novelty is that both of them are growing and trying to absorb the transnational movement of populations (tourism, legal migration, refugees from conflicts and repression) through the necessary control and repression of illegal immigration and of bogus or economic refugees. This amounts to a criminalization, perhaps even militarization, of matters regarding the transnational movement of persons. Many Western leaders seem to fear that these migrations, by disturbing border control, directly affect state structures and internal homogeneity, themselves the basis of proper citizenship. They are (or seem to be) afraid that these movements may lead to the very destruction of the state framework in democracies. What is the real situation? Is the state endangered or not? Apart from right-left posturing, this seems to be the question around which authors and politicians position themselves.[13] Governments seem to react to these challenges essentially by taking recourse to traditional coercive measures, by amplifying them, and by arranging intergovernmental cooperation in order to remain in command. Whether this is the best strategy is extremely doubtful, given the limited usefulness of coercive measures in a multicentered and no longer state-centered world.

The Post-Hobbesian State

In fact, it can be argued that we are heading toward a new form of governance, a new type of state. The *post-Hobbesian state*, which many saw as a model for the European Community, is developing under our very eyes. This state is obliged to be open to economic and population movements because economic prosperity is its primary legitimization. At the same time, it is obliged to be less openly militaristic and can no longer legitimize itself through warfare. It can no longer contain within its own territorial control both coercive resources and a concentration of capital because their dynamics are contradictory.[14] Does this mean that it might abandon coercion and be satisfied with an enlightened surveillance as envisaged by some federalists for a European Federal Union?[15]

On the contrary, at the moment there seems to be a fixation with security at all levels. This is not some by-product of outdated nationalism but a policy expressed by the United Nations, the Council of Europe, and in the European

Commission and Parliament as *preventive diplomacy*. It is a fixation with the relation between internal security and open borders at the national as well as at the European levels. The police assume a major role and replace the army as the central instrument of coercion. The enemy is no longer some foreign state but a world of crime, drugs, and illegal immigrants. The post-Hobbesian state is therefore quite possibly a new reality and every bit as security-conscious as its predecessor; it merely introduces new concepts, methods, and systems of control.

4. Freedom of Movement and the Myth of Effective Border Controls

Schengen, Maastricht, and various bilateral agreements, as well as the resulting changes of national legislation, have created a particular situation within the European Union where freedom of movement of people and security problems are linked by the notion of *the absolute necessity to have compensatory measures*—to compensate by more checks at the external borders of EU. In that way, it differs considerably from the NAFTA context in North America. The rhetoric is different; the legitimization of the reinforcement of the controls against immigrants takes different paths, but at the same time, in both situations, we can see that we are situated at an intersection, a significant crossroad, leading away, in every single case, from the traditional relations between the state, on the one hand, and its population and its borders, on the other. In both cases the nature of the state has to change because transnationalization and this transformation toward a post-Hobbesian state engage in new forms and technology of controls, which are less and less the traditional border checks.

This important fact is too often ill-perceived and interpreted in a narrowly technical or political perspective. While these perceptions are of unquestionable importance, they are less fundamental than the development of multiple allegiances (such as to regions, communities, ethnic, and religious identities) that challenge the concept of single allegiances to a given nation-state. It is not only a question of immigration policies, rights of asylum, and police cooperation but of the entire system of interaction that links them and explains why the state cannot continue in its traditional coercive role.

Furthermore, *identity borders* no longer correspond to state borders. This upsets not only those who arrive from abroad (with their culture, their ideologies, their religious practices, and so forth), but also those who receive them, those who previously thought in terms of asymmetric relationships with the others without questioning the pertinence of the polarization that turns the immigrant into a stranger. This is perhaps quite new because it questions definitions of the nation-state where identity, majority, and citizenship are supposed to coincide.

However, the isolated states created by the more or less forced nationalization of populations within borders, putting populations into cages (in the words of Michael Mann [1993]), no longer really constitute national identity, if they ever did in any real sense. This identity did, however, fulfill a symbolic role because it allowed majorities to think of themselves as having a central and integrating role. It is thus not sufficient to recall the history of migrations and to point out that even nations like France never ceased being countries of immigration, and that the French nation had difficulty imposing itself in border regions like Britanny, Corsica, and the Basque country. It has to be recognized that the crumbling of the national concept originates elsewhere, and that the question of border control arises from a general upheaval of the relations between the state and the transnational.

From Freedom of Movement to a Security Deficit: The Uniqueness of the European Situation

Transnational and globalizing phenomena disturb borders. They imply a network logic and microdecisions by autonomous players while traditional authority is weakened or diluted. Thus, there is a need for a new and more general framework to deal with these changes, for example, in the form of the EU and NAFTA. The construction of the European Union, through *spillover* effects, has become an illustration of what states can do to adapt themselves to new economic conditions. In a way, this construction has become a local answer to the world-wide phenomenon of transnationalization. Frontiers have lost their meaning much as did tolls levied by feudal lords. They have become a hindrance to development and have lost their meaning as *differentiators* of economic, consumer, and cultural homogeneity, which has created a factual continuum in border regions of various countries. If not abolished, they could at least be tempered to ease movement of goods, capital, and labor. This latter point is important. The free movement of persons was at first limited to workers in the private sector, but the principle of the European Community (Rome Treaty) was modified by the Single Act of 1986 to include all workers. The Maastricht Treaty of 1993 extended this right to all persons living within the European Union, hence also resident alien populations. This free movement of persons (no longer restricted to labor) interfered with the basic and rapid change in population flows between developed and developing countries.

Cross-border movements exploded in the 1960s (immigration, refugees, but mainly tourism, and frontier workers) and were hardly affected by the mid-70s crisis. These movements are linked to demographic differentials, economic development, media-created images, as well as attempts to escape from authoritarian regimes and regional conflicts. They have created a problem of quantitative control of persons at the borders of prosperous democratic states. At first, the movements were seen in terms of a labor force free of national fetters, therefore more mobile and adaptable to economic needs. Later, it was realized that the free movement of persons could not be limited to its economic aspects, but that it implied the arrival of men and women with their own different values, cultures, and identities. When border control had to be viewed from its cost angle, the whole structure of security, collective identity, citizenship, and democracy became endangered.[16]

From then on, reactions were manifold, often disorderly, and contradictory, because they were highly segmented (in Europe more by economic interests than by nationality). Security imperatives were advanced, although the difficulty of merely increasing resources was recognized. Should Europe's inner borders be softened for the sake of prosperity and its outer borders strengthened for the sake of security? There appear to be some contradictions of principle and unspoken assumptions of bad augur for nationalism, xenophobia, and racism. Is it justifiable, for the cause of security, to strengthen outside borders but as a counterpart weaken inner borders? Can one develop a Europe of police and security, and, at the same time, promote free movement? Is there such a thing as a *perimeter of security*? Is it possible that asylum seekers should be subject both to an entry visa and to an exit visa without sliding into a wartime attitude?

There exists an ambiguity to the extent that enemies of European integration approve measures toward stricter security while refusing advances toward free movement. These are basic questions that are often neglected by the drafters of legislation in an effort to be pragmatic, but the problems arise necessarily with time. The absence of overall coherence may ruin the whole project by exacerbating contradictions and by constructing a fortress Europe, homogeneous inside, cut off from the outside, even from its closest neighbors. Such a project appears ethically incoherent and ill-adapted to the world situation. Why use the argument of weaker borders for greater prosperity among Europeans, and refuse it at a global level? Why should free movement be good among Europeans, but bad with our neighbors? Conversely, if security is so important, why deprive ourselves of national borders? One cannot change the line of argument according to whether we deal with inner or outer borders.

Moreover, the displacement of border controls from internal to external borders seems difficult to realize. Who controls the borders now, and who will do so in the future? Is the control effective? Can one trust another state with one's own security while there is no central political structure in the European Union? Should one, or should one not, create a European police force, and what should be its powers? Would it not be dangerous to create a European police force while there is a lack a unified penal code and real political structures (government, parliament, court of justice) capable of controlling it? Is there not a danger that European police networks composed of groups of specialists achieve a degree of autonomy that places them outside national interests while not yet under effective European control? Despite its fragmentation, the European police network is the embryo of a powerful and relatively independent bureaucracy beyond state allegiance, mainly intent on the pursuit of its own corporatist interests. Despite the diversity of these structural characteristics, a complex reality has been restructured into a simplified view easily accepted by the players because it follows old footsteps, while giving them the aspect of something new. With the aid of new semantics (gray zone, tidal wave of migrants, global mafia, bogus refugees, minority criminality), this view integrates the transnational aspect, which had not previously been taken into account, and presents it as part of the end of bipolarity and the disintegration of the Soviet Union. A new enemy has been identified, and a global meaning has been given to the events reflected in the media. Reassurance and protection are promoted by reducing uncertainty, although the creation of an artificial enemy may cause anxiety toward the world in which we live.

Discourse in Europe has shifted from freedom of movement of people to the ideology of a security deficit and the necessity of compensatory measures. This implies an overlapping of internal and external security functions. A *security-deficit* ideology becomes more prevalent. Struggles between various agencies inside the global security field are more and more important, while their specific roles become less and less clear.

5. Overlap between Internal and External Security

Presently, debate on the state's role in guaranteeing national security is characterized by dissenting viewpoints. The more traditional ones tend to ignore changes due to transnationalization and aim at simply reinforcing control methods. Structural changes are seen as the perverse effect of one or several enemies that have to be identified. Bellicose stereotypes are reused, presenting the confrontation of wills as a means of settling socio-economic situations. The army is proposed as a substitute for the police. This is the war against drugs, against infiltration by religious fanatics, and the systematic search for signs of nonconformity for police and political control.[17] The Cold War logic is restored as a matrix, but the *East* is replaced by the *South* and Islam—especially since the United States has also fallen victim to Islamic extremism (den Boer 1992).

New discourses on political violence still largely rely on the definition of geographically and socially identifiable enemies (the red threat of Moscow, the green threat of Teheran, the white threat of Medellín, and so forth). Unable to define terrorism or drug trafficking, analysts have grouped these under the term narcoterrorism. At the same time, observers have been unable to understand transnational movements of persons and migratory movements and have assigned them the role of a fifth column, stealthily invading democracies and bringing terrorism, drugs, crime, AIDS, and so on. Transnational phenomena, in some cities, have become the source of all dangers. Transnational players become the enemy of the state They are viewed as an infiltrating, omnipresent enemy that can be found in businesses and banks, among individuals and minorities—whichever is the paranoia of the moment. A flagrant example is the interlinking of terrorism, drugs, mafia, organized crime, illegal immigration, legal immigration, young second-generation immigrants, urban rioting, economic crisis, bogus refugees, and asylum seekers (Bigo, forthcoming). The discourse on gray zones where different intelligence services search for post-Cold War enemies has been developed by experts into a seemingly new concept. It is, in fact, clumsy propaganda, obsolete thinking, and reactionary rhetoric.

For once, this type of discourse is not an American import into Europe. The strength of the neorealist approach and of the theoreticians of unipolarity in the United States limited, for some time, discourse on a *southern threat* to a select and small group (e.g., specialists of Limited Intensity Conflict school). While Europeans worried over developments in Central Europe, the Balkans (Yugoslav crisis), and the Maghreb (Algeria, Morocco, Tunisia, Sudan), Americans had reason to be optimistic about developments in South America. The first elements of a concept of civilizational confrontation are to be found in Europe and in France.

A Threat From the *South*

It is a well-known fact that this vision characterizes the French extreme right, which is more or less inspired by racism. What needs explanation is the fact that this idea has broken loose from its origins, taking on global pretensions and imposing itself as a general and legitimate theoretical framework—even to someone like Régis Debray (1990: 44–45), old revolutionary comrade of Ernesto "Che" Guevara and adviser to François Mitterrand on Latin America. Apart from McCarthyites, Debray was one of the first to create a geopolitical view of the world that justifies civilization and culturalist approaches and promotes the idea of a threat from *all azimuths*. As early as 1989, he described two main threats to the stability of Western Europe.[18] The first came from the East and consisted of Europe being torn apart by the implosion of the Soviet empire. The second, and more recent one, came from the South. Resulting from a switch of the East-West axis to a North-South one, this danger is more insidious because it is unfamiliar. In the words of Debray (1990):

The public was used to a great reassuring fear and is unprepared for a series of small threats, seen as peripheral...The end of the US/USSR dyarchy moves us from a world with a (planned) risk of world war, but deviated into regional conflicts, towards a world of regional conflicts, with a danger of deviating into an unprogrammed world war. In this polycentric chaos, disarmed and demobilized nations will not be sheltered, and France, like its neighbors, will need its earlier strength.

The various threats from the South combine to form a manifold threat, changing but dangerous for the internal security of our states. These include local conflicts, religious fundamentalism, terrorism, weapons of mass destruction, even immigration and the demographic differential between the two sides of the Mediterranean, the urban crisis, and so on.[19] These require mobilizing the population, vigilance, and the understanding that maintaining security is no longer the exclusive prerogative of the military but calls for multidimensional measures. André Brossard refers to the same phenomenon of "transborder multidisciplinary criminality" and their favorite haunts (Golden Triangle, Amazonian border regions, the Bekaa plain, the Moroccan Rif, and others) and speaks of the projection of this criminality into the world by means of relays in hostile countries, all this being part of a strategy of the South against the North. In short, there exists an unexpected, infiltrating, unseizable enemy.

Debray (1990: 196) refines the idea and anticipates Huntington:

Because of its subordination to Atlantic priorities, NATO Europe strengthened its German flank, but left its South exposed. In every respect, and not only militarily speaking, we are tough when facing the soft, and soft when facing the tough. Broadly speaking, green has replaced red as the rising force, but we concentrate our attention and our decisiveness on a secondary front facing a defensive opponent; and we spare our means on more sensitive fronts with potentially offensive opponents. Tense in a calm zone, relaxed in a tense zone, we can, as usual, be attacked from the rear. The nuclear and rational North deters the nuclear and rational North, not the conventional and mystical South.

To sum up, the new threat is in the South, on the other side of the Mediterranean, in the Maghreb, where archaic religion coalesces with ultramodern technology.

A Clash of Civilizations

This discourse can of course also be developed in the United States, but never to the extent of rousing and mobilizing public opinion, which is undoubtedly its unavowed or involuntary aim. The Maghreb, Russia, and Yugoslavia are too remote. It is not opportune to present Central Americans as barbarians, even though some discussion on organized crime and drugs, in fact, does just this. Islamic fundamentalism has been presented as an enemy in the case of the Iranian revolution. This argument, though, cannot be extended to Iraq, Sudan, and Libya; insisting that these states constitute a threat would ridicule the United States itself. If, however, this threat could be associated with another, more powerful state, it might become plausible. For some days immediately following the coup against Gorbachev in Russia, the idea of a "put-up show" flourished: the USSR had planned the end of the Warsaw Pact to receive American aid and would now ally itself with Islam and all other anti-Western nationalisms in order to take advantage of the West. However, this argument did not find a receptive audience.

Samuel P. Huntington found another *alliance* that would bring credibility to the southern threat: a *Confucian-Islamic* connection would attack the West. The rest of the world might also rise in revolt against the West. China and North Korea (both, it was overlooked, officially and for the public, maintain their affiliation with the Socialist camp) became the Confucian conveyor that would assist the Islamic conveyor, strengthened by religious revival. The proof? Arms sales by China to Iraq, Pakistan, and Algeria.[20] Hence, the connection exists. The entire post-bipolar period can be reexamined through this perspective. The phrase "the West and the rest" (of the world) is often found in American editorials[21] probably because of its effective rhyme. As with Francis Fukuyama, had Huntington's article not been such a popular success, had it not summarized the feel of the moment, it certainly would have been ignored.[22] Huntington legitimizes the discourse of fear and common sense in the media, which reflects in a somewhat deformed manner the apprehensions of Western politicians. He allows them to take root in refurbished pre-World War II traditions. The civilizational theories of De Gobineau and the geopolitical theories of Ratzel have been barely modified, explaining that the clash of civilizations and cultures, rather than ideological and political cleavages, will determine tomorrow's conflicts. In any case, a civilization has to be defined as a living cultural entity with its variants and subjective identification criteria, but disposing of sufficient objective elements (language, history, religion, customs, institutions) to be immediately identifiable and placed on a map within a given territory.

This thesis was largely applied by Huntington's followers to the Yugoslav conflict where minorities were seen as well-constituted religious, ethnic, and linguistic groups going back to the dawn of time.[23] Minorities are necessarily agents of disorder. Even nonviolent groups with a religious identity are also subject to suspicion.[24] It is assumed that they follow the logic of proselytism and are incapable of mutual tolerance. Confrontations between the religions of the Book, with Islam facing Christianity, are unavoidable. Out of respect for symmetry, and to stigmatize the Islamic opponent, there is readiness to identify oneself as *Christian* where, earlier on, *modernist* or *free-thinker* would have done.[25]

Views of the world in terms of a civilizational clash are neither sustained by real events nor by an analysis of cultural dimensions, so often ignored by globalists. They do not deal with the right questions (cultural relations), nor can they provide their own wrong answers (necessary confrontation) because they define culture in geographical terms, i.e., tracing borders in order forcibly to exclude, instead of accept, culture as a code with each individual participating in several cultures (national, regional, professional, social class, and other) and not reducible to a single cultural identity. For some, these views are a reaction of extreme pessimism following the optimism of 1989. They are neither an explanatory principle nor even a description, but a process of adjustment of actors in the security field facing changes that they have difficulty admitting. For others, this confrontational world view assumes a central position by creating a feeling of insecurity, undoubtedly in relation with positions held by the main actors in the field of security. It provides the latter with a justification against peripheral critics and permits them to reconvert the techniques used in East/West relations for use in North/South relations.

The Clash-of-Civilizations Ideology: Rationale for Its Development

The ideology of a global threat conveyed by Islam (and Confucianism) was developed soon after the consequences of the new international context became evident to security professionals. It originated among those who had the most to lose after the disappearance of the Soviet threat: Strategists, secret service organizations with an East/West specialization, Kremlinologists, experts in terrorism, and others who had difficulty applying their knowledge elsewhere. These individuals and institutions faced financial difficulties, a loss of social relevance, and, as a result, a loss of influence on power through the production of knowledge and world views.

John Kenneth Galbraith (1990) was among the first to detect the role of bureaucracy behind some of the debate on disarmament. He explained how American conservatives, the military, and industrialists close to the Pentagon (especially associated with the Strategic Defense Initiative [SDI] program) were suddenly confronted with the new situation and found themselves devoid of a replacement doctrine. They desperately hung on to the threat from the East and Gorbachev's guile, and were temporarily unable to respond to the peace ideology and the growing demands to justify their budgets. But disorder in the Soviet Union and developments in the Middle East soon provided arguments in their favor. As they could not accept a shrinkage of their budgets or criticism of their parasitic nature and social uselessness, they soon developed reasoning around new potential threats that could unite the Atlantic Alliance against a new enemy.[26]

We have already tried to expose the nature of this discourse, not only in terms of interests, but also in terms of identity structures.[27] Military and national identities have, for a long time, been confused. Losing the enemy could thus be perceived as a risk of losing national identity. Hence, the nostalgic reaction of some to the Cold War. This would be ridiculous, if it were not significant in other ways. Pascal Bruckner (1990) develops the idea that, for some, the absence of an enemy means that life has no meaning. The enemy is "stock for the future, a way of ensuring the cohesion of a group, of striking a posture of opposition" (Bruckner 1990). Without an enemy, a state of melancholy and malaise can develop. To reestablish identity, different risks have to be synthesized within a new discourse, into a matrix that creates imaginary links between disparate phenomena. This matrix was quickly found. It imposed itself through force of evidence. The threat from the East was recycled into a threat from the South using Cold War arguments: dictatorships were in ascendancy with a growing military potential that threatened American superiority, and their revolutionary ideology united a bloc of countries against liberal democracies, already operating a fifth column within the United States.

The idea of a threat from the South, of a clash of civilizations, and of the infiltration of alien values through immigration and asylum seekers, permits the transfer of a new insecurity objective onto the practical know-how acquired during the bipolar period in terms of management of threat. It rejustifies inequality in distribution of resources, power, and knowledge in search of legitimacy. This is unquestionably one of the explanations why these views have found acceptance outside the extreme right and have repeatedly assured the electoral success of any party (whatever its position on the political chessboard) that advocated a firm policy with regard to the movement of persons and foreigners. This explains the political outbidding on this theme and the loss of credibility of those who attempt to restrain polarization in favor of security at the expense of citizens' rights. In fact, recent political concessions are such that this present discourse resembles that of their opponents earlier on. A striking example is the position of the French Socialists on European security, police cooperation, controls of identity, and asylum discourse on free movement turning into a justification of the opposite: security and border control (Bigo 1991).

Impacts on Internal and External Security Policy

American specialists of the theory of low-intensity conflicts (LIC) were the first to consider that the proliferation of nuisance actions by perpetrators without clearly defined political links could become as significant as the traditional Soviet threat (Hoffman 1992). However, as stated before, their position within the security field was subordinated to that of strategists. Relegated to peripheral conflicts, and without competence in central theaters, they were choice auxiliaries. Guerrilla war in Latin America, the lost war in Vietnam, the Iranian revolution followed by the Iran/Iraq war, none of which fit into the concept of conflict as an indirect strategy of the great powers, provided them with the opportunity of regaining influence with the *no-war* strategists and with regard to the disarmament problem. Starting in the 1980s, they emphasized the *warlike* value of the military, as opposed to its role of accountant of the balance of terror and psychologist of dissuasion. The military was thus characterized as waging real wars but not as exclusive agents in protecting the West against all forms of subversion.[28] This argument was strengthened when influential strategists took it up after 1990 in order to counter the *peace dividend* notion. Instead of admitting their social irrelevance, the strategists portrayed terrorists and organized crime as future enemies. Guarding the borders would keep personnel occupied and the fight against drugs would maintain manpower, budgets, and an identity.

However, the military are not alone in claiming the role of fighting terrorism, drugs, and immigration. They have to share these responsibilities with the police and are compelled to accept a modified security role. The enemy is not overly powerful. The problem is not one of harnessing large forces, but of localization and identification. The enemy cannot be immediately identified; he has *infiltrated*, he is inside and outside. This is the origin of the military malaise. Some in the military feel diminished by accepting a *cheap* threat.

The police, however, see in all this a magnificent opportunity. They no longer consider themselves restricted to their precincts to keep law and order, but, with the internationalization of the world, can now expand their work beyond the national scale. Although for many years the difference between the military and the police has not been convincing, the concept of keeping law and order and the restricted use of weaponry have, nevertheless, given the police an image of themselves that is not one of auxiliaries of the military. Now the police consider that the dangers facing society and the state justify a role at least as important as that of the military. Their know-how in dealing with the civilian population is more useful than that of the military. There is no longer any meaning in the difference between the local, societal, limited knowledge of the police and the international, political, statesmanlike knowledge of the military. The police are now engaged in the international political game and contribute significantly to the affirmation of state sovereignty.[29]

This explains why they have intensified international cooperation—in contrast to traditional notions of police as a force turned essentially inwards. Many criminal investigations are no longer local or even national; as soon as major traffic is involved, they cross borders. Whether in the fight against terrorism, drugs, major crime, stolen cars, or works of art, all specialized services that operated earlier on the sidelines or were superimposed on traditional national police activities now have to work with their foreign colleagues in order to be effective. This has obliged interior ministries to have their own foreign policies and contacts beyond Interpol. International police training was organized to provide specific know-how. Sometimes it became necessary to act outside the rules of cooperation and in violation of national sovereignty in order to infiltrate transborder networks. This has led to the constitution of unstructured police networks outside national sovereignty, where the police are primarily responsible for upholding public order, freed from political considerations.

The fight against terrorism and drugs has contributed to the broadening of the police domain at the expense of the military. As well, it has challenged the boundaries between the two organizations because of the altered conception of the role of borders in the world. This was beneficial to the police in France, whereas in the United States it is perhaps more beneficial to the military who are now involved in controlling the southern border. The fight against illegal immigration and, more generally, policies concerning the movement of persons and the granting of asylum, have given interior and justice ministries broader authority at the expense of other institutions and have led to internal restructuring inside these ministries. At the same time, intelligence activities have adopted new approaches that cross the internal/external division, and the police have had to deal increasingly with external intelligence, for example, the traditional field of the army. This institutional development has caused much agitation and generated difficulties in the adaptation of agencies conceived to wage secret wars against an identified enemy, using the compartmentalization principles of the past. This became a delicate question for services specializing in internal political intelligence whose task it has become to observe particular population groups coming from abroad. The police are thus, together with the LIC theoreticians, the most enthusiastic supporters of the notion of a threat from the South and of a clash of civilizations as it strengthens them against the military world, which earlier had been privileged.

6. Concluding Remarks: Security Concerns and Institutional Rearrangements

Unable to break out of their state-centered view and limited by state borders, the police have in the past sought to involve themselves in the activities of other security agencies. Now they have gone international (while the military has become *introverted*), but without ever examining the real meaning of these deviations from their initial missions. They have preferred to view this as an extension of their traditional tasks, marginal activities, so to speak, although in terms of time, personnel, and budget spent they assume a constantly growing importance. The army, for instance, no longer sees its functions only in terms of interstate conflict or block-to-block confrontation, but, under the pressure of politics, is obliged to assume new tasks: antiguerrilla strategy, antiterrorism, international police operations-styled peace maintenance, protection of nationals, or humanitarian action.

Strategists and specialists of low-intensity warfare have debated one another on who is to deal with *real wars* and other important business. Until 1989, strategists clearly had the upper hand in this debate. Since the end of the Soviet threat, the balance has moved against them. Another debate has raged concerning the structure of the army, its professionalization (abolition of compulsory military service), and the future of the nuclear deterrent. Without going into detail, it should be noted that the deterrent has rendered world war with classical weapons more or less obsolescent, upsetting centuries-old Western military theory.[30] Wars have changed in nature. Strategists call them limited, contained. Even though guerrilla wars, *coups d'état*, and civil wars have multiplied, their nature has changed. They have become more complex owing to the interplay of internal/external factors.

Conflicts have become intertwined and can no longer be regulated through the trusted system of balance of power.[31] On the contrary, certain local problems have disturbed the equilibria established in the interest of central players. Furthermore, as these central players have continued to act on the basis of preestablished models, their actions have also often tended to destabilize rather than balance the situation. The politics of deterrence deprived European and American military leaders of the possibility of engaging in traditional warfare. As a result, they resorted to strategic "gesticulations" and the promotion of an armaments race.[32] Strategy became total and global, testing the willpower of the opponent. Discourse, symbolism, and posturing replaced actual combat. In the post-Cold War period, the military are increasingly aware that their secular mission of interstate confrontation is in decline and has little to do with their present tasks as rescuers in natural catastrophes, humanitarian helpers, buffer forces, and peace soldiers—who, in the cases of Lebanon and Yugoslavia, have remained witnesses to combat, prohibited from using their weapons.

Some military staff hoped to find a new justification for their existence in low intensity conflicts. Starting with guerrilla war, the term *low intensity conflict* covers all external operations, allowing the strong to win the day without engagement in all-out war and all actions against terrorism and drug mafias.[33]

European and American military leaders were thus led to intervene in police matters: the enemy is never overpowering; the problem does not lie in the amassing of forces, but in localization and identification. The police have also had to broaden their horizons. They can no longer be restricted to the precinct and to the maintenance of public order. They are concerned with the internationalization of the world and are often involved in research beyond the national scale. As such, the police consider that the dangers facing society and the state give them a more important role than that of the army because of their better experiences and knowledge in dealing with the civilian population.[34] There is no longer any meaning in the local, societal, limited approach of the police as opposed to the international, political state approach of the military. The police are now engaged in international political issues and contribute significantly to the affirmation of state sovereignty.[35]

Foreign police forces have received training in specific fields. Sometimes transborder networks have been infiltrated despite rules of collaboration and concerns about state sovereignty. At other times, similar services of different nationalities (but sharing a common outlook) have collaborated better with one another than different services of the same nationality. This is especially the case in countries where the various services dealing with security (in the case of France: police, gendarmerie, customs) are directed by highly differentiated ministries. As a result, groups within police agencies have developed that are guided by considerations of maintenance of public order outside the political framework, rather than by national considerations. Action against terrorism and drugs has been the main cause of this enlargement of the police domain at the expense of the military, at least in France. In the United States, the opposite seems to have occurred. Actions against illegal immigration, and migration and asylum policies in general, are likely to enlarge the fields of ministries of the interior and of justice at the expense of other ministries and lead to major internal restructuring of these ministries.

At the same time, intelligence has broken away from the traditional internal/external dichotomy, and the police have increasingly dealt with external intelligence, previously a military function. These developments of intelligence agencies were accompanied by institutional infighting and difficulties of adaptation, given their original design for secret war against an identified enemy, using the age-old principles of seclusion.[36] This was especially difficult for services specializing in internal political intelligence that were called upon to control immigrant groups.

These transformations require redefinitions of army and police missions. In some specific—and so far marginal—cases, such as repression of international terrorism, action against mafias, action against drugs in production and transit zones, control of illegal immigration, and expulsion of refugees, there is much competition among security agencies. Essentially—and this is our hypothesis—there exists a dynamic correlation of cooperation and conflict, a redefinition of activities, and a change of tasks for all forces at the intersection between police and military.

The originality of this combined approach lies in its analysis of the transformation of police and military functions as affected by changes in types of violence within the context of globalization trends and the end of state supremacy over outside actors. The transnational nature of certain types of violence and the bureaucratic interplay among institutions result in the interpenetration of the two institutions and in the creation of a security continuum that unites the worlds of crime and war. To analyze them separately no longer conforms with reality. They have to be examined together because they share the same field, carry out similar tasks, and because their strategies, policies, and methods of action are related.

Notes

1. Some of the author's hypotheses are based on the work of Michel Foucault, especially on his course at the College de France.

2. Didier Bigo (Paris) is responsible for the research network for the EC Commission; partners are Malcolm Anderson (Edinburgh), Heiner Busch (Berlin), Donatella della Porta (Florence), and Professor Benyon (Leicester).

3. See Raymond Aron (1984). The long preface deals with the distinction between the internal—dominated by the civil state and its relation with the individual—and the external—dominated by anarchy between states.

4. See Charles Tilly (1991).

5. See the different studies and articles of James Rosenau (1990; 1992).

6. See Didier Bigo (1993).

7. See the HESI report of Didier Bigo and Rémy Leveau (1992).

8. It is all very well for the United States, in the NAFTA agreement, to have refused free movement of persons; their border control nonetheless remains ineffective and tends toward a control of the Hispanic population, regardless of nationality. See Didier Bigo (1992).

9. Examples are the border passages between the United States and Mexico, or between Germany and Poland. Even France would be economically unable to ensure effective border control.

10. Anthony Giddens (1984).

11. For example, the effect on the Algerian population of the introduction of parabolic antennae.

12. Bertrand Badie and Marie Claude Smouts (1992).

13. The term "state" is taken to be the form of government adopted in Europe on the basis of the theory of sovereignty.

14. See, for example, Charles Tilly (1991).

15. Schmitter uses a now classical line of argument that compares the economic and the military, emphasizing the decline of the latter. But all studies that compare economic to military power fail to take into account the socio-political transformations and the historical trajectories

that melt the military into the police universe, and the economic into the social. Security is, thus, no more a function of the military than prosperity of the economic. It would be an interesting challenge historically to reintegrate the various components of security and of prosperity without limiting them to the military and the economic. Even Charles Tilly seems to fall into this trap in his otherwise highly synthetic study mentioned above.

16. The origin of Schengen was an agreement between the French and German ministries of transportation as a result of truck drivers' strikes in 1984.

17. See Denis Duclos (1991).

18. An ancillary threat consists of Europe being asphyxiated by American domination.

19. See Didier Bigo (1993).

20. To expose the weakness of the argument, it suffices to compare arms sales by China with arms sales by France and the United Sates to the same countries.

21. Kishore Mahbubani (1992).

22. This was the case for many eminent American academics, but not journalists. Thus, it became necessary to publicly refute such theses. Zaki Laïdi did this in France through Libération.

23. To cite one person, see Philippe Moreau Desfarges (1993) and an interview with Ms. Desfargues in *Cahiers français* "Ordre et désordre dans le monde," No. 263, December 1993.

24. For a critical approach to these views, see Ted Gurr and Barbara Harff (1993).

25. Gilles Kepel (1992) shows the irrelevance of this type of thinking. Although quoted by Huntington, he is critical of culturalist views. He shows up the strategies of the culturalist and religious activists for what they are, instruments of the religious for political ends.

26. Régis Debray, an enemy of the Atlantic Alliance, uses the same arguments, but to justify the specific role of France (1990:196): "Overseas is outside the zone; we are in the front line, without a program, without established partners. Here (in the East) the Alliance could, in a pinch, do without us. There (in the South) we have to do without it and no one will defend us in our place."

27. Didier Bigo and Daniel Hermant (1990).

28. See Jean-Louis Dufour (1990).

29. See Didier Bigo (1995b).

30. See the studies by General Poirier published by the Fondation pour les Etudes de Défense Nationale.

31. On the intertwining of conflicts, see Didier Bigo and Daniel Hermant (1989).

32. See the studies of Alain Joxe and in particular "Le cycle de la dissuasion 1945–1990; essai de stratégie critique" (1990).

33. One of the most significant aspects of research in this field is the development of low-intensity conflict theories and the involvement of European and American military staff in problems of terrorism and drugs. Some of this appears in Bigo and Hermant (1991). Studies by Michael Klare, Johnson, Bruce Hoffman, Jean-Louis Dufour, and Latin American authors could serve as the basis for a systematic examination, including American concerns and their replication by French military staff. Another instructive item is the preparation of the White Book on Defense.

34. This point is covered by a significant bibliography. See, in particular, the studies by Dominique Monjardet, Loubet del Baye, Journes, Gleisal, Brodeur, and Gary Marx.

35. Didier Bigo and Rémy Leveau (1992).

36. See the studies of Michel Dobry on "le renseignement politique" for IHESI, May 1992.

References

Aron, Raymond. 1984. *Paix et guerre entre les nations* (8th edition). Paris: Calman Lévy.

Badie, Bertrand, and Marie Claude Smouts. 1992. "Le retournement du monde." *PFNSP*.

Bigo, Didier. 1991. *L'Europe des polices et de la sécurité intérieure*. Brussels: Complexe.

Bigo, Didier. 1992. "Interpénétration entre sécurité intérieure et sécurité extérieure: enjeux américains et européens." Report for FEDN.

Bigo, Didier. 1993. "Le discours sur la menace et ses ambiguïtés." *Cahiers de l'HESI* 15 (October).

Bigo, Didier. 1995a. *Polices en réseau l'exemple européen*. Paris: Presses de la Fondation Nationale des Sciences Politiques.

Bigo, Didier. 1995b. "Terrorisme, drogue, immigration: la construction de la menace." *RIAC*. Québec.

Bigo, Didier, and Daniel Hermant. 1989. "La métamorphose des conflits." *Etudes Polémologiques* 50.

Bigo, Didier, and Daniel Hermant. 1990. "Les lectures de la conflictualité." *Stratégique* 47 (3)

Bigo, Didier, and Rémy Leveau. 1992. "L'Europe de la sécurité intérieure." Report for the IHESI. June.

Bruckner, Pascal. 1990. *La mélancolie démocratique*. Paris: Seuil.

Debray, Régis. 1990. *Tous azimuts*. Paris: Odile Jacob/FEDN.

den Boer, Monica. 1992. "The Quest for International Policing: Rhetoric and Justification in a Disorderly Debate." *ECPR*.

Duclos, Denis. 1991. "Les déplacements de la menace." *Cultures et Conflits, L'idéologie de la menace du Sud* 2.

Dufour, Jean-Louis. 1990. *Les vraies guerres*. Paris: La Manufacture.

Galbraith, John Kenneth. 1990. "Comprendre ce qui se passe en URSS et aux USA." *Le Monde Diplomatique* (February).

Giddens, Anthony. 1984. *The Constitution of Society*. Cambridge: Cambridge Polity Press.

Gurr, Ted, and Barbara Harff. 1993. *Minorities at Risk*. Washington, D.C.: USIP.

Hoffman, Bruce. 1992. *An Agenda for Research on Terrorism and LIC in the 1990s*. San Diego: San Diego State University.

Joxe, Alain. 1990. "Le cycle de la dissuasion 1945–1990; essai de stratégie critique." *La Découverte*.

Kepel, Gilles. 1992. *Les politiques de dieu*. Paris: Seuil.

Mahbubani, Kishore. 1992. "The West and the Rest." *The National Interest* (Summer).

Mann, Michael. 1993. "The Nation-State in Europe and Other Continents: Diversifying, Developing, not Dying." *Daedalus* (Reconstructing Nations and States) (Summer).

Moreau Desfarges, Phillipe. 1993. "Relations internationales," Points Seuil and interview in *Cahiers français* "Ordre et désordre dans le monde" 263 (December).

Rosenau, James. 1990. *Turbulence in World Politics*. Princeton: Princeton University Press.

Rosenau, James. 1992. "Les constitutions dans un monde en proie aux turbulences." *Cultures & Conflicts* 8.

Rupnik, Jacques. 1993. *De Sarajevo à Sarajevo*. Brussels: Complexe.

Tilly, Charles. 1991. *Coercion, Capital and European States*. Cambrige: Cambridge Polity Press.

III

Border Regions and Transboundary Cooperation in Europe

Dutch-German Euroregions: A Model for Transboundary Cooperation?

James Scott

1. Introduction

The development of transboundary cooperation in Western Europe is inextricably linked to political and economic integration within the European Union (EU); in attempting to deal with common problems, even the most conservative EU member states have agreed to a limited suspension of sovereignty. This de-emphasis of nationally oriented policy-making has opened up new prospects for border regions. Indeed, transboundary cooperation is now a high-priority area within European regional- and spatial-planning policy

The slow evolution of transboundary interaction in Western Europe from informal encounters among local officials to more structured and institutionalized forms of policy-making has been widely documented and assessed (Scott 1989, 1993; Hansen 1992; Martínez 1986; Strassoldo and Delli Zotti 1982; Anderson 1982). As a result, Europe has witnessed an increasingly vocal transboundary regionalism culminating in the creation of semi-official transboundary associations or *Euroregions* and gradually establishing a political agenda for greater central-government support of transboundary cooperation. At the same time, European Union policy reflects a reevaluation of the political, economic, and cultural roles of border regions. Official European discourse on transboundary cooperation tends to be rational in nature, emphasizing the political necessity of finding problem-solving mechanisms that transcend the institutional limitations of nation-states. More recently, the idea that there exist hidden but compelling economic incentives to transboundary cooperation has been raised.

In fact, it is argued here that a clearly definable border-region policy is materializing within the EU based on a pragmatic philosophy that stresses international-policy coordination, solution of day-to-day problems at different administrative levels, and creation of new regional growth opportunities through transboundary cooperation. According to this philosophy (based on principles described here as integration, subsidiarity, and synergy), the nation-states have, furthermore, a crucial role to play in supporting efforts at the local and regional levels.

Over the past 30 years, Dutch-German border-region associations have established an impressive track record in the area of transboundary planning cooperation. This has enabled them to assume a pioneer role in the institutionalization of transboundary cooperation, whereas other international regions are only now beginning to make headway in the area of spatial planning. Indeed, it is on the Dutch-German border that the first international and local parliamentary bodies—albeit advisory in nature—were established. The Dutch-German EUREGIO, with its unique transboundary parliament, the EUREGIO Council, has been offered as proof that, for the public and private sectors, cooperative output is greater than the end result of unilateral action. As such, it is often seen—and touted—as a model to be emulated.

Pragmatism implies that transboundary cooperation emphasizes issues of mutual interest and activities that benefit all parties involved. While this argument appears rational enough, history, language, culturally defined perceptions of border regions, as well as other elements that create specific transboundary contexts, must be considered in order to make the *synergy paradigm* politically feasible (Scott 1993). Based on the experiences of transboundary regional-planning attempts on the Dutch-German border, this article attempts to venture some observations on the cross-cultural transferability of transboundary cooperation "models," discussing strengths but also limitations of EU border-region policy.

2. The Evolution of a European Border-Region Policy

The end of World War II brought with it the breakdown of historical military rivalries among the countries of Western Europe. This fact, along with the monumental task of postwar reconstruction and reconciliation, has made transboundary cooperation possible in a way hitherto inconceivable. As postwar Europe evolved within the framework of the NATO security community and the Common Market, the slow emergence (or reemergence, as the case may be) of a "supranational" rather than strictly national perception of economic and political interests helped change the status of national borders. This, along with increasing economic interaction, the creation of truly European institutions, and the elimination of internal controls within the "Schengen Seven" states in March 1995,[1] has considerably diminished the defensive character of national borders.

Transboundary cooperation in regional development and other policy areas has unfolded accordingly. Presently, transboundary cooperation within the EU is characterized by activity at virtually all levels of government as well as among private associations, interest groups, and businesses. Moreover, the long-term efforts of harmonizing spatial planning concepts of the individual EU member states emphasize the strategic role of border regions as zones of integration and economic synergy. This is reinforced by official EU policy and, most recently, by regional development initiatives specifically aimed at supporting transboundary cooperation.

It would be incorrect to assume that all barriers to planning coordination within international border regions have been eliminated. Despite the progress of the past decades, national interests often prevail over the most ambitious attempts at cooperation in—among other important areas—transboundary environmental protection and transport planning. Given time, however, and assuming continued momentum toward European integration, transboundary cooperation will eventually surmount even these persistent obstacles.

From Local Initiatives to Euroregions

Euroregion is a more or less generic term that refers to government associations dedicated to the cause of transboundary problem-solving. Euroregions are, in most cases, initiated by local governments but have also been created by regional and/or national authorities. They are, without exception, informal bodies with an advisory and promotional function. As such, their primary objectives are to influence public opinion by popularizing the concept of transboundary regionalism and to lobby for greater national-government support of transboundary cooperation. Generally speaking, Euroregions achieve this through a variety of activities including cultural and other events that emphasize international neighborliness, commissioning studies on border-region problems, promoting visions of future transboundary development, and intensifying local-government contacts across national borders. In this, Euroregions can often—but by no means always—count on the support of local and regional media. Apart from creating a sense of inclusive, European, regional identity (and hence the word Euroregion), these activities serve political aims, such as publicizing the need for more forceful, transboundary planning mechanisms at the local level (Scott 1989).

Initially, Euroregions developed as a local-level manifestation of the spirit of European cooperation that emerged after the end of World War II. It is not surprising, therefore, that transboundary cooperation initiatives gained greatest momentum in the core area of the European Community—most notably the BeNeLux states, France, and West Germany.[2] Consequently, much of the research that has been conducted on European border regions has focused on attempts to establish institutions of transboundary planning and problem-solving in the Upper Rhine Valley and along the Dutch-German border. This geographical nexus of cooperation is particularly important in that here transboundary planning has developed simultaneously with that at various levels of government—a development that in large measure has been facilitated by the ground-breaking activities of the Regio Basiliensis, the Dutch-German Euregios, and other associations.

Pioneers of transboundary cooperation in postwar Europe made no attempt to conceal their objectives—generally to improve communications, economic ties, and working relationships with government officials across national boundaries. From its inception in 1963, the Regio Basiliensis—widely documented for its attempts to bring the trinational Upper Rhine Valley closer together—has insisted on promoting a supranational regional identity. Operating basically as a nongovernmental organization (NGO) with official backing of the Swiss cantons of Basel-Town and Basel-Land, it has created a dense network of formal and informal working relationships among local authorities, businesses, universities, and representatives of senior government in the region (Briner 1986). The Regio's local-level partners in France and Germany, located in the cities of Colmar and Freiburg, respectively, attempt to reinforce this network through their own access to national lobbies and senior governments.

At the same time, Hans Briner, former Director General of the Regio, has admitted quite openly that Basel, a large but geographically peripheral city within Switzerland, itself a staunchly neutral nonmember of the European Union, had to take the initiative in order to avoid economic and political isolation. Basel's "unabashed" self-interest did, for a time, generate skepticism on the part of its French and German partners as to the Regio's sincerity in promoting a trinational regional identity.[3] However, skepticism about Basel's motives in promoting transboundary cooperation within the Upper Rhine Valley has perhaps never been as critical an issue as some have made it out to be; the greatest present difficulty facing cooperation lies in actually establishing Upper Rhine Valley regional policies. These have been largely stymied by the sheer institutional inertia of the three nation-states (Germany, France, and Switzerland) and their various organs of planning authority. The Regio's attempts to establish a trinational, metropolitan, public-transportation network are a case in point: the colossal task of coordinating investment decisions and tariff policies among three large and strategic national institutions (the railway companies of Germany, France, and Switzerland) defies a local-level solution, even when supported by senior government representatives.[4]

The experiences of the Regio Basiliensis demonstrate the limitations of local-level transboundary cooperation. An alternative strategy to the trilateralism practiced by the Regio and its French and German counterparts has been the establishment of Euroregions based on agreements among *associations* of local governments. Indeed, this appears to be the strategy favored by many European policymakers. On the whole, Euroregions are private law organizations and, as such, as politically informal as the Regio Basiliensis. However, because they are supervised by local governments, Euroregions theoretically enjoy greater legitimacy and influence. As in the case of the trinational Upper Rhine Valley, Euroregions evolved out of a multitude of low-key contacts between municipal authorities and community groups motivated by a need to join forces in solving a variety of local problems. The first of the Euroregions were established along the Dutch-German border in the 1960s and 1970s. From there, the model spread to other parts of Europe, first to the French, Belgian, and Luxembourgeois border areas and then, eventually, to the EU's external borders with Poland and Czech Lands.

As the momentum of local-level transboundary cooperation increased, it was realized that the interests of border regions could only be effectively promoted if a certain unity of purpose were established. To this end, a group of politicians, planners, and researchers, including Hans Briner, Viktor Freiherr von Malchus, and Alfred Mozer, founded the Association of European Border Regions (AEBR) in 1971. At that time, AEBR received considerable impetus from efforts of the Dutch and German governments to sponsor local transboundary pilot projects in the area of cultural exchange and social activities. Since that time, the AEBR has developed into an important NGO whose members include local-government representatives, European and national MPs, as well as designated representatives of the Euroregions themselves. The organization, thus, has more or less direct access to the European Commission and the Council of Europe in addition to its close contacts with regional and national authorities. Events since 1971 have borne out the strategic role of the AEBR in influencing European debate on regional policy and, more specifically, on development policies aimed at transboundary regions on the EU's internal and external borders.

Transboundary Planning Cooperation among Senior Governments

The local level has played a decisive role in promoting transboundary regionalism. A discussion of transboundary cooperation within Europe, however, would be incomplete without mentioning the increasing interaction of senior governments, that is to say, nations, states, and provinces, in the regional-planning arena. There are several examples of bilateral and multilateral commissions whose aim is to facilitate the coordination of national policies with international ramifications. Again, these international bodies have developed most rapidly in the core area of the European Union and include the French-German-Swiss,

Transboundary Associations (Key to Figure 1)

1. Nordkalotten (N, S, SF)	29. South-Upper Rhine-Alsace (F, D)
2. Mitt Norden (N, S, SF)	30. Moyenne Alsace-Breisgau CIMAB (F, D)
3. Kjolen-Nordland-Västerbotten (N, S)	31. Hochheim and Lake Constance (D, CH)
4. ARKO (N, S)	32. Regio Basiliensis (F, CH, D)
5. Östfold-Nordliga Bohuslän (N,S)	33. Jura (F, CH)
6. Kvarken (S, SF	34. Lake Geneva Region (F, CH)
7. Skärgardsprojecktet (S, SF)	35. Ticino (CH, I)
8. Øresund (DK, S)	36. Alps Working Community /ARGE Alp (D, A, I, CH)
9. Bornholm-Sydostra Skåne (DK, S)	
10. Vestnorden (DK, Faroe Islands)	37. Alps-Adria Working Community (A, I, D, H, SLO, CRO, CH also includes the memberstates of ARGE-Alp)
11. Åbenrå-Flensburg (DK, D)	
12. Ems Dollart (NL, D)	
13. EUREGIO (NL, D)	38. Valle d'Aosta-Haute Savoie-Valois (I, F, CH)
14. Rhein-Waal (NL, D)	39. Assoziazione Franco-Italiana delle Alpi (F, I)
15. Rhein-Maas-Nord (NL, D)	40. Alpazur (F, I)
16. Maas-Rhein Euroregion (NL, D, B)	41. West Alps Cantons and Regione Working Community (CH, F, I)
17. Interlimburg Maasland (NL, B)	
18. Weert-Noord-Limburg (NL, B)	42. Pyrenees Regional Conference (E, F, AND)
19 Kemperland (NL, B)	43. La Manche-Dover Calais (GB,F)
20. BENEGO (NL, B)	44. Northern Ireland (GB, I)
21. Nord-Pas de Calais (F, B)	45 Euroregion Pomerania (D, PL)
22. Lille-Roubaix-Tourcoing (F, B)	46. Euroregion Pro-Europa Viadrina (D, PL)
23. Eifel and Ardenne European Union (F, B, L, D)	47 Euroregion Spree-Neisse-Bobr (D, PL)
24. Arlon-Longwy-Esch (F, B, L)	48. Euroregion Neisse/Nysa (D, PL, Cz)
25. Westpfalz Planning Community (D, F)	49. Euroregion Elbe/Labe (D, Cz)
26. Saar-Lorraine-Luxemburg (D, F, L)	50. Euroregion Erzgebirge (D, Cz)
27. Rheinpfalz Planning Community (D, F)	51. Euroregion Egrensis (D, Cz)
28. Upper Rhine-Alsace (F, D)	52. Region Triagonale (A, H, SVK).

A (Austria)	DK (Denmark)	NL (Holland)
AND (Andorra)	E (Spain); F (France)	PL (Poland)
B (Belgium)	GB (Great Britain)	S (Sweden)
CH (Switzerland)	H (Hungary)	SF (Finland)
CRO (Croatia)	I (Italy)	SLO (Slovenia)
Cz (Czech Lands)	L (Luxemburg)	SVK (Slovakia)
D (Germany)	N (Norway)	

French-German, Dutch-German, and Belgian-German planning commissions. In all of these commissions, representatives of central, regional, and local governments meet to discuss ways of coordinating planning decisions taken within common border regions.[5]

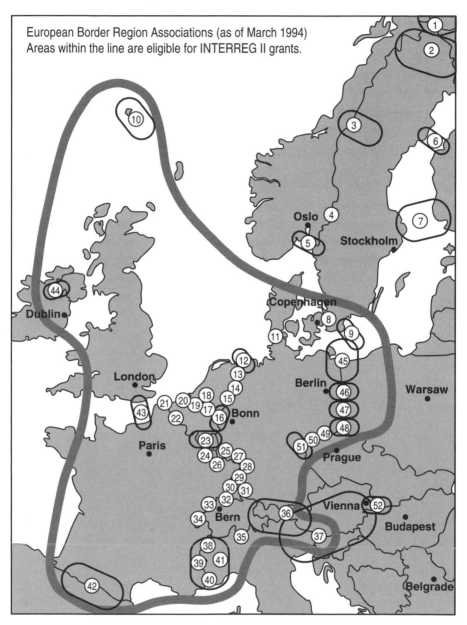

European Border Region Associations (as of March 1994)
Areas within the line are eligible for INTERREG II grants.

Figure 1. Euroregions, Interregional Working Groups,
and other Border Region Associations in Europe

A further element in the development of a European border-region policy has been the activities of the Council of Europe. Established in 1949, the Council was originally conceived as a supranational parliamentary institution, but it never acquired legislative authority.[6] This has allowed it to develop into an advisory body devoted to problems of global importance and unfettered in its activities by day-to-day politicking. Attempts at intergovernmental cooperation between nation-states, including the harmonization of spatial planning and regional-development policy within the European Union have been a priority objective for the Council of Europe. It has also been one of the most vocal promoters of greater political support of transboundary regionalism, sponsoring a number of European conferences on border regions and producing an impressive body of policy studies on the perspectives of transboundary cooperation. With respect to border-region issues, the greatest achievement of the Council to date has been the elaboration of an Outline Convention on Transfrontier Cooperation (Council of Europe 1983). This Convention, passed by the Council in 1980 and since ratified by most member states, provides contractual models for local governments to enter into formal cooperative agreements with their counterparts across national boundaries.[7] To date, however, the only precedent for actually creating the public-law frameworks envisaged by the Council of Europe has been the Dutch-German Treaty of Transboundary Cooperation among Local Governments, ratified in 1991 (Scott 1993: 57).

New Regional-Policy Paradigms

The creation of a European regional policy in 1975 was deemed an important element in the creation of a cohesive and economically balanced common market. Subsequently, the European Regional Development Fund (ERDF) is an institution whose management has required an increasing degree of harmonization of development targets, award procedures, and criteria governing the geographical disbursement of grants. During the first years of the ERDF's existence, community moneys collected from member states were redistributed by way of a system of quotas back to national governments. In this way, the ERDF did little else than basically support nationally oriented policies toward backward areas (e.g., Italy's Mezzogiorno, Ireland, and Greece) or regions in crisis (for example, Clydeside and Tyneside in the UK and the Belgian and French coal and steel producing areas).

In later years, and particularly after the reformation of Europe's structural policies in 1989, regional policy focus began to shift from direct transfers of wealth to the creation of new opportunities for locally and regionally generated (*endogenous*) growth. One of the primary reasons for this change was the realization that the international economic context had been supplanting strictly domestic factors in determining regional outcomes. The mobility of production factors, determined by a variety of global considerations, was deemed too limited to hold out promise for the more underdeveloped regions in Europe. At the same time, and influenced by Europe's economic recession of the late 70s and early 80s, policymakers feared that fiscal constraints could eventually make a policy of direct regional transfers detrimental to the general welfare of nation-states.

By 1980, suggestions for the support of endogenous growth strategies by mobilizing local resources were making the rounds in Brussels (Commission of the European Communities 1981). The debate on regional policy that ensued centered on the role of innovation, small-and medium-sized enterprises, retraining schemes, alternative-energy sources, and new opportunities for agriculture.[8] In the actual changes in regional policy that followed, emphasis shifted from large national projects and long-term support of problem regions to strategic development initiatives that could be employed flexibly and with greater accountability.

Regional policy in Europe has also been greatly affected by a desire for greater transparency and "grassroots-level" participation in the development of community policies. In keeping with the New Community Approach ultimately enshrined by Article 5 of the 1991 Maastricht Treaty, a "regionalization" of regional policy is taking place that involves a shift in regional-development focus not only toward endogenous growth strategies but also toward closer involvement of regional bodies, including transboundary associations, in the policy-making process. At the same time, the political principle of "subsidiarity" implies a reevaluation of the most efficient level of government for the execution of specific tasks and a new partnership between various levels of government within the EU.[9]

These regionalization trends indicate that national and European attitudes toward border regions as a special regional development have been shifting as well. As early as 1981—and due partially to the insistent prodding of the Council of Europe and AEBR—the EC Commission was recommending that transboundary cooperation at the local and regional levels be recognized as a regional-development activity in and of itself and thus eligible for development grant support. Although tangible progress in this area is of more recent date, the Commission did help finance ground-breaking transboundary activities in the Dutch-German border area during the 1980s—most importantly in supporting the elaboration of transboundary development programs.

One Step Further: The Concept of Synergy

Fears for the future competitiveness of European industry against a North American and Japanese onslaught have helped prompt EU preoccupations with technological innovation and endogenous growth potential. Simultaneously, due to their potential ability to adapt to new economic circumstances, great importance is being attached to regions and cities as innovators and catalysts of economic development.

However, the issue of balanced regional development still looms large within the EU, where socio-economic cohesion is seen as a prerequisite for integration. The Europa 2000 project is an initiative of all EU member-state ministries responsible for regional affairs to analyze spatial development and regional problems on a pan-European level with the intention of establishing guidelines for coordinated planning and policy frameworks. The first report has established that several spatial trends are unfolding that could have grave consequences for many peripheral regions of the EU (Commission of the European Communities 1993). Among the findings are: *(a)* formerly a vital development factor, new investment is now generally avoiding the European periphery, and *(b)* at the same time, investment in those sectors considered to be the most locationally independent—services, in particular—appears to be concentrating on easily accessible core regions of the EU. One conclusion that can be drawn from these observations is that labor-cost differentials play a much less important role in influencing the locational decisions of firms than do optimal combinations of hard and soft factors.

In order to achieve the twin goals of growth and spatial balance, regional-policy debate in Europe has centered around the feasibility of pooling local and regional resources in promoting development and combating unemployment. Similarly, the subsidiarity argument holds that it is not only more democratic but more efficient to allow communities to do what they can do best and to solve those problems that can be more clearly addressed at the local level. In this way, the exploitation of complementarities through interregional cooperation, regional marketing, and public-private partnerships is seen as a means of improving infrastructure and providing the basis of innovative and regionally based development initiatives. Synergy, a relatively new watchword of European regional policy, implies that cooperation, and not the costly duplication of competitive efforts, holds the key to development in disadvantaged and peripheral regions. Not surprisingly, the concept of synergy has become a central issue in border-region policy and one increasingly used to emphasize the importance of transboundary cooperation in regional development

Among the first strategies based on paradigms of endogenous development and economic synergies to be explicitly devised for European border regions were those originating from the AEBR and the Council of Europe and were based on the work of economists such as Jacques Robert and Charles Ricq. In a brochure produced by AEBR, Robert (1982?) summarized the most important aspects of border region development policy. These involved promoting transboundary cooperation in areas such as education and vocational training, creating regional financial institutions tailored to the needs of small- and medium-sized businesses, "bio-agriculture," research and development, and provision of services.

In more recent years, a respectable body of research on synergy effects within international border regions has accumulated, undertaken primarily by experts personally involved in border-region associations. Riccardo Cappellin, an Italian economist active in the Alps-Adriatic Working Community, has identified several benefits that interregional and transboundary cooperation can provide (1993, 20). Among them are:

1. The reduction of transaction costs and other obstacles to economic relations.

2. The development of network economies that allow exchanges of information in areas of common interest and, as a result, help create cooperative alliances.

3. The joint utilization of common resources (water, forests, rivers, etc.) and a more efficient approach to addressing transboundary environmental problems.

4. A pooling of resources in the provision of certain strategic public goods and services (airports, universities, international fairs, research facilities, transportation infrastructure, etc.) that can prevent costly duplications of investment

5. In the case of direct geographical proximity, the overcoming of specific-size thresholds and/or the exploitation of specific economies of scale in the creation of those public services whose provision within smaller "catchment areas" would be exorbitant.

6. The management and/or limitation of potentially damaging interregional competition.

Of particular interest to local-level transboundary actors, adds Cappellin, is the fact that bargaining power at the subnational level is oftentimes only possible in an interregional context that allows for joint bargaining power and lobbying.

Van der Veen (1993: 94–95) carries this argument further. He maintains that cross-border cooperation among local governments brings with it value-added (surplus-value) effects, particularly the combination of equity and efficiency goals in regional/local development and in the strengthening of cultural and regional identities. In the design of regional policy, income distribution and other socially oriented (equity) policies have traditionally conflicted with growth- and innovation-oriented (efficiency) strategies. By supporting transboundary cooperation, argues van der Veen, national governments can employ national public-investment instruments to improve accessibility and other locational factors of peripheral border regions. However, in doing this, national governments open up new regional-cooperation possibilities that, in the long run, will improve the competitive positions of their core regions as well. Euroregions and particularly the Dutch-German EUREGIO, are, in van der Veen's estimation, proof that, for the public and private sectors, cooperative output is greater than the end result of unilateral action.

The INTERREG Initiative

These paradigm shifts in regional policy are changing the way the European Union views the economic and political roles of borders and border regions. Starting in 1990, several new programs aimed at establishing transboundary networks were inaugurated. This can be seen as proof that a more "enlightened" perception of transboundary cooperation is forming the basis of actual EU policy. The main objective of LACE (Linkage Assistance and Cooperation for the European Border Regions), an EU pilot project implemented by AEBR, is to promote the exchange of information and experience in local-level transboundary cooperation by providing technical advice and assistance. Participants are local governments, chambers of commerce, trade-union organizations, and "all other organizations and initiatives with the aim to promote cross-border cooperation" (AEBR 1991).

However, the most important regional-policy innovation in this regard is the community initiative INTERREG, now in its second four-year phase (1995–1998). This program funds transboundary planning and development and capital-investment projects in all border regions but focuses primarily on areas particularly affected by unemployment and industrial decline or, in the case of rural areas, by underdevelopment. The objectives of INTERREG are: (1) to prepare border regions for the introduction of the single market, (2) to terminate the economic and social isolation of border regions through direct problem-solving measures, (3) to promote transboundary cooperation and networking, and (4) to prepare border regions on the external boundaries of the EC for their role as gateway to the single market.

The regional development goals of the initiative paraphrase those outlined by the AEBR more than fifteen years ago, namely, the creation of alternative employment opportunities by exploiting the unique synergy potentials of the border. Within the scope of INTERREG, a wide variety of transboundary projects has received funding in such areas as environmental protection, rural-enterprise development, tourism, communications infrastructure, and transborder information networks. With EU contributions of over 1.5 billion ECUs (matched by a similar amount provided by national and regional governments), INTERREG is by far the largest European regional-policy initiative. Nevertheless, it must be said that while INTERREG has been welcomed by all supporters of transboundary cooperation, the initiative has received ample criticism with regard to its actual implementation. (For a brief analysis of the INTERREG Program, see the annex at the end of this paper.)

3. Dutch-German Transboundary Cooperation: From Passive to Active Transboundary Planning

When studying the development of European border-region policy, one must keep in mind that throughout the period in discussion here, events were greatly influenced by the experiences of local authorities in transboundary cooperation. Local transboundary actors, either through AEBR, the Council of Europe, and, in some cases, proximity to national and European institutions, have had and continue to enjoy direct access to the highest echelons of decision-making power within the EU. In no other case is this as evident as in the development of Dutch-German transboundary cooperation.

The first municipal organizations (councils of government) to include transboundary cooperation on their agendas were founded in Germany and Holland in the 1950s. By 1980, four binational Euroregions (Ems-Dollart, EUREGIO, Rhine-Waal, Rhine-Maas-North), a trinational (Belgian-Dutch-German) Euregio Maas-Rhine, a Dutch-German intergovernmental agency, and a cross-boundary natural preserve were in full operation. Transboundary cooperation on the Dutch-German border has thus established a precedent for the vertical integration of planning so desired by the European Commissions. Similarly, the participation of local governments and their associations all along the common border in establishing regional development goals represent considerable progress in the horizontal coordination of transboundary planning.

Dutch and German senior governments officials make up the first tier of transboundary actors. Indeed, after the formal signing of the Dutch-German Border Treaty in 1960, contacts between the two countries in the area of regional planning have steadily increased. The most important institution of this binational cooperation is the Dutch-German Planning Commission (DGPC), established in 1967. The primary objective of the DPGC is to coordinate spatial and sectoral development plans, provide relevant information to formal planning agencies, and elaborate general development goals for the common border region (Malchus 1985). Directly involved in the DPGC are representatives of Dutch central planning offices, the German Federal Ministry of Planning, and those of the German states of North Rhine-Westphalia and Lower Saxony.

The Commission is not a political body with police powers; it merely has an advisory role, recommending specific policies for the common border areas to formal organs of planning authority. Regional planning is an exclusive task of German states and is shared by the Dutch central government and the provinces.

However, due to the mere fact that several formal planning institutions are involved in the DGPC, its *de facto* administrative role is considerable (Malchus 1985).

On the more formal level, a treaty—the only one of its kind to date—was concluded between Holland and Germany establishing a framework for European transboundary cooperation based on public-law institutions at local and regional levels. The Dutch-German Treaty on Transboundary Cooperation between Regional and Local Authorities was signed in May 1991, by the Dutch Home and Foreign Ministers, the German Foreign Minister, and the Prime Ministers of the German states of North Rhine-Westphalia and Lower Saxony. The treaty defines three possible areas in which transboundary cooperation can be covered by international law. These are: (1) cooperation between special districts or councils of government (COGs), (2) the conclusion of specific international agreements by local and regional governments, and (3) the creation of international working groups and committees. Because of their governmental character, special districts and COGs are the central institutions of transboundary cooperation designated by the treaty (EUREGIO 1992).

Transboundary Development Programs

The aim of integrating European regional development objectives and instruments as well as regionalizing the regional-planning process requires a methodical and reproducible means of obtaining input from the local and regional levels. Among other ways, this is being achieved by a system of incentives that literally obliges regions to elaborate regional-development strategies or programs. These strategies must include socio-economic and geographical analyses of existing regional situations (strengths and weaknesses) and development problems, the enumeration of future development goals, and, finally, concrete measures and projects that can be undertaken with which future goals can be achieved. Furthermore, these regional-development programs are now a prerequisite for obtaining funds from the ERDF—as the specific projects listed in the programs form the basis for concrete grant proposals.

It is no coincidence that the first of these development programs were produced for the Dutch-German border area. Already in 1981, the European Commission recommended that the German and Dutch governments continue their efforts at transboundary cooperation by supporting the formulation of transboundary development goals for the common border region (Malchus 1992: 6). Financial support for pilot projects was subsequently provided. After several initial pitfalls, the Transboundary Development Program of the Euregio Rhine-Maas was presented to the Commission in 1985. By 1991, programs for the other

Dutch-German associations as well as the Belgian-Dutch-German Euregio Maas-Rhine were also approved.

The INTERREG initiative has proven instrumental in the development and implementation of Dutch-German Transboundary Action Programs. Through it, a variety of projects involving tourism, transboundary databanks and electronic mailboxes, vocational training, biomedical technology, environmental protection (including the establishment of the transboundary wetlands preserve Maas-Schwalm-Nette), as well as numerous other measures were made possible. In total, the Dutch-German Euroregions received during the first INTERREG cycle 72.8 million ECUs[10] from EU and national sources. Furthermore, these moneys have been disbursed under the direct supervision of the Euroregions themselves.

The Dutch-German INTERREG Agreement of 1991 effectively transferred responsibility for the execution and supervision of INTERREG measures undertaken between the two countries to the German state of North Rhine-Westphalia and steering committees representing the three Dutch-German transboundary associations. Signatories were the state of North Rhine-Westphalia and the Royal Dutch Government as represented by the Minister of Foreign Trade and Regional Policy. Moreover, participation within the individual regional steering committees is shared by all levels of government (national, state/provincial, Euroregional), in an attempt to achieve an optimal coordination of the various development goals targeted by INTERREG projects. As stipulated by the Agreement, the German partner also has responsibility for managing Dutch-German INTERREG funds through a public investment institution. This has greatly simplified financial technicalities. However, it is the Euroregions who have the central task of overseeing the selection of transboundary projects for support; they receive, evaluate, and select proposals to be approved by the appropriate steering committees.

The EUREGIO and Its Transboundary Parliament

The EUREGIO, centered around the Dutch city of Enschede and the German town of Gronau, is the oldest of the Dutch-German border-region associations. Transboundary cooperation here dates back to the mid-1950s, when the regional council of government (COGs) on the German side (the Kommunalgemeinschaft Rhein-Ems) initiated bilateral consultations with representatives of Dutch communities. The EUREGIO was formerly established in 1965 as a voluntary association comprised of two Dutch COGs and the KG Rhein-Ems (Scott 1993).

Presently, the EUREGIO represents 109 jurisdictions (towns, cities, and counties) in Germany and Holland and a population of roughly 1.9 million. The most important transboundary policy innovation attributed to the organization is its local parliament, the EUREGIO Council, created in 1978 and comprising 29 Dutch and 31 German representatives chosen by the municipalities. The Council, a consultative and coordinating body without a direct political mandate, supervises various areas of Dutch-German cooperation and attempts to coordinate local-government actions in this respect (see Figure 2).

The Council is an international private-law organization and, as such, has no formal legislative or executive powers. Instead, the Council operates on the principle of volunteerism and on the good faith of its members to adhere to decisions taken by it. Additionally, the Council remains in close contact with municipal officials through the three local councils of government who elect council members. At senior government levels, the Council operates as a well-organized lobby, submitting recommendations for improvements in regional transportation, land-use planning, drug enforcement, public safety, disaster relief, and other areas of transboundary cooperation. Advisory members of the Council include representatives of the European Parliament, the Dutch and German governments, the German states of North Rhine-Westphalia and Lower Saxony, and the Dutch provinces of Gelderland and Overijssel.

Through the agencies of its Council, the EUREGIO has avoided many of the bureaucratic and legal problems that can often hinder comprehensive transboundary cooperation. Tied together by a private-law agreement and a desire to cooperate, the three public-law COGs represent their own sovereign jurisdictions and translate EUREGIO policy agreed by the Council into local action (Gabbe 1992a). Other elements of the EUREGIO Council are its working group, of which 20 senior civil servants from Dutch and German local governments are members, and a Steering Committee that includes representatives of European institutions and senior governments of both countries. The work of the Council is very much problem- and project-oriented. A variety of committees oversees cooperation and table recommendations relating to the environment, social problems, transportation, agriculture, tourism. and other development issues of local relevance.

Finally, the EUREGIO maintains administrative offices directly on the border, which, at the same time, lies between the communities of Gronau and Enschede. Operational and financial responsibilities are shared equally by the Dutch and German member communities who contribute close to 1.2 million DM (US$900,000) yearly to the EUREGIO's budget. Moreover, these contributions help not only to finance administrative operations but also cultural activities, EUREGIO-related services (information offices, schools, adult-education centers, libraries, etc.), and economic-development programs. Many of these programs are also funded through grants provided by the Dutch and German governments and matched by EU moneys.

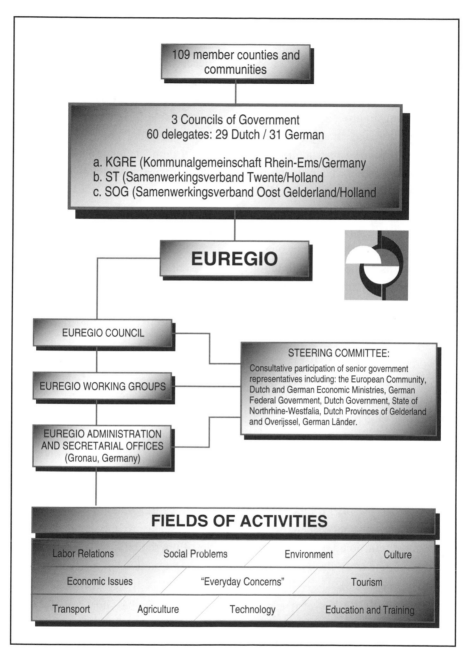

Figure 2. Organizational Structure of the EUREGIO

Results of EUREGIO Activities

Initially, the EUREGIO experienced greatest success in organizing cross-border cultural events and educational exchanges. This was and remains necessary, in order to promote mutual understanding and a sense of transboundary regional identity among the citizenry. As the prospects and means for transboundary planning improved, the EUREGIO was later able to involve itself more forcefully with the strategic issue of public transportation and with general aspects of industrial restructuring as a means to combat unemployment.[11] A certain degree of coordination among fire protection, health agencies, and other local public services was achieved as well.

It is, of course, evident that the EUREGIO is not solely responsible for progress in economic, social, and cultural matters—it cannot nor does it desire to supervise all local-level transboundary activities. Instead, the EUREGIO sees itself more as a forum for attracting public attention to and focusing public opinion on important regional issues (Gabbe 1992b: 198–99). In this way, the EUREGIO can act as a transboundary lobby, presenting coherent *regional* arguments in favor of solutions to border-related problems. Furthermore, this strategy has brought results.

Some examples of EUREGIO activities in economic and socio-cultural areas have been mentioned. In addition, the EUREGIO appears to have played a vital role in improving the accessibility of the regions as well as the mobility of their inhabitants. Vital road links, such as the European Highway 30 (Rotterdam-Hannover), as well as the Emsland Highway, which joins the region with urban areas north and south of it, have been either built or finished ahead of schedule because of constant local pressure on the responsible national authorities (Gabbe 1992:198). Similarly, planned suspensions of passenger and commercial rail service by the German *Bundesbahn* on several lines traversing the EUREGIO communities—not only an environmentally obtuse measure but also one which would have reinforced the peripheral character of the region—were halted after numerous round table discussions with the responsible national ministries (Gabbe 1985: 96; 1992: 198).

The EUREGIO has also succeeded in improving the situation of local cross-border commuters, of which there are approximately 2,000. These persons have to deal with two different sets of public bureaucracy and, because they work and pay taxes in another country, do not have access to tax benefits or cheap loans on their own. Thus, various problems related to unemployment benefits, health insurance, disability payments, as well as obtaining subsidized loans for home building or purchasing recur with alarming frequency.[12] While not able to resolve all the problems, the EUREGIO has, again in round table discussions with the respective national authorities, helped introduce simplified registration and payment procedures, hence reducing the insecurity of cross-border workers (Gabbe 1992:199–200).

Finally, joint grant sourcing and project funding has been an increasingly important area of transboundary cooperation and one that has been quite successful. This is, in no small measure, attributable to the support of Dutch and German senior governments and new grant programs of the EU. In the area of vocational training, the EUREGIO has secured financial support in excess of four million DM for programs in the textile, metalworking, and plastics trades as well as in important services such as nursing, catering, restauranteering, and the hotel trade. Thanks to INTERREG, an ambitious transboundary tourism development and marketing scheme has been recently initiated (EUREGIO 1991; Malchus 1992: 11–16; European Communities 1993).

4. On the Transferability of the EUREGIO Model

The assumption that a model European border-region policy indeed exists is not primarily based on explicit EU treaties or legislation. Instead, it has been prompted by the evolution of regional-development priorities within the EU and by changing national attitudes toward subnational diplomacy at the local and regional level. Summarizing the information presented earlier, three essential elements of this model are integration, subsidiarity, and synergy.

Integration is a concept in which transboundary cooperation activities at the local and regional levels are seen as bridging gaps between nations. Thus, local attempts at planning and regional-development cooperation set precedents for a more comprehensive international coordination of spatial-planning goals and act to stimulate greater economic interaction between nation-states. The socio-cultural aspect figures prominently as well; border regions are seen as areas of mutual understanding and profound cultural knowledge and, consequently, as microcosms of international diplomacy.

Subsidiarity is an element that refers to the institutional structure of transboundary cooperation, whereby a partnership between local and senior governments is deemed necessary to promote cooperation. The horizontal coordination achieved by Euroregions and other actors at the local level is to be matched by a vertical integration of regional and national policies. Each level of transboundary interaction is responsible for specific tasks within its own administrative sphere of action. At the same time, continual dialogue between the various administrative levels—including input from nongovernmental actors—makes for improved overall coordination of policy, allows for critical evaluations of transboundary cooperation, and enhances the democratic nature of the process.

Finally, the synergy element implies that criteria of mutual benefit and greater economic and administrative efficiency emphasize the importance and desirability of transboundary cooperation. The "synergy paradigm" adds political legitimacy to the efforts of transboundary actors as they attempt to solve local problems, provide public services, and realize new economic potential through cooperation and a more optimal use of available resources.

These requirements have been fulfilled by the EUREGIO and other European border region associations. For this reason, experiences in Dutch-German transboundary cooperation have been promoted by the European Commissions—as well as Dutch and German progenitors of the EUREGIO—as a general model for border regions in Europe.[13] If the experiences of the EUREGIO and Dutch-German cooperation are accepted as having a model-like character, then it is important to identify the reasons for its success.

Determinants of EUREGIO Development

Common problems of economic marginality have helped promote a transboundary regional identity. A traditional textile-manufacturing area, the region has experienced industrial decline for over two decades. Symptomatic of most European regions in crisis, job growth in the service sector has not compensated for the diminishing importance of industry and agriculture. Unemployment has, at times, reached 18 percent particularly affecting school dropouts and other younger members of the work force. A number of determinants of EUREGIO grew out of this economic context:

1. The binational political and cultural context is characterized by a *lack* of socio-economic, structural, and administrative asymmetry, as well as commonalities of economic, social, and environmental problems. Despite residual resentment among certain sectors of the Dutch population, there is a very low level of binational conflict. Furthermore, problems of international asymmetry between Holland and Germany have not been as acute as elsewhere. Dutch provinces and German states, responsible for supervising municipal affairs, enjoy a considerable degree of political and financial autonomy. The EUREGIO has been able to capitalize on these advantages.

2. The economic context is characterized by similar sectoral and cyclical problems on both sides of the border that have led to a relative marginalization of the region both nationally and binationally.

3. In the European context, the economic and political integration is a global objective, and redistributive mechanisms have been created to lessen the impact

of polarization. The existence of a European political superstructure and NATO has promoted international cooperation and hence decreased national sensitivities to sovereignty and internal security issues. Furthermore, supranational institutions allow border regions the chance to redress above the level of their respective national governments.

4. Similarly, national interests within the EU are much less defined by security issues and the control of territory than they are by economic (and, to an extent, cultural) issues. Peaceful economic competition allows considerable room for cooperation.

5. The EUREGIO was among the first of the international associations to promote transboundary cooperation as a goal of integration at the community level through networking and lobbying activities. With the active support of the Dutch and German governments, it has thus been able to establish vital institutional ties to European agencies. As a result, the EUREGIO has been able to influence European border-region policy at crucial moments and precisely at the time when role models of transboundary-cooperation practice are being sought to act as policy guides. In this way, the EUREGIO, which also houses the European Association of Border Regions, has been able to create a framework for *good practice* in transboundary cooperation based on its own experiences.

Transboundary Synergies in the Polish-German Border Region?

The precedent established by the EUREGIO has motivated several local governments on the external boundaries of the EU to create their own Euroregions and/or zones of transboundary cooperation. A case in point is the cooperative effort among the former East Germany, Poland, and the Czech Republic. Here, transboundary regionalism is developing under very difficult conditions, largely attributable to the process of transformation from state socialism to parliamentary democracy within a market economy. Since 1993, four Euroregions have been established on the Polish-German border (see Gruchman and Walk's essay in this volume). These Euroregions are structured along the lines of Dutch-German associations, based on voluntary cooperation among towns and municipal associations. Similarly, a Polish-German Planning Commission has been established that provides recommendations for the coordination of long-term regional planning goals in the common border area.

The promoters of transboundary economic cooperation—particularly in the German state of Brandenburg, where two of the four Polish-German Euroregions have their offices—speculate on the role increased East-West commerce and trade will play in the region's development. Since 1991, various proposals for Polish-German economic development projects have been suggested. With the support of Brandenburg, for example, a complex plan for establishing a binational industrial park in Eisenhüttenstadt was drawn up that would have operated similarly to *maquiladoras* on the U.S.-Mexican border, combining the advantages of new sophisticated infrastructure, proximity to Berlin, and attractive Polish wage levels. Included in the initial plans were proposals for joint Polish-German investments to modernize steel production in Eisenhüttenstadt and Kattowitz. These concepts, clearly motivated by the "synergy paradigm," were intended to improve transboundary cooperation by emphasizing mutually beneficial regional-development effects for Polish and Brandenburg regions.[14]

While not completely abandoned, these projects have made little headway. This has been partially due to political reasons and mistrust of German intentions, and also due to lack of funds for capital investments, disinterest at the national level, and insufficient coordination among agencies responsible for telecommunications, railways, customs, and other vital areas of national authority. Recently, Polish-German transboundary cooperation has picked up some momentum through the INTERREG II program that is now funding projects here, including the construction of a binational water treatment plant for the border cities of Guben/Gubin. Still, progress in the area of transboundary regional-development issues has been and will probably remain slow.

In attempting to establish the legitimacy required to bring Polish and German local governments together, as well as to become an effective regional-development forum, the Polish-German Euroregions must deal with a variety of hindrances to closer transboundary cooperation. Unfortunately, cooperation among the partner communities—cooperation upon which the Euroregion institution is based—has not developed as harmoniously as its promoters had hoped. Some of the more tenacious problems facing Polish-German cooperation can be generalized as follows:

1. The controversy of the border. The opening up of national borders between Western and Central Europe and at the same time introducing new restrictions through the Schengen Agreement has created problems in local commercial traffic and angered the Poles. Since 1990 and the elimination of visa restrictions for Poles to enter Germany and vice versa, the border has been associated with illegal immigration; the smuggling of drugs, weapons, radioactive materials, and cigarettes; car thefts; and the influx, often illegal, of cheap labor onto German job markets. The stigma of the border will take some time to disappear.

2. Psychological barriers. These barriers are rooted in Polish-German history and the trauma of World War II—particularly among older Poles. Thus, there is fear of German hegemony and a loss of national sovereignty. Political interests (*"Euroregions will bring about the fifth partition of Poland"*) orchestrate public hysteria by exploiting this insecurity.[15] This Polish-German contradiction main-

tains, in effect, a mental border that for many is exclusionary and serves to protect cultural identities.

3. International asymmetry. German states, counties, and municipalities do not have equal partners on the Polish side. Wojewodships, the Polish equivalent of French departments, are basically functional appendages of the central government and are neither independent nor strong. This weak intermediate level of government basically creates a power vacuum between Warsaw and local governments—a source of legal uncertainty regarding transboundary cooperation. Furthermore, the planning function is very weak in Poland, complicating cooperation attempts at the national level. This political asymmetry is compounded by an immense gap between the economies, standards of living, and the financial resources available to local governments in Germany and Poland.

Clearly, time is required for Poles and Germans to develop a sense of trust and to discover each other's culture. Possibly, progress toward the integration of Central European states into EU might expedite matters. Unfortunately, events are moving much more rapidly, and local communities are subject to much greater pressures today than three or four decades ago. Polish-German Euroregions do not have the opportunity of developing gradually and cautiously within a context of rapid economic growth and increasing prosperity as did their Dutch-German counterparts.

Euroregions: Their Limitations as a Model

One of the principal underlying premises of research on transboundary cooperation is that individual citizens and governments have an innate propensity to interact with their counterparts across national boundaries in order to deal with issues of mutual interest. Furthermore, this propensity to interact increases with the degree of functional and/or cultural interdependence within international border regions. Barring situations where ethnic and religious conflicts influence popular sentiment, this desire to interact, then, can only be impinged upon by the jealous actions of national governments who see their primary responsibility in the maintenance of cultural cohesion and territorial sovereignty. In other words, the will to cooperate across boundaries is often seen in terms of a logical and rational form of behavior often confronted by the territorial policies of the nation-state or, even worse, by political expressions of emotion and ideology.[16] However, while utilitarian and apparently rational arguments are frequently used to lend support to the idea of transboundary cooperation, one cannot simply ignore history, language, culturally defined perceptions of borders and border regions, and other elements that create specific (and partially unique) contexts for transboundary cooperation.

Information on specific border situations must be circulated in order to promote a more global understanding of border regions as zones of contact between nations and peoples. Economic history indicates, for example, that social networks have been essential in the development of the market economy. Thus, the importance of historical and cultural factors (e.g., the existence of agricultural-cooperative traditions) should, in Hansen's opinion, be emphasized. "Economic networking in (innovative regional milieux) ... cannot be forced by outside parties. It can be encouraged, but essentially it has taken place spontaneously on the basis of existing social networks ... that generate and reinforce milieux where there are high levels of mutual trust and reciprocity" (1992: 101–02). Hansen adds that "trust and reciprocity have not implied a zero-sum game; rather, they have involved increasing returns to the relevant regions. This is probably the heart of the matter: cooperation engenders increasing returns" (1992: 104).

This paradigm of increasing returns and the mutual benefits of cooperation helps explain the apparent paradox of cooperation and competition existing side by side in close regional proximity. Hansen's remarks, however, imply that utilitarian arguments of *surplus value* effects of interregional cooperation cannot overlook basic preconditions for successful cooperation—preconditions that are not always explainable in terms of *rational* economic decision making or *technical* problem solving. Cappellin also puts particular stress on the existence of common values and interests as well as on cultural similarities, "given that any form of cooperation can only develop when built on a foundation of mutual knowledge and trust" (1993: 20). Consequently, cultural affinities, mutual trust, and psychological aspects of cooperation acquire particular importance in transboundary contexts. In order to analyze the potentials of transboundary and interregional synergy, there must be a definition of factors that affect the quality of transboundary cooperation.

Finally, criticism of this interdependence/synergy argument has been voiced for other reasons than those previously mentioned. Friedmann and Morales (1984) see in this argument—at least in the case of the United States and Mexico—a possible political and economic strategy for a large, powerful nation to secure its interests in a weaker and smaller neighboring state. This implies a very one-sided form of cooperation, where one wealthy partner is the "provider" and determines most of the conditions for cooperation while the other, poorer partner is forced to accept a subordinate role in exchange for financial and technical assistance. For this reason, Friedmann and Morales have warned that the intractable asymmetries between Mexico and the United States preclude the development of transboundary planning and regional-development initiatives on the scale of European border-region associations. These observations may appear unduly pessimistic and yet, experiences on the German-Polish border have at least partially confirmed them.

Summarizing the information presented above, it can be said that the Euroregion model of transboundary cooperation contains several limitations that must be taken into consideration when attempting to apply West European experiences to other transboundary contexts. Among the weaknesses of the model are:

1. While gradualist, this model presupposes the existence of harmonious bilateral relations, of mutual trust and understanding, and a convergence of local and regional interests in transboundary contexts.

2. Only international treaties concluded by nation-states can pave the way for institutionalized transboundary cooperation. Legal assurances can only be based on national legislation and it has become clear that model transboundary legislation is useless unless backed by an agreement between two or more states. To date, only the Dutch-German Treaty on Transboundary Cooperation between Regional and Local Authorities has established a framework for European transboundary cooperation based on public-law institutions.

3. Regional issues: the fact that border-region associations, particularly those operating under difficult circumstances, need a broader geographical and political base of support than local governments or an association of local governments similar to those that constitute the backbone of the EUREGIO.

5. Concluding Remarks

International research on borders and border regions indicates that the elimination of barriers to cooperation ultimately requires the elimination or reduction of international asymmetries. However, as experiences in North America and Europe have demonstrated, this is a task that dwarfs the problem-solving capacities of local transboundary cooperation. At the same time, the present author (Scott 1993) and other border-region observers such as Hayes (1991) have concluded that formal international treaties allowing local-government participation are a precondition for the development of comprehensive transboundary problem solving. Political solutions, often favored by central governments for their expediency and enhancement of national sovereignty, are generally unsuitable for establishing a long-term, transboundary, regional-planning dialogue.

The institutionalization of transboundary cooperation at the local and regional level, far from being an idealistic goal, is essential in addressing ecological, economic, and social problems that affect everyday life in border regions, regardless of the overlying political circumstances affecting cooperation. Ultimately, transboundary cooperation can only develop if nation-states mutually agree to suspend sovereignty over certain aspects of domestic policy.

It is not suggested here that European experiences in transboundary cooperation can be indiscriminately applied to situations in other parts of the world. Supporters of the EUREGIO concept themselves advise other border regions against slavish imitation. Gabbe (1992a: 184) has warned that a slow, piecemeal approach is always preferable to more radical, but politically controversial attempts to institutionalize transboundary cooperation.

Future developments in Europe as well as in other parts of the world will tell whether or not pragmatic approaches can form the basis of a general strategy of transboundary cooperation. From the perspective of international and comparative research, it will be fascinating to see to what extent transboundary cooperation can develop along the lines of integration, subsidiarity, and synergy. Continuing globalization, intensifying competitive pressures on cities, regions, and nations, as well as increasing subnational diplomacy, would appear to confirm new political and economic roles for border regions. However, the volatile political situation in many areas of the world—characterized more by conflict than cooperation—and the recent upheavals in the world's emerging markets warn against over-optimism. In the end, the solution of global problems will require a cooperative spirit that transcends the integrationist logic of the European Union.

Notes

1. At the time of this writing, internal border checks in Spain, Portugal, France, Germany, and the BeNeLux states have been eliminated. Italy and Greece will also join once technically equipped to perform the necessary external-border controls. Austria, Finland, and Sweden will most likely join as well. Great Britain and Denmark still refuse to comply with the Schengen accords and maintain border controls for EU traffic.

2. These countries, together with Italy, were known as the "Six." They created the European Steel and Coal Community in 1951 and the EEC and Euratom in 1958.

3. See, for example, Susan J. Koch's remarks on this issue (1984: 33–34). Still, this does not seem to have inhibited cooperation, and the Regio Basiliensis, together with its German and French partners, has achieved a respectable degree of success in project-oriented activities such as cultural exchanges, land-use planning around the regional airport in Mulhouse (France), cooperation among universities in the area of research and higher education, as well as monitoring air quality in the Upper Rhine region.

4. Indeed, the Regio's apparent insistence on promoting this difficult but vital project has been criticized as the wrong kind of strategy for a public-private planning advocacy approach to transboundary cooperation. Hopes that a regional heavy-rail system could be achieved by coordinating existing services were raised when the heads of states of Germany (Helmut Kohl), France (Francois Mitterand), and Switzerland (Jean-Pascal Delamuraz) converged on Basel

on December 15, 1989, to sign a declaration in support of transboundary cooperation. The fact that these three statesmen could be brought together for this occasion is a sign that the activities of the Regio Basiliensis and its partners have not gone unnoticed. On the other hand, there is still no indication that a regional transit system is anywhere near realization.

5. See Briner (1986: 47–53) for a short discussion of the bipartite (French-German) and tripartite (French-German-Swiss) commissions.

6. This was due primarily to the perseverance of political forces who believed that only a limited integration was possible within Europe and then only within the framework of *international coordination*. Thus, the idea of shared sovereignty within European institutions would have to wait for the development and maturation of the European Community in the 1960s and 1970s. Since then, the Council has established its *raison d'etre* primarily as an international—paraparliamentary—forum within which various political, economic, social, environmental, and other issues can be discussed. Members of the Council include several non-EU states as well, such as Cyprus, Iceland, Liechtenstein, Malta, Norway, and Turkey.

7. This document does not represent a circumvention of national sovereignty. Contracting partners in the sense of the European Outline Convention are national governments. Only when model interstate agreements have been agreed by the respective nations, i.e., when bilateral or multilateral treaties on transboundary cooperation have been formally signed, can the local level take advantage of the legal opportunities offered by the Outline Convention.

8. See, for example, Robert (1982?) and Council of Europe (1982).

9. See Renzsch (1991) for a provocative discussion of subsidiarity and how it is being applied within the context of European integration.

10. Approximately US$110 million.

11. For example, the EUREGIO succeeded in obtaining "crisis area" status for a large portion of its jurisdiction, thereby securing from the EC and Dutch and German governments badly needed economic development funds for the textile industry (Gabbe 1992).

12. See, for example, Charles Ricq (1986), for a concise description of the various difficulties facing cross-border commuters. It remains to be seen whether European integration will ultimately eliminate disadvantages for people who work and live in different countries.

13. This fact is borne out by the AEBR's and the EUREGIO's central roles in managing the LACE initiative, which, by definition, is an informational and educational exercise aimed at assisting border regions in improving transboundary cooperation. The AEBR, the LACE Secretariat, and the EUREGIO's administrative offices presently have the same address: Gronau (Germany)/Enschede (Holland).

14. These synergy concepts are clearly documented in materials circulated by the Brandenburg Ministry of the Economy. See, for example, Brandenburgisches Ministerium für Wirtschaft, Mittelstand, und Technologie (1993).

15. An interesting side note: between 1991 and 1993, a pilot study financed by local sources and the state of Brandenburg was carried out, the aim of which was to evaluate the feasibility of a commercial and housing estate on a former Soviet base on an island in the Oder River, directly on the Polish-German border. The idea was to create an environmentally sensitive *maquila*-like environment that would dynamize the region economically and attract new residents. The project, in fact, received official backing by German and Polish authorities and a Japanese investor eventually showed interest in setting up a production site there. However, considerable delays in getting necessary approvals to begin construction and a fatal error in translation of documents, leading Polish authorities to believe that German Customs

were to "annex" Polish territory in order to affect border controls there, took up so much time that the investor abandoned his plans and the sponsors withdrew their financial support.

16. Experts of the U.S.-Mexican borderlands (Stoddard, Herzog, Clement, Ganster), for example, have for years championed an alternative border-region policy that recognizes the interdependencies of the borderlands urban system and economy and thus allows local transboundary actors to overcome traditional institutional barriers to cooperation.

References

Anderson, Malcolm. 1982. "The Political Problems of Frontier Regions." *West European Politics* 5 (4).

Association of European Border Regions. 1991. Informationsbroschüre: EG-Pilotprojekt "LACE."

Association of European Border Regions. 1993. "Expertenseminare zu INTERREG II." Lace-Info, no. 2.

Brandenburgisches Ministerium für Wirtschaft, Mittelstand, und Technologie, ed. 1993. *Industriepark Oderbrücke: Mosaikstein eines deutsch-polnischen Gemeinschaftsprojektes* (Elements of a German-Polish Joint Project). Potsdam: MWMT.

Briner, Hans J. 1996. "Regional Planning and Transfrontier Cooperation: The Regio Basiliensis." In *Across Boundaries: Transborder Interaction in Comparative Perspective*, Oscar J. Martínez, ed. El Paso: Texas Western Press.

Cappellin, Riccardo. 1993. "Interregional Cooperation and Internationalization of Regional Economies in Alps-Adria." In *Development Strategies in the Alps-Adriatic Region*, Gyula Horváth, ed. Pécs, Hungary.

Commission of the European Communities. 1993. "Cross-Border Cooperation." Information package on the INTERREG Program distributed by the EU. EU: Brussels.

Commission of the European Communities. 1993. "Europa 2000: Spatial Perspectives of European Integration." Discussion paper prepared by Commissar Millan for the informal working session of ministers responsible for regional policy and planning in Liege, Belgium. (12–13 November).

Council of Europe. 1982. "Mobilizing the Endogenous Potential of Disadvantaged Regions." Report by the Council of Europe, Study Series 40.

Council of Europe. 1983. "European Outline Convention on Transfrontier Cooperation between Territorial Communities or Authorities." European Treaty Series No.106, Madrid, 21 May 1980. Strasbourg: Council of Europe.

Duchacek, Ivo. 1990. "Perforated Sovereignties: Towards a Typology of New Actors in International Relations." In *Federalism and International Relations. The Role of Subnational Units*, Hans J. Michelmann and Panayotis Soldatos (Hg.), eds. Oxford.

EUREGIO. 1992. Geschäftsbericht 1991. Gronau, Germany: Euregio.

Friedmann, John, and Rebecca Morales. 1984. "Transborder Planning: A Case of Sophisticated Provocation?" Working paper WCP 8. Los Angeles: University of California at Los Angeles, Graduate School of Architecture and Urban Planning.

Fry, Earl H. 1993. "States and Local Governments in the International Arena." *Annals of the American Association of Political and Social Science* 509 (5).

Gabbe, Jens. 1985. "EUREGIO—regionale grenzüberschreitende Zusammenarbeit auf kommunaler Ebene" (EUREGIO—Regional Transboundary Cooperation at the Local Level). In *Staatsgrenzen überschreitende Zusammenarbeit des Landes,* Institut für Landes-und Stadtentwicklungs-Forschung des Landes Nordrhein-Westfalen, ed. NRW Dortmund: ILS.

Gabbe, Jens. 1992a. "Institutionelle Aspekte der grenzüberschreitenden Zusammenarbeit (Institutional Aspects of Transboundary Cooperation)." In *Grenzübergreifende Raumplanung: Erfahrungen und Perspektiven der Zusammenarbeit mit den Nachbarstaaten Deutschlands,* Akademie für Raumforschung und Landesplanung, ed. Hannover: ARL.

Gabbe, Jens. 1992b. "EUREGIO—Regionale grenzüberschreitende Zusammenarbeit an der Basis (EUREGIO—Regional Transboundary Cooperation at the Grassroots)," in Akademie für Raumforschung und Landesplanung (ed.), *Grenzübergreifende Raumplanung: Erfahrungen und Perspektiven der Zusammenarbeit mit den Nachbarstaaten Deutschlands* Hannover: ARL.

Hansen, Niles. 1992. "Competition, Trust and Reciprocity in the Development of Innovative Regional Milieux." *Papers in Regional Science: The Journal of the RSAI* 71.

Hayes, Douglas L. 1993. "The All-American Canal Lining Project: A Catalyst for Rational and Comprehensive Groundwater Management on the United States-Mexico Border?" *Transboundary Resources Report* 1 (Spring).

Herzog, Lawrence A. 1991. "International Boundary Cities: The Debate on Transfrontier Planning in Two Border Regions." *Natural Resources Journal* 31 (3).

Koch, Susan J. 1974. "Towards a Europe of Regions: Transnational Political Activities in Alsace." *Publius: The Journal of Federalism* 4 (Summer).

Malchus, Viktor. 1985. "Zusammenarbeit auf dem Gebiet der Raumordnung—Bilanz und Perspektiven der Raumsordnungskommissionen (Cooperation in Spatial Planning—Results and Perspectives of the Work of the Intergovernmental Commission)." In *Staatsgrenzen überschreitenden Zusammenarbeit des Landes NRW,* Institut für Landes-und Stadtentwicklung des Landes Nordrhein-Westfalen, ed. Dortmund: ILS.

Malchus, Viktor, Freiherr von. 1992. "Strategische Zielsetzungen der grenzüberschreitenden Zusammenarbeit unter Auswertung der belgischen, deutschen und niederländischen INTERREG-Programme (Strategic Goals of Transboundary Cooperation as Defined by Belgian, Dutch and German INTERREG Projects)." Paper presented at the LACE-Seminar in Maastricht, Holland (13 February).

Martínez, Oscar J., ed. 1986. *Across Boundaries: Transborder Interaction in Comparative Perspective.* El Paso: Texas Western Press.

McDonnel, Valerie, and Marie Garnier-Raymond. 1990. *Business Cooperation and Development in Border Regions.* Sachbericht für die EG-Kommission. London: LRDP (Local and Regional Development Planning, South Bank Technopark, 90 London Road, London SE1 6LN, UK).

Renzsch, Wolfgang. 1991. "Europa der Regionen: Institutionelle Grenzen, aber politische Spielräume." Reihe Eurokolleg der Friedrich-Ebert-Stiftung 11.

Ricq, Charles. 1986. "Les travailleurs frontaliers en Europe" (Transboundary Workers in Europe). Institut für Landes- und Stadtentwicklung des Landes Nordrhein-Westfalen, ed. Third European Conference of Frontier Regions. Dortmund: ILS.

Robert, Jacques. 1982(?). Wirtschaftliche Entwicklungsstrategie für die europäischen Grenzregionen: Anpassung ihrer Wirtschaftsstruktur an die Zwänge und Möglichkeiten der 80er Jahre (Economic Development Strategies for European Border Regions: Accommodating their Economic Structures to the Exigencies and Possibilities of the 1980s). Brochure published by the Association of European Border Regions. Bonn.

Scott, James. 1989. "Transborder Cooperation, Regional Initiatives, and Sovereignty Conflicts in the Upper Rhine Valley." *Publius: The Journal of Federalism* 19 (Winter).

Scott, James. 1993. "The Institutionalization of Transboundary Cooperation in Europe: Recent Developments on the Dutch-German Border." *Journal of Borderlands Studies* 8 (1).

Scott, James. 1994. "Aspekte der wirtschaftlichen Entwicklung im deutsch-polnischen Grenzraum" (Aspects of Economic Development in the German-Polish Border Region). Schriftenreihe des Instituts für Ökologische Raumentwicklung (IÖR) 9.

Seele, Günter. 1992. "Europa der Regionen—ein Holzweg?" *der Landkreis*62 (8–9).

Soldatos, Panayotis. 1993. "Cascading Subnational Paradiplomacy in an Interdependent and Transnational World." In *States and Provinces in the International Economy*, Douglas M. Brown and Earl H. Fry, eds. Berkeley: Institute of Governmental Studies, University of California.

Strassoldo, Raimundo. 1982. "Frontier Regions: Future Collaboration or Conflict?" *West European Politics* 5 (4).

Van der Veen, A. 1993. "Theory and Practice of Cross-Border Cooperation of Local Governments: The Case of the EUREGIO between Germany and the Netherlands." In *Regional Networks, Border Regions and European Integration*, R. Cappellin and P. W. J. Batey, eds. London: Pion.

Appendix: Notes on the INTERREG Program

Although widely hailed as a success, there are indications that INTERREG has failed to achieve many of its original political objectives—in particular the aim of decentralization. Indeed, after a study of the preliminary results of the program, one provocative question persistently arises: Has INTERREG helped border regions develop closer ties and promote regional problem solving, or has it been co-opted by national governments as a source of additional infrastructural-development funds? In attempting to address these border-region issues, it is hoped that new light will be shed on the actual progress transboundary cooperation is making in Europe.

Some of the most salient research questions that can be asked are the following:

1. To what extent have local and regional associations of transboundary cooperation been involved in project management?

2. Were there any obvious geographical patterns regarding the distribution of INTERREG funds?

3. How were INTERREG grants employed?

Summary Evaluation of INTERREG

With regard to the first question, it is indeed interesting to analyze the levels of government involved in the INTERREG Program, as this demonstrates rather variegated geographical patterns. Generally speaking, four participation patterns emerged, including *(a)* projects supervised by Euroregions and other local-level associations in cooperation with senior governments, *(b)* project management by regional authorities, *(c)* projects carried out solely by central governments, and *(d)* the participation of different levels of government in different countries. In total, 31 border regions received financial aid between 1990 and 1994. The breakdown of total distributed funds according to project priorities was as follows:

Communications	45.5%
Enterprise Development	16.9%
Tourism	10.4%
Environment	10.0%
Rural-Area Development	6.2%
Social	5.8%
Transboundary Institutions	4.0%
Management	1.2%

The other main points can be summarized as follows:

1. INTERREG proved a very popular program; demand exceeded available funds by 35 percent.

2. The lion's share of INTERREG funds went to improving *hard* locational factors in the European periphery and particularly to bolstering communications infrastructure in Greece's border areas and to improving communications between Spain and Portugal. In Spain, Greece, and Portugal, the issue of developing institutions of transboundary cooperation was only marginally addressed. INTERREG projects here received almost 53 percent of total funds and 63 percent of the EU contribution.

3. In only a few cases, such as the Dutch-German and Danish-German border regions, was INTERREG administered by local authorities working together with senior governments. In most cases, the programs were managed by regional authorities and/or national governments.

4. Generally, one year was required by Brussels to process proposals for INTERREG. This caused uncertainty as to the prospects of receiving aid and as to the choice of priorities agreed upon by the border regions seeking assistance.

5. Joint administration of funds by national agencies proved difficult, and unclear guidelines concerning the cofinancing of projects delayed work. Basically (and insofar as they were involved), border regions with little experience in transboundary cooperation and largely dependent on senior governments for guidance had considerable difficulty in managing projects under INTERREG guidelines.

Although welcoming INTERREG, many, including Cappellin (1993: 43–44), have criticized "traditional" aspects of the initiative that have diverted funds away from the promotion of a more solid, transboundary regionalism. Among others, the following shortcomings of the initiative have been emphasized:

1. The project appears to have been heavily oriented either to strictly bilateral forms of cooperation or to multilateral projects within a small geographic area. Cooperation among three or more regions in different countries appears to have been intentionally excluded from the program, an issue that has been raised by supporters of the Alps-Adriatic Working Group.

2. The requirement that national governments review transboundary projects submitted by regions contradicts the general objectives of decentralizing regional policy and facilitating local-level transboundary cooperation. Local and regional authorities are forced to work through central authorities, which, inevitably, can negatively influence the character of local-level cooperation.

3. Furthermore, while certainly of crucial importance, economic growth and capital investments in peripheral areas of the EU have been overemphasized, thus diminishing the innovative quality of INTERREG. Too little attention has been paid to institutional, legal and social barriers to transboundary cooperation.

Figure 3. Regional Patterns in INTERREG I Participation
(1990–1994)

Area	Agency	Priorities	Cofinancing in MECU	as % of INTERREG Total
Spain-Portugal	National Planning Offices (Madrid, Lisbon)	Communications 76.4% Environment 7.7% Transboundary Structures and Studies 6.7%	EU: 411 S/P: 182	593 MECU 33.5%
Greece	Ministry of the National Economy (Athens)	Communications 67.4% Enterprise 16.9% Rural 9.2% Social 6.1%	EU: 242.2 GR: 97.2	339.5 MECU 19.2%
Spain-France (Pyrenees)	National Planning Offices (Madrid, Paris)	Social 50% Communications 30% Tourism 20%	EU: 31.2 S/F: 31.2	62.4 MECU 3.5%
France - Italy (Alpine and Mediterranean)	French National Planning Office/Italian Office of European Affairs (Paris, Rome)	Enterprise 42% Social 27.3% Rural 16.7% Communications 6.3% Environment 5.2%	EU: 22.3 F/I: 39.5	61.8 MECU 3.5%
Germany-France-Switz. (S. Alsatia, S. Baden, Cantons of Basel	French National Planning Office; European Office of the State of Baden; City of Basel (Paris, Stuttgart, Basel)	Enterprise 44.4% Environment 28% Transboundary Structures and Studies 14.3% Communications 13.3%	EU: 9.4 G/F/S: 9.5	18.9 MECU 1.06%
Germany-Holland (EUREGIO)	Euregio Office in Gronau/Enschede in cooperation with the state government of Northrhine-Westfalia (Düsseldorf) and Dutch government (The Hague)	Communications 44.5% Enterprise 17.3% Tourism 13.3% Environment 12.5% Social 10.2%	EU: 11 G/H: 15	26 MECU 1.5%

Source: Directorate General 16 of the European Commissions (1993)

Recommendations for the Improvement of Future European Transboundary Initiatives

1. Establish programs that specifically support—both financially and politically—local and regional structures of transboundary cooperation.

2. Require central, regional, and local-government partnerships in drawing up and supervising transboundary development projects that are submitted for funding by the EU.

3. Aim for greater clarity of and better access to information regarding the conditions that apply to grants, as well as to the amount of money actually available for specific areas of transboundary activity.

4. Lessen emphasis on "hard" economic factors by requiring a more balanced mix of priorities and increased attention to areas of social action (hospitals, day care centers, care for the elderly, youth centers, vocational training, language and general adult education, etc.).

5. Promote interregional cooperation by allowing associations based on multilateral forms of transboundary cooperation to participate in INTERREG and similar programs.

References

Cappellin, Riccardo. 1993. "Interregional Cooperation and Internationalization of Regional Economies in Alps-Adria." In *Development Strategies in the Alps-Adriatic Region*, Gyula Horváth, ed. Pécs, Hungary.

Commission of the European Communities. 1993. "Cross-Border Cooperation" Information package on the INTERREG Program distributed by the EU. EU: Brussels.

Malchus, Viktor, Freiherr von. 1992. "Strategische Zielsetzungen der grenzüberschreitenden Zusammenarbeit unter Auswertung der belgischen, deutschen und niederländischen INTERREG-Programme" (Strategic Goals of Transboundary Cooperation as Defined by Belgian, Dutch and German INTERREG Projects). Paper presented at the LACE-Seminar in Maastricht, Holland. (13 February).

da Silva Santos, Paulo. 1992. *Einschätzung der INTERREG-Initiative in den Grenzregionen an den Außengrenzen der Europäischen Gemeinschaft* (Evaluation of the INTERREG Initiative in the External Boundaries of the EG). Internal LACE document prepared by Local and Regional Development Planning. London.

The Evolving Political Role of Borders and Border Regions in Central Europe[1]

Kristian Gerner

1. State Building in Central Europe: A Recurring Problem

The dissolution of the Warsaw Pact and COMECON that took place between 1989 and 1991 initiated a process of state reconstruction and state building in Central Europe. The lodestars were democratization and nationalism, and the goal was to reestablish sovereignty. This stood in glaring contrast to the simultaneous process of European integration signaled by the signing of the Maastricht Treaty. Put in provocative terms, while in the eastern half of Europe the last vestiges of Byzantium disappeared, in the western half a reconstruction of the West Roman Empire—in the guise of the European Union—was under way. Nevertheless, in both parts of Europe the nation-state was the principal actor.

In Central and Eastern Europe, issues of state boundaries and national minorities have again come to the fore much as they did after the end of the two world wars. The process of state building in the post-Warsaw Pact states has striking similarities with the processes 70 and 45 years earlier, including a basic conceptual confusion. This has to do with the different political implications of concepts that denote territory and ethnicity.

In the course of the nineteenth century *ius soli*, the principle of domicile and historic administrative boundaries as a basis for establishing citizenship and defining the state, and *ius sanguinis*, the principle of ethnic origin as a basis for nation-building and the granting of citizenship, became the two main ideologies guiding the creation of nation-states. The crux of the matter lay in the apparently oppositional nature of the two principles: should democracy and territoriality or ethnicity and origin define citizenship and the state?[2] When the Ottoman,

141

Habsburg, Romanov, and Hohenzollern empires were defeated, the leaders of Western and South Slavs, Balts, and Romanians demanded the establishment of sovereign states on the ruins of the multinational empires. They did so in the name of the principle of national self-determination.

At the Paris Peace Conference in 1919–1920, the interpretation of the concept of national self-determination was influenced by an American perspective. *Democracy* and *national self-determination* were understood to be two sides of one coin, i.e., sovereignty for a historically given territory.[3] The establishment of the United States served as an implicit model; here, there was no conflict between the principles of *ius soli* and *ius sanguinis*, between citizenship and ethnicity, as the basis for state legitimacy. *National* referred to a certain, delimited territory and to the population within it, regardless of ethnic origin.

However, the political leaders in the successor states in Central and Eastern Europe interpreted the principle of national self-determination according to the rule of *ius sanguinis*. The ethnic majority became the *owner* of the state. Those of different ethnic origin became *minorities*. Czechoslovakia was also defined as a national state for the Czechoslovak nation. Serb leaders regarded the United Kingdom of Serbs, Croats, and Slovenes as a Serbian state.

After the First World War, the states in Europe were regarded as ethnic, with the exception of Belgium and Switzerland. Old territorial states such as France and Sweden had become linguistically and culturally homogenized during the nineteenth century as a result of democratization, education, and the infusion of ethnic nationalism. However, when the new state boundaries were drawn in Central and Eastern Europe after the First World War, the principle of national self-determination was not applied with regard to the core nations of the Habsburg and Hohenzollern empires, the Germans and the Hungarians.[4] They were not only defeated but also deemed to be responsible for the outbreak of the war. Where ethnic groups lived together, or when historical boundaries were regarded as sacrosanct, as was the case with Bohemia, the rule was that Germans and Hungarians should become citizens in *alien* states rather than the other way around. As a consequence, the states next to Germany, Austria, and Hungary received huge German and Hungarian minorities.

After coming to power in Germany in 1933, Hitler could use the argument of defending the ethnic Germans in Czechoslovakia and Poland as a pretext for his expansionist policies. The Western powers now accepted the validity of the ethnic argument also with regard to the Germans. This was demonstrated in the Munich agreement in 1938 on the partition of Czechoslovakia. Poland and Hungary followed the German example and reclaimed parts of Czechoslovakia in the name of historical and ethnic rights.

The case of Poland was rather special because in 1938 this state was both an aggressor and a victim. The second republic was the historical heir to the multinational Jagiellonian empire, but its leaders used ethnic and pre-Jagiellonian arguments in the conflict with Czechoslovakia over the Teschen Silesia area. Already in 1918–1920, the Polish government laid claims to the whole region, arguing that it had belonged to the Piast dynasty and that the majority was ethnic Polish and Slonzak (the latter being considered to be Poles who had lost sense of their origin). The region was divided in 1920, with Czechoslovakia getting the lion's share. In 1938, Poland conquered most of this lot, the so-called Zaolzie.

The old Hungarian kingdom was defined as comprising the dominions of the crown of St. Stephen. This included contemporary Slovakia, Croatia, Transylvania with the Banat, Slavonia, and Vojvodina. After 1867, the ethnic minorities in Transylvania and Slovakia—i.e., the majority in these regions—were subject to continued policies of magyarization, whereas Croatia was able to assert itself within the framework of a special agreement, the *Nagodba*, between Zagreb and Budapest in 1868, defining Croatia as "a political nation possessing a special territory of its own" (Nyström 1984: 159).

After the loss of two-thirds of its prewar territory in the Treaty of Trianon in 1920, Hungary became an irredentist state, and its foreign policy was aimed at resurrecting the former nation. This goal was partly realized when Hungary, under German tutelage, reconquered parts of Slovakia and Transylvania as well as Transcarpathia and Vojvodina in 1938-1941. This time *ius sanguinis* was adopted as the basic political principle. Hungary adopted racist, anti-Semitic laws in 1938 and in 1940 carried out a population exchange with Romania, aimed at ethnic purification of the reconquered parts of Transylvania.

The outbreak of the Second World War may be seen as the result of the failure to build a viable system of nation-states in Central and Eastern Europe. One reason behind the failure was the inherent contradiction between the principles of *ius soli* and *ius sanguinis*. Ethnicity and historical mythology took the upper hand over democracy and territoriality as legitimizing principles behind state-building and foreign policy.

After the Second World War, state boundaries were redrawn once again in Central and Eastern Europe. Ethnicity was regarded as a self-evident, legitimizing principle, but military reasons were also taken into consideration. The USSR could take both northeast Prussia, eastern Poland, and Transcarpathia (from Czechoslovakia), thus improving its defenses in the west. Poland was moved westward, with large Polish populations moved from the prewar eastern parts to the postwar western parts, which in turn were *cleansed* of Germans. Similarly, the Ukrainians in southeast Poland were *pacified* and dispersed throughout Poland.

In 1945–1947, the greatest ethnic-minority problem was dealt with by the expulsion of sizeable German populations in Czechoslovakia, Poland, Hungary, Romania, Yugoslavia, and the Baltic states. Those individuals who remained, primarily in Poland, became "invisible." A similar solution was initiated with regard to the Hungarians in Czechoslovakia but never completed. The Hungarians remained the main minority group among the nation-states in Central Europe. After the Cold War, a third attempt at state building was initiated in Central Europe. This time, the inherited state boundaries were taken for granted. The creation of the new states of Czechia and Slovakia transformed an internal border into an international one. The ethnic principle was taken for granted as the basis for citizenship. Examples are to be found in the new constitutions of Croatia (1990), Romania (1991), and Slovakia (1992). These states are defined as the state of the Croats, the Romanians, and the Slovaks, respectively.

In contrast, the new and democratically elected Hungarian government tried after 1989 to reconcile the principles of *ius sanguinis* and *ius soli* by demanding collective minority rights and autonomy for the Hungarians in the neighboring states, but without raising the question of boundary changes. With the exception of the ambitions of the Hungarian politicians both among the Hungarian minorities and in Hungary, the political actors in Central Europe have behaved in a way that has tended to reify existing state borders and enhance their significance as dividing lines. As a consequence, border regions have remained peripheries. They have not been seen and exploited as potential links between political and economic centers, not to mention as potential states in their own right.

However, developments in Western Europe seem to portend a diminished role for nation-states. The European Union is an example of suprastate integration. The emergence of Euroregions, such as Regio Basiliensis, Euregio Maas-Rhein, Saar-Lor-Lux, and Région Transmanche, means the return of historically defined, ethnically mixed regions as subnational actors. Both these tendencies should be of interest when discussing the future of Central and Eastern Europe.

2. Regions in Europe

A region can be defined by objective geographic criteria. However, a more politically relevant definition might be based on subjective social criteria. Historically, regions have been cognitive constructs—based on interpretations regarding the coherence and continuity of a given area. They thus may have established historical ("Christian") names. In addition to states, which in certain cases can be regarded as regions, Europe also consists of historical/cognitive regions at three different spatial levels. In terms of ideology and world view, Europe has been seen as divided into two *macroregions*, defined by Eastern and

Western Christianity. The border between the two runs through contemporary east Central Europe, from the Adriatic Sea and Bosnia across Transylvania and Galicia to the Baltic Sea and the Kaliningrad and St. Petersburg areas.

In terms of political and economic networks of long duration, Europe can, furthermore, be divided into four *mesoregions*, the North Sea, the Baltic Sea, the Mediterranean, and the Black Sea regions. The third level consists of *microregions*, i.e., areas that have certain distinct historical characteristics but are not identical with today's nation-states. Such regions may be located entirely within one state or constitute a part of two or more neighboring states. Politically, they might be characterized according to ethno-nationalist or historic criteria, depending on whether the population or the territory is the defining element of the region. Of course, a combination of both aspects is possible.

3. The Two Halves of Europe[5]

After the death of Emperor Theodosius I, in A.D. 395, the Roman Empire was split into two halves—a Latin West Rome and an Orthodox East Rome. The line was drawn in the western Balkans, along the river Drina. The split was completed in 1054, when the Pope in Rome and the Patriarch in Constantinople issued mutual excommunications. Although both Rome and Constantinople remained Christian empires, in several other crucial respects they developed in highly divergent directions. Rivalries between missions from Orthodox Constantinople and Catholic Rome defined a lasting conflict between East and West. Two Christian churches would compete throughout the centuries for the "true" interpretation of the faith. From the very outset, the other side was defined as heretical and as a mortal enemy. With an analogy from geology, one might regard the respective cultural spheres of Eastern and Western Christianity as two tectonic plates, set in continuous change and motion. Friction along the fault line has repeatedly caused conflicts, which at times have escalated into major wars.

After the last Roman emperor ended his rule in A.D. 476, spiritual and secular power was separated in the West. While the pope remained in Rome, the emperor moved north. The west Roman Empire was succeeded by the Empire of Charlemagne and by the Holy Roman Empire of German Nation, with varying capitals in the German and West Slavonic areas. The fact that Rome could remain a center of the faith even after the relocation of the emperor was due to the status of the pope as the successor to the Apostle Peter. This "apostolic" criterion defined the role of the church as the universal ideological center of the new states that succeeded the Roman Empire. The attempt by the French monarchy to constrain papal power by moving the pope to Avignon symptomatically ended in failure.

Western European history came to be marked by a struggle between spiritual and secular power. The result was political pluralism.

In this process, language played an important role. Since missions from Rome utilized Latin, spoken by both religious and political elites, the spreading of the faith also brought in its wake a spreading of the classical heritage as a whole. The Roman church could thus fill an important function not only in the field of religion, but also in the secular process of societal development and state-building. By coincidence, also the pagan Greek intellectual heritage was salvaged by the church fathers. Similarly, the highly cultured Arabs of Spain preserved the Greek classics, a heritage which would be reclaimed by the Europeans after Poitiers.

From Rome, the basic principles of Roman law concerning notions such as private property and civil rights were passed on to the Empire of Charlemagne, the Holy Roman Empire, and the subsequent territorial states of Western Europe. The Roman tradition was thus blended with the heritage of Germanic common law. From the latter came, most importantly, the institution of legislative and judicial popular gatherings. Both kings and emperors were elected, albeit from a rather narrow circle.

In the twelfth century, the Catholic church developed the notion of a purgatory, a place where souls were tested and purified before the final ascension to heaven or descent into hell. Dante's *Divina Commedia* is the first literary and widely spread expression of this ideological innovation. The importance of introducing a middle stage between heaven and hell, a time of trial between earthly life and the afterlife, can hardly be exaggerated. As a result, a graduated practice of justice, a sophisticated penal system, and a sense of personal responsibility could develop. Fundamental notions such as *individual*, *law*, and *politics* were given solid theological-ideological foundations, built on the existing basis of Roman law and Germanic common law.

By introducing the notion of a purgatory, it was also possible to transform the original Christian binary view of the world. The previous clear-cut division into good and evil, strong and weak, ruler and ruled was replaced by a ternary view. The introduction of a middle ground was important, above all, in the sense that it was well in tune with the increasing social differentiation of Western European society, where the burghers of the cities emerged as a separate category between the nobility and the peasantry.

The notion of a purgatory also helped promote an individualistic attitude which, in turn, allowed further development of the concept of a citizen (*citoyen*). It became possible to calculate individual chances and to take risks. The road was thus laid open for a process of secularization, where rationality was focused on social analysis. Both the Catholic and the Protestant worlds became oriented toward material research and exploitation. The latter observations in particular provide a powerful illustration of the highly dynamic nature of Western European development. With regard to obligations of the citizen to the state, a central concept to the Roman Republic, subsequent development added the notion of responsibility to society. Between the *civis romanus* of ancient Rome and the *citoyen* of the French revolution there lies a world of difference, and the process certainly did not stop in 1789.

The main point in developing these thoughts lies in the fact that Russia has remained largely on the periphery of the processes just described. The Soviet socialist system was, in many respects, a continuation of Tsarism. Tsarism, in turn, drew heavily on Byzantine traditions. In that millennial continuity, a world view was formed that differs form Western perceptions of democracy, market economy, and the constitutional state.

With Emperor Constantine the Great, the basic foundations were laid for a relation between church and state that would remain unchanged throughout the history of the Orthodox world. As the church was turned into a state institution, the imperial capital was also made the center of the church. The patriarch was appointed by the emperor, and Orthodoxy was made the criterion of citizenship. No other legal grounds were needed to define the relation between the state and its citizenry.

As was mentioned previously, the decisive break between the two Christian churches occurred in 1054. The cause was a conflict over the nature of the Holy Spirit, over the notion of *filioque*. According to Western interpretations of the Holy Trinity, the Spirit was derived from the Father and the Son. In the Eastern version, the three are one. The Spirit is seen as a manifestation of the union between God and the congregation. The Greek term *koinonia*, "togetherness," denotes the presence of the Spirit in the congregation. The church is not only a union in faith between individuals, but also a *koinonia* in God and with God. In the Orthodox tradition, emphasis is placed on "perfection" and "holiness," rather than on legality and individual morality.

In the Orthodox view, there is no purgatory between heaven and hell, no shades of gray between good and evil. Since the very notion of purgatory was irreconcilable with the notion of unity in *koinonia*, it was refuted by the Orthodox church; only the church could be free of sin. Since the Son of God had suffered and died for the sins of man, the individual could not free himself from sin. The absence of purgatory in the Orthodox tradition implies that there is little room for compromise and that there is no clear dividing line between politics and morals. This stands in stark contrast to the development of political pluralism that came to mark the Western parts of Europe.

In order fully to appreciate the isolation of Russia, we must also take into account the role of missions. We may recall the important secular role played by the Roman church, pursuing its mission in Latin. When the Orthodox mission spread to Russia, Slavic vernacular was used, severing all bonds with the classical cultural heritage. Against this broader background, it is natural that Russian Orthodoxy could never be reconciled with the role of promoting secular education. Instead of theology and law, there came an extreme letter worship, where emphasis was placed on the ritual and purely emotional components of church life.

Another important dimension is that, according to Orthodoxy, truth was once revealed to man by God in the Bible. Since the Holy Scripture contained answers to all questions, no further seeking after truth was necessary. Since the Russian tradition rejected the Greek philosophical heritage as a whole, it could not match the increasing Western rationality that marked the development of science in the Western world. The response of the Russian Orthodox world was increasingly rigid and ritualized readings and interpretations of the Bible. The strong role of the church precluded any form of secularization in Russia.

Scholasticism, the Reformation, the Renaissance, the Baroque, and the Enlightenment—all manifestations of profound changes in Western mentality in the direction of secularization—passed by Russian culture without leaving much trace. Before the eighteenth century, there were no secular schools or universities, no secular arts or sciences. Hence, room for individual initiative and responsibility remained miniscule, both in politics and in the economy. The land and the people, including the nobility, were regarded as the personal property of the Tsar, for him to dispose of at will. Crucial notions such as rationality, constitution, and the law-based state remained alien to this "patrimonial" system.

During the two crucial centuries between Peter I and Stolypin, repeated attempts were made to modernize Russia by way of *Westernization*. They were all initiated from above, and they all ended in failure. Time and time again Russian tradition demonstrated its resistance to such attempts at transformation. When the Bolsheviks took power in Russia, via the coup of October 1917, and the victory in the ensuing civil war, Marxism-Leninism was put in the place of Orthodoxy as state ideology. Behind the façade of Communist symbolism, however, the basic continuity of the Orthodox view of the world was maintained; the Bolsheviks skillfully adapted the liturgy for their own political ends. Party congresses were modeled after the Orthodox mass, and processions of the Holy Cross and icons were replaced by public parades where portraits of politburo members were carried.[6]

Deep-seated Russian suspicions of Western concepts of capitalism, democracy, and law were thus promoted by the new regime. Under the Communist order, the notion of unity in the congregation was replaced by an appeal to mob rule, expressed in mass meetings and demonstrations, as well as in xenophobia, expressed in campaigns of focused hate. After the Second World War, two generations of Central Europeans would be forcefully drawn into this community.

Central Europe, which had been part of the western tradition until 1945, experienced four decades of easternization/sovietization. The weight of this heritage in the minds of the people makes transition to democracy, the market economy, and the law-based state precarious. Regional identity has remained important in western culture through the millennia. In the Russian and Soviet empires people learned to identify more with the Church/Party and the Emperor/Party leader than with the ethnic or the local. Identification with regions beneath the state or Soviet-republic level was minimal.

The East-West cultural dichotomy manifests itself, among other things, in an extensive border area where people belonging to the respective denominations live intermingled. It stretches from the Adriatic Sea to the Baltic Sea. Conflict along this old border between eastern and western Christianity may develop if and when west Christians in east Central Europe, by invoking old, pre-Soviet traditions and a common world view, succeed in joining western Europe (the European Union). Thus, west Christians could become examples of successful modernization, at the same time that east Christians remain destitute and deprived of possibilities to develop a civil society but cognizant of developments on their border to the West.

Mesoregions

During antiquity, the Romans elaborated the doctrine of *mare nostrum* for the Mediterranean. This meant that they regarded the area as a "natural" region under Roman rule. The Mediterranean united many peoples and territories in southern Europe, west Asia, and North Africa. After the demise of the Roman Empire, Venice and Genoa served as the unifying economic center in the region. During the Spanish Habsburg era, in the sixteenth and seventeenth centuries, the Mediterranean region partly regained its political unity for a time, except for the eastern part which was under Ottoman rule.

In the Black Sea region, the Byzantine Empire was succeeded by Ottoman rule, with the Greeks acting as the unifying economic bond. During the fourteenth, fifteenth, and sixteenth centuries, this area was a Turkish *mare nostrum*. Around the North Sea, in the fifteenth and sixteenth centuries, England and Holland emerged as leading political and economic actors. After the defeat of the Spanish Armada in 1588, the North Sea became a Dutch and British *mare nostrum* for three centuries.

In the Baltic Sea region several historical actors have tried to establish a *mare nostrum*, with none being completely successful. Among these were the kingdoms of Denmark, Sweden-Finland, Poland-Lithuania, and Russia, the Teutonic Order, and the Hanseatic League. After 1871, the Second German Reich emerged as a potential hegemon. After 1945, the Soviet Union was the regional great power, but the region as a whole was divided between the Western and Eastern blocs, with Sweden and Finland as buffers.

Of these four mesoregions, the Mediterranean and the Baltic directly concern Central Europe. In the late Cold War period, tendencies of regional cooperation and conscious attempts to further a sense of regional identity across the East-West divide could be discerned in both these regions. The tendencies were an expression of the reemergence of German presence east of the Oder and Leitha rivers. The pattern from the early 900s to the early 1900s was recalled. However, this time the Germans did not come as crusaders, monks, burghers, and farmers, but in the guise of capitalists.

More recently, there have emerged a German-Prussian project in the Baltic region and a German-Austrian and Italian initiative in the Adriatic part of the Mediterranean region. The former is known as the *New Hansa* and the latter as the *Alpe-Adria*. As both projects are well known (and discussed elsewhere in this book), their history or any details will not be dwelt on, and only a few aspects of fundamental interest will be highlighted. Both the New Hansa and the Alpe-Adria build upon the notion that people have common interests in furthering their material and spiritual well-being and that this might be achieved not only within the confines of the respective nation-states but through regional cooperation. Two factors allowed these movements to gain momentum in the late 1980s. The first was the ongoing dissolution of the Soviet bloc, which meant that the western areas could count on better access to the eastern areas and that the latter could embrace the West without being punished by Moscow. The second factor was more a political event than anything else. It so happened that the German state of Schleswig-Holstein in the Baltic region and Friuli-Venezia in the Alpe-Adria region saw the emergence of charismatic politicians who believed that regional notoriety would carry them to the pinnacles of national power: Björn Engholm and Gianni de Michelis, respectively, have since fallen from power. It is conspicuous that with the exit of these charismatic figures much less has been heard of the New Hansa and the Alpe-Adria.

Still, the New Hansa and the Alpe-Adria probably will have a lasting impact, having helped Europeans on both sides of the old Iron Curtain overcome Cold War division. Under the auspices of these transnational-cooperation initiatives, Estonians, Latvians, Lithuanians, and Poles, as well as Czechs, Hungarians, Slovenians, and Croats, were drawn into the orbit of Germans, Scandinavians, and Italians, with both sides profiting even before the fall of the Berlin Wall. Through these arrangements, east Central Europe partly became functionally reunited with Western Europe.

The so-called Višegrad group is a special mesoregion, situated at the interface between the Baltic and the Adriatic-Mediterranean regions. While well publicized, it remains rather feeble at present and need not be dwelt upon at length in the present context. It is enough to recall that it was created in February 1991 as a very loose form of cooperation among Poland, Czechoslovakia, and Hungary with the double aim to coordinate security policies vis-à-vis the ailing but still dangerous Soviet Union and economic policies vis-à-vis the European Community. When Czechoslovakia split up, the group became known as the Višegrad Four. The cooperation was not institutionalized; it received a lukewarm reception from the Czech government under Vaclav Klaus while Slovenia, ill at ease with Czechia and Hungary and rather cool towards Poland, looked to Austria for guidance.[7] What remains is the nostalgia of Polish-Hungarian historical relations and friendship (the two do not have any common boundary).[8] The enduring importance of the Višegrad group is that it has helped to define Poland, Czechia, Slovakia, and Hungary in terms of a special group of Central European states, with better prospects for the future than the rest of the former Soviet bloc. This mesoregion thus became the easternmost part of the Western macroregion, constituting a sort of link between "East" and "West." Strictly speaking, Czechia, separated from the East by Slovakia, does not form part of this link. Václav Klaus has been the first to stress the importance of this fact; according to his view, Czechia is more Western and "European" than Germany.[9]

Microregions

There are many different ways of defining microregions: through intrastate administrative boundaries, functional interdependencies, or as peripheral areas (Bretagne, Laponia, and so on).[10] The Council of European Regions, founded in 1985, today has more than 200 members of these different kinds, ranging from large German *Länder* to small British counties.[11] In this analysis, the focus is on historically defined regions in Central Europe that are divided between contemporary nation-states.

Several regions in Central Europe have a long history, a specific cultural and social identity, are situated at the present state boundaries, and have changed state identity in the twentieth century. Among these are Upper Silesia, Teschen Silesia, East Prussia with the Königsberg district, the Vilna district, Galicia, Transcarpathia, Transylvania, and the Vojvodina. If the local vernaculars, for example, in Silesia and Transcarpathia had been recognized as distinct languages at the time of the creation of the successor states in 1918–1920, both Slonzaks and Ruthenians might have aspired for separate statehood for these regions in the name of their right to national self-determination. With the help of historical arguments, a similar claim could have been made for Transylvania, which enjoyed a degree of autonomy in the old Hungarian kingdom, under the Turkish Sultan, and under the Austrian Emperor. It did not become an integral part of Hungary until after the *Ausgleich* between Vienna and Buda in 1867; in 1920 it became part of Romania.

In the present period of national economic reconstruction, border regions in Central Europe are acquiring a potentially more dynamic role than during the Soviet period, when boundaries presented considerable obstacles to transboundary cooperation. In the process of creating a national identity in post-Soviet circumstances, ethno-nationalism has resurged. The regions in question are populated partly by minorities whose brethren are national majorities in neighboring states: Hungarians in Slovakia and Germans in Poland are cases in point.

Economic considerations should favor low boundary significance, whereas fear of minority disloyalty and potential irredentism from across the border point in the other direction. In the following, recent developments with a bearing on the economy and national minorities in some border regions involving Poland and Hungary will be discussed. As has been indicated previously, these two states are situated at the dividing line between eastern and western Christianity and between the Adriatic Sea and the Baltic Sea regions. Historically, both have been multinational empires. The main difference is that whereas Poland has (been) moved from West to East and back to West again, Hungary has been reduced to a core area. Together, these states constitute the heart of Central Europe. Developments in their border regions are crucial for future cooperation in the area and for the West's relations with the East.

The Poland that emerged after the Second World War was rather homogeneous ethnically; only a few individuals of Jewish descent remained, Soviet Ukraine, Belorussia, and Lithuania having acquired most of the territories with mixed populations and the Germans having been expelled. Those Germans who remained basically disappeared as an ethnic group, to reemerge only when opportunities to emigrate to West Germany were offered. In the 1950s, Poland discontinued the collection of census data based on nationality.

After 1989, however, Germans and Ukrainians, in particular, have reemerged in Poland, and the Polish minorities in Lithuania, Belarus, and Ukraine have also made themselves much more visible than before. As a consequence, Poland's border regions have become dynamic. Prospects for economic cooperation have opened up at the same time that ethnic tensions have been revived. In 1991–1994, Poland concluded friendship and cooperation agreements with all neighboring states. Boundary stability, thus, was secured. However, nostalgic interest in the former eastern regions of Poland, the Kresy, has been revived. Excursions into this area are arranged by *friends*, i.e., descendants of Poles from Wilno, Grodno, and Lwów, that is, contemporary Vilnius, Grodno, and L'viv.[12] Among the Polish minorities in Lithuania, Belarus, and Ukraine, the Catholic priests have emerged as spokesmen for their nationalities. Poland's state flag flies above the churches in the Kresy.[13]

On the Polish side of the border with Ukraine, religious strife broke out in 1991 in Przemysl over the right to use the Carmelite church. It used to be Uniate (Ukrainian), but had been taken over by the Catholics (Polish). The Pope tried to solve the problem by giving the garrison church to the Ukrainians. They were not particularly amused, because over the altar was written in Polish *Bog, Honor, Ojczyzna*, a slogan that certainly was not pro-Ukrainian. Tit for tat, the Ukrainian congregation reopened a war cemetery, celebrating those who had fallen in the Ukrainian Galician Army that had fought the Poles in the 1918–1920 war.[14]

The Polish minority in the Vilnius region caused considerable tension between Poland and Lithuania in 1991–1992, because its leaders were rather Moscow-oriented (!) and because the Lithuanian authorities reacted by way of gerrymandering the election districts and with other petty harassments. However, after much protraction, a Polish-Lithuanian friendship treaty was finally signed by presidents Brazauskas and Walesa in Vilnius on April 26, 1994. It confirmed the current boundary and obliged both countries to be fair to their ethnic minorities. When signing the treaty, Brazauskas underlined the "Lithuanian character" of Vilnius and claimed that in the interwar years, Vilnius had belonged to Poland *"de facto* but not *de jure."* However, Lithuania abandoned a previous claim that Poland should explicitly condemn its occupation of Vilnius in 1920 (Vinton 1994).

Belarus has not adopted a border-region policy in any real sense. Thus, Poland's eastern border is characterized at present by relative calm, except for the ubiquitous bazaar trade, smuggling, and illegal border crossings. Indeed, Poland's main ambition is to preserve political order by reinforcing boundary controls and to stop migrants from Ukraine and beyond from crossing Poland on their way to Germany. Meanwhile, Poland's western border regions acquired new significance at the time of the revolutions of 1989, with the prospect of a democratic Poland bordering on a (truly) democratic Germany. At the very time of the fall of the Berlin Wall, Chancellor Helmut Kohl was in Warsaw to sign an agreement with Poland. Poland received credits in the order of two billion German marks. In return, the existence of a German minority in Upper Silesia was acknowledged, as well as its rights to church services and school education in German. People began to change their family names from Polish to German and the German minority increased considerably in number.[15]

In 1990, a bilingual newspaper, *Glazeta Gornoslaska/Oberschlesische Zeitung* was launched in Upper Silesia. The radio stations in Opole (Oppeln) and Katowice (Kattowitz) started to broadcast programs in German.[16] The Germans are back on the political stage in Upper Silesia. In addition, the Slonzaks have reemerged. These are local people, speaking a special variety of West Slavonic. Having difficulties in defending Silesian autonomy, they have tended, historically, to rely on the "opposite" state to get protection. In the interwar years, they tended to side with the Germans. After 1945, they became Polish, but a total amalgamation between them and the incoming Galician Poles never took place. In the eyes of many Polish nationalists, the Slonzaks are potential national renegades, a German fifth column. It caused some concern among Polish intellectuals in Warsaw when Slonzaks voiced their misgivings over Warsaw's neglect of Upper Silesia under the economic restructuring program. Sociologist Jadwiga Staniszkis even warned that Upper Silesia sooner or later would demand another plebiscite (after the one in 1922) on uniting with Germany.[17]

During the Communist era, Upper Silesia was a relatively prosperous region, the miners and the steelworkers being the labor aristocracy of the socialist state. Provincial pride was further bolstered when Edward Gierek, who was from the region, ruled Poland from 1971 to 1980. In post-Communist Poland, political leaders have come from the Warsaw and Gdansk areas. In addition, the new economic policy has meant relative neglect of dirty heavy industry and the coal mines of Upper Silesia. In this situation of relative—or even absolute—deprivation, people have begun to question their Polishness; it might be more useful to be a German or at least a Slonzak to be able to get attention—and money—not only from an alarmed Warsaw but also from Germany. As a reaction to this tendency, a certain reservation has become evident in Poland with regard to the new Euroregions along the western border, *Pomerania, Pro-Europa-Viadrina, Spree-Neisse-Bober,* and *Neisse-Nisa-Nysa.*[18] The argument against close cooperation is that it might undermine the Polish identity of these western border regions and encourage separatism.[19]

A further aspect to take into consideration is that the costs of reconstruction of the five new *Bundesländer* have surpassed all expectations. Prospects for some regions in eastern Germany look dim indeed, not the least for those further East. Thus, Amber Sayah (1994: 39), correspondent with the German weekly *Die Zeit,* could say after visiting Görlitz on the Oder/Odra border:

> The city has little to offer that might attract investment capital. While there is considerable cross-border crime, cigarette-smuggling, and car thievery, employment is scarce—there is hardly any trade or industry. Life itself has abandoned the crumbling walls of the city.

In terms of regions and borders, the trouble spots for Hungary are to be found in its relations with Romania, Yugoslavia (Serbia), and Slovakia. With Ukraine there exists an agreement on equal or preferential treatment of national minorities (Hungarians in Transcarpathia outnumbering Ukrainians in the upper Tisza [Tisa] region by at least ten to one), and with Austria, Slovenia, and Croatia, relations reportedly are in good order.[20]

In the historical Hungarian provinces of Transylvania and Vojvodina, in Romania and Serbia, respectively, the Hungarian population, to a large part, live some distance from the border. It is hard to imagine ethnically motivated irredentist claims by Hungary on these areas today (quite apart from the fact that there is no political reason to expect any such claims). Moreover, the nationalist Hungarian MDF government at the end of its rule made clear that in spite of incursions into the rights of the Hungarian minority after 1991, it would respect Serbia's military might and considered it not to be in Hungary's interest to pose a threat to an isolated Serbia. In return for this magnanimity, Serbia was expected to respect certain basic rights regarding its Hungarian minority.[21]

The new Hungarian government of Socialists and Free Democrats, which came to power in June 1994, underlined Hungary's wish to pursue a policy of good relations with all its neighbors. The incoming foreign minister, László Kovács, declared that "minority groups living outside Hungary's border are part of the nation" and should "pursue happiness wherever they live." He underlined that the new Hungarian government would strive to secure the rights of Hungarian minorities through bilateral negotiations and involvement in international fora.[22]

Transylvania (Erdély) might be compared with the L'viv/Lwów and Wilno/Vilnius areas in several respects. The respective regions belong to the core national mythology of Hungary and Poland, respectively.[23] The former two regions now are situated firmly within east Christian states that are rather unstable but where it would be politically impossible for Poland and Hungary to demand back lost territories, even if they so desired.

What remains as an acute problem for Hungary is Slovakia. It is a new state, even if Slovaks like to view it as a reincarnation of the Great Moravian State of the ninth century. Its international status, thus, is somewhat unclear. Its capital, Bratislava, was once the capital of the Hungarian Habsburg kings during the Turkish occupation of Buda in the sixteenth and seventeenth centuries. It has a minority of close to 600,000 Hungarians, more than ten percent of Slovakia's total population, and although the Hungarians do not live in one compact settlement, they live rather close to Hungary, especially in *Északmagyarorzság* ("Northern Hungary") just north of the Danube. Moreover, Slovakia and Hungary are deeply involved politically in the conflict over the Gabcikovo (Bös)-

Nagymaros hydroelectric project. The border region between the two states for all these reasons can be regarded as one of the most intriguing in all Central Europe.

The hydroelectric project at Gabcikovo on the Danube was near completion on the Slovak side, when Hungary canceled its involvement in the project at Dunakiliti and Nagymaros. The arguments used were ecological, but they had clear ethno-nationalist connotations. Nationalist Hungarians argued that the project would destroy Hungarian settlements and further weaken the Hungarian population in Slovakia. This argument was accepted in Hungary across the political spectrum, especially as it became linked to the conflict in Slovakia over the linguistic and political rights of the Hungarian minority.[24]

In October 1992, the Gabcikovo dam and a new channel diverting the water to the Slovak side were finished and the hydropower plant put into operation. Hungary protested, among other things, with the argument that the change of the course of the river violated the boundary agreement in 1947. In the end, the parties agreed to relegate the solution of the conflict to the International Court in the Hague. It will take years to reach an agreement. Meanwhile, tensions have remained high regarding the situation of the Hungarian minority in Slovakia. Even after the nationalist Vladimír Meciar was forced to resign as Slovak premier for a second time in March 1994, to be replaced by the more conciliatory Jozef Moravcik, the Slovak authorities continued to harass the minority.

Slovakia was admitted to the Council of Europe in June 1993 with the provision that Hungarian villages should be allowed to have bilingual signs. However, Meciar refused to fulfill this requirement. When the question at last came up for a vote in the Slovak parliament in June 1994, it was rejected by a majority of one. This rather unpromising outcome was further compromised by the fact that two of the Hungarian deputies abstained from voting and one voted against. The obvious conclusion is that Slovak and Hungarian extreme nationalists acted in collusion, both seeking potential advantages from an intensification of conflict.[25]

The idea of a Carpathian Euroregion was launched in 1991. Two different projects were discussed at an international conference in the North Hungarian town of Nyiregyháza in May 1992. No Romanian representative was present. Whereas Poland, Ukraine, and Hungary sent government officials in addition to the local representatives, Slovakia was represented only by local leaders from Kosice, Presov, and Bardejov. The Romanian absence was motivated by discontent with Hungary's refusal explicitly to deny any irredentist ambitions. The lukewarm Slovakian attitude may have been prompted by related concerns.

The proposal for the Carpathian Euroregion presented by the Hungarian Academy of Sciences encompassed six Polish, two Slovakian, three Hungarian, seven Romanian, and five Ukrainian districts. Its total area would have encompassed 193,900 km^2 and included a population of 18 million. In terms of territorial share, 10.2 percent of the Euroregion would be Hungarian, 15.1 percent Slovak, 16.6 percent Polish, 21.9 percent Romanian, and 36.3 percent Ukrainian. In terms of population, the percentage would be 10.2 percent Hungarian, 14.0 percent Slovak, 18.2 percent Romanian, 21.7 percent Polish, and 35.9 percent Ukrainian. An American-based nongovernmental organization, the Institute for East-West Studies, presented a much more modest plan where the respective parts of the states were of the same size in terms of both area and population. It was accepted by the participants of the conference. When the Carpathian Euroregion finally was established by the signing of an agreement at a meeting in Debrecen in February 1993, no Romanian representative took part.[26]

It is highly significant that reservations regarding Euroregions in Central Europe are connected with Czech, Polish, Slovak, and Romanian fear of German and Hungarian revisionism and irredentism. Czech leader Václav Klaus, for example, explicitly criticized the emerging Euroregions in the Bohemian-Bavarian area as a German attempt at "creeping" reconquest of the Sudetenland.[27] This is the enduring ideological legacy from the German and Austro-Hungarian empires before 1918, and from the German and Hungarian occupations during the Second World War.

As far as Hungary is concerned, there is a conceptual solution to the problem of potential irredentism. In Hungarian political language, the policy aiming at diminishing boundary significance was once called "the spiritualization of frontiers." In 1988, when the question of the Hungarian minority in Transylvania was discussed in the Hungarian parliament, a deputy recalled an idea of the Hungarian left of the 1930s that the nationality question in the former Hungarian Kingdom, that is, the fate of the Hungarian minorities in the successor states, should be solved by "spiritualization of frontiers" (Boldizsar 1988: 55).

German and Hungarian national aspirations cannot be fulfilled according to the formula "one nation, one state." Irredentism in the literal sense is out of question. The formula "spiritualization of frontiers," which has been repeated time and time again after 1989 by Hungarian intellectuals and politicians, implies the solution of abolishing the ethnic and cultural significance of international boundaries. In this perspective, the establishment of transboundary Euroregions acquires a special significance.

The homogeneous nation-state which has evolved in Europe over the last 200 years has implied greater boundary significance not only economically but also culturally and linguistically. Repeatedly, people have been asked, ordered, or compelled to be Frenchmen and Germans, Danes and Poles rather than Alsatians, Saarländers, Schleswigians, or Silesians. Many local actors in these

old historical regions today identify with the respective nation-state rather than
with the people across the border. Whereas a regional identity may be preserved
in the periphery in relation to the core regions and capitals of any nation, it is
much harder to develop a specific, transboundary, regional identity.

The significance of international boundaries must be diminished in order that
peripheral regions of potential transboundary cooperation within the nation-
states may develop and acquire dynamics of their own. Diminished boundary
significance could alleviate minority problems in border areas. Now as in the
interwar period, this problem concerns primarily the German and Hungarian
minorities in the successor states.

4. Conclusions

Since 1989, state borders have become more transparent between the former
Soviet bloc states in Central Europe and between these and their neighbors in the
west. There have also been attempts by local politicians to lower boundary
significance and to initiate transborder-development projects. On the macro level,
the old divide between eastern and western Christianity has acquired new
significance with the disappearance of the Iron Curtain. The events of October
1993 in Moscow, the election results and the adoption of an authoritarian
constitution in December of the same year, as well as the internal and foreign
policies of the Yeltsin regime in 1994, have once again stymied Russian attempts
to cooperate more closely with Europe.

It is often controversial in the West to argue that Russia has proved unable
to develop institutions of democracy, market economy, and the legal state
(*Rechtsstaat*). Central Europeans, however, tend to be less inhibited in this
respect, as has been noted recently by the chronicler of contemporary Central
European history, the Englishman Timothy Garton Ash (1994:18). He records a
conversation with a Lithuanian MP:

> And what is Europe? Strutting up and down, he barks a short and definite
> answer: '*Europa ist...nicht-Russland!*' Europe is not-Russia! Well, that is one
> definition, and far from just a Lithuanian one. (It's just that the Lithuanians are
> naive enough to say so).

A few years after the end of the Soviet system, the states in the former Soviet
blocs parted ways. Those to the west of the Christian divide turned into the normal
post-1945 pattern of politics in Western Europe, as conservative governments
had to give way to social democratic ones in Lithuania, Poland, and Hungary.
Social democratic beliefs asserted themselves also in the new *Bundesländer* in
the European elections on June 12, 1994. This did not imply a return of

Communists, only that the pendulum had begun to swing as it had swung in Western Europe for half a century.

However, in Russia, Ukraine, Romania, Bulgaria, and Serbia, democracy came to imply authoritarian rule, in spite of democratic forms. The tendency to identify the state and its citizens with Orthodoxy was evident not only in Russia, where the subsequently dissolved parliament in mid-1993 issued a law against west Christian missions among Russians, but also in Bulgaria, Romania, and Greece, where the security services warned against west Christian subversion.[28] Thus, the binary world view of Orthodoxy was reinforced, and the significance of the state boundaries as a shield against intrusion from abroad was enhanced. On the other hand, this did not imply any restriction on expansionist foreign policy, as was evident from both Serbia's policy and from Russia's defense doctrine with its description of its west Christian neighbors as living in a "near abroad," where Russia had the right to intervene militarily if need be.

On the macro level, a new sharp ideological boundary, thus, has emerged to the east of the Baltic states, Poland, Slovakia, and Hungary. On the meso level, Central Europe has been affected by three regional configurations, the New Hansa, the Alpe-Adria and the Višegrad Four. The latter two are incorporated in the still looser Central European Initiative, in its turn an outgrowth of the previous *Pentagonal* and *Hexagonal*.[29] Apart from furthering cooperation in fields such as culture and environmental monitoring, education, and development of the infrastructure, the establishment of these regions has served to reconnect the Central European states with Western Europe and to distance them from the Orthodox countries. The Kaliningrad and St. Petersburg districts have not been integrated in deep, meaningful cooperation in the Baltic region. The Russian military has exerted its veto right, and Moscow has been extremely reluctant to loosen its grip over these outposts on western soil.

Meanwhile, the Višegrad Four have emerged as a distinct group in the eyes of outsiders. Through increased contacts with Hungary and Czechia, Slovenia is drawn into the group. Slovakia may fall out, should the political and economic situation deteriorate. On the other hand, Czechia's government has tried to distance itself from the group, arguing that the Czech Republic is more developed and mature for "Europe" than the other three.[30]

On the micro level, cooperation in the form of Euroregions has been hampered by remaining mutual suspicion between, for example, Poles and Germans, Czechs and Germans, Poles and Czechs, and Slovaks and Hungarians. However, in a sense, Hungary has been an exception. Precisely because its MDF government was nationalist, it advocated cross-border cooperation and "spiritualization" of the boundaries, in order to let the Hungarian minorities prosper.

Hopefully, the future political role of border microregions will include the freedom to self-define specific identity beyond the ramifications set by ethnic nationalism and the mononational state. This is possible if individuals are allowed to emancipate themselves from the notion that there is only one identity and that one is born with it. It should be recognized that one might be a Pole in one setting, a Slonzak in another, a German in a third, and a Jew in a fourth, that is, if the individual happens to have ethnic roots, a territorial background, linguistic skills, and religious beliefs that allows her or him to identify with any of these categories, according to circumstances. The *usefulness* of transboundary regions, thus, would be to serve as an antidote to the war-prone ethnic nationalism that has ravaged Europe during the last two centuries.

Notes

1. Central Europe here is defined as contemporary Poland, Czechia, Slovakia, and Hungary and the areas bordering on these states.

2. For a theoretical survey, see Tägil et al. (1977).

3. In this paper, we will not discuss the theoretical and conceptual aspects of the concept of national self-determination. For an elaborate discussion, see István Bibó (1967–1970).

4. Hungarian stands for ethnic Hungarian (Magyar), not for citizens of Hungary.

5. This section is largely based on a manuscript by the present author and Stefan Hedlund (1994), "Homo Oeconomicus Meets Homo Sovieticus," Uppsala: Department of East European Studies, June. See also, "The Role of Dual Models in the Dynamics of Russian Culture (Up to the End of the Eighteenth Century)," by Ju. M. Lotman and B. A. Uspenskij (1984), in *The Semiotics of Russian Culture*, Ann Shukman, ed. Ann Arbor: Department of Slavic Languages and Literature, University of Michigan.

6. "Scientific socialism," in fact, could be interpreted as a Communist version of the Orthodox belief that all truth had once been revealed by God to man in the Bible. The Party assumed the role of the priesthood in interpreting the faith, and the "eternally living" (*vechno zhivoi*) Lenin took the place of God. Symbolically, pictures of Lenin replaced the icon in the traditional icon corner.

7. See Milada Vachudova (1994).

8. Višegrad was chosen as a meeting place in 1991 because of historical connotations. In this royal Hungarian castle, John of Luxemburg, king of Bohemia, Charles Robert of Anjou, king of Hungary, and Casimir the Great, king of Poland, met in 1335 to coordinate their foreign policy.

9. Berthold Kohler, "Füreinander bereit? Die Tschechen, die Deutschen und der Traum von vereinten Europa," *Frankfurter Allgemeine Zeitung*, June 14, 1993.

10. An overview is to be found in Ingemar Karlsson, "Regionernas Europa—den enes dröm, den andres mardröm." *Världspolitikens dagsfrågor* 3 (1994). Stockholm: Utrikespolitiska institutet.

11. "Regionalisierung als Allheilmittel? Der Katalane Pujol fordert eine dritte Ebene in der EG," *Frankfurter Allgemeine Zeitung,* January 21, 1993.

12. See for example Ryszard Chanas and Janusz Czerwinski (1992). The foreword begins with asserting that the guide deals with places and events "close to the Pole's heart" (p. 9).

13. Werner Adam, "Lauter neue Nachbarn. Die Reformstaaten in Osteuropa finden sich auch untereinander nicht ohne Schwierigkeiten zurecht," *Frankfurter Allgemenie Zeitung,* June30, 1993.

14. See Frank Golszewski (1994: 89–91).

15. See the reports "Belagerte Festung" and "Ewige Verehrung. Die deutsche Minderheit fordert die Polen hinaus—mit Grossmansucht und Heldendenkmälern," *Der Spiegel,* no. 24, 1991, and no. 45, 1992.

16. Golczewski (1994: 97).

17. Jan Dzialul (1992), "Autonomiczny, regionalny czy nemecki? W Slaskim kotle," *Polityka,* October 3, 1992.

18. For an overview of these regions, see Bohdan Gruchman and Franz Walk, "Transboundary Cooperation in the Polish-German Border Region," in the present volume.

19. See Jan B. de Weydenthal (1993).

20. See Michael Frank (1991).

21. See Stan Markotich (1994).

22. See Karoly Okolicsany (1994).

23. The place in the romantic nationalist imaginations of Endre Ady, Julius Slowacki, and Adam Mickiewicz!

24. See Edith Oltay (1994).

25. "Umstrittene Minderheitenrechte in der Slowakei. Scheitern eines Gesetzes für zweisprachige Ortstafeln," *Neue Zürcher Zeitung,* June 8, 1994.

26. For an overview, see Alexander Duleba (1993).

27. Bernhard Kohler, *Frankfurter Allgemeine Zeitung,* June 14, 1993.

28. Wendy Slater and Kjell Engelbrekt (1993).

29. See Alfred A. Reisch (1993).

30. Berthold Kohler, "Ohne Bremser nach Westen. Prag hält das 'Višegrad'-Konsept für überholt," *Frankfurter Allgemeine Zeitung,* June 18, 1994.

References

Adam, Werner. 1993. "Lauter neue Nachbarn. Die Reformstaaten in Osteuropa finden sich auch untereinander nicht ohne Schwierigkeiten zurecht." *Frankfurter Allgemenie Zeitung* (30 June).

Vachudova, Milada. 1994. "The Višegrad Four: No Alternative to Cooperation." *RFE-RL Research Report* 2 (34).

Bibó, István. 1991. "The Principle of Self-Determination: Critiques and Justification (1967–70)." In *Democracy, Revolution, Self-Determination,* Károly Nagy, ed. Boulder: Atlantic Research and Publication, Columbia University Press.

Boldizsar, István. 1988. "In a Good Cause." *New Hungarian Quarterly* 29 (111).

Chanas, Ryszard, and Janusz Czerwinski. 1992. Lwów. Przewodnik, Wroclaw: Zaklad Narodowy im. Ossolinskich Wydanictwo.

de Weydenthal, Jan B. 1993. "Controversy in Poland over 'Euroregions.'" *RFE-RL Research Report,* 2 (16).

Duleba, Alexander. 1993. "Karpatsky Euroregión—genéza projektu transhranicnej spoluprace." *Medzinárodné Otázky* 2 (4).

Dzialul, Jan. 1992. "Autonomiczny, regionalny czy nemecki? W Slaskim kotle." *Polityka* (3 October).

Frank, Michael. 1991. "Rund ein Drittel aller Ungarn lebt im Ausland." *Süddeutsche Zeitung* (22 August).

Garton Ash, Timothy. 1994. "Journey to the Post-Communist East." *New York Review of Books* 41 (12).

Golszewski, Frank. 1994. "Nationale Minderheiten in Polen und die Wende." *Nationalities Papers* 22 (1).

Kohler, Berthold. 1993. "Nur Häme gibt es umsonst. Erster Tiefpunkt im Verhältnis von Tschechen und Slowaken." *Frankfurter Allgemeine Zeitung* (18 March).

Kohler, Berthold. 1993. "Füreinander bereit? Die Tschechen, die Deutschen und der Traum von vereinten Europa." *Frankfurter Allgemeine Zeitung* (14 June).

Kohler, Berthold. 1994. "Ohne Bremser nach Westen. Prag hält das 'Višegrad'-Konzept für überholt." *Frankfurter Allgemeine Zeitung* (18 January).

Lotman, Ju. M., and B. A. Uspenskij. 1984. "The Role of Dual Models in the Dynamics of Russian Culture (Up to the End of the Eighteenth Century)." In *The Semiotics of Russian Culture*, Ann Shukman, ed. Ann Arbor: Department of Slavic Languages and Literature, University of Michigan.

Markotich, Stan. 1994. "Autonomy for Vojvodina Hungarians." *RFE-RL Research Report* 3 (6).

Nyström, Kerstin. 1984. "Regional Identity and Ethnic Conflict: Croatia's Dilemma." In *Regions in Upheaval*, Lund Studies in International History, vol. 22, Sven Tägil, ed. Kristianstad: Esselte Studium.

Okolicsanyi, Karoly. 1994. "Budapest's Minority Policy in the Making." *RFE-RL Research Report* 3 (29).

Oltay, Edith. 1992. "Minorities as Stumbling Block in Relations with Neigbours." *RFE-RL Research Report* 1 (19).

Reisch, Alfred A. 1993. "The Central European Initiative: To Be or Not to Be?" *RFE-RL Research Report* 2 (34).

Reisch, Alfred A. 1994. "Consensus on Hungary's Foreign Policy Frayed by Elections." *RFE-RL Research Report* 3 (20).

Sayah, Amber. 1994. "Der Fall Görlitz." *Die Zeit Magazin* 24 (39).

Slater, Wendy, and Kjell Engelbrekt. 1993. "Eastern Orthodoxy Defends Its Position." *RFE-RL Research Report* 2 (35).

Tägil, Sven et al. 1977. *Studying Boundary Conflicts. A Theoretical Framework.* Lund Studies in International History, vol. 9. Kristianstad: Esselte Studium.

Tolstaya, Tatyana. 1994. "Boris the First." *New York Review of Books* 41 (12).

Vinton, Louisa. 1994. "Polish-Lithuanian Treaty Signed." *RFE-RL Research Report* 3 (18).

The Evolution of Cooperation in the Kuhmo-Kostamuksha Region of the Finnish-Russian Border

Veikko Tikkanen
Jyrki Käkönen

Introduction

During the Cold War period, interregional and transboundary cooperation in the Baltic Sea region was basically limited to the open and democratic societies of Scandinavia and West Germany. Security concerns dominated by the East-West confrontation led to a high degree of militarization of the region and restricted opportunities for multilateral dialogue. Starting with the period of Perestroika in the Soviet Union, and especially after 1989, the decline of confrontational politics has allowed not only increased and more open international dialogue between truly sovereign states, but also opened up new possibilities of East-West cooperation at the local level.

Although far from being freely traversable, the present-day Finnish-Russian border is no longer the hermetically sealed zone of noncooperation it was during the Cold War period. Today, it is an external boundary of the European Union and, as such, is a possible springboard for greater European cooperation and integration. Karelia has been opened up to tourism and foreign investment, joint ventures are being encouraged, and transborder trade has increased. This more relaxed international atmosphere has given local governments new opportunities to establish cooperative transboundary relationships. One example is the activities of the Finnish town of Kuhmo and its Russian sister city of Kostamuksha.

Kuhmo is located in the northeastern Finnish administrative district of Oulu. Area-wise it is the largest town in Finland, but its population is only 13,000. Kostamuksha is located in the northwestern Russian Republic of Karelia. It is a new mining town established in the 1970s and now has a population of 30,000. The distance between the centers of these two towns is about 80 kilometers, and the border between the towns is also the border between Finland and Russia.

Interregional Frameworks for Cooperation on the Finnish-Russian Border

The border between Kuhmo and Kostamuksha was already fixed in 1495 in the peace treaty of Pahkinasaari. Since that time, the border has separated people with the same ethnic and cultural origin into two different countries. Historically, the region has been populated by the Karelian people with their own Finnish-related language. However, the history of the region has not been a peaceful one. Its history is full of violent raids from both sides across the border to the villages and centers on the other side of the border. It is equally true that while the states (Russia and Sweden) fought their wars further in the south, the local population made their own border peace.

Until the construction of the mining town of Kostamuksha, there were no real urban centers in the region. It has always been scarcely populated. People lived in small villages along the lakes and rivers, which is a Karelian tradition. Some of the traditional villages, called Karelian villages, can still be found on the Russian side of the border. On both sides of the border people shared common traditions and culture. The border was open until 1920. In the late nineteenth and early twentieth centuries, Finnish anthropologists and other collectors of traditional oral poetry moved freely on both sides of the border. The material for the Finnish national epic, *The Kalevala*, was mostly found in this region.

Within the last several hundred years, the political, cultural, and economic significance of the border between Finland and Russia has gone through marked changes. Domination of Finland by Sweden, then Russia, was followed by independence in 1917. After the border between Finland and Soviet Russia was closed in the 1920s, it became a genuine barrier to everyday interaction. While Finnish independence inaugurated an intensive process of nation-building, it was also followed by the calamities of World War II with considerable losses of life and territory. After 1945, the Karelian Isthmus was incorporated into the Soviet Union. Finland lost important Baltic and Barents seaports. Over 400,000 Finns from the lost territories were resettled elsewhere in Finland, and the new border between both countries became an almost impenetrable ideological and militarized boundary.

The closing off of the border region for more than three generations has left indelible marks in the popular imagination, particularly since Karelia is perceived as being the *cradle* of Finnish culture (Paasi 1994). The Finnish-Russian border fortifications were higher, wider, and even more impenetrable than the Berlin

Wall. The picture of Finnish-Russian relations that official propaganda transmitted to the rest of the world was extremely positive. In reality, the only gap in this hermetically sealed boundary was the connection between both nations' capitals, Helsinki and Moscow. Through that gap, and only through that gap, did Finnish and Soviet leaders interact. This left no room for transboundary exchanges at the local level.

The border became not only a separating, but also an isolating factor for the municipalities located alongside it. The Finnish-Russian border region thus became an economic periphery, predominantly rural, sparsely populated, neglected by both Helsinki and Moscow, and largely cut off from international trade. Indeed, the painful loss of Karelia—central to the Finn's collective consciousness—and Finland's ambiguous geopolitical position in the Cold War order (where the question of whether Finland was part of the *East* or the *West* provoked frequent debate) until recently made the issue of transboundary cooperation rather academic (Paasi 1994).

Points of Departure: Perestroika and Local Level Transboundary Cooperation

The discovery of significant iron ore deposits in the Kostamuksha region had a major impact on transborder development in the area. Although these deposits were found during World War II, it took decades for the Soviet authorities to open a mine in the Kostamuksha forest area. Due to the scarce population of the region, the Soviet government was willing to begin a large project in cooperation with Finland as a manifestation of the 1948 Finish-Soviet Pact of Friendship, Cooperation, and Mutual Assistance. An agreement on a joint construction project was signed at the top political level by Secretary General Leonid Brezhnev and President Urho Kekkonen. Finnish enterprises and workers got a chance to participate in the construction of the mining plant and the new town. The planning for the project started in 1973, and construction took place from 1977 to 1985.

The project provided work for 16,000 Finns. It was a great economic boom for the town of Kuhmo. A railway and a road connection were constructed and opened between Kuhmo and Kostamuksha. The border became a temporary crossing point between Finland and the Soviet Union, and in 1973–1988 there were altogether 2.5 million border crossings. On an official level this implies a real cross-border cooperation between Finland and the Soviet Union. The cooperation increased economic welfare on both sides of the border However, the cooperation remained mostly on a very formal level.

During the construction phase there was no real cooperation between people involved in the construction work or between the local communities. The cooperation remained at the official, state level, although the firms had to have day-to-day contacts. One factor that exemplifies the poor human contact is the low number of mixed marriages. In the years 1973–1984, there were only eight mixed marriages in Kostamuksha. Human contact remained on a formal level. People's knowledge about one another across the border did not increase during the project (Kinnunen 1995: 53). The workers could get together only in organized festivities. The Soviet authorities were not interested in letting people meet one another in less than official situations.

Since 1985, changes in the relations between the superpowers have been the most important prerequisites for the development of cooperation between local authorities in Finland and Russia. "Glasnost" and "Perestroika" permitted greater local-government autonomy and thus created new possibilities for local-level initiative in the Soviet Union. Theoretically, the economic reforms based on the decisions made during the 27th Party Congress also provided a framework for greater local and regional cooperation in economic development. One element of this was the extension of foreign-trade rights to authorities of border-region districts and communities. As such, local administration acquired a limited ability to engage in border region diplomacy with prospects for greater autonomy. Mikhail S. Gorbachev inaugurated a notable cooperation program for the peoples of the northern regions in Murmansk on October 1, 1987. The program was aimed at improving international relations within the greater region and the promotion of extensive cooperation at various levels in order to utilize the region's natural resources on an ecologically sustainable basis. Respect and maintenance of minority cultures was one of the guiding principles behind this envisaged cooperation.

As economic and political changes transformed the Soviet Union, the Cold War eased off, and an improvement in U.S.-Soviet relations began. Preconditions for the development of cooperation on local and regional levels in the most original and genuine spirit of the Helsinki CSCE were made possible. At the Washington, D.C., meeting of December 8, 1987, Gorbachev and Ronald Reagan exchanged opinions on measures that would expand contacts and cooperation on issues concerning northern regions. They stated their support of bilateral and regional cooperation among the "circumpolar" countries. This cooperation was to include the coordination of scientific research, nature conservation in the region, cultural cooperation, and tourism.

The INF Treaty, concluded in Washington, D.C., in December 1987, had a direct impact on the political and attitudinal latitude within which the local and regional cooperation between countries of different social systems could develop. Consequently, in his Finlandia Hall address of October 1989 in Helsinki, Gorbachev predicted the emergence of new forms of interregional cooperation stating that, in the preconditions of republic and regional cost-effectiveness, the most vigorous development would take place in the contacts of Finland and its different regions with the interior of Russia, Karelia, the Komi autonomous republic, as well as with the Soviet Baltic states. However, transboundary cooperation—as a formal policy concept—had not yet been established.

The Context of Baltic and Nordic Cooperation

As Pertti Joenniemi has mentioned elsewhere in this book, the Baltic Sea region[1] today represents a zone of post-Cold War interregional cooperation, bound together by a common, endangered waterway and natural resources. Since 1990, attempts to reverse the alarming environmental deterioration of the Baltic Sea and to promote the economic development of peripheral regions, as well as to reestablish normal working relationships among governments of East and West, have provided much of the rationale for cooperation. The Barents Euro-Arctic region in the far north also represents a new zone of cooperation between Russia and Scandinavia. Here, the Nordic countries are attempting to reconcile their environmental-development concerns with Russia's economic-development ambitions in realizing the long-term cooperative goals of sustainable-resource exploitation and pollution abatement (Holst 1993). Multilateral, interregional cooperation in these European mesoregions is a relatively new development and has only been possible with changes in the perception of the essence of national security. This is in large part due to the realization that nation-states are dependent on one another for their well-being and that the solution of transboundary environmental problems is central to the welfare of individual nation-states. In Europe, bioregionalist paradigms of transboundary and international cooperation are crucial elements in attempts to establish a future, comprehensive, spatial-planning strategy within the expanded EU.

These visionary approaches to international cooperation are evident in interregional attempts to deal with a complex array of problems ranging from water resources management and urban development to the restructuring of post-socialist economies in crisis. In a first major effort to promote a sustainable environmental and economic future for the Baltic Sea region, for example, the ministers for spatial planning and development of the 11 Baltic Sea states have agreed to a global and flexible strategy to achieve this sustainable balance, Visions and Strategies for the Baltic Sea Region (Scott 1995).

This gives evidence of increasing and multidimensional possibilities for interstate interaction, particularly at the local level. In the last few years, a plethora of *Baltic* organizations have either been newly established or expanded that clearly fit the new regionalist mold, among them the Council of Baltic Sea

Figure 1. The "Self-defined" Baltic Sea Region

States; the Helsinki Commission (for the protection of the marine environment), the Baltic Sea Chambers of Commerce Association, and the Union of Baltic Cities.

Kuhmo with Kostamuksha: Redefining the Role of the Border

With the gradual (if partial) legitimization of subnational foreign policy, functional concepts of the border and transboundary cooperation are evolving that stress the integrative and unifying potential of national boundaries. The foremost example of this is, of course, the process of integration within the EU. While much remains to be done in the Baltic and Nordic areas, a critical mass of transboundary interaction is being built up that it is hoped will overcome political and attitudinal barriers to cooperation. In addition to the interregional efforts previously mentioned, a local-level tier of transboundary cooperation is developing between "sister" cities on international borders and within more or less informal networks of partner municipalities.

Local-level cooperation on the Finnish-Russian border has slowly achieved a certain degree of political legitimacy. During the Cold War years, it was important, even necessary, to justify cooperation by referring to diplomatic arrangements agreed by both sovereign states. The 1948 Agreement of Friendship, Cooperation, and Mutual Assistance, which formally established Finland's geopolitical status as a neutral country between East and West, is today often condemned as having placed Finland in the Soviet Union's direct sphere of influence. Nevertheless, the fifth article of this document was important in that it unambiguously expressed the will of both parties to develop and expand economic and cultural relations in all respects. It should be emphasized that this Agreement manifested a desire to reduce international-security risks and that increased and more varied cooperation was seen as a means of achieving this.

With respect to city partnerships, another important interstate agreement is the long-term program (PAO), which will continue until the year 2000. It calls for concrete action in the development of trade, construction of industrial and other units, scientific-technical cooperation, as well as the fields of energy, traffic and transport, communications, environment protection, geology, and so forth. The most recent interstate point of departure is the transboundary cooperation agreement (officially known as the Nearby Region Agreement) that was signed between the Russian Federation and Republic of Finland on January 1, 1992, and ratified in August of the same year. This document marked the first time that the term *transboundary cooperation* was formally used in the context of Finnish-Russian relations. Another notable factor is that the agreement recognizes the authority of municipalities to engage in a cooperative dialogue with local governments on the other side of the border. Cooperation at the local level has acquired a wider, regional dimension and a dynamic functional position.

At present, towns and municipalities located on international borders, such as the Finnish community of Kuhmo and the Russian-Karelian city of Kostamuk-sha, seem to be very well suited for the purpose of expanding interstate coopera-tion in this phase of cautious rapprochement. It has already been mentioned that these two cities alongside the Finnish-Russian border are located in a European periphery distant from primary transportation axes and characterized by a limited economic base. Regional and urban development here, however, has been motivated by Russian resource-exploitation schemes that have necessarily in-volved Finnish expertise and labor. The growth of Kostamuksha can, in fact, be seen as a direct product of project-oriented cooperation between both coun-tries—in this case the construction of an iron ore smelting plant and worker housing in Russian Karelia (Sweedler 1994).

Both cities remain deeply concerned about their economic futures and, indeed, there are few alternatives to closer cooperation in economic and regional development issues. However, after the Kostamuksha iron ore smelter project was completed in 1985, there were no direct attempts to continue cooperation. Contractual agreements regarding further elements of the joint project, such as maintenance and municipal engineering, were not finalized. At the same time, the economic crisis of Russia has clearly demonstrated the vulnerability of Kostamuksha's economic monostructure. Because the Kostamuksha project had been an exceptional event, the idea of continuing cooperation was greeted with caution at the national level. Finnish reservations about taking advantage of the Near Region Agreement to promote local-level transboundary dialogue were, nevertheless, finally abandoned due to the gradual inclusion of Finland in the Council of Europe and its closer ties to the EU.[2]

Since 1986 and the conclusion of the iron smelter project, Kuhmo and Kostamuksha have overcome the initial shock of realization that exogenously driven economic momentum would not secure the long-term well-being of the region. They have been involved in an increasing number of joint initiatives and have promoted greater cooperation among regional firms. While the Finnish and Russian governments have partially supported these efforts, it is primarily local action and initiative that have created an atmosphere of transboundary regionalism between the two cities.

After 1985, a great deal of work at the local level was needed in order to continue regional cooperation across the border. The Perestroika in the Soviet Union gave a chance for this. In a way, cooperation had become a precondition for the welfare of Kuhmo. On the other hand, Kuhmo had something to offer Kostamuksha, which had to find a new way for surviving in the changing Soviet

Union. Therefore, the local authorities partly replaced the central state authorities and established cooperative connections based on local interests on both sides of the border.

Already in 1986 the local authorities signed an agreement on cooperation between the two sister towns. At the beginning, the agreement was more a statement of intention. Later on, it became a base for real cooperation. In 1990, a Swedish town, Robertfors, joined the cooperation, which became trilateral. New forms for border-region cooperation were explored. The initiative was moved to the local level, and the role of the state actors was minimized. However, the states were still needed. The preconditions for intensive cooperation, such as permission to cross the border, were still controlled by the states.

During the time of changes, new institutions were established. In 1987, an organization afterward called the Kuhmo Summer Academy was founded. Many new ideas and initiatives for border-region cooperation were launched in the sessions of the Summer Academy, which has been a meeting place of international scholars, local and national politicians, and bureaucrats from both sides of the border as well as representatives of grassroots organizations. Since 1988, the Summer Academy has been held in Kuhmo, Kostamuksha, and twice in Petrosavodsk, the capital of Russian Karelia. This way, the Academy has been a part of the cooperation across the border.

One of the goals in organizing the Kuhmo Summer Academy on both sides of the border was to influence state authorities, especially on the Finnish side, to make the existing customs station between Kuhmo and Kostamuksha an official crossing point. This goal was achieved the same year that Finland and Russia signed an agreement on cooperation. The very same year the foreign minister of Finland visited Kuhmo, among other border-region communities, in order to find out about already existing border-region cooperation or foreign policy of these communities. That is, Kuhmo became an example of the more decentralized and localized foreign policy of Finland.

Since 1992, however, cooperation on the local level has not become any easier than it used to be during the Soviet regime. On the Finnish side, state authorities have concentrated the financial resources devoted to regional cooperation in the hands of the state organizations. Therefore, most of the cooperation in the border region is now managed by provincial and district authorities, and it has remained formal. On a local level, cooperation has to be financed by the municipalities or local enterprises. However, the situation is still better than it was compared to the period of the Finnish-Soviet friendship. Today there already is a functioning network that interconnects Kuhmo and Kostamuksha.

On the level of enterprises, one already sees important joint ventures trying to find their place in the markets in Finland and Russia and even in the global economy. One example is Karnor, which produces wooden houses. Wood is also the base for a joint enterprise producing furniture. Another example is a plant for producing fashion textiles mostly for Russian markets. Finnish farmers are functioning as experts and consultants in developing local agriculture in the northern part of the Karelian Republic. During the Soviet period, agriculture was a neglected sector in Karelia. The revitalization of local agriculture has already given new life to some of the old Karelian villages around Kostamuksha. Also, the cultivation of the rainbow trout has been started by a joint enterprise at Lake Njuk in Russian Karelia.

Individuals and some organizations in Kuhmo have actively participated in programs that aim to revitalize the almost dead Karelian villages. These villages were a major source for the Finnish national epic, *Kalevala*, as noted earlier. Finnish activists are trying to get funding from UNESCO for maintaining and renovating these traditional villages. The idea is to get these villages into the world-heritage programs of UNESCO. One aspect of these activities is small-scale cultural tourism. Groups of 10 to 20 people will be taken into different traditional "Kalevala" villages. These tourists will then follow the footsteps of those people who collected the Karelian heritage in the region in the late nineteenth and early twentieth centuries.

Increasing tourism is one of the factors that lead to the establishment of regular bus connections between Kuhmo and Kostamuksha. The regular line goes twice a week. In addition to tourism, there are Finnish people who live in Kostamuksha where living costs are much lower than in Finland. Also, the increasing connections make it possible for those people to do part of their shopping in Kuhmo where there still is much more available than in Kostamuksha. In spite of the growing connections and increasing traffic between Kuhmo and Kostamuksha, negative effects, such as transborder-related crime, have increased only marginally.

Transboundary activities that have taken place include the establishment of a Finnish-Russian Friendship Park, cooperation in environmental studies, and a UNESCO-sponsored project for the preservation and restoration of monuments and historical buildings in Karelia. A veritable boom in transboundary traffic has taken place since 1991 with the opening up of Russian Karelia to "nostalgic tourism" (Paasi 1994). This, in turn, has intensified cultural and commercial contacts within this border region and allowed the establishment of new, inter-regional tourist services. Several Russian-Finnish joint ventures are now in operation. Furthermore, Kuhmo, along with the Finnish regional center of Kajaani, is contributing to cross-border knowledge transfer by accommodating Russian students at its technical institutes.

Action Models

Unlike the situation in Western Europe, transboundary relations on the Finnish-Russian border have not been formalized by the creation of Euroregions or other similar institutions. This is perhaps not a suitable model for local-level cooperation in this part of Europe at the moment. Instead, the main goal of this cooperation is to establish and build networks of policy coordination in various areas (economy, infrastructure, culture, environment, etc.) that can reduce the peripherality of the region. In this respect, it has proved beneficial to use existing bilateral agreements as a framework of sorts within which one- or two-year programs can be developed and carried out.

This informal exercise in regional cooperation possesses considerable potential for geographic expansion in terms of an interregional problem-solving mechanism. Kuhmo and Kostamuksha are clearly becoming more interdependent. From these two cities, the pattern of transboundary regionalism could be spread to other cities in the Nordic and Baltic regions. Interesting in this sense are the alliances developing between the northwestern towns of Russia and Scandinavia via Finland. The towns of Kuhmo, Suomussalmi, and Kuusamo are forming a mutual-border municipality strategy concerning a common line of action in order to benefit from greater economic interaction. As each municipality has its own contacts with Scandinavia and with both Eastern and Western Europe, the Finnish-Russian border-region strategy naturally involves mediating between cities outside the immediate zone of cooperation.

The long-term goal is to create an administrative-structural foundation for regional cooperation in northern regions through the establishment of East-West cooperation at the local level. Both Kuhmo and Kostamuksha are members of the League of Cities of the North, an attempt to create a network of cities in Scandinavia and Russia. The municipal partners concerned could, for example, exert pressure in obtaining assistance for the improvement of the communications network. The relations between towns and municipalities are themselves a basis for establishing the multifaceted, interregional communications necessary for economic development. Special emphasis must be put on new telecommunications and railroad infrastructure (especially between northern Finland and the Murmansk areas), as well as on international air traffic between northern Scandinavia and northern parts of Russia. The importance of the Lietmajärvi-Kotskoma railway connection for the development of the northern regions should also be stressed. It has the same importance as the St. Petersburg line did for the economic development of Finland in the 1870s.

Furthermore, the exchange of extensive expertise between partner municipalities in the fields of administration, planning, economy, and management skills is necessary. Tourism, as a form of interaction and international relations involving different layers of society, helps meet the marginal conditions for cooperation. To develop a varied communication network, it is necessary to include postal and telecommunications, roads and railway connections, air traffic, as well as satellite connections. This network is important, for example, in conducting large conferences and negotiations. Last but not least, regional cooperation is a necessary tool in the battle against possible marginalizing effects that European integration might have for regions on the EU's external boundaries.

In the event that Finish-Russian relations develop positively, it can be expected that regional cooperation will also have a chance to become more intensive. On a local level in Kuhmo, there are expectations that border-region cooperation could be a base for the economic development in Kuhmo. One of the future options is in a gateway approach. The border between Kuhmo and Kostamuksha has all the required facilities for transit and transportation. The railway already connects the Russian centers via Kuhmo and Finnish harbors to Central Europe.

In a much wider context, the border region between Russia and Finland is still a meeting place. Even today, the Eastern and Western cultures meet each other in Karelia in a fruitful way. In the context of the Europe of regions, Karelia on both sides of the border has a chance to become the region where Orthodox and Slavic Europeans meet peacefully. It is in the interest of the EU to connect Russia into Western structures and processes. Regional cooperation gives a chance for this. On the other hand, one must acknowledge that still today the infrastructure is not constructed for East-West cooperation. The existing infrastructure connects Russian Karelia to Moscow and Finnish Karelia to Helsinki.

Conclusions

Persistence and patience are required in establishing a long-term pattern of transboundary regionalism in the Finnish-Russian border region. Local-level cooperation and even neighborly interaction here still remain quite vulnerable to different populist and centralizing trends. Practice has brought us toward cooperation and interaction among associations, organizations, enterprises, and administration, and even among ordinary people. This is a good trend. But it has been, and still is, necessary that cooperation have a basis in local administrative agreements that focus directly on common interests and opportunities. Variations from this practice involving entirely open and unchanneled avenues of cooperation or exclusively centralized forms based on interstate agreements would not allow for an optimal exploitation of cooperation possibilities.

New cooperation attempts follow a new logic of interstate diplomacy. It is an approach to interregional cooperation that contrasts starkly with centralist, statist, and narrowly defined, security-obsessed attitudes that stress the primacy of national sovereignty and, until recently, of regional hegemony. Since transboundary cooperation has begun to develop, the border has taken on a new significance. A separating factor has become a connecting one, an isolating factor an integrating one. At the same time, increasing transborder interaction and cooperation between Kuhmo and Kostamuksha are creating new centers of activity. According to the international division of labor, their location near the border helps fight centralizing tendencies as well as continuously generating new economic perspectives that counteract dangers of political and economic marginalization.

Notes

1. Going from West to East these are Norway, Denmark, Germany, Sweden, Poland, Lithuania, Latvia, Estonia, Finland, and Russia (St. Petersburg and Kaliningrad districts and the Karelian Republic).
2. Among the Council of Europe's goals are the promotion of local and regional participation in European policy debate and the promotion of municipal "foreign policy" and international interaction.

References

The Baltic Institute. 1994. *Visions and Strategies Around the Baltic Sea 2010. Towards a Framework for Spatial Development in the Baltic Sea Region*. Karlskrona, Sweden: The Baltic Institute.

Holst, Johan Jørgen 1993. "The Barents Cooperation: A Regionalization Project in the Euro-Arctic Region." Statement prepared by Norway's Minister of Foreign Affairs for the Nordic Council Arctic Conference, Reykjavik (August).

Kinnunen, Perti. 1995. "A Look Across the Border. The Views and Expectations of the People in Northern Finland and North-West Russia." In *The East-West Interface in the European North*, Margareta Dahlstrom, Heikki Eskelinen, and Ulf Wiberg, eds. Uppsala, Sweden: Nordisk Samhallsgcographisk Tidskrift.

Paasi, Anssi. 1994. "The Development of the Finnish-Russian Border and its Changing Role in the Social Consciousness of the Finns." In *European Challenges and Hungarian Responses in Regional Policy*, Zoltán Hajdú and Gyula Horváth, eds. Pécs, Hungary: Center for Regional Studies.

Scott, James. 1995. "Environmental Protection and Interregional Cooperation in the Baltic Sea Region: The VASAB Initiative." Paper presented at the conference "International Boundaries and Environmental Security: Frameworks for Regional Cooperation," June, National University of Singapore (to be published).

Sweedler, Alan. 1994. "Conflict and Cooperation in Border Regions: An Examination of the Russian-Finnish Border." *Journal of Borderlands Studies* 9 (1).

Transboundary Cooperation in the Polish-German Border Region

Bohdan Gruchman
Franz Walk

1. Introduction

At present, the border between Germany and Poland along the Oder and Neisse rivers plays a double role. It is a border between two countries that historically have witnessed more hostility than friendly relations. Simultaneously, it is the border between the European Union, an international confederation of great economic potential, and Poland, one of the Central and East European countries evolving from state socialism to a much more efficient market economy. On February 1, 1994, Poland, along with Hungary, acquired the status of associated member of the EU.

Before 1945, both sides of the current border were part of the same national economic space, belonged to the same economic and administrative regions, and developed an integrated settlement system along the Oder and Neisse rivers. After 1945, and as a consequence of the Second World War, the two rivers became heavily guarded dividing lines between the German Democratic Republic (GDR) and Poland, which also became a socialist state.

For 45 years, the current border divided two countries that tried to develop their economies along the same highly centralized planning principles. Even though economic relations developed between East Germany and Poland over the years, they were largely governed by bilateral treaties between Warsaw and East Berlin and, hence, highly centralized. There was little room for direct contacts or local-level cooperation between border communities and regions. If such contacts were initiated, they were organized mainly for political and propaganda reasons with little economic effect.

There was, however, one important exception to this general rule. Due to a critical shortage of manpower, the East German authorities encouraged Poles to work in the large industrial plants located close to the border. In some localities, such as the twin cities of Guben/Gubin or Görlitz/Zgorzelec, both on the Neisse River, commuting to work became a major economic activity, even if restricted territorially.

In the 1970s, there was a brief period of relative freedom for the inhabitants of both countries to cross the frontier without a passport and visa. Owing to differences in market supply and prices, this arrangement generated an immense flow of "tourists" and subjected the local East German economies to considerable pressure. Therefore, at the request of the GDR, this experiment in open borders was soon stopped, and the intensity of direct contacts diminished rapidly to the previous restricted level.

Generally speaking, the Polish-German border was an effective obstacle to wider transfrontier cooperation between local communities. The negative consequences of this situation, which prevailed during the postwar period, were many. Regional- and local-development potential went unutilized, the scant number of border crossings restricted the flow of transboundary traffic, twin cities were divided without common utilities and infrastructure, the Oder River was neglected as a possible waterway, and ecological problems accumulated as neither side felt responsible for protecting the natural environment. Such was the inheritance from the socialist era and the situation facing Germany and Poland when, after the collapse of state socialism in 1989, possibilities for transfrontier cooperation and development were reestablished.

2. Overall Characteristics of the Polish-German Border Regions

Within the Polish-German border region one can distinguish several zones, in which certain specific features dominate. There is first the immediate border zone comprising Polish communities adjacent to the border and others neighboring them and, on the German side, the counties (hereafter referred to by their German name, *Kreise*) directly on the border (see Figure 1). It is estimated that this border zone on the Polish side covers over 8,000 km² with a population of 910,000 inhabitants (1989). On the German, side the border zone covers 9,200 km² with a population of 949,000 people (1990).[1]

Intensive border traffic is the outstanding feature of many of these areas touching the border. This traffic has two distinct components: on the one hand, there is a heavy truck flow in both directions generated by the expanding trade between Poland and Germany and in transit between the European Union and

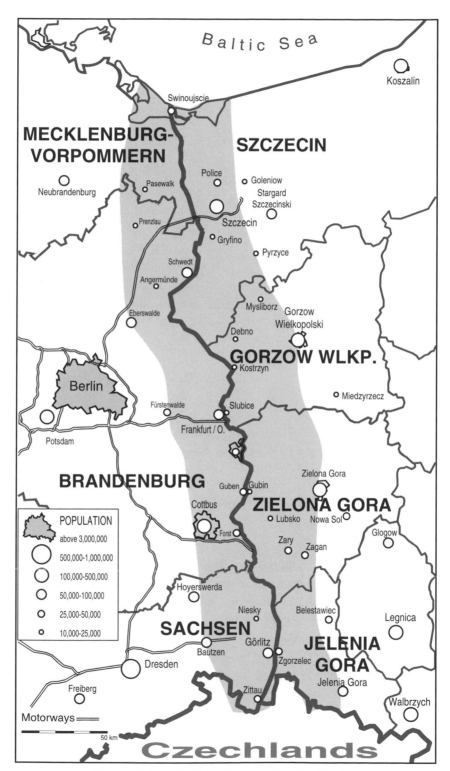

Figure 1. The Polish-German Border Region

Russia and other East European countries. On the other hand, there is currently heavy local traffic generated by considerable price differences for consumer goods. Prices on the Polish side are generally much lower than on the German side. Hence, inhabitants of German border areas commute regularly to expanding trade centers on the nearby Polish side, leaving there considerable amounts of deutsch marks. This is particularly true with regard to a number of twin cities, which before 1945 were developing as single entities and now belong to different national spaces.

The second border zone extends much deeper inland on both sides of the frontier. On the Polish side it covers entire *voivodeships* (administrative districts of the second order) adjacent to the border (including the previously mentioned communes), such as the *voivodeships* of Szczecin, Gorzow, Zielona Gora, and Jelenia Gora. They cover an area of 32,000 km^2, approximately 10 percent of the area of Poland. This entire area has 2.7 million inhabitants, or 7 percent of the entire Polish population.

On the German side, it is more difficult to trace a similar second order-border zone. Nowadays, this zone includes certainly the new larger *Kreis* created by reforms introduced in 1993. They cover an area of 19,500 km^2 (approximately twice that of the previous border counties), with a total population of 1.6 million inhabitants (about 60 percent more than previously). The major decisions regarding transboundary cooperation are taken in the capitals of the border Länder-Mecklenburg Vorpommern, Brandenburg, and Sachsen; in Schwerin, Potsdam and Dresden. On the Polish side, all similar major decisions have to be undertaken by the Polish government in Warsaw, as the governors of the *voivodeships* have limited discretionary power. This asymmetry in the administrative divisions of the border areas and, more importantly, in the decision-making powers on each administrative level on both sides of the border, is a major obstacle to more effective direct cooperation.

Finally, there is the wider hinterland of the border zones that in many ways plays a backup role in transboundary cooperation. This is particularly true with regard to the development of institutions of higher education, scientific research, and various research and development (R&D) centers. On the German side, the scientific landscape after 1990 has been substantially changed. New academic institutions have been organized, among them the European University "Viadrina" in Frankfurt (Oder). The institutions of higher learning and research on the Polish side have existed for a longer period, but many of them need strengthening and incorporating into an international network of similar institutions. Thus, from this point of view, the hinterland of the border areas stretches on the Polish side beyond the scientific center of Szczecin to the university cities of Poznán and Wroclaw. On the German side, cooperation networks of higher education extend at least to Berlin (only 100 km away from the border) and Dresden.

The entire border area, both at the macro and microregional levels, is currently in a process of deep structural change. This has particularly affected industrial and agricultural enterprises as well as public utilities—institutions and organizations developed under a centralized-command economy. On the German side, rapid privatization of mostly large enterprises has been carried out by the special trust agency or *Treuhand*. In the course of this process, production profiles have been changed dramatically and the number of employees substantially reduced. A good illustration of this process is the huge EKO steelworks in Eisenhüttenstadt, located close to the border. Here, the work force was reduced from over 10,000 persons to slightly over 2,000. In agriculture, the often highly specialized collective farms have been dissolved, with the land and buildings offered to private farmers and other entrepreneurs.

On the Polish side, industry, with the exception of Szczecin, was not as well developed as on the other side of the border. Small-scale and middle-sized enterprises were dominant. The privatization process of the latter has been slower than on the German side, but, on the other hand, Polish privatization has been characterized by rapid growth in new private enterprises. While there were no collective farms in Poland, the share of land belonging to state-owned farms was relatively high along the border, necessitating a parallel privatization process on a scale unknown in other parts of Poland.

The restructuring process on both sides of the border has brought with it high unemployment. Measured against the Polish national average of 15.7 percent at the end of 1993, unemployment reached 14 percent in Szczecin, 21.2 percent in Gorzow, 18.1 percent in Zielona Gora, and 18.6 percent in Jelenia Gora.[2] On the German side, with an average of 17.1 percent unemployed for all new *Länder* as of February 1994 (compared with only 8.9 percent for the old *Länder*), unemployment rates stood at 19.2 percent for Mecklenburg-Vorpommern, 17 percent for Brandenburg, and 17.3 percent for Saxony.[3]

Unemployment on both sides of the border is primarily a consequence of the transformation process, but it is also the consequence of the marginalization of the border region during the postwar period. Transboundary cooperation is presently looked upon as a means to improve locational advantages, create new jobs and, hence, reduce out-migration. A more area-specific approach to such cooperation is, thus, required.

3. The Establishment of Euroregions

After an initial period of individual and often intensive day-to-day contacts across the border among various administrative entities, economic and social institutions, enterprises, and local governments on both sides of the border began to systematize and institutionalize their mutual cooperation. They followed the example of existing Euroregions that cover border areas of member states of the European Union, particularly those established between Germany, on the one hand, and Holland, Belgium, and France, on the other.[4] However, many West European arrangements, developed within the framework of European integration, have proved nontransferable, particularly in view of Poland's nonmembership of the EU.[5]

The Neisse-Nysa Euroregion

This Euroregion was the first to be established in February 1992, as a follow-up to a three-country cooperation conference held in May 1991. It covers adjacent areas of approximately 12,000 km² with a population of 1.6 million along the borders of Germany, Poland, and the Czech Republic (of this, the German part covers 4,378 km² with 518,000 inhabitants). The legal framework has been established by the autonomous territorial administrative units: on the German side it is the Association "Kommunalgemeinschaft Euroregion Neisse—Sektor BR Deutschland," on the Polish side an association comprising 40 communes of the Jelenia Gora *voivodeship*, and finally on the Czech side a similar communal union. Together, all three parties form a 30-member Council of the Euroregion that is headed by a presidency of three persons. In order to deal with separate, different issues affecting the region, seven working groups have been established. The common seat of the Euroregion with its secretariat is located in Zittau (Germany).

The Neisse-Nysa Euroregion is relatively well represented by mining and industry: open-pit lignite mines with electricity works on the German and Polish sides, glass and construction materials in all three parts, textiles and clothing industry on the German and Czech sides, as well as engineering, electrotechnical, and metal industries in each zone. Currently, industrial enterprises are undergoing substantial transformation adapting themselves to new market conditions. Transboundary cooperation, particularly with respect to technological innovation, will help many to survive and to grow. In all three parts, agriculture plays a relatively minor role while tourism is a major sector with considerable potential for future development, particularly since the Euroregion is strategically located along the transportation route, linking southern Europe with Scandinavia. One major problem in this part of Europe is heavy air pollution (power plants) and damage done to the environment (open-pit mining). Therefore, measures to protect the environment are high on the action agenda of the Euroregion's Council.

The Pomerania Euroregion

This Euroregion was created informally in November 1992, through agreements between respective German and Polish municipal associations.[6] On the German side, membership consisted of nine *Kreise* and townships from Brandenburg. The communal association on the Polish side includes 54 communes and towns of the Szczecin *voivodeship*. The total area of the Pomerania Euroregion is over 17,000 km² with approximately 1.5 million inhabitants.[7]

With the exception of the Szczecin industrial agglomeration, the entire area represents a peripheral zone in need of development. Nature is still relatively unspoiled in many parts of the region, particularly along the Oder River where plans to establish a nature park on both sides of the border are being implemented. The seacoast of the region is a valuable asset as a holiday area. Industry is represented primarily by shipyards. Cooperation potential in higher education and research exists between Szczecin with its 25,000 students and the German university centers along the Baltic coast of Greifswald and Rostock and also Berlin, which is only some 120 km away.

There are plans to extend the Pomerania Euroregion to the north in order to include the nearby territorial units of Denmark (the island of Bornholm) and Sweden. Regular daily ferryboat connections bring the latter close to the Polish and German parts of the Euroregion.

The Spree-Neisse-Bober (Szprewa-Nysa-Bobr) Euroregion

This Euroregion was formally launched on September 21, 1993. The German founders included three *Kreise* and the cities of Cottbus and Eisenhüttenstadt. On the Polish side, members included 18 cities and communities belonging to a municipal association in the *voivodeship* of Zielona Góra. The total area is close to 7,500 km² of which two-thirds are located on the Polish side.[8] The main centers of the region are the industrial, commercial, and service cities of Cottbus and Zielona Góra. For twin cities such as Guben/Gubin, where demand for common infrastructural facilities is particularly great, the creation of the Euroregions promises to be especially beneficial.

The area of the region has soil of relatively poor quality. More than half of the entire territory is covered by forests. On the German side, the dominant economic activity is exploitation of brown coal in open pits and subsequently production of electricity in several power plants. Industry is represented by iron and steel works, glass, chemical, construction materials, and machine industries. On the Polish side textile, wood-processing, construction materials, and metal-working industries dominate. These are generally smaller than their German counterparts and therefore more adaptable to the difficulties of transformation.

The region is blessed with natural amenities conducive to the promotion of tourism, including large wooded areas with numerous lakes. It has some tourism infrastructure, which is in need of modernization and extension in order to attract more tourists from nearby Berlin, Poznán, and elsewhere. It is hoped that coordinated actions in this field, and also in other areas of the economy, will bring synergy effects to both sides of the border.

The Pro-Europa Viadrina Euroregion

This is the last transboundary association to have been established (formally or informally) along the Polish-German frontier. It was founded on December 21, 1993, by the association "Mittlere Oder e. V.," whose original members were the cities of Frankfurt (Oder) and Eisenhüttenstadt and four counties. On the Polish side, founders of the new Euroregion are the community associations of Ziemia Lubuska and Gorzow. The entire Pro-Europa Viadrina Euroregion (Viadrina is the Latin name of the Oder River) covers an area of 9,730 km^2 with a population of 795,000 inhabitants.[9]

The economy of the Euroregion is strongly differentiated. Its main centers on the German side are Frankfurt (Oder), Eisenhüttenstadt, Fürstenwalde, Bad Freienwalde, and Seelow. On the Polish side, the centers are Gorzów, Kostrzyn, Sulecin, Debno, and the Polish counterpart of the German city of Frankfurt, Slubice.

The industry of the area is represented by the following: wood processing, paper and printing, engineering, electrotechnology, textiles, clothing, leather, food processing, and chemicals. Agriculture plays an important role on both sides of the border. All these sectors and branches are currently undergoing substantial changes connected with privatization and technological transformation within their respective national spaces. An unwanted result of these changes is a relatively high level of unemployment and underutilized industrial and agricultural potential on both sides of the border.

The aim of the Euroregion is to change this situation through coordinated action and the pooling of available resources. The Euroregion should also benefit from the fact that it is situated along the main East-West route. Work is under way to improve the existing congested border crossing (primarily at Frankfurt/Swiecko) and to establish new ones.

Figure 2. Objectives of the Pro-Europa Viadrina Euroregion

Overall Objective				
Improvement of Living Standards and Economic Performance and the Promotion of European Integration by Creating an Integrated Transboundary Region				

Primary Objectives				
Strengthening Regional Potential and Reduction of Unemployment		Promoting Good Neighborliness	Promoting a Regional Identity	Promoting the Cause of European Integration
Economic Cooperation	Environment and Infrastructure			

Individual Objectives				
1. Establishment of integrated site development procedures	1. Creation of a transboundary commercial transport network	1. Short-term measures to increase capacities of border crossing points	1. Cooperation in urban land use planning and in development of rural areas	1. Establishment of new institutions affiliated with and managed by the Euroregion
2. Promotion of transboundary business cooperation	2. Modern cross-border communications infrastructure	2. Joint German-Polish public events and cultural and sports activites	2. Promotion of social, cultural, and recreational infrastructure	2. Optimal utilization of available programs, initiatives, and grants from EU
3. Development of tourism	3. Joint energy, water, and waste disposal management schemes	3. Establishment of regional German-Polish institutions of research and education	3. Establishment of a process of transboundary regional planning	3. Hosting of regional events that publicize the EU and its activities
4. Establishment of German-Polish business associations	4. Introduction of European environmental norms	4. Public relations measures to popularize the idea of cooperation	4. Establishment of professional methods of urban and regional marketing	4. Cooperation with European institutions: European Parliament & Commission, Council of Europe, etc.
5. Promotion of innovation and technological development	5. Integration of concepts for transboundary environmental and natural area protection	5. Measures to support international significance of the Europa-University in Frankfurt (Oder)	5. Decentralized development	5. Cooperation with other Euroregions on the German-Polish border
	6. Protection of the Oder River and its biotopes		6. Initiation of education programs that increase cultural knowledge and language proficiencies	

Source: Software Union (1993), Wissenschaftliches Arbeitsgemeinschaft Politikberatung WAGP, Berlin (1992)

A major development with far-reaching consequences for the future has been the opening in October 1992 of the Europa University Viadrina in Frankfurt (Oder) with at least a one-third Polish student body. Just across the Oder River in Slubice work has already begun to establish a Collegium Polonicum, which will be part of the Viadrina University. With a sizable foreign faculty, this university will help not only to change the scientific landscape of the border area, but also to transform the economy of the region.

4. The Scope and Level of Transboundary Cooperation

A noteworthy feature of the new Euroregions is that they have been established by voluntary associations of local territorial units equipped with a certain degree of autonomy, such as communes, and on the German side also by *Kreise* adjacent to the border. Unfortunately, the latter have since been abolished with the creation of new larger counties. The new counties need to be incorporated into the existing framework in order to strengthen the legal base of the Euroregions.

It is at the municipal level that transboundary cooperation along the Polish-German frontier can take concrete shape. This is the conclusion one can draw from the following list of major goals and tasks for implementation in the border regions (see Figure 2). This list is a synthesis of various development schemes prepared for the Pro-Europa Viadrina Euroregion since 1992.[10] The hitherto formulated goals and tasks for the other Euroregions largely coincide with this list so that the goals and tasks listed on the chart can be regarded as representative for all Euroregions along the Polish-German border.

In order to contribute to the establishment of the common European area, seven main goals have been set for the Polish-German frontier regions. They include economic and infrastructural aspects as well as cultural, political, and environmental ones. The main goals are subdivided into concrete tasks that, in turn, can be implemented through detailed action programs. The goals and objectives defined by the four Polish-German Euroregions also reveal a high degree of consistency. These reflect rather well the specific situation along the Polish-German border.

Although the main role in Polish-German transboundary cooperation is assigned to the municipalities, there is need to support their actions from above, both from the regional as well as the central levels. This has been done until now by the existing Polish-German Intergovernmental Commission. The Commission is comprised of two committees: one devoted specifically to transboundary cooperation, with its members representing Polish *voivodeships* and German *Länder* situated along the common frontier, and the other dealing with interregional cooperation with members representing similar units from the remaining territory of both countries.

The Intergovernmental Commission has, among other things, worked out coordinated schemes for the expansion of border crossing points, now being implemented—albeit slowly—by the respective regional authorities. It has also been instrumental in the establishment in March 1994 of a special Polish-German Economic Development Association (Polsko-Niemieckie Stowarzyszenie Wspierania Gospodarki) that operates as a limited company according to Polish law. The main task of the Association is the elaboration of a development program for the entire Polish-German border area and support of individual projects and schemes important for transboundary cooperation. Financial support is available from special funds set aside for the Association by the following banks: The German Kreditanstalt für Wiederaufbau (KfW) and the Polish banks Polski Bank Rozwoju, Wielkopolski Bank Kredytowy (WBK), and Pomorski Bank Kredytowy. The seat of the Association is in Gorzów. Its operations are supervised by a joint Polish-German board of directors.

5. Programs of the European Union

The work that remains to be done along the Polish-German border is considerable. It requires strong popular support, the active involvement of many enterprises and institutions operating in the area, and no small amount of outside assistance. Such assistance within the European Union is channeled through Structural Funds, Action Programs, and other schemes especially designed to help in the development of border regions. However, since Poland is not a member of the European Union, border-region development schemes already in operation must be reconsidered and/or modified to accommodate the particular situation of the Polish-German border. Fortunately, the European Union seems determined to bridge the gap between it and the adjacent areas of non-Union members.[11]

Among the EU programs, INTERREG II (1995–1999) should prove particularly helpful. It is targeted for border regions both within the European Union and at its external boundaries. INTERREG II allows for the pooling of EU regional aid and regional grants destined for Central European states and, thus, (theoretically) for equal participation of Poland and Germany in border-region projects. Its general aim is to help solve development difficulties stemming from isolation from growth poles within particular countries. In particular, this program contains measures to help Euroregions. With reference to those on the outskirts of the European Union, such measures deal with local infrastructure, the protection of the environment, technology transfer, and also foreign travel and agrotourism. This program belongs within the category of EU initiatives.

Applications for assistance have to be directed to the European Commission through the respective national governments.

A different category, the "Action Programs," is represented by OUVER-TURE/ECOS. Its aim is to support the cooperation between regions and cities of the European Union with those in Eastern Europe. This program is particularly focused on the development of local economies, the improvement of local administration, and regional and urban planning. In addition, it assists in environmental protection. In order to benefit from this program, cooperating applicants must represent at least two territorial units from the European Union and one from a Central or East European country. Here again, applications must be submitted directly to Brussels.

A similar procedure with cooperating territorial units from at least three EU countries is required in order to benefit from another Action Program that supports exchange of experience (PEE) between local and regional territorial units. Here, the priority is given to know-how exchange in the implementation of EU policies toward public administration, the transport sector, applied research and technology, cooperation of academic institutions and enterprises, local resources, energy, and the environment. In addition to this, support can also cover the organization of fairs, seminars, exhibitions, and the hiring of experts and consultants.

There are also programs to promote particular industrial sectors or cooperation in specific policy areas. For example, Action Programs exist for the promotion of tourism, the development of transboundary environment policies (LIFE), and the restructuring of areas hitherto specialized in the textile and clothing industry (RETEX). All three programs are highly relevant to the Polish-German border regions.

Finally, one should mention here the PHARE program, a scheme of the European Union especially launched to assist Central and East European countries in their transformation to a market economy. Originally conceived as a technical-assistance program in various areas (e.g., in developing privatization programs, restructuring the banking system, reforming agriculture), it has evolved into a program substantially supporting selected areas. For 1994, the total amount of PHARE assistance to Poland was 305 million ECU.[12] Although the involvement of PHARE assistance is still directed according to sectoral and not territorial principles, two of its subprograms can be relevant to the transboundary cooperation along the Polish-German frontier.

The first is the subprogram STRUDER through which the European Union is assisting Polish regions with high unemployment. The first installment of STRUDER assistance did not include any of the border areas, since the highest unemployment regions are situated elsewhere in Poland. However, it may indirectly influence the labor market of the *voivodeship* of Jelenia Góra because it covers the nearby coal-mining region of Walbrzych. There is a high possibility that in the future, with an increase in PHARE assistance, the latter will also include selected areas of the border zone.

The other PHARE subprogram is TEMPUS, established to help institutions of higher education in Central and East European countries to modernize curricula and to prepare teaching staff accordingly. TEMPUS requires the participation of at least two universities from EU countries with one or more academic institutions from Central and East European countries. Under this program, there is an opportunity to establish academic institutions from the Polish-German border regions. Some are already in operation, such as the one linking the European University Viadrina and the University of Bochum with the universities of Wroclaw, Poznán, and Szczecin.

Outside assistance granted under the previously mentioned program or others can be of great help to transboundary cooperation. However, it remains limited in comparison to perceived needs. The main support has to come from internal sources: within the border regions or from other parts of the country. Given the relatively low level of economic activity along the Polish-German frontier, assistance from the countries' interiors becomes crucial. In this respect, the German side is in a much better position than the Polish one. Currently, the Polish economy generates little capital for investment, and the priorities of the government's regional-development policies lie elsewhere.

6. Concluding Remarks

The process of transforming the Polish-German frontiers from a barrier to a vital link between two countries is not an easy one. Many problems mentioned earlier have to be solved before marked progress can be achieved. There is no other way than systematically improve locational factors in the border regions and to strengthen them through consistent and coordinated policies on both sides of the frontier. To this effect, it is particularly important that the frontier should be made more permeable. In practical terms, this requires more border crossings to be opened as soon as possible, existing ones improved, and border crossing procedures streamlined. Another crucial task is the development of the settlement systems on both sides of the border in a coherent fashion so that settlements of regional importance can be assigned functions serving both sides of the border.

The crucial role in all these endeavors must be played by the towns and communities on both sides of the frontier zone. They have been the founding fathers of existing Euroregions. The future of the latter will greatly depend on how they will continue to function and grow. It is at the local level that synergy effects can best be generated that may be decisive for future development. This is particularly true with the encouragement of innovations, a vital element of the contemporary framework of regional development.[13] The Polish-German border area fulfills many preconditions for such local development. However, necessary links to international-innovation networks can be established, exploiting the increasing flows of people and goods that daily cross border region areas in all directions

Notes

1. According to IAW (1992: 10).

2. GUS (1994: 129). Data calculated as percentage of economically active persons.

3. *Berliner Morgenpost*, 9 March 1994/H.

4. The beginnings of transboundary cooperation in these areas can be traced back several decades. See: *Èconomie Régionale sans Frontiere, Actes du Colloque Scientifique Belgo-Allemand d'économie Régionale*, Liege October 1965, Editions Sciences et Lettres, Liege.

5. This situation formally resembles that existing along the Swiss-Italian border. Compare: Alberto Bramanti and Remigio Ratti (1993).

6. At the time of editing this manuscript, August 1995, no Pomerania Euroregion as yet formally exists.

7. Econometrica GmbH (1993).

8. See Dormier Deutsche Aerospace (1993: 14).

9. According to Software Union GmbH (1993: 21).

10. Among others, a special working group of representatives of various institutions and associations under the leadership of Professor Franz Walk from the Free University of Berlin, were involved (Walk 1993).

11. This is the main conclusion of a Commission of European Communities' study written by Dieter Höbler (1993).

12. According to *Rzeczpospolita*, a daily dated 1 April 1994.

13. See Remigio Ratti (1992).

References

Bramanti, Alberto, and Remigio Ratti. 1993. *Verso un' Europa delle Regioni. La cooperazione economica transfrontaliera come opportunita e sfida* (Toward a Europe of the Regions. Opportunities and Challenges of Transboundary Economic Cooperation). Milano: Franco Angeli.

Dormier Deutsche Aerospace. 1993. *Entwicklungs- und Handlungskonzept für die Euroregion Spree-Neisse-Bober* (Development and Strategic Concept for the Euroregion Spree-Neiße-Bobr). DDA: Friedrichshafen.

Econometrica GmbH. 1993. *Europaregion Pomerania. Operationelles Programm* (Europaregion Pomerania. Operational Program). Berlin: Econometrica.

GOPA-Gesellschaft für Organisation, Planung und Ausbildung GmbH. 1991. *Förderkonzept Oder-Raum* (Development Concept for the Oder-Region). Berlin: BG-Berlin-Consult.

GUS (Central Statistical Office of Poland). 1994. *Buletyn Statystyczny*. Rovznik XXXVI (Statistical Bulletin 36). Warsaw.

Höbler, Dieter. 1992. *Renewal versus Decline—The Changing Face of the German New Länder and their Eastern European Neighbours* (Fast Dossier: Continental Europe Science, Technology and Community Cohesion, vol. 3). Brussels: European Commission.

Institut für Angewandte Wirtschaftsforschung e. V (IAW). 1992. *Die deutsch-polnischen Grenzgebiete als regionalpolitisches Problem* (The German-Polish Border Regions as a Regional Policy Problem). IAW Forschungsreihe 2.

Ratti, Remigio. 1992. *Innovation technologique et développement regional; Base théoretique et étude de cas* (Technological Innovation and Regional Development: Theoretical Foundations and a Case Study). Bellinzona, Méta-Editors S.A.

Software Union GmbH. 1993. *Entwicklungs- und Handlungskonzept für die Euroregion Pro Europa Viadrina* (Development and Strategic Concept for the Euroregion Pro Europa Viadrina). Software Union: Berlin.

Stasiak, Andrzej, and Krzysztof Miros, eds. 1993. "Podstawy rozwoju zachodnich I wschodnich obszarow przygranicznych Polski" (Aspects of the Development of Regions on Poland's Eastern and Western Borders). *Bulletin of the Polish Academy of Sciences*, Institute of Geography and Spatial Economy 1 (May).

Walk, Franz, ed. 1993a. *Europa-Region im Deutsch-Polnischen Grenzgebiet*. Institut für kommunale Politikberatung und regionale Entwicklung, FU Berlin Schriftenreihe B, Heft 1.

Walk, Franz, ed. 1993b. *Wirtschaftsentwicklung im deutsch-polnischen Grenzgebiet* (Economic Development in the German-Polish Border Region). Working Papers of the Institute of Communal Policy and Regional Development (Free University of Berlin) Series B (3).

Walk, Franz. 1993. "Mutations de l'espace économique et politique de la région frontaliere germano-polonaise et de Kaliningrad" (Changes in Economic and Political Space along the German-Polish Border). *Les Cahiers de L'Observatoire de Berlin*, Centre Franco-Allemand de Recherches en Sciénces Sociales 25 (November).

Walk, Franz. 1994. *Grenzüberschreitende Zusammenarbeit im deutsch-polnischen Grenzgebiet, Zusammenfassende Darstellung aus deutscher Sicht* (Transboundary Cooperation on the German-Polish Border from a German Perspective). Unpublished manuscript.

Winiarski, Boleslaw. 1993. "Zachodnie regiony Polski—Szanse I zagrozenia" (Western Regions of Poland: Opportunities and Dangers), in Kuklinski, Antoni (ed.). *Polonia, quo vadis?*, Studias Regionalne I Lokalne, 12 (45), Warsaw: University of Warsaw (European Institute of Regional and Local Development).

Emerging Conflict or Deepening Cooperation? The Case of the Hungarian Border Regions

Zoltán Hajdú

1. Introduction

Border-related issues and transboundary cooperation are of particular significance to Hungary. In a sense, the whole country can be considered a "borderlands society." Out of Hungary's 19 counties, only five do not share borders with a neighboring state. Even the capital city, Budapest, with a population of two million, is located only 50 kilometers from the present-day Hungarian-Slovakian border.

The preservation, and, in some cases, establishment of relatively open state borders has been and remains a question of national political importance. It is especially important for the survival of those Hungarian minorities who found themselves citizens of foreign countries after the signing of the Trianon Peace Treaty and the subsequent dissolution of Hungary's historical borders in 1920. Since Trianon, transboundary cooperation between Hungary and its neighbors has been rather slow to develop. Throughout the period of state socialism (1949–1989), bilateral frontier cooperation was generally not very intensive. Concepts for trilateral border development on the Hungarian-Czechoslovak-Soviet and Hungarian-Czechoslovak-Austrian borders, proposed with the aim of deepening socialist territorial integration or as a gesture of good will and *détente*, could not be implemented due to the stubborn insularity of socialist economic and planning policy.

The changes since 1989 as well as Hungary's intention to join the European Union make necessary new approaches to transboundary cooperation in this part of Europe. Along with the other former socialist countries, Hungary must solve its historical problems as well as clarify the status of national minorities and find new and peaceful forms of coexistence with its neighbors.

2. Geopolitics and Hungary's State Borders: The Historical Tumults of the Twentieth Century

Generally speaking, Hungary's borders were, from the establishment of the Christian kingdom in 996 until the end of World War I, relatively stable. These borders, defined by the natural barrier of the Carpathian mountains, were, in fact, among the most permanent in Europe. This permanence is still embedded in Hungary's collective consciousness: the concept of the "Thousand Year Border" has consequently formed an important part of national policy. By contrast, the most characteristic features of twentieth-century Hungarian history have been frequent and radical changes in national boundaries. For this reason, border-related issues have become a crucial element of Hungarian domestic and foreign policy, as well as of social and political geography.

The present Hungarian state borders have only a short history. The Austro-Hungarian Empire was one of the powers suffering defeat in World War I and was literally torn asunder in compliance with the interests of the great powers. At the same time that the Empire ceased to exist, Hungary recovered its independence, but only about one-third of its original territory. Ultimately, six states received a share of the former Hungary: Austria, Czechoslovakia, Yugoslavia, Poland, Italy, and Romania. Of the 325,411 km^2 once occupied by Hungary, only 92,833 km^2 remained within Hungarian sovereignty after 1920. Similarly, the number of inhabitants decreased from 20,886,387 to only 7,606,971.

The multiethnic Hungarian state was split up in such a way that the new post-Empire states (Czechoslovakia, Yugoslavia, and Romania) also became multinational. As a consequence, the characteristics of Hungary's borders changed fundamentally. The historical Hungarian state, largely delimited by natural boundaries, had after 1920 only two physical boundaries, the Danube and Drava rivers. The entire length of the Hungarian-Romanian border, for instance, was politically and thus artificially determined (Palotás 1990). With regard to ethnography, only the Hungarian-Austrian state border coincided entirely with natural linguistic borders; about 60 percent of Hungary's borders (that is, virtually all of the Hungarian-Slovak, four-fifths of the Hungarian-Romanian, and 30 percent of the border with the former Yugoslavia) cover linguistically and culturally cohesive regions.

Before and during World War II, Hungary's borders were again—if only temporarily—revised. In 1937, the length of Hungarian state borders was 2,266 km. In 1938, the First Vienna Decision transferred control of the southern zone of the former Upper Hungary and Sub-Carpathia from Czechoslovakia back to Hungary, so that the length of the state borders increased to 2,734 km. In 1940, as a result of the Second Vienna Decision, Northern Transylvania, ceded to Romania by Trianon, was reincorporated into the Hungarian state. With the collapse of the Yugoslav state after Hitler's invasion in 1941, Hungary regained territory in the south as well, as a result of which the length of its borders increased to 3,491 km. After the Second World War the borders created in 1920 were reestablished. The Paris Peace Treaty, signed between Hungary and the allied powers, not only abrogated the Vienna Decisions but also ceded three additional settlements of the Pozsony (Bratislava) district to Czechoslovakia (see Figure 1).

These radical border changes have also been accompanied by important political rearrangements affecting Hungary's neighbors. As a part of the Austro-Hungarian Monarchy, Hungary bordered only on Romania and Serbia. After the territorial changes of 1920, Austria, Czechoslovakia, and Yugoslavia became Hungary's new neighbors. Austria itself became, as a result of the Anschluss in 1938, a part of the German Reich until 1945. During the spring of 1939, Slovakia declared its independence for the first time. Furthermore, with the disintegration of Yugoslavia in 1941, Serbia was occupied by Germany, and Croatia became an independent state on Hungary's southern border. After the Second World War, Sub-Carpathia was ceded to the Soviet Union, making the USSR a "Carpathian basin country" for the first time in its history and, for more than four decades, Hungary's dominant neighbor.

As a result of the recent political and economic changes in Central and Eastern Europe, Hungary's surroundings have yet again completely changed. Through the disintegration of Czechoslovakia, Slovakia again became a neighbor as an independent state, as did Ukraine after the breakup of the Soviet Union and Serbia, and as did Croatia and Slovenia after the collapse of the former (socialist) Yugoslavia. Besides the changes of state borders and surroundings, the fundamental and continual changes in the position that Hungary has occupied in the European power structure should be noted. The Austro-Hungarian Monarchy ranked as a European great power during the first decade of the twentieth century. Historical Hungary played an important geopolitical role within Europe. Geographically the sixth largest country in Europe, it had the seventh largest population. By comparison, the new Hungary of 1920 occupied only fifteenth place in terms of territory and eleventh in terms of population within the European concert of nations.

In the period between the two world wars, Hungary's primary political ambition—if not obsession—was to regain lost national territory. The unambiguous proclamation of this goal necessarily turned its neighbors against Hungary. They naturally sought to keep the acquired territories in their possession. How-

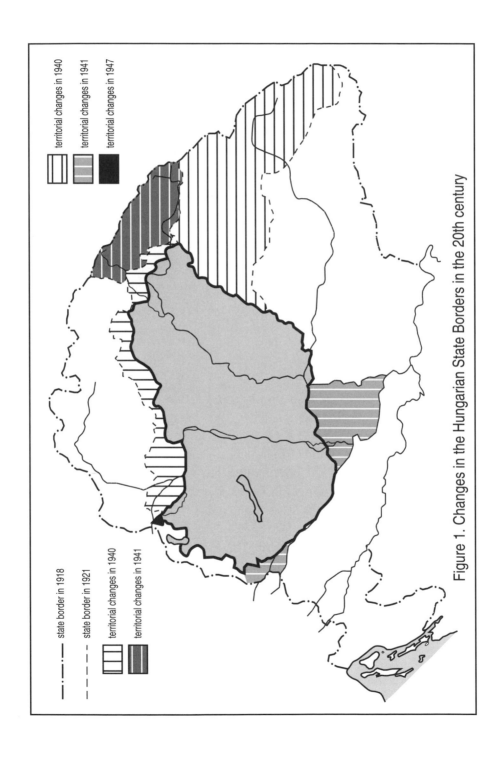

Figure 1. Changes in the Hungarian State Borders in the 20th century

ever, there was no real military force behind Hungarian revisionist aims. Hungary, weaker than any of its neighbors, found itself surrounded by a more or less unified group determined to keep it at bay. Consequently, Hungary was only able to achieve its goals working within German and, to a lesser extent, Italian power politics. This help from the axis powers eventually compromised Hungary, leading to German occupation in 1944, to repeated defeat in war and, finally, to the occupation by the Soviet army. Thus, after World War II, Hungary became a part of the Soviet Union's zone of influence, first as an occupied country and later as a member of the socialist political, economic, and security community. Border-region issues were not openly discussed among the socialist countries, the political vocabulary having acquired the ideological terminology of "socialist friendship and cooperation."

For a variety of historical and geopolitical reasons, the concept of a "borderlands situation" is currently enjoying wide application in Hungarian scientific literature. There are about 320 settlements and cities—about 10 percent of all Hungarian settlements—located directly along the 2,242 km-long state borders. These are considered, in a sociological sense, as "frontier settlements." The main social and economic characteristics of these settlements are determined by the border (Kovács 1993). Hungarian military geography (Kozma et al. 1993) theoretically considers a 25 km-wide strip along the state border as a topographical zone, and a 50 km-wide strip as a strategic borderland area, defining both as danger zones. This consideration appeared in our modern history many times, especially in the 1950s. Hungarian settlement and borderland development policy and practice were influenced by this theory.

3. Borderland Situations in the Period of State Socialism (1949–1989)

During the period of state socialism, the country's political-geographic situation and the nature of its state borders were determined by many different actors. Among them were the effects of Soviet hegemony in Hungary's external affairs, the Cold War and the evolution of a bipolar world, and, later, the process of *détente*. Crises and changes within the socialist bloc (the exclusion of Yugoslavia at the end of the 1940s, the Czechoslovak crisis in 1968, and the independent policy-making of Romania), as well as events in Hungary (the revolution of 1956 and the economic reforms in 1968), also had considerable impact on Hungary's political status. Finally, the economic crisis and internal liberalization at the end of the 1980s, processes that spelled the end for state socialism, again changed the political environment in and around Hungary.

In the period of state socialism, the possible fields of cooperation between regional administrative units were strictly defined by the centralized state. Contacts between borderland areas were determined, beyond the global international surroundings, by prevailing bilateral interstate relations. Similarly, central governments determined the ability of citizens to cross international borders and implemented strict controls on travel during the first years of socialist rule. The state was the main player in economic life and, at the same time, the initiator and supervisor of business contacts as well.

Within COMECON, basically a socialist version of the European Common Market, the issue of common development initiatives for the borderland areas of member states was first raised in 1960. A report delineating various aims of border-regional development was published in the early 1960s and submitted for official consideration by COMECON within the framework of the so-called Complex Program. The Complex Program was a long-range development plan for COMECON countries that included a problem-oriented approach to border regions. However, no real attempt was made to promote or even emphasize the importance of day-to-day contacts within international border regions.

Functional Changes of the Hungarian-Austrian Border

In 1945, the Austrian territories adjacent to Hungary were occupied by the Soviets. At this point, the Hungarian-Austrian borderlands were controlled by the same foreign power. The internal role of the occupying army, however, differed considerably in the two countries. Intervention in the internal affairs and in the economic development of Austria was significantly more moderate than in Hungary's case. Austria was relatively *free*, and its borders were *open* toward the West. After the takeover of power by the Communists in 1948–1949, Hungary's relations with Austria deteriorated, adversely affecting the common border areas.

After the Austrian treaty in 1955, the occupying Soviet troops were withdrawn from Austria, which regained its sovereignty and became an independent but neutral country within the capitalist system. Its 356-km common border with socialist Hungary became an almost completely impenetrable frontier between the capitalist and socialist worlds. The Iron Curtain came down and all along the border minefields were set. The border checkpoints of Hegyeshalom and Sopron were maintained only for managing the international rail and road traffic, itself reduced to a minimum.[1] The first cracks in the Iron Curtain appeared during the Hungarian Revolution of 1956, even if for only a very short time. The borders were opened, and more than 200,000 people emigrated.

From 1960 onwards, Hungarian-Austrian relations gradually improved, although positive effects of this improvement were slow to reach the border regions. The reestablishment of interstate contacts started from the top down. After the ice had been broken during the 1960s, new and deeper forms of cooperation were able to develop in the 1970s with contacts among local governments, cities, and private citizens gradually increasing. By the 1980s, binational relations at all levels and in most aspects of everyday life had, by and large, been normalized.

Similarly, the Hungarian-Austrian border zone, controlled by frontier guards and characterized by dozens of administrative regulations, became more permeable and less restrictive. The negative attitudes of political leaders toward transboundary cooperation mellowed, the economic development of frontier areas became more intensive and, finally, new border checkpoints were opened. Out of the Iron Curtain evolved the Iron Door, and a growing number of Hungarians discovered the benefits of cross-border travel.[2]

The Hungarian-Austrian borderlands became model areas for the peaceful coexistence of countries with different political and economic systems. Research on border-region problems and transboundary regional-planning studies began already in 1967 but, due to the initial lack of interest on the part of Austria, these efforts were stopped in 1972. The issue of common development of the frontier was raised again in the 1980s and eventually was incorporated into the policy-making process, both at the interstate and regional-administration levels. During the 1980s, the initiative for forming more intensive frontier relationships came from the Austrian side, generated, to an extent, by the growth of large-scale transboundary shopping. Cross-border commuting also intensified, first in the form of contracted workers and later in large flows of inexpensive Hungarian labor.

As a consequence of these developments, the Hungarian counties located closest to the western borders of Hungary were the first in contact with the Alps-Adriatic Working Community (an association dedicated to interregional cooperation including the Alpine and Adriatic coastal areas of Switzerland, Austria, Germany, Italy, Slovenia, and Croatia) through their relations with the neighboring Austrian state of Burgenland. Eventually, the Hungarian counties of Baranya, Györ-Moson-Sopron, Somogy, Vas, and Zala became members of the organization. By 1985, the Hungarian-Austrian border had become the easiest to pass and the busiest between East and West. Because of the rapid economic and political changes taking place, Austria and the Austrian border became a vital gateway for Hungarian traffic and international trade and, at the same time, the most accessible western country for Hungarian citizens. In 1989, the Iron Curtain opened not only for Hungarians but for East German citizens as well, eliminating any remaining rationale for maintaining a defensive border between the two countries.

The Hungarian-Yugoslavian Border

By the end of the 1940s and with Stalin's censuring of Tito, the common border between Yugoslavia and Hungary, 631 kilometers in length, became a border of heightened political, ideological, and military confrontation. As was the case on the Austrian-Hungarian frontier, minefields were laid here initially as well. Even as tensions have eased, this border has remained problematic with regard to security as well as economic and social concerns. At the end of the 1950s the Yugoslavian border was still largely sealed off. Regulations here were, in many respects, even stricter than along the borders with Austria. Small-scale confrontations and clashes were a common occurrence. Both interstate relations and contacts between the respective Socialist parties (the decisive ones during this period) improved only slowly, and it was not until the early 1960s that comparatively stable and balanced binational political relations began to develop.

Research on the territorial development along the Hungarian-Yugoslav border, as well as work on a common border-region development policy, first began in 1966. In 1970, the two countries established the Standard Committee of Urban and Regional Development, and, in the course of its activities, coordinated at government level, long-term regional-development goals were identified and a harmonization of public investment policy was initiated. Most successful in this respect were activities along the frontier with Slovenia, where political leaders demonstrated the greatest openness for transborder cooperation. Furthermore, a variety of agreements were concluded in the 1970s between Hungary and Yugoslavia, supporting such cooperation efforts. A good example of this was the processing of Hungarian sugar beets in Yugoslav factories for reimport and/or marketing in third countries. Direct contacts between universities and other educational institutions were encouraged. At the same time, transborder shopping boomed.

The national minorities living in the frontier areas profited from this increased freedom of movement and were able to reestablish traditional and familial ties. Minorities were helped in their activities in order to create bridges between the two countries. This was supported by a significant reduction of restrictions on local cross-border traffic.

The Hungarian-Soviet Border

Despite the economic, political, and military alliance that existed between Hungary and the Soviet Union, the Hungarian-Soviet border (215 km in length) was at least as impermeable and, at times, as hermetically sealed off as the Hungarian-Austrian border. On the Soviet side of the border a Socialist Iron Curtain was, in fact, established that was less visible than the "real" Iron Curtain at the Hungarian-Austrian border. Sub-Carpathia (in the Ukraine) became a strategic zone with high troop concentrations. The Soviet military presence was, of course, not directed against Hungary itself, but nevertheless it had a significant negative effect on transboundary communications.

Transboundary cooperation between small regions was hindered by many factors, the most important of which were the fear of Hungarian agitation and the presence of about 200,000 ethnic Hungarians living very close to the border on the Soviet side. Along this border there was only the Záhony road and railroad checkpoint serving larger regional centers. Border-crossing facilities operating here in the period of state socialism were so few and far between as to effectively close the border to local interaction.

The Hungarian-Romanian Border

According to official propaganda, the Hungarian-Romanian border should have been an area of friendship and cooperation between socialist brothers. However, because of differing attitudes toward the issue of minority rights during most of the period of state socialism, the Romanian-Hungarian border symbolized alienation and even downright hostility. Poor binational relations limited everyday local-level interaction here as well—despite the fact that the peripheral situation of the common border logically should have provided incentives to cooperate. The fact that the Hungarian-Romanian border transects Hungarian linguistic areas could also have eased the establishment of transboundary cooperation. But in practice it became the main hindrance to closer cooperation. For the Romanian government, it was more important to change the frontier's ethnic character than to allow and encourage cross-border contacts. Romania restricted even the maintenance of civil relations through very strict administrative measures.

The Hungarian-Czechoslovakian Border

The character of the Hungarian-Czechoslovakian border (608 km in length) has changed several times since 1945. The years following the end of World War II were an emotionally charged period of deportation and forced emigration. Citing the legally and morally questionable principle of "collective responsibility," the authorities in Czechoslovakia expelled about 40,000 Hungarians from the Sudetenland. Simultaneously, over 100,000 people were sent from other parts of Czechoslovakia to Hungary. The sizeable Hungarian community that remained in the country was effectively deprived of citizenship until 1948. Because of this legacy, attempts to establish transboundary contacts between Hungary and Czechoslovakia were not energetically pursued until the end of the 1950s.

As transboundary cooperation then slowly developed, it was influenced by the specific characteristics of the border region. As such, the Hungarian-Czechoslovakian border (in practice, the border between Hungary and the Slovakian half of the Czechoslovak Federal Republic) could be divided into three different subunits: the Danube, an area of contiguous Hungarian settlement characterized by joint use of the river and heavy transboundary traffic; the central area, dominated by the Budapest metropolitan region; and the eastern border zone, in which cooperation in heavy industry was quite pronounced.

The zone along the Danube is a principal transport and development axis within Hungary. It is an industrialized area, very attractive for the neighboring Slovakian territories settled by Hungarian minorities. Labor moved quite freely across this part of the border in what was a rather unique binational relationship for the period. Nevertheless, the cooperation had its clear limits. The bridge across the Danube at the Hungarian city of Esztergom, destroyed during World War II, was never rebuilt, although the issue was brought up several times. Another important element of cooperation involved joint investments in the Gabcsikovo-Nagymaros hydroelectric dam. This project, which drew considerable criticism on environmental grounds, would eventually affect political relations between Hungary and the new Slovak Republic.[3]

The most important characteristic of the central part of the Hungarian-Czechoslovakian border is the attractiveness of Budapest. The Hungarian capital city would have dominated the neighboring Slovakian territory in all respects had the present border not materialized. Whether officials were willing to admit it or not, the political management of the *Budapest problem* caused many headaches during the period of state socialism, as the city represented a natural center for Hungarian minorities living in the southern part of Slovakia.

Significant areas of the eastern border with Czechoslovakia can be described as peripheral regions and agrarian in character. However, in other areas heavy industries predominate on both sides of the border—a fact that, in the past, has prompted Hungarian-Slovak cooperation. This area remains one of potential cooperation, primarily between the regional centers of Miskolc and Kosice, although bilateral cooperation between other cities in this border region is developing in the field of tourism.

In 1971, the two countries established a Permanent Working Committee for Regional Development, which in 1977 prepared a medium-range development concept for the common border (1977–1990). Only a few elements of the concept were implemented; political and environmental movements protesting the construction of the Danube hydroelectric power station and dam, as well as severe economic difficulties (debt crisis), hindered implementation on the Hungarian side. Indeed, controversy surrounding the Gabcikovo-Nagymaros project made relations between the two governments very difficult during the last phases of state socialism.

4. Frontier Relations and Perspectives during the Period of Democratic Transformation

The collapse of the bipolar world, the fall of state socialism either by evolution or revolution, the breakup of the Soviet Union, Yugoslavia, and Czechoslovakia, and the withdrawal of occupying Russian troops from the area were all factors that contributed to a completely new situation around Hungary, creating, in turn, new conditions for cooperation with an increased number of neighbors. Beginning in the 1990s, new cooperative ambitions appeared in attempts to establish new interstate relations (Višegrad Three, Višegrad Four, Pentagonal, Hexagonal, and, finally, the Central-European Initiative) among the former Central European satellites of the Soviet Union. These activities were aimed, in part, at avoiding a political vacuum in Central Europe and motivated out of distrust of Russia's long-term ambitions in Europe. They also resulted from the necessity—often grudgingly acknowledged—to establish new multilateral forms of economic and political cooperation hitherto restricted by Soviet hegemony.

However, one should not forget that future integration into the EU could foster greater cooperation. The articles of association that apply to Hungary, the Czech Lands, Slovakia, and Poland carry with them the possibility of establishing common political and social values. These new initiatives and agreements promise to create a better basis for transboundary cooperation despite the fact that, in most cases, such cooperation does not command much attention at the national level. Some of the newly independent countries are primarily concerned with internal issues (organizing the state, institutionalization, and economic and financial crisis management). As such, the purposeful development of frontier relations has not been a policy priority (Figure 2).

The Hungarian-Austrian Border in Transition

Post-Socialist transformation has affected the Hungarian-Austrian border in many respects. General research characterizes it as Hungary's *open border* (Rechnitzer 1990) and one where intensive economic, social, and local political interaction is developing. New possibilities for cooperation are best symbolized by the Adam Opel factory (an automotive subsidiary of General Motors) recently established in the border city of Szentgotthárd.

In particular, the privatization of the Hungarian economy has brought with it an inflow of Austrian capital, some of which is being put to use in illegal ways. This frontier region is, for example, affected by the unlawful purchasing of cropland by Austrians. Hungarian law forbids the purchase of land by foreigners. Austrian farmers on the frontier acquire land with so-called *pocket contracts*, hoping to assume full title to their properties once legal restrictions are suspended. *Double ownership* was typical of the situation between the world wars, when land owners had their properties split up by a new international border.

Austria's membership in the European Union, effective since January 1, 1995, will certainly create new conditions and modify transboundary relations with Hungary, since the border now separates Hungary from the European Union. Due to the requirements of the Schengen Agreement, in force since April 1995, frontier controls will probably become stricter. One can only hope that no new barriers to cooperation will be erected.

The Hungarian-Ex-Yugoslavian Border

The events connected with the disintegration of Yugoslavia have made the Hungarian frontier here very unstable. The international community maintains a long-term presence, with NATO scout planes patrolling the ex-Yugoslavian area from Hungarian airspace. Due to UN sanctions imposed on Serbia, international observers now control traffic on the Danube. Furthermore, the acute problem of refugees requires international attention.

The relations among Serbia, Croatia, and Slovenia—and between Serbia and Croatia in particular—have strongly influenced Hungary's southern border regions. During the civil war that was fought in close proximity to Hungarian territory, Hungarian areas came under fire. Bombardments and the violation of Hungarian airspace were common.

According to international law, the area that is confined by the Danube and Drava rivers, known as the Baranya Triangle, belongs to Croatia, but Croatia cannot enforce its sovereignty here due to Serb occupation. This part of the Hungarian-Croatian border is currently perhaps the most impenetrable border in Europe, and transboundary cooperation has been suspended indefinitely. The most important issue in the Baranya part of the Hungarian-Croatian border is when and by what means Croatia will attempt to re-establish control over the region. Should this be possible only through a show of force, then frontier war may again become a reality.

In the meantime, UN sanctions against Serbia have had considerable impact on transboundary traffic on the Hungarian-Serbian border. Smuggling has greatly

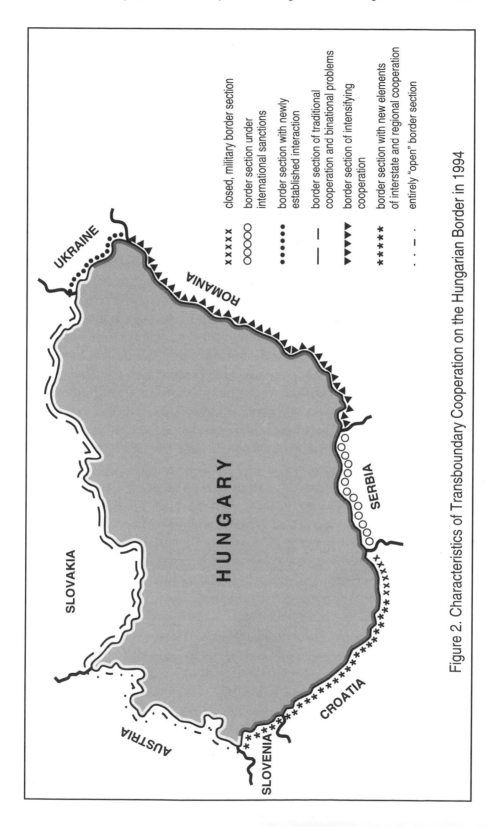

Figure 2. Characteristics of Transboundary Cooperation on the Hungarian Border in 1994

increased, bringing with it a host of problems. Indeed, the Hungarian border city of Szeged must live under *Balkan* conditions. With crime and violence on the increase, long-term investment in Szeged has been discouraged. In contrast to this, the Hungarian-Slovenian border is relatively problem-free; in fact, it is a region of expanding economic and social contacts and of little conflict between the long- and short-term ambitions of the population. The existence of national minorities living on both sides of the border has tended to promote rather than hinder transboundary cooperation.

The Hungarian-Slovakian Border

The establishment of an independent Slovak state has produced an entirely new situation on the northern border of Hungary. The first democratically elected governments of Hungary and Slovakia were not able to resolve differences between the two countries, involving minority rights and the formal recognition of mutual borders—differences inherited from the previous system. Thus, they could not provide a new basis for interstate relations through an international treaty. In the meantime, the proportion of Hungarian-speaking persons compared to the total number of citizens has increased in the new Slovakian state. About 3.8 percent of the former Czechoslovakia's total population was of Hungarian nationality. In sovereign Slovakia, ethnic Hungarians make up 10.7 percent of the total population, concentrated mainly in a narrow strip along the Hungarian-Slovakian border. From the standpoint of Slovakians, the Hungarian minority's ambitions for autonomy therefore increase the danger of possible future territorial losses.

In the context of rather strained relations between the two countries, the issue of opening up border crossing points became an important political one. Of the four additional border crossing points demanded by the Hungarian population only one was opened by August 1994 (despite the fact that the mayors of the two Hungarian settlements on either side of the border went on a hunger strike to emphasize these demands). The inauguration of this crossing point was presided over by the heads of state of Hungary and Slovakia, underlining the political (as opposed to technical) character of the event.

An inherited problem of this border region is the Danube hydroelectric power plant, which has put relations between the two countries under severe stress. If the two countries cannot reach an agreement of their own accord, the decision of the Hague International Court will probably be final. However, systemic change and economic transformation have also allowed greater possibilities for social contacts between residents of the border region. Travel is now without restriction, and cooperative relationships between private companies have begun to develop.

The Hungarian-Ukrainian Border

With the collapse of the Soviet Union, this border region has experienced considerable change. This is primarily because the sovereign state of Ukraine has adopted new approaches to dealing with its border regions and transboundary cooperation with its neighbors. It has also been quite lenient with regard to the status of Hungarian and other national minorities. The binational treaty between Ukraine and Hungary in 1991 has formed the basis for long-term and friendly relations, containing, among others, border guarantees pertaining to the respect of territorial sovereignty and the assurance of minority rights. In 1993, extraordinarily heated and harsh discussions took place in the Hungarian parliament about the treaty. In fact, members of the parliamentary majority accused their own government of capital treason, and ratification was only secured by support from the opposition.

Despite objections to recognizing the Soviet status quo, benefits to the local community on the Hungarian-Ukranian border (once hermetically sealed) have been appreciable. It is now possible for the Hungarian population living in Sub-Carpathia to visit Hungary for the first time since 1945. In addition, four new border crossing points have been opened up within a short period of time. Cross-border passenger traffic has increased, and, in the Hungarian border cities, businesses catering to the needs of visitors have developed rapidly.

The Hungarian-Romanian Border

The expectations of better interstate relations and more liberal border-region policies raised during the period of the Romanian Revolution (1989–1990) have only been partly fulfilled. The past few years have proved insufficient for the leaders of the two countries to improve historically cold relations. Asynchronously, the liberation of individuals has rapidly increased mobility, and transboundary interaction has become more intensive than at any time before.

At the time of writing (1995), Hungary and Romania have not yet concluded a binational agreement. However, the period of artificial restraint has ended, and negotiations regarding a basic treaty are underway. Both countries consider their own ambitions of joining the European Union as important, and integration into the European community of interests and values could contribute to the improvement of bilateral relations between Romania and Hungary. But top down conformity cannot resolve all binational tensions. In fact, it could serve to cover them up. Therefore, it is very important for both nations to intensify direct interaction along the common border, because only initiatives coming from the bottom up and good relations established with popular support will last in the long term.

The Challenge of a Carpathian Euroregion

The idea of establishing the Carpathian Euroregion was first raised by geographers at the end of the 1980s and was a result of the reestablishment of full national sovereignty in the Central European states of Hungary, Czechoslovakia, Romania, and Poland. It was an attempt to follow the good example of the Alps-Adriatic Working Community and one in which expectations of generous Western support were raised. During the period of state socialism, the Carpathian-Tisza region was a common periphery of Czechoslovakia, Poland, Hungary, the Soviet Union, and Romania. Simultaneously, however, it served as an area of interstate interaction. Large transportation and other physical infrastructure networks emanating from the Soviet Union (e.g., oil and gas pipelines, electricity grids) crossed through this region without integrating it.

While the Euroregion concept was being developed, various political, economic, environmental, ethnic, and other issues began to bear heavily on relations between post-socialist countries. Arguably, supporters of the Euroregion idea did not properly consider the difficult and tumultuous history of the region. One need only look at developments in the twentieth century to understand that the Carpathian-Tisza basin is a large regional periphery with no stable and dominating center or capital; it changed hands many times after 1914 and has seen an endless host of rulers, including Austria, Hungary, Slovakia, Czechoslovakia, Germany, Romania, Poland, the Soviet Union, and Ukraine. As a result, the region is characterized by complicated spatial relationships and linguistic and ethnic heterogeneity.

The scientific research that accompanied political attempts to establish the Euroregion relied on broad-based cooperation between research institutes and universities of the countries involved. The proposals for joint action that emanated from this cooperative work de-emphasized local level cooperation, concentrating instead on the wider regional context. The Hungarian development concepts, for example, would have affected an area of about 200,000 square km and 18 million inhabitants (Illés 1993). This mesoregional approach encountered not only Romanian opposition (Romania took umbrage to geographical reference to the "most Hungarian" of rivers, the Tisza, in the official name of the Euroregion) but also the problem that it included nearly half of the territory of the newly created Slovak Republic.

The Euroregion was formally established in 1993, at a conference of the Hungarian, Ukrainian, and Polish foreign ministers in the Hungarian city of Debrecen. Slovak and Romanian representatives declined the invitation. Almost immediately after the agreement was signed, heated parliamentary debate ensued over the political significance of the Carpathian Euroregion in all the countries

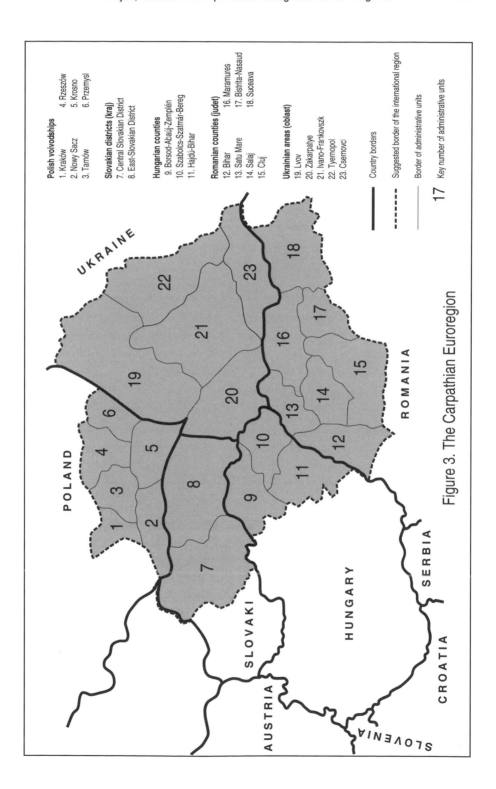

Polish voivodships
1. Kraków   4. Rzeszów
2. Nowy Sacz   5. Krosno
3. Tarnów   6. Przemysl

Slovakian districts (kraj)
7. Central Slovakian District
8. East-Slovakian District

Hungarian counties
9. Borsod-Abaúj-Zemplén
10. Szabolcs-Szatmár-Bereg
11. Hajdú-Bihar

Romanian counties (judet)
12. Bihar   16. Maramures
13. Satu Mare   17. Bistrita-Nasaud
14. Salaj   18. Suceava
15. Cluj

Ukrainian areas (oblast)
19. Lvov
20. Zakarpatye
21. Ivano-Frankovszk
22. Tyernopol
23. Csernovci

Country borders

Suggested border of the international region

Border of administrative units

17 Key number of administrative units

Figure 3. The Carpathian Euroregion

involved. Here, historical resentments and rivalries rather than the consideration of the potential long-term economic advantages of cooperation dominated and almost prevailed. This comes as no surprise in this part of the world; history is not an academic issue here, but a part of everyday politics.

5. Conclusions

The twentieth century has brought enormous and rapid change to Hungary's geographical surroundings, as well as spatial and functional transformation of its borders. Neighbors and borderlines have been of little permanence. Hence, one cannot speak of historically balanced, long-term transboundary cooperation and experiences in this region. The beginning of the 1990s brought yet again a rearrangement in the political geography in the area around Hungary. This process proceeded along the southern borders of Hungary under circumstances of a bloody war and along the northern and eastern borders in a peaceful way.

Along the Hungarian borders, the tendencies of integration (primarily into the European Union) and of disintegration are present at the same time. We will most likely have to reconcile ourselves to the prolonged coexistence of these two tendencies and, primarily at the southern borders, to long-term uncertainty, even perhaps with the possibility of violent frontier conflicts resurfacing. In the meantime, it is quite likely that transboundary cooperation along Hungary's other borders will develop and, with time, emulate the success of West European Euroregions.

Notes

1. It was a peculiar element in the frontier relations, that the Gyôr-Sopron-Ebenfurt railway, an Austro-Hungarian joint property, was nationalized. During these years, this railway functioned as a window toward the West.

2. As the "Iron Door" gradually became penetrable, the slogan that "Hungary is the brightest barrack in the Soviet camp" began to make the rounds.

3. See Galambos (1993) and Assetto and Bruyninckx (1995) for an overview of the issues involved.

References

Assetto, V. J., and H. Bruyninckx. 1995. "Environmental Security and Social Conflict: Implications of the Gabcikovo/Nagymaros Barrage System for Hungarian-Slovak Relations." Paper presented at the conference "International Boundaries and Environmental Security: Frameworks for Regional Cooperation," June 1995, National University of Singapore (to be published).

Berényi, I. 1988. "A határmenti területek kutatásának szociálgeográfiai aspektusai" (Socio-Geographical Aspects of Research on the Frontier Regions). In *A sajátos helyzetü térségek terület- és településfejlesztési problémái*, Ferenc Erdösi and József Tóth, eds. Pécs: MTA Regionális Kutatások Központja.

Erdösi, F. 1988. "A határmenti térségek kutatásáról" (About Research on the Frontier Regions). In *A sajátos helyzetü térségek terület- és településfejlesztési problémái*, Ferenc Erdösi and József Tóth, eds. Pécs: MTA Regionális Kutatások Központja.

Erdösi, F. 1990 "Entwicklungspolitik in den Grenzgebieten Ungarns" (Development Policies in Hungarian Border Regions). *Specimina Geographica* 1.

Galambos, J. 1993. "An International Environmental Conflict on the Danube: The Gabcikovo-Nagymaros Dams." In *Environment and Democratic Transition*, A. Vári and P. Tamás, eds. Netherlands: Kluwer Academic Publishers.

Hajdú, Z. 1988. "Az államhatárok és a határmenti területek politikai földrajzi kutatása" (Political-Geographical Research of the State Borders and the Frontier Regions). In *A sajátos helyzetü térségek terület- és településfejlesztési problémái*, Ferenc Erdösi and József Tóth, eds. Pécs: MTA Regionális Kutatások Központja.

Horváth, Gy.1993. "Restructuring and Interregional Cooperation in Central Europe: The Case of Hungary." In *Regional Networks, Border Regions and European Integration*, R. Cappellin and P. W. J. Batey, eds. London: Pion Limited.

Illés, I. 1993. "A Kárpátok Eurorégió." (The Carpathian Euroregion). *Valóság* 6.

Kovács, T. 1993. *The Borderland Situation as It is Seen by a Sociologist*. Discussion Paper No. 18. Pécs: Centre for Regional Studies.

Kovács, Z. 1989. "Border Changes and Their Effect on the Structure of Hungarian Society." *Political Geography Quarterly* 8.

Kozma, E., I. Héjja, and F. Stefancsik. 1993. *Katonaföldrajzi kézikönyv* (Handbook of Military Geography). Budapest: Zrínyi Kiadó.

Lackó, L. 1994. "A határmenti együttmûködés helyzete és perspektívái Közép-Európában" (The Situation of Cooperation along the Borders and Its Perspectives in Central-Europe). *Magyar Közigazgatás* 44.

Matheika, M. 1989. "Magyarországnak a trianoni békeszerzôdés által megállapított országhatárairól" (About the State Borders of Hungary Set by the Trianon Peace Treaty). *Egyetemi Szemle* 11.

Ministry for Environment and Regional Policy. 1991. *Regional Planning in Hungary*. Budapest: Ministry of Environment and Regional Policy.

Palotás, Z. 1990. *Trianoni határok* (The Trianon Borders). Budapest: Interedition.

Rechnitzer, J. 1990. *A nyitott határ. A gazdasági és szellemi erôforrások innovációorientált fejlesztése az osztrák-magyar határmenti régióban* (Open Border. The Innovation Oriented Development of Economic and Intellectual Resources in the Austrian-Hungarian Frontier Region). Györ: MTA RKK Észak-dunántúli Osztály.

Süli-Zakar, I. 1992. "Az államhatár társadalmi-gazdasági fejlôdést akadályozó hatásának vizsgálata ÉK-Magyarország határ menti területein" (A Study of State Borders as Factors Blocking Socio-Economic Progress in North-Eastern Hungary). *Földrajzi Közlemények* 116.

Tóth, J. 1993. "Conception of the multidisciplinary studies in connection with the Carpathian-Tisza region." In *Regional Problems in East-Central Europe after the Political Changes*, A. Aubert, F. Erdösi, and J. Tóth, eds. Pécs: Department of General Social Geography and Urbanistics, and Center for Regional Studies of Hungarian Academy of Sciences.

Zala, Gy. 1988. "A határmenti együttmûködés szükségessége, eddigi fôbb eredményei és problémái" (Necessity of Frontier Cooperation, Its Main Results and Difficulties). In *A sajátos helyzetü térségek terület- és településfejlesztési problémái*, F. Erdösi and J. Tóth, eds. Pécs: MTA Regionális Kutatások Központja.

Zsiga, T. 1991. *Burgenland, vagy Nyugat-Magyarország?* (Burgenland or West-Hungary?). Oberwart: Burgenlandi Magyar Kultúregyesület.

Kaliningrad: A Russian Exclave in Search of a New Role

Lyndelle Fairlie

1. Introduction

Russia's Kaliningrad *oblast* has been significantly affected by the dissolution of the Soviet Union. Formerly a member of the Baltic Military District and the Gosplan Baltic Economic Zone, which included Estonia, Latvia, and Lithuania, Kaliningrad is now separated from its Baltic Economic Zone partners and from "mainland" Russia. On the east, the Kaliningrad exclave is separated from Greater Russia by Lithuania and Belarus. On the north, Estonia, Latvia, and Lithuania lie between Kaliningrad and St. Petersburg.

Kaliningrad's separation from the rest of the Russian Federation has been worrisome for Moscow for several reasons. The loss of control over ports in the newly independent Baltic states means that Kaliningrad is now Russia's only ice-free Baltic port. The bombing in Lithuania of the railroad line linking Moscow to Kaliningrad and St. Petersburg in late 1994 drew attention to the fragility of access. There are also fears of increased smuggling through Kaliningrad which is seen as a hole in Russia's western borders and where goods destined for Kaliningrad end up in Belarus and the Baltic states. Lastly, Moscow worries that history may repeat itself. Recalling that Kaliningrad was part of the German province of East Prussia until 1945, Moscow is concerned about the role German investment plays in the *oblast*'s fledgling civilian-economic development.

Arguably, Russian post-Soviet attitudes toward Kaliningrad and its political and economic role are characterized by a Maginot-Line approach; threats are seen coming primarily from Germany although problems or opportunities may arise from unexpected sources. Russian eagerness to retain sovereignty over Kaliningrad leads Russian authorities to seek assurances that foreign governments have no unsettled claims on the territory. In addition, Russia is ever mindful of former Soviet citizens of ethnic German origin who are moving to Kaliningrad. Russian nationalists are reportedly encouraging fear that the *oblast* will be handed over to Germany and that Kaliningraders will be deported to "mainland" Russia (Biryukov 1994). There is, in fact, some fear that even if there were no direct threat to Russian sovereignty, a *de facto* takeover by German economic interests could be possible.

The opportunities for Kaliningrad offered by Poland and the Baltic states should not lead to an underestimation of Germany's importance. Throughout Central and Eastern Europe and the Baltic states, the role of German trade and investment is important, and Kaliningrad is part of this bigger picture. Germany is now the leading trading partner of all of the former Warsaw Pact/COMECON states (Atkinson 1994). In Kaliningrad, Germany reportedly accounts for 40 percent of all foreign investment (Viviano 1994) and is second to Poland as a foreign trading partner for Kaliningrad.

Trade with foreign countries could lead to economic relationships comparable to the "spontaneous character" of economic cooperation that has developed between the Russian Far East and China "without a coordinated long-term strategy" (BBC Summary 1994a). In the Russian Far East, these economic ties have led to the idea of separating from Russia and integrating into the economic system of the Asian-Pacific region as a "junior brother."[1] Perhaps it is the possibility of what might be called "spontaneous, incremental, spillover integration" that helped motivate the Russian Security Council to recognize the need to "take urgent steps to improve the economic situation in the Kaliningrad region and strengthen its ties with other members of the Russian Federation" (BBC Summary 1994b).

In summary, this paper analyzes changes in Russian border areas after the opening of the borders in the post-Soviet period. It focuses on Kaliningrad but also raises the broader question of whether the dissolution of the Soviet Union, the rise of Germany[2] as one of Russia's principal trading partners in 1993, previous borderland integration, and porous borders may imply that sovereignty of states and trading blocs such as the EU cannot be sustained in their current form.

2. Developments in the Kaliningrad Exclave

Kaliningrad is the westernmost *oblast* of Russia. Until 1991, Kaliningrad was closed to foreigners, and many areas were closed to nonresident Russians. Only Soviet ships docked at the commercial port. Kaliningrad was linked with the outside world mainly by its large fishing fleet and the Navy base at Baltiysk.

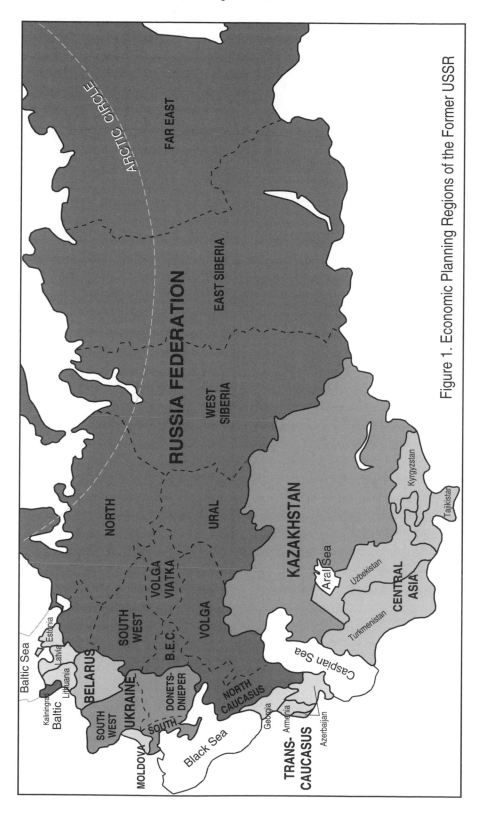

Figure 1. Economic Planning Regions of the Former USSR

The border with Poland was closed except for small-scale diplomatic traffic. Kaliningraders were oriented primarily toward Moscow, the sea, or toward their Baltic Republic economic-zone partners. During the Soviet period, roughly half the population worked in fishing and half worked in the military or enterprises related to the military.

In the Gosplan Baltic Economic Zone, the link with Lithuania was particularly strong not only due to geographic proximity but also because "at the beginning of the sixties the Council of National Economy (special body of territorial planning and industrial management) of the region (Kaliningrad) was included into the Lithuanian Economic Council so that the control of the Kaliningrad region was primarily exercised from Vilnius" (Kropinova n.d.: 5). Connections to Moscow continue to be central to the economy, partly because of the military and the importance of subsidies.

Kaliningrad researchers report that the *oblast*'s economy was linked to the Baltic Republics in such important sectors as transportation, fishing, food processing, energy, and building construction. In the transportation sector, for example, Vilnius handles air-traffic control. In the energy sector, the Lithuanian Ignalina nuclear power plant, which supplies 80 percent of Kaliningrad's electrical energy, was originally built with the goal of supplying the entire Baltic Economic Zone. In the food-processing industry, fruits and vegetables from the Baltic Republics were shipped to a plant in the city of Sovietzk for processing, then returned to the Baltic Republics (Kropinova n.d.: 5). In building construction, the shortage of raw materials for bricks led to the closing of brickworks in Kaliningrad and the shipment of the brick-making equipment to Lithuania. Bricks were then supplied to Kaliningrad by Lithuania. Surrounded by closed Soviet borders, an economy based on the ruble zone, and economic and political alliances with its East European allies, Russia did not experience the problems or opportunities in the Soviet period that western countries have as a result of open borders and an open economy.

Kaliningrad in the Post-Soviet Period

All of these links were disrupted with the dissolution of the Soviet Union. In the transport sector, for example, Lithuania threatened to deny Russia access to Lithuanian airspace while electrically powered locomotives became unavailable since hard currency instead of rubles was demanded. Disruptions have also occurred in other sectors. Kaliningraders report that, in the past, Lithuania has threatened to disrupt the supply of electricity to Kaliningrad. Symptomatically, the *oblast*'s food-processing plant no longer processes the fruits and vegetables from the Baltic states. Bricks and other construction materials have been in short supply due to periodic interruptions in delivery. All the blame for deteriorating

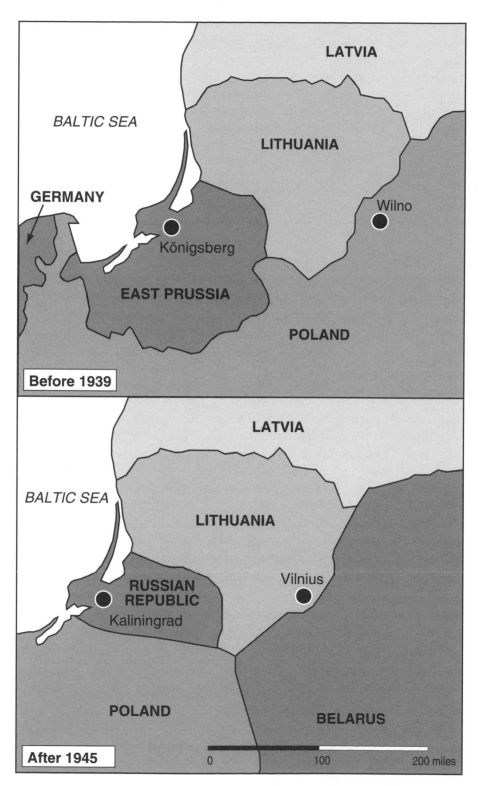

Figure 2. Boundary Changes: The Geopolitical Genesis of Kaliningrad

relations should not be placed on Lithuania. From the viewpoint of the Baltic states, Russia has contributed to tensions by threatening to disrupt the supply of energy or raise prices. All of these economic links, formerly arranged within the Soviet Union and the Baltic Economic Zone, are now issues for bilateral or multilateral negotiation among foreign countries.

Ambiguities in evolving foreign economic relations, disruption of former economic ties, reduced subsidies from Moscow, and defense-budget cuts have all adversely affected the Kaliningrad economy. Regional-administration statistics show that in the first six months of 1994, production in industry declined by 35 percent. The energy sector declined by 9 percent, food by 12 percent, pulp and paper by 54 percent, construction by 51 percent, and machinery by 80 percent. This resulted in the elimination of 11,500 jobs or 14.2 percent of the workforce.[3] Unemployment estimates vary widely. An unofficial unemployment level of 30 percent was estimated in 1995 (Kaminski 1995), but other estimates indicate a rate of 2 to 3 percent real unemployment as most people have four or five jobs.[4]

All of these factors meant that in the immediate post-Soviet period, it was not clear if the *oblast* would be viable as a Russian exclave. The need for transit corridors between Kaliningrad and "mainland" Russia via Lithuania raised issues reminiscent of the questions raised as to the viability of West Berlin in the aftermath of World War II. Kaliningrad Governor Yuri Matochkin estimated that the region had lost around 800 billion rubles because of its exclave position (Yurkin 1994). Partly because of these uncertainties, a variety of possible scenarios regarding the future of the exclave has been suggested.

Kaliningrad Defense Issues in the Post-Soviet Period

Moscow's response to these changes has been unequivocal on the basic issue of sovereignty and defense. Russian officials have made it clear to foreign countries that Russia regards Kaliningrad as essential to Russia's security and economic interests. It is a high-stakes issue. Foreign diplomats and Russians recall that if Russia lost Kaliningrad it would be back to the time before Peter the Great when Russia had limited access to the sea. Partly for this reason, Moscow has sought and received assurances that foreign governments have no unsettled claims to the Kaliningrad territory.

Nevertheless, the immediate post-Soviet period was a difficult period in Russian relations with Lithuania, partly because of sovereignty issues involved for both sides. The most prominent issues were withdrawal of Russian troops stationed in the area and treatment of Russian minorities. Because the Baltic states were not parties to the 1990 Conventional Armed Forces in Europe Treaty, these negotiations took place primarily on a bilateral basis although Russia and the Baltic states often brought the issues up in a wide variety of multilateral meetings.

Partly because of the asymmetrical power relationship between Russia and the Baltic states, and because Lithuania controls the historical land access to Kaliningrad from Moscow and used this power lever to its advantage, relations between Russia and Lithuania started off on a contentious basis. The negotiations between them regarding economic and military issues illustrate that both Russia and Lithuania have made use of economic retaliatory measures; these are far from the confidence-building measures one would like to see in a post-Cold War period.

After the departure of Russian troops from Lithuania in 1994, Russia's request for transit access for military and equipment across Lithuania, as well as Lithuania's demand that Russia ratify a bilateral, most-favored-nation treaty, remained areas of binational disagreement. Lithuania's need for such a treaty with Russia is self-evident: "Forty percent of what Lithuania produces is sold to Russia. In turn, Lithuania buys about half its raw material and energy resources from Russia, and moreover, Russia attaches a draconian 30 percent tariff to these imports" (Lashkevich 1994: 1). Poland was drawn into the dispute between Russia and Lithuania regarding access to Kaliningrad as well. Russia has attempted to reduce Lithuania's ability to hold Kaliningrad "hostage" (Turek 1994) by exploring agreements with Poland which would provide for alternative access to Kaliningrad via routes through Belarus and Poland. Russia delayed implementing the most-favored-nation trade agreement with Lithuania until the two countries could agree on transit rights for military personnel and equipment across Lithuania to Kaliningrad. The Lithuanian government was under pressure not only from Russia but also from its opposition parties who rejected the transit agreement the Lithuanian government submitted to Russia. They were concerned that specific articles in the agreement would "create a precedent for the establishment of Russian military control not only over airspace but the entire territory of Lithuania as well" (Turek 1994).

Agreement between the two governments was reached in January 1995 when Lithuania agreed to extend current military-transit regulations until the end of 1995, and Russia implemented the most-favored-nation trade status for Lithuania (Girnius 1995). The Lithuanian prime minister said that Lithuania was willing to continue the present arrangements because military transportation from the Kaliningrad region to Russia make up 95 percent of Russian military transit and only 5 percent of the traffic is from "mainland" Russia to Kaliningrad. This traffic pattern presumably indicates that Russia is primarily engaged in withdrawal of its military from neighboring countries, and this policy is compatible with Lithuania's interests. It is hoped that the resolution of the military-transit issue will end the conflictual period of relations between Russia and Lithuania and will begin a new period of cooperation on trade and other economic issues. The European Union had urged both Russia and Lithuania to resolve the matter.

Economic Issues in the Post-Soviet Period

Moscow has given mixed signals regarding Kaliningrad's foreign economic relations. On the one hand, Russian authorities would like a healthy economy in the area. President Yeltsin signed several decrees that set the stage for Kaliningrad to become the Yantar (Amber) Free Economic Zone. The *oblast* also participates in transportation plans which include a Via Hansa, connecting Kaliningrad with Poland and Germany, and a Via Baltica, that would connect it with the Baltic states and Helsinki.

On the other hand, Moscow, urged on by nationalists, seems to fear that too much foreign trade and investment might surreptitiously weaken Russian sovereignty in the *oblast*. Ambivalence can be seen even in the remarks by Russian reform leader, Yegor Gaydar, who is Chairman of the Democratic Choice Party. Visiting Kaliningrad in September 1994, Gaydar expressed the opinion that while the region deserved special status, "this should not be detrimental to other regions and should not destroy the state's unity and ties with the common national market" (BBC Summary 1994b). In speaking about a draft of a law pertaining to the *oblast*'s economy, Gaydar said, "For the time being it is a collection of intentions without any consideration given to the possibility of implementing them" (BBC Summary 1994b). It is partly this uncertain status of the Yantar Free Economic Zone that prevents Kaliningrad from attracting more foreign investment. Recent reports indicate that the entire Free Economic Zone system may be revised. A draft of the law reportedly suggests "creating compact and specialized economic zones" in border areas (BBC Summary 1994a).

Potential foreign investors are concerned not only about ambiguity but also about policies that can be quickly and easily changed. The recent abolition of customs privileges by presidential decree is an example. A brief historical review puts the problem in perspective. Partly because Kaliningrad was separated from mainland Russia, it was "exempted from customs duties for a period of ten years by earlier-issued presidential decrees and injunctions of the Russian Supreme Soviet. This allowed it to pay quite considerable sums for the transit shipment of goods through the Belarus republic and Lithuania and to keep the local prices for consumer goods at the average Russian level" (BBC Summary 1994d).

In an austerity move, Yeltsin signed a presidential decree in March 1995 abolishing all customs privileges in Russia (BBC Summary 1994c). A joint statement by the head of the Kaliningrad administration, Yuri Matochkin, and the speaker of the regional Duma deplored this move, stating that it "places the enclave in an unequal position in respect to the internal regions of Russia. It will boost local prices for prime necessity commodities ... will cause substantial economic and political damage" (BBC Summary 1994c).

Moscow's major role is also evident in its rejection of plans to lower regional taxes. In addition, Moscow must approve any joint venture over 100 million rubles. The privatization regulations, "whereby a foreign proprietor may not own more than 49 percent of the shares ... has so far been holding back operations by the German Krupp concern which was offered a mere 23 percent."[5] "The five-year tax holiday and custom duty exemption for most goods produced in the region are not backed by law, only presidential decrees" (Kaminski 1995).

The exclave status and the politics of economics are frustrating for Kaliningraders because their deep-water ice-free port and their European- and Russian-width railway gauges make the *oblast* a theoretically ideal port of access to Russia and Ukraine. The foreigners who go to Kaliningrad are usually either German nostalgia tourists returning to visit their homeland or business people who go to assess its potential as a Gateway City. Recognizing these opportunities, the Russian Free Economic Zones Association describes Kaliningrad, St. Petersburg, and Vladivostok as "land's end" zones. Similarly, the brochure of the Kaliningrad Sea Commercial Port is titled "Kaliningrad: A Bridge between Europe and Russia ... A Crossroad of East-West Trade Routes." As one German analyst states clearly, "Basically, the region (Kaliningrad) is of little significance to the German economy as a market, but it is of some interest as a location" (Bingen 1993: 46). For this reason there is discussion of handling commercial cargo at the deep-water navy base at Baltiysk, and a new 200-hectare port facility will reportedly be built with foreign investment (Zavarsky and Minin 1994).

Moscow's ambivalence is also evidenced in its attitude regarding the approval of foreign consulates in the *oblast*. Polish and Lithuanian consulates were opened in 1994 with an honorary Danish consul appointed in 1995. However, plans for a German consulate have been put on hold. Scandinavian officials say that Russian authorities are trying to get Scandinavian economic interests participating in Kaliningrad in order to offset the economic influence of Germany. Because Russia's leading trading partners in 1993 were Germany and China, these countries are often now seen as providing the greatest opportunities but also the greatest risk to Russian political and economic sovereignty.

The concern about the influence of Germany is best understood if foreign trade and investment are viewed in a broad perspective. The dissolution of the Soviet Union and CMEA had a substantial impact on Kaliningrad's trade. It is reported that the former close relationship with Lithuania has deteriorated to the point where "Lithuanian exports to the region amount to only 5 percent while imports are even less" (Afanasyeva 1994). The Lithuanian Consul in Kaliningrad,

Siditas Sileris, reported that "the optimum moment for conquering the Kaliningrad market had already passed (BBC Summary 1995b). He said that "leading positions in the Kaliningrad market were being taken by Poland ... and by Germany" (BBC Summary 1995b).

A Russian report indicates that, since 1993, Poland has become Kaliningrad's principal trading partner (Afanasyeva 1994). In 1994, bilateral trade was valued at 60 million U.S. dollars (Petrov 1995), while, in 1993, it accounted for more than half of joint enterprises, 19 percent of exports and 57 percent of imports" (Afanasyeva 1994). One Polish source estimates that more than half of Kaliningrad's food was imported from Poland (Ratajczyk 1995). In addition to consumer goods, "they [Poles] bring sugar, flour, canned food, and vegetables and take away raw materials, metals, and timber" (Afanasyeva 1994).

Germany is second to Poland as a foreign-trade partner for Kaliningrad. In 1993, Germany was the destination for 17.6 percent of Kaliningrad's exports and was the source of 24.7 percent of its imports. Total trade turnover (exports plus imports) for the *oblast* in 1993 was an estimated $210,400,000 (Barinov and Sberegaev n.d.: 3). It is generally agreed that the most important exports are in the categories of cellulose, timber, paper products, fish, and related processed foods.

Although Poland is Kaliningrad's leading foreign-trade partner, Germans lead as investors. Russian analysts report that the Poles are mostly active in commercial-trade joint ventures whereas Germans prefer to invest in manufacturing and services (Barinov and Sberegaev n.d.: 5). According to 1994 data, of the enterprises with foreign participation registered in the *oblast*, 151 are German (21.9%) and 262 are Polish (38%) ("Yantar" 1994), but German sources reportedly account for almost 40 percent of the foreign investment (Viviano 1994). Most joint enterprises are small, their starting capital rarely exceeding two-thousand dollars. Overall, it is estimated that the total value of foreign participation is limited partly because it is not possible for foreigners to own land, even if their enterprise is occupying the land.

In various reports, numerical data available raise more questions than they answer. Figures are sometimes given in rubles, and sometimes no base year is indicated. Trade data may be merely estimates because, as one Polish source said about trading in Russia, generally, "most transactions are carried out in cash, with money passed from hand to hand. Small transactions, very often done under the counter, never go through banks" (Styczek and Staniszewski 1994). This may be the case in Kaliningrad although recently Investbank, a Moscow-based bank (reportedly serving Polish and German customers), has opened a branch in Kaliningrad. The first foreign bank in Kaliningrad was the Rolbank, a Polish bank based in Poznan. It was reportedly used by Polish people but was suspended by Poland's central bank in February 1995 when its liabilities exceeded its assets.

Population

Russian borders are now open and porous, making movement of people and trade possible between East and West. If the population composition of the *oblast* changes significantly, there is the possibility that in the future the people might use the self-determination process to express their preference about whether the *oblast* should remain part of Russia. Even without a major change, Russian elections might entail a bargaining process similar to past elections when regions gained additional rights because of politicians' need for support in the regions.

In the post-Soviet period, migration patterns have changed in the Kaliningrad *oblast*. Poles, Germans, and other nationalities, as well as Russians, some of whom were military personnel and their families leaving the Baltic states and other parts of the former Soviet Union, have been increasingly coming to Kaliningrad. The focus of publicity has been on the alleged re-Germanization and the overwhelming Russian military presence. This implies that the composition of the population is an important factor affecting the future of the *oblast*.

Estimates of the number of ethnic Germans in the Kaliningrad *oblast* vary widely. One analysis states that less than 5 percent of the city's population is made up of ethnic Germans who were born there. Another 7,000 Volga Germans were allegedly resettled in the *oblast* in 1989 (Viviano 1994). Most Kaliningrad authorities estimate that 4,000 to 5,000 ethnic Germans now live in the area, with an annual increase of some 1,000 coming mostly from Central Asia and Kazakhstan (Afanasyeva 1994). Nationalists aware of this development may seek to limit the number of Germans in Kaliningrad in order to avoid such a concentration. The trend probably became controversial because some people suggested that Kaliningrad should become a Baltic German republic. At the September 1994 "First Congress of Patriotic Forces" under the slogan "Russian Boundary: From Kaliningrad to the Kuriles," speakers reportedly "scared the audience with an imminent transfer of their enclave to Germany and their deportation to Russia" (Biryukov 1994).

Ethnic Germans who are in Kaliningrad are reportedly not viewed negatively by Russians. In a public opinion poll, "more than half of the polled residents of the city view the arrival of Germans favorably" (Afanasyeva 1994). This may be partly because they provide some economic opportunity for Russians. In the town of Jasnaja Poljana, where a German community is developing, the Russians at first "looked mistrustfully at the new arrivals. But this changed once they saw that the new settlement also provided them with jobs" (Marsch 1994). The arriving ethnic Germans are not necessarily political activists. In fact, "the new settlers are not fully aware of the connections to the rightist scene in Germany or of the possible political repercussions" (Marsch 1994).

The issue of humanitarian aid provided to ethnic Germans by German organizations and the German government is complex. This policy is a subject of controversy between the German Foreign and the Interior ministries. "The Foreign Office fears that the granting of humanitarian aid by the Federal Ministry of the Interior to ethnic Germans resettling in the region—even if meant only as a response to an existing situation and not as an incentive to resettle—occasionally leads to misunderstandings between the two ministries" (Bingen 1993: 48).

The Foreign Ministry would prefer to avoid conflict with Russia, but the Interior Ministry, which determines who is eligible for German citizenship, would like to avoid having to consider petitions from a large number of former Soviet citizens attempting to prove their German ancestry. Some Russians of German heritage are allegedly moving to Kaliningrad as a stepping stone to moving to Germany. Some voices within the Russian government claim that Germany is essentially subsidizing the *re-Germanization* via humanitarian associations, although experts note that Gorbachev began the resettlement policy at a time when he was trying to improve relations with West Germany.

The German immigration phenomenon can be kept in perspective if one observes the migration of other population groups into the *oblast*. Although estimates vary, immigration data show that in 1991, of the approximately 800,000 people then living in the *oblast*, approximately 20 percent were non-Russian. About half, 81,000, were Belorussian. Ukrainians were the second largest group with approximately 62,700, and Lithuanians were third with 18,100, constituting about 11 percent of the minorities.[6] A Polish minority of about 5,000 is also present (Polish Press Agency 1994).

The overall data show that, although German Russians are moving to the area, so are other nationalities, and there is speculation that more Russians who now live in the Baltic states may be moving to the *oblast* if they perceive that socio-economic conditions for Russians will worsen in the Baltic states and CIS republics. On the other hand, if the Baltic states join the EU, minority rights will be strengthened as a result of the norms and rules that flow from the recent "Stability" conference that the EU designed for prospective members in the hope of heading off any more Yugoslavia-style conflicts. Although Kaliningrad is receiving Russian immigrants, the opposite trend is that Russians keep moving to the Baltic states. According to 1994 data, 43 percent of the 50,000 immigrants to Lithuania over the last five years were Russians (Lashkevich 1994)—perhaps attracted by the possibility of the Baltic states' membership in the EU and the prospect of better economic opportunities.

3. Scenarios for the Future of Kaliningrad

Post-Cold War western analysis of Kaliningrad has focused on the extent to which the area is militarized. Indeed, scenarios of Kaliningrad's political and economic future roles could be directly affected by the development of Russian defense policy in the Baltics. By contrast, depending on whether the Russian government takes decisive action to move the region clearly in the direction of democracy and market reforms based on laws that are implemented locally, alternative scenarios could be viable. Still other scenarios are possible should the region remain unable to clearly define its role in foreign economic relations. Furthermore, a worst-case scenario could envisage a return to authoritarian control.

Military-Dominant Scenarios

The first scenario that will be considered is that which current Russian government officials envision regarding the level of militarization in the *oblast*. In August 1994, Vyacheslav Kostikov, Yeltsin's Press Secretary, said that Russia intends to have only a level of militarization in Kaliningrad that is "determined solely by Russia's defense needs and its commitments under the Treaty on Conventional Armed Forces in Europe" (Current Digest of the Post-Soviet Press 1994). "Defense Minister Pavel Grachev indicated that, if Russia were given concessions on the flanks, it would be prepared to cut considerably the number of troops and arms in Kaliningrad oblast" (Clarke 1994). Reductions in the fleet are apparently also being contemplated.

Russia is not likely to carry demilitarization in the *oblast* too far because both Russian and foreign officials are quick to point out that the loss of Kaliningrad would put Russia back to the time before Peter the Great, when Russia had limited access to the sea. Perhaps for this reason, Foreign Minister Kozyrev was quoted as saying "that Russia needs to maintain an 'imposing presence' in Kaliningrad in order to avoid being 'squeezed out' of the region" (Dawisha and Parrott 1994: 217). His concern might be increased if NATO admits the Baltic states in response to the troop withdrawals the Russians have already made. In addition, according to Kaliningrad Governor Yuri Matochkin, one must not carry demilitarization too far because the military have been instrumental in stopping some of the smuggling attempts (Yurkin 1994).

Westerners do not agree about how much demilitarization might be needed in order to allow for significant expansion of the civilian economy. There are two sides to the argument. Some experts argue that foreign trade and investment would only be secure and profitable in the *oblast* if it has a peaceful environment and access to the land and labor force needed to make significant changes in the local economy (Wellman 1994: 14). Other experts argue that substantial demilitarization is an unrealistic expectation considering that people who live in military-base areas worldwide are generally against base closures because of the potential damage to the local economy (Hansson 1993: 18).

A change in the western approach may have been signaled at the August 1994 meeting of Nordic and Baltic foreign ministers. The conference, held in Lithuania, welcomed the Russian departure of troops from Estonia and Latvia. The Baltic foreign ministers made the usual call for the demilitarization of Kaliningrad, but the Nordic foreign ministers "did not issue the expected joint communique calling for the demilitarization of Kaliningrad (Girnius 1994). The former Swedish Foreign Minister simply said that in the Russian military concentration there was "an absolute anomaly ... incongruous with stability."[7] Toning down western calls for demilitarization of the area may be wise because such a call might play into the hands of Russian nationalists.

The likelihood of a military scenario depends not only on Russian politics but also on developments in other areas such as Lithuania. If nationalists come to power in Lithuania, Russia may be more inclined to adopt one of the militarization scenarios previously outlined.

Economics-Oriented Scenarios

It is not clear how far Russia will move toward a market economy and democracy. Federalism is also a high-priority issue that will continue to focus on the question of how much authority the central government should have in comparison with the regions. So long as these issues are on the agenda, the Russian government and the Kaliningrad *oblast* will have to address the questions that continually arise in western countries. For example, to what extent should the quest for economic growth be allowed to affect a country's sovereignty by permitting too much direct foreign investment, immigration, subordination of the nation-state to trading blocs such as the EU, or regional authority for border areas to make public policy?

These problems and/or opportunities have been exacerbated because in 1993 Russia's leading foreign-trade partners were Germany and China. This situation would put even the most stable, well-run country in a difficult position. The U.S. and the European Union examples illustrate the point. United States territorial integrity continues partly because no matter how annoyed the regions become with Washington, they know that neither Mexico to the south nor Canada to the north offers a more desirable economy with which to affiliate. Similarly in the European Union, no matter how irritated members might become with Brussels, it is common knowledge that neither Africa to the south nor eastern Europe and Russia to the east offer a more attractive alternative trading-bloc affiliation.

By contrast, in the Russian case, prosperous Russian peripheral areas might be able to argue with some credence that their long-term prospects would be better if they were detached from Russia and linked with the trading bloc nearest to them in Europe or Asia. For example, the Russian Far East might find Asia a more plausible natural economic territory in the long term than the current link with European Russia. It has, indeed, been suggested that prosperity in peripheral areas may be inversely related to the cohesiveness of Russian federalism (Fairlie 1993). Even in the short term, separatist risks loom. Sergei Shakhrai has recently suggested that without initiatives to populate the area, Russia could lose Siberia and the Russian Far East in 20 years due to migration out of the area.[8]

Seen in this light, it might be plausible to argue that Kaliningrad could be wooed away from Moscow, particularly if neighboring Poland and Lithuania develop closer relations with the EU. Theoretically, Kaliningrad could also be enticed away from Moscow by Baltic commercial opportunities even if Germany were not prominently involved. In this scenario, Kaliningrad might be an important conduit, not only between Russia and Germany but also between Russia and the EU via the Baltic states. This scenario could become even more probable if the Russians succeed in getting these changes: "automatic dual citizenship for Russians abroad; Russian to be an official language; and treaties guaranteeing the rights of 'Russian-speakers'" (a wider category than Russian citizens or ethnic Russians) (n.n. 1994: 48).

Economic scenarios involving the possible development of an informal and/or illegal service industry (Supir 1993: 51) have gained in credibility and urgency in light of the attempted smuggling of plutonium out of Kaliningrad. In analyzing other nuclear-smuggling attempts involving Germany, the press has speculated that there may be "links between criminals and the old East German secret police, who may have helped set up smuggling routes across the Baltic" (Frankland 1994) smuggling that reportedly occurs as Russian business people export from "mainland Russia" to Belarus and the Baltic states under the guise of naming Kaliningrad as a final destination for material. Russian authorities say that "… of more than 6,000 organizations which exported goods from Russia to Kaliningrad in 1993–1994 it was found that not less than half of the exported goods were 'left' in Belarus and the Baltic states" (Frankland 1994). Authorities suggest that a substantial number of strategic materials are illegally exported from

Russia with the participation of commercial structures which are specially being created by criminal elements.

Finally, incipient foreign investment and the EU TACIS-Program symbolize an "incremental economic spillover" scenario of the future of Kaliningrad. Indeed, incremental change involving more interaction with the European Union is likely unless Russian policy changes. Now that Finland and Sweden have joined the European Union, the Commission is trying to promote a coordinated Baltic policy. The EU's programs in part extend to northwest Russia, defined as the area including Kaliningrad, St. Petersburg, Novgorod, Pskov, and Murmansk, as well as Karelia (Commission of the European Communities 1994: 1). In July 1994, the Management Committee of the EU's TACIS initiative[9] adopted a program that will give 10 million ECU to Kaliningrad (Euro-East 1994). The projects scheduled for implementation include development of Kaliningrad's Free Economic Zone, post-privatization assistance to enterprises, development of the transport and energy systems, reconstruction of the fishing industry, and development of a business-management department at Kaliningrad University.[10]

4. Conclusion

The range of future scenarios indicates that the future of Kaliningrad is rather uncertain. The exclave could experience peace and prosperity if democracy and market-economy reforms gain a sure foothold in Russia. On the other hand, it could become a battlefield if nationalist and anti-reform leaders gain control in Russia or Lithuania.

Moscow's attitude toward Kaliningrad has varied from ambivalence and inaction to the hasty issuing of presidential decrees. This creates uncertainties that risk a loss of commercial attractiveness as competing areas develop in nearby foreign countries. The regional perspective is that the Baltic states' transport system and Kaliningrad provide the principal transport links among Russia, Belarus, Ukraine, Germany, and the Baltic Sea routes. Changes in the Baltic states, as well as changes in Russia and in the nearby Polish port of Gdansk, can all affect Kaliningrad's competitiveness.[11]

Circumstances may change. Finland has joined the European Union, and Russia is now on the external border of the EU. In the past, Russia has tended to regard EU interests in Kaliningrad as synonymous with German interests. Future EU debate regarding the status of Kaliningrad will presumably have more of a Baltic and Nordic component. This could encourage a Russian shift away from its Maginot-Line focus on an alleged German threat to sovereignty.

Finnish and Swedish membership in the EU insures that the Nordic and Baltic areas, including Kaliningrad, will be a region in which the Russian *near abroad* meets the EU *near abroad*. Even before the EU's Scandinavian enlargement, Vladimir Shumeiko suggested to the Danish Minister for Housing and Nordic and Baltic Cooperation that an international conference on Baltic region cooperation and the development of Kaliningrad be held. The Danish Minister welcomed the initiative and expressed the hope that the other members of the Nordic Council would be interested. But more than conferences will be needed to insure that Kaliningrad does not become a forgotten land while the other Baltic ports, such as Gdansk, Ventspils, and Klaipeda, develop.

In any case, dealing with Kaliningrad is not an option but a requirement. The interface of the EU's *near abroad* with Russia's *near abroad* is part of the reality of daily life. The Baltic states are now discussing the possibility of operating joint air-traffic control. This may link Finland, the EU, and Russia partly because Estonia asked Helsinki to help with its air-traffic control in the post-Soviet period, and Vilnius operates Kaliningrad's air-traffic control as it did during the Soviet period. Because of the need to cooperate on issues like these, it would be helpful if the Baltic states and westerners would tone down the complaint that Russia's interest in the Baltic states is neo-imperialistic. Although there may be some Russian nationalists who would like to reconquer the Baltic states, there are probably many more Russians who are now just trying to solve the many problems that occurred in Russia's economy when the Baltic states separated from Russia.

In spite of all of its problems, Kaliningrad is still functioning. Apparently, there is nothing inherently unstable about the exclave status. However, an indication exists that the military may regard Kaliningrad's exclave status as a weakness and a liability. Admiral Yegorov reportedly said that "with Lithuania and Belarus now independent states, the remoteness of the Kaliningrad *oblast* from other Russian regions has become a fact. This created an acute need for a base that would accumulate supplies and prepare reserves on the Russian mainland. The Leningrad Naval Base will play the role of such a logistics base" (International Intelligence Report 1994).

These future scenarios do not imply that any foreign government presently poses a threat to Kaliningrad. There is no evidence that responsible government officials in Germany, Poland, or Lithuania intend to try to take over Kaliningrad either directly or indirectly. However, in the post-Cold War world, potential threats have to be taken into consideration. Nationalist minorities in Lithuania and Germany have expressed an interest in recovering Kaliningrad. These views, along with the November destruction of the rail link between Moscow and Kaliningrad, give Russia ample reason to maintain a substantial military presence in the *oblast*.

However, Russia's focus should not be on external threats. The Olshansky analysis of separatist trends in Russia shows that the greatest threat to Russian territorial integrity comes not from outside but from Russia itself. Circumstances such as the fall of the ruble and the lack of decisive action to provide Kaliningrad with economic and political stability will try the patience of Kaliningraders of the future. Even now, Russians in Kaliningrad, Murmansk, Karelia, and other areas are probably concerned when they learn of Yeltsin's March 1995 presidential decrees abolishing the customs privileges that they had previously received.

But Russians are famous for their patience and tolerance. In addition, the government has clearly demonstrated that mother bears do not like to be separated from their cubs. Memories of Grozny and the lack of short-term economic alternatives will prevent Kaliningraders from making a quick dash for the exit, but they cannot be blamed for fantasizing about more promising economic and political affiliations than they now have. Perhaps a Kaliningrad affiliated with northwest Russia may be Russia's best realistic hope in the long run. In the short term, however, Kaliningrad will continue to be a microcosm of the conflicting pressures of centralization and decentralization. Only time will tell whether or not Kaliningrad can build a bridge or will become a *cordon sanitaire* between Europe and Russia.

Notes

1. Valliant (1994: 93) quoting *Kommersant Daily*, 26 May 1994, 3/FBIS SOV, 94/103, 27 May 1994, 37.

2. Valliant (1994: 33) quoting "Russia Plans to Further Develop Economic Ties with China," TASS, 23 May 1994/FBIS Sov, 94/100, 24 May 1994, 15. FBIS is the abbreviation for Foreign Broadcast Information.

3. Data accumulated from a press conference by the Regional Administration where the latest official statistics were made public (reported in *Kaliningradskaya Pravda*, 19 July 1994, p. 1, trans. Vladimir Lisniak).

4. Valentin Korneyevets, economic geographer at Kaliningrad State University, interview by author, interpreted by Vladimir Lisniak, Kaliningrad, Russia, July 1994.

5. Petrov (1995). The company reportedly intends to get involved in "local metal working enterprises, the Vtorchermet joint-stock company and the Baltmet JV."

6. All of this information is from Mr. Valentin Korneyevets. Most of it drawn from his revisions which will be submitted for the publication *Urban Systems and Rural Areas Report* from Vision and Strategies around the Baltic Sea 2010, 2nd Conference of Ministers for Spatial Planning and Development, Gdansk, Poland, 14–15 December 1993, p.17. The information in these reports is prepared by individuals who represent each of the Baltic areas in The Group of Focal Points. The report on Kaliningrad was given to me by the Kaliningrad representative on the Group of Focal Points, Mr. Valentin Korneyevets, the Scientific Research Institute of Complex Studies of Regions. I am especially grateful to Mr. Korneyevets who met with me for many hours on three occasions over the 10-day period of my research in Kaliningrad.

7. Girnius (1994). Swedish elections have occurred since this meeting was held and a new Foreign Minister is now in office.

8. Shakhrai is former minister for nationalities and regional policy and has reportedly said that he will run for the post of Head of the Administration of the Kaliningrad Region. Information quoted here is from Nadezhda Potapova, "Russia May Lose Siberia, Far East in 20 years—Shakhrai Warns," TASS, 23 February 1995. [Online]. Available: NEXIS Library: EUROPE File: ALLEUR.

9. TACIS is the acronym for Technical Assistance for the Commonwealth of Independent States. The program "provides technical assistance in a number of key areas to underpin the transition to a market economy and a democratic society."

10. Information provided by Sylvia S. Gurova, Head of Foreign Economic Department, Administration of Kaliningrad Region, Free Economic Zone "Yantar" Development Committee in an interview with Lyndelle Fairlie in Kaliningrad, July 1994.

11. There are tentative plans to develop a new port, Ust-Luga, near St. Petersburg to relieve congestion in that area. Nearby, the Lithuanian port of Klaipeda and the related road and rail network will benefit from the $46.5 million infrastructure-enhancement project to be funded by the European Bank for Reconstruction and Development, the Export-Import Bank of Japan, and the Lithuanian Ministry of Transport.

References

Afanasyeva, Galina. 1994. "Russia on the Baltic." *Moscow News* (24 January) .

Atkinson, Rick. 1994. "Germans Invest in East Europe but Curb Image of Empire; Auto, Chemical Firms at Forefront; $2 Billion Effort Trails Americas." *The Washington Post* (17 April).

Barinov, A., and N. Sberegaev. n.d. "Tendencies of the Development of International Activity of the Kaliningrad Region—Development Trends under Circumstances of Exclave." Translated by Oksana Shestakova.

BBC Summary of World Broadcasts. 1994a. "Russian Deputies Call for Further Development of Ties with China." 9 May, sec. Part 1 Former USSR; Russia; SU/1992/B, citing source as ITAR-TASS news agency (World Service), Moscow, in English 1851 gmt 6 May [Online]. Available: NEXIS Library: EUROPE File: ALLEUR.

BBC Summary of World Broadcasts. 1994b. "Russia's Regions; Gaydar Sets Off for Tour of Regions, Explains Its Purpose." 12 September, sec. Part 1 Former USSR; Russia; SU/2098/B; citing Moscow, in Russian 1400 gmt 5 September [Online]. Available: NEXIS Library: EUROPE File: ALLEUR.

BBC Summary of World Broadcasts. 1994c. "Russian Security Council Discusses Federal Policy." 4 October, sec. Part 1 Former USSR; Russia; internal affairs; SU/2126/B quoting Interfax news agency, Moscow, in English 1439 gmt 12 October [Online]. Available: NEXIS Library: EUROPE File: ALLEUR.

BBC Summary of World Broadcasts. 1995a. "Russian Government Approves Draft Law on Economic Zones." 30 January, sec. Part 1 Former USSR; Russia special; economic affairs; SU/2214/C; citing Interfax news agency, Moscow, in English 1402 gmt 26 January [Online]. Available: NEXIS Library: EUROPE File: ALLEUR.

BBC Summary of World Broadcasts. 1995b. Sileris verbatim as reported in "Lithuania Misses Opportunity to Organize Trade with Kaliningrad." 4 March [Online]. Available: NEXIS Library: EUROPE File: ALLEUR.

BBC Summary of World Broadcasts. 1995c. "Yeltsin Abolishes Export Restrictions and Customs Privileges." 8 March, sec. Part 1 Former USSR; Russia Special; Economic Affairs [1]; SU/2246/C; citing ITAR-TASS news agency (World Service), Moscow, in

English 1546 gmt 6 March [Online]. Available: NEXIS Library: EUROPE File: ALLEUR.

BBC Summary of World Broadcasts. 1995d. "Other Russian Regions: Kaliningrad Leaders Criticize Presidential Decree Abolishing Customs Privileges."14 March, sec. Part 1 Former USSR; Russia; SU/2251/B; citing ITAR-TASS news agency (World Service), Moscow, in English 1457 gmt 11 March [Online]. Available: NEXIS Library: EUROPE File: ALLEUR.

Bingen, Dieter. 1993. "The Kaliningrad Region (Königsberg): An Inventory of the Present Situation and Prospects for the Future." *German Viewpoints* (II), Bericht des BIOst 25 (Summary in English).

Biryukov, Valery. 1994. "Opposition Plans Joint Actions to Oust Yeltsin by May." The Telegraph Agency of the Soviet Union (hereafter abbreviated TASS), 16 September [Online]. Available: NEXIS Library: EUROPE File: ALLEUR.

Clarke, Doug. 1994. "Russia to Keep Up Pressure on Arms Treaty." RFE-RL Daily Report No. 174 (13 September).

Clement, Norris. 1992. "Local Responses to Globalization: New Opportunities for the San Diego-Tijuana Region." CIBER Working Paper 94-1. San Diego: Center for International Business Education and Research, San Diego State University.

Commission of the European Communities. 1993. *Europe in a Changing World: The External Relations of the European Community.* Brussels: EC.

Commission of the European Communities. 1994. "Orientations for a Union Approach Towards the Baltic Sea Region." Communication from the Commission to the Council, Sec. (94) 1747 final. Brussels (25 October).

Current Digest of the Post-Soviet Press. 1994. 10 August 1994, sec. The Russian Federation; Military Affairs; Volume XLVI, No. 28; p. 20 citing Vyacheslav Kostikov, "In the Dunes of Baltic Policy," Sevodnya, 12 July 1994, p. 10 excerpt [Online]. Available NEXIS Library: EUROPE File: ALLEUR.

Dawisha, Karen, and Bruce Parrott. 1994. *Russia and the New States of Eurasia: The Politics of Upheaval.* New York: Cambridge University Press.

Economist. 1994. "Leaning on the Balts." (27 August).

Euro-East, European Information Service. 1994. "New Action Programme for CIS Adopted and Funds Diverted for Chernobyl." 20 September, sec. No. 25 [Online]. Available: NEXIS Library: EUROPE File: ALLEUR.

Fairlie, Lyndelle. 1993. "Center-Periphery Issues in the Russian Far East." *Relazioni Internazionali* (June).

Foreign Economic Department. 1994. "Yantar." Kaliningrad Region.

Frankland, Mark. 1994. "The Great Plutonium Chase." *The Observer.* London (21 August).

Girnius, Saulius. 1994. "Meeting of Baltic and Nordic Foreign Ministers." *RFE-RL Daily Report*, no. 166 (1 September).

Girnius, Saulius. 1995."Lithuania and Russia Agree on Military Transit." *OMRI Daily Digest* no. 14, Part II (19 January).

Hansson, Ardo. 1993. "Commentaries." *Council of Baltic Sea States Newsletter* , sec. International, no. 4.

International Intelligence Report. 1994. "Commander Says Baltic Fleet Vital to Interests." 8 July, citing as source Russia/CIS Intelligence report citing Kaliningradskaya Pravda in Russian [Online]. Available: NEXIS Library: EUROPE File: ALLEUR.

Kaminski, Matthew. 1995. "Kaliningrad Opens its Fortress Gates." *Financial Times* (15 February).

Kresl, Peter. 1992. *The Urban Economy and Regional Trade Liberalization.* New York: Praeger.

Kropinova, Helena. n.d. "The Place of the Kaliningrad Region in the Community of the Baltic States." Unpublished manuscript.

Lashkevich, Nikolai. 1994. [Online] Available: NEXIS Library: EUROPE File: ALLEUR.

Lashkevich, Nikolai 1994. "Lithuanian Politicians Threaten to Cut Kaliningrad off from Russia." *The Current Digest of the Post-Soviet Press* (10 August).

Lashkevich, Nikolai. 1994. "Russia Will be to Blame for Possible Russian Exodus from Lithuania." *Russian Press Digest* (12 August). Available: NEXIS Library: EUROPE File: ALLEUR.

Marsch, Renate. 1994. "Germans Start to Resettle Former East Prussia." Deutsche Presse-Agentur, 20 September, BC Cycle 04:05—Central European Time, sec. International News. [Online]. Available: NEXIS Library: EUROPE File: ALLEUR.

Petrov, Vladimir. 1995. "External Capital Displays Interest in 'Amber.'" RusData Dialine-BizEkon News (10 February).

Polish Press Agency. 1994. "Polish Provinces, Kaliningrad to Tighten Cooperation." PAP News Wire, 21 January 1994 [Online]. Available: NEXIS Library: EUROPE File: ALLEUR.

Potapova, Nadezhda. 1995. "Russia May Lose Siberia, Far East in 20 Years—Shakhrai Warns." TASS, 23 February [Online]. Available: NEXIS Library: EUROPE File: ALLEUR.

Ratajczyk, Andrzej. 1995. "Chernomyrdin Visit: The Result of Heated Agreement." *The Warsaw Voice* (26 February).

Rosenau, James N. 1993. "Coherent Connection or Commonplace Contiguity? Theorizing About the California-Mexico Overlap." In *The California-Mexico Connection*, Abraham F. Lowenthal and Katrina Burgess, eds. Stanford: Stanford University Press.

Sapir, Jacques. 1993. "References economiques regionales, transition et politique de stabilisation en Russie." *Revue d'etudes comparatives Est-Ouest* 24 (1).

Styczek, Dariusz, and Mariusz Staniszewski. 1994. "After Comecon: Old Partner, New Partner." *The Warsaw Voice* (27 March).

Turek, Bogdan. 1994. "Lithuania: Russia Obstructs Trade." United Press International (20 May).

Valliant. Robert, ed. 1994. "Special Economic Regime Proposed for Primorskii Krai." *RA Report* 17 (July). Honolulu: Center for Russia in Asia, School of Hawaiian, Asian & Pacific Studies, University of Hawaii at Manoa.

Viviano, Frank. 1994. "Lost Empire May Be on Rise Again: Inhabitants of Central Europe Unnerved by 'Germanization.'" *San Francisco Chronicle* (17 January).

Wellmann, Christian. 1994. "Market Place or Garrison? On the Future of the Kaliningrad Region." In *Towards a Baltic SeaCurity Community*, Björn Hagelin, ed. (no place furnished).

Yurkin, Anatoly. 1994. "National Wealth Stolen on Pretext of Militarization." TASS 29 March [Online]. Available: NEXIS Library EUROPE: File: ALLEUR.

Zavarsky, L., and V. Minin. 1994. "Russia: Kaliningrad Port in Fever." *Reuter Textline Novecon*, 2 August [Online]. Available: NEXIS Library: EUROPE File: ALLEUR.

IV

Transboundary Cooperation Issues in North and Central America

On the Road to Interdependence? The United States-Mexico Border Region

Paul Ganster

1. Introduction

The territorial interface between the United States and Mexico is one of the most dynamic and complex border regions of the world. It is an area of rapid population growth, accelerated urbanization, political change, and economic expansion. Two very different systems meet at the boundary between Mexico and the United States: the developed, industrialized world meets the developing world. It is where the North meets the South. One of the most distinguishing features of this border region is its economic asymmetry. It has the strongest contrasts in the entire world in terms of economic differences from one side of the boundary to the other. Although this border was created by war and characterized by conflict over many decades, it is nonetheless a binational region that shows evidence of growing integration and increasing levels of transborder cooperation. This process accelerated with the implementation of the North American Free Trade Agreement (NAFTA) among Mexico, the United States, and Canada on January 1, 1994. This paper will summarize the historical development of the region. Then, the major features of the contemporary border, including the major conflictual issues, will be detailed. Finally, the growing transborder interdependence and integration will be discussed.

2. The Physical Context of the Border Region

From a physical perspective, the borderlands lack clear definition. The western half of the border region is characterized by natural features that trend north-south. The far west is occupied by the Pacific Coastal Range, and eastwardly is the interior basin and range region. Then, continuing toward the east, is the Sierra Madre Occidental, followed by the *meseta central* (central plateau) of Mexico that gradually decreases in elevation from some 8,000 feet in central Mexico to about 4,000 feet at El Paso-Ciudad Juárez on the international boundary. Still farther to the east is the broken, dissected range of the Sierra Madre Oriental that dies out just north of the border in the Big Bend area of Texas. Finally, on the far eastern edge of the border, are the gulf coastal plains, sloping gently towards the Gulf of Mexico.[1]

The U.S.-Mexican border region is arid. Rainfall on the western edge at San Diego is approximately ten inches per year. That figure increases slightly in the coastal range, decreases in the interior deserts, rises a bit in the Sierra Madre Occidental, is low for the Chihuahua desert region, and rises moderately on the moister gulf coastal plain. The Rio Grande and the Colorado River systems provide most of the water of the region used for human consumption, but water is scarce and is a problem for future growth and development of the border.

These natural features tend to facilitate northerly and southerly movement of humans, and to frustrate movement eastwardly and westwardly. The western half of the international boundary is simply a surveyed line cutting across mountains and deserts. Only a small stretch of the Colorado River forms the boundary between the two countries, but is not a barrier or a transportation route of any importance. On the east, the boundary follows the Rio Grande, an intermittent body of water at its upper reaches. Although the lower Rio Grande is a large year-round river, it is not big enough to be an effective natural barrier or to serve as a usable inland water transportation route.

3. Historical Overview of the Border Region

The U.S.-Mexican border region initially was the northern fringe of the Spanish colony of New Spain and then, after 1821, of the newly independent republic of Mexico.[2] Characterized by sparse settlements based on mining and ranching, the northern region was never effectively settled or occupied by Mexico, a new nation that experienced nearly a half century of internal disorder after independence. Mexico lost much of its northern territories, first through a revolt of Anglo settlers in Texas in 1835, and then through a war between Mexico and the United States in 1846. The Treaty of Guadalupe Hidalgo that was signed in 1848 to end the war ceded much of the north to the United States. This, along with the sale of parts of New Mexico and Arizona by the Gadsden Purchase in 1854, established the international boundary between Mexico and the United States that endures today.[3] Figure 1 shows the location of the boundary line, along with the U.S. and Mexican states and cities that have developed in the region.

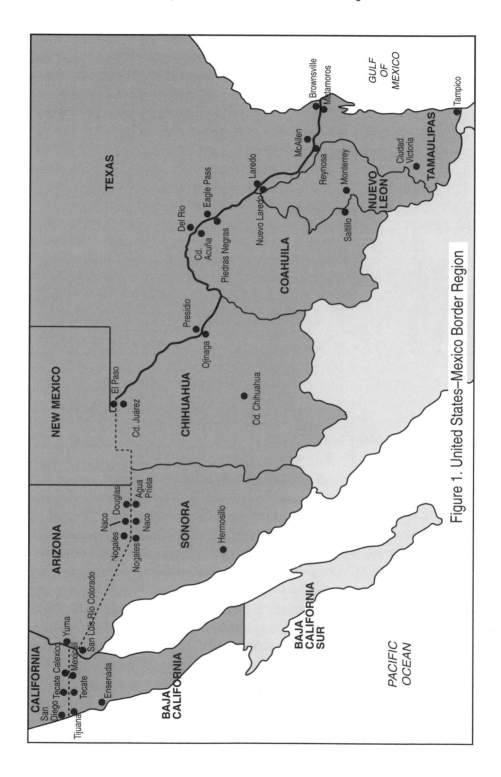

Figure 1. United States–Mexico Border Region

Early Border Development

The conclusion of the war with Mexico in 1848 opened a vast area to the dual forces of Manifest Destiny and the dynamic U.S. economy. Economic cycles of mining, ranching, and agriculture—in combination with the building of extensive railroad networks and urban centers—led to rapid economic development of the Southwest of the United States in the late nineteenth century. The linking of transportation networks of the United States and Mexico encouraged the development of border cities. At every major transportation route crossing the international boundary, customhouses and service industries for trade developed on both sides of the border. These gave rise to population centers that eventually emerged as the twin-city settlement pattern that characterizes the region today as clearly portrayed on the map of the border region.

The interdependence of the U.S. border region with Mexico was evident relatively early. Increasingly, trade was a factor, but also important was the fact that much of the labor for the economic development of the southwestern border region came from Mexico. The flow of labor was conditioned, of course, by the dual push-pull factors of lack of jobs in Mexico and labor needs in the United States. Since Mexico's north was isolated from the national economy, the United States was the historical trading partner for Mexican northerners. Mexican border urban centers developed in response to economic stimuli from across the border, and Mexican border urban growth became dependent upon the U.S. settlements and regions to the north. These elements have been present in the border region for more than a century and continue in significant ways today.

The first several decades of the existence of the border region were characterized by lawlessness, Indian raids, banditry, and lack of strong governmental controls. Relative peace and order finally came to the region by the 1880s along with extension of railroads throughout the U.S. border region, economic development, and defeat and confinement to reservations of most of the marauding Indian groups. In Mexico, a half century of internal disorder was brought to a close with the rise to power of Porfirio Díaz who was to dominate Mexican politics until 1910[4] Díaz ruthlessly suppressed rural violence, restored order to the nation's border, and opened the country to foreign investors. In the northern border regions of Chihuahua, Sonora, and Baja California, foreign and Mexican companies acquired huge tracts of land for agricultural, mining, and urban development purposes from the Díaz government.[5]

The violent upheavals in Mexico during the 1910 revolution affected the border region. Mexican revolutionaries often operated from safe bases in U.S. border towns. Mexicans of all classes fled the violence, and many settled on the U.S. side of the border and remained even after restoration of relative peace in

Mexico by the 1920s. Everywhere, the revolution reinforced and strengthened the Mexican communities in U.S. border towns.

Prohibition, the period from 1920 through 1933 in the United States when sale, manufacture, or transportation of alcoholic beverages was prohibited, provided stimulus for economic growth in Mexico's northern border cities as they became the sites of tourism development centered on gambling, entertainment, and alcohol.[6] Although during the 1920s Mexican border towns grew and their economic bases broadened with the creation of agricultural industries and other enterprises, development was very much dependent upon the twin city across the border. With the ending of Prohibition and the deepening Great Depression, the Mexican border towns were hard hit, exposing their extreme dependence on the adjacent U.S. border towns. Tijuana, with a narrow economic base linked to tourism and isolated from the Mexican economy, was particularly affected. Mexican border cities did not recover until the World War II era brought prosperity that continued with the impressive economic expansion of the U.S. Southwest in the postwar period. Mexican border cities grew rapidly, so that by 1960 their populations were relatively large: Mexicali (281,333); Ciudad Juárez (276,995); Tijuana (165,690); Matamoros (143,043); and Reynosa (134,869).

Labor Flows

Flows of Mexican labor across the border supported the economic development of the U.S. Southwest and provided a safety valve for Mexico's unemployed and poor masses. Welcomed during periods of economic expansion, these laborers were rejected during economic downturns. With the Great Depression, large-scale forced-repatriation programs returned Mexican workers across the border.[7] This was a pattern that was repeated every time there was an expansion and recession cycle in the United States. These episodes have been the source of bitter feelings on the part of Mexicans and have disturbed the lives of border residents. Immigration continues to be a source of conflict between Mexico and the United States. To a large extent, immigration is a border issue since the flows are across the border, the U.S. border states receive most of the undocumented workers, and the migratory flows have great impacts on both Mexican and U.S. border cities.

In 1942, in response to the wartime labor shortage in the United States, the Mexican and the United States governments agreed to a guest worker program to allow contracts for Mexican laborers to work temporarily in the United States, initially in agriculture, but later in other occupations. The program, known as the Bracero Program, was extended beyond the wartime emergency and was terminated only in 1964. Nonetheless, driven by poverty and lack of jobs in Mexico and attracted by employment in the United States, the flow of Mexican labor northward has continued to the present time in the form of illegal migration. The movement of Mexican migrants into the United States has profoundly affected border communities and today constitutes a key issue for the border region.[8]

Over the years, as many Mexicans acquired visas for work in the United States and as many border Mexicans acquired U.S. citizenship, a significant group of commuter workers developed along the entire border region. Living in the Mexican twin city and commuting to work at jobs in the United States, these workers are an important regional economic force. For example, in the San Diego-Tijuana region there are approximately 30,000 men and women who cross daily to work in the United States. These commuter workers who work in San Diego constitute about six percent of Tijuana's economically active population. Approximately eight percent of the employed people in Mexico's northern border cities work across the border in the United States. Paid in dollars, these individuals account for important retail purchases in the United States. In addition to providing high quality and low cost labor, these workers benefit the U.S. border cities in another way. San Diego, for example, has a serious shortage of affordable housing and for the commuter workers, Mexico provides that basic infrastructure need.[9] Shared labor flows and shared low ¢ost housing infrastructure are but two examples of the interdependence and integration of border cities.

The Border Industrialization Program

Mexico, fearing significant unemployment as the Bracero Program ended and guest workers returned from the United States, established in 1965 the Border Industrialization Program (BIP). Designed to generate jobs in Mexican border cities through establishment of assembly plants, or *maquiladoras*, the program initially enjoyed modest success. BIP was the Mexican manifestation of the globalization of the world economy and the shift toward export processing zones. U.S. and Mexican tariff codes allowed for components to be imported duty-free into Mexico where they were assembled with low-cost labor and then exported back to the United States, paying duties only on the value added in Mexico.[10] Beginning in 1983, stimulated by simplified regulations and lower wages in dollar terms brought by the devalued Mexican currency, the industry saw increases in employment that averaged 14.4 percent on an annual basis, as seen in Figure 3.

The importance of the *maquiladora* industry to the border region should not be underestimated. Initially, *maquilas* were restricted to the border and even today approximately eighty percent of the plants are in the border zone. On the Mexican side of the international boundary, the industry stimulated significant job creation and produced a group of managers and technical personnel in an industry that was competitive on a world level. Other areas of Mexican industry were not globally competitive since Mexican economic development policy from the 1940s favored import substitution industrialization, heavy protection for national producers, and great state participation in the economy through parastate industries. The *maquiladora* industry, through job creation and investment, helped the northern border become one of the most economically dynamic regions of Mexico, even during the severe economic downturn of the 1980s.

Figure 2. Number of Plants and Workers in the *Maquiladora* Industry, 1974–1994

Year	Number of Plants	Annual Growth Rate of Plants	Number of Jobs	Annual Growth Rate of Plants
1974	455		75,970	
1975	454	-0.2	67,210	-11.3
1976	448	-1.3	74,500	10.8
1977	443	-1.1	78,430	5.3
1978	457	3.2	90,700	15.6
1979	540	18.2	111,370	22.8
1980	620	14.8	119,550	7.3
1981	605	-2.4	130,970	9.6
1982	585	-3.3	127,050	-3.0
1983	600	2.6	150,860	18.7
1984	672	12.0	199,680	32.4
1985	750	13.1	211,970	6.2
1986	890	17.1	249,830	17.9
1987	1,130	26.4	305,250	22.2
1988	1,400	24.1	369,490	21.0
1989	1,670	18.6	429,730	16.3
1990	1,938	17.1	460,260	7.1
1991	1,910	-1.2	467,350	1.5
1992	2,080	8.4	505,700	8.2
1993	2,170	4.4	540,930	7.0

Source: Comisión Económica para América Latina y el Caribe, 1994: Figure 30 (based on data from Instituto Nacional de Estadística, Geografía e Informática).

Figure 3. Average Annual Growth Rate of Plants and Jobs in the *Maquiladora* Industry

Year	Average Annual Growth Rate of Plants	Average Annual Growth Rate of Jobs
1974-1978	0.1	4.5
1978-1984	6.6	14.1
1983-1993	10.9	14.4

Source: Comisión Económica para América Latina y el Caribe 1994: Figure 30 (based on data from Instituto Nacional de Estadística, Geografía e Informática).

The expansion of the *maquiladora* industry in the early 1980s coincided with a decline in Mexican retail purchases in the United States. Many local officials in U.S. border communities noted the positive economic impact of the establishment of *maquiladoras* in adjacent Mexican twin cities and began actively to recruit U.S. and other companies to relocate to the Mexican side of the border. For the first time in U.S. border communities, many business and political leaders, as well as members of the general public, became aware of the symbiotic relationship with their Mexican neighbors. Beginning in the mid-1980s, then, U.S. border communities began to see significant opportunities in expanded economic relations with Mexico. This was particularly true in the smaller U.S. border communities such as those along the lower Rio Grande in Texas where regional economies were narrowly based on agriculture and Mexican retail purchases.[11] This new outlook led to strong support in border communities for the North American Free Trade Agreement. It also led to enhanced border interactions in areas other than those strictly related to trade and commerce, pushing U.S. and Mexican border communities to increased cooperation on many fronts.

Restructuring the Mexican Economy

Over the course of the last decade, Mexico has undergone a profound revolution in its economic development policy It has changed from a highly protected domestic economy, with strict controls on imports and foreign investment and heavy state participation in many sectors of the economy, to an open economy with liberalized import and investment laws. These measures liberalizing the Mexican economy produced a significant increase in U.S.-Mexican trade that accelerated with NAFTA. Since most bilateral trade moved goods by land transportation, trade-related activities boomed in the border cities. At the same time, infrastructure in the border cities, including customs facilities, ports of entry, and roads, became saturated.

North American Free Trade Agreement

In the spring of 1990, President Carlos Salinas of Mexico requested that the United States discuss implementation of a free trade agreement between the two countries. Canada, which already had a free trade agreement with the United States, joined in and the three countries negotiated the North American Free Trade Agreement. Debate over approval of NAFTA was particularly intense in the United States Congress and for the first time focused national attention on environmental conditions in the border region and potential impacts of the treaty on border communities. In response to strong criticism of existing governmental efforts on the border environment, U.S. and Mexican authorities developed the *Integrated Environmental Plan of the U.S.-Mexico Border Region* (IBEP).[12] Other important actions included negotiation by Mexico and the United States of side agreements to NAFTA that led to the establishment of the North American Development Bank (NADBank) and the Border Environment Cooperation Commission (BECC). The BECC analyzes border environmental issues and certifies priority infrastructure projects for funding by NADBank. By 1997, these two new binational institutions had begun to have an impact in the border region.

The recent history of the border region, culminating with the NAFTA process, has seen a fundamental change in the role that the border region plays domestically within Mexico and the United States and also internationally in the bilateral relationship. Historically, the border has been politically marginalized in the polities of Mexico and the United States. The NAFTA process helped transform the border from a region that merely received policy from Washington, D.C., and Mexico City to a region that began to initiate actions that became national and bilateral policy. The border was key to the passage of NAFTA and will likely retain a strategic role in the unfolding economic integration of the two partners.

After more than two years of NAFTA, many of the hopes of its supporters have been realized with respect to Mexico-United States trade. During the first nine months of NAFTA, American exports to Mexico grew 22 percent and imports from Mexico expanded 23 percent. America's surplus on this trade was $1.8 billion and the U.S. Department of Commerce estimated that this expansion of exports to Mexico accounted for 130,000 U.S. jobs.[13] At the end of 1994, a note of uncertainty was interjected into NAFTA as Mexico fell into a severe economic crisis. This situation was exacerbated by the transition from the Salinas presidency to that of Ernesto Zedillo on December 1, 1994, and a continuing series of political crises, including the Chiapas rebellion, disputed gubernatorial elections, and the assassination of several prominent political leaders. A sharp devaluation of the peso at the end of the year and early in 1995 had predictable impacts on the border region in terms of decreases in Mexican shoppers in U.S. border cities. The devaluation severely affected the middle class in Mexico's border cities, where many expenses such as rents are pegged to the value of the dollar. Despite the economic shock, trade between Mexico and the United States recovered in 1996. Most analysts agree that NAFTA has created jobs in both nations, has stimulated new investment in Mexico, and has significantly increased bilateral trade.

3. Major Characteristics of the Border Region

Historical forces have produced a border region of considerable diversity from east to west. For example, on the U.S. side, the eastern half of the border is poorer, more Hispanic, and with a more narrow economic base than on the western end, which is wealthier, has a broader economic base, and is more Anglo in population and culture. On the Mexican side, there is also some east-west differentiation, principally with respect to economic development. The western end of the Mexican border is more dynamic economically than elsewhere along the border. There are also strong contrasts from north to south across the border. The human settlement of the borderlands is one of twin cities separated by expanses of lightly populated deserts, mountains, or in the lower Rio Grande, agricultural land or undeveloped rolling plains with scrub vegetation. The map in Figure 1 illustrates clearly the twin city settlement patterns of the border region.

While the natural systems extend seamlessly across the border, the international boundary marks a very clear dividing line between two very different human systems. Some features of these systems do not extend across the border; others demonstrate a surprising degree of transboundary interaction with counterpart features from the other country. A review of the different components of the Mexican and U.S. systems that meet at the border will serve to highlight the extent of integration present in this transboundary zone.

Political and Legal Systems

The juxtaposition at the border of the highly centralized Mexican political system with the decentralized federal U.S. political system has broad implications for the daily lives of border residents. The differences in the two political systems have hindered bilateral cooperation on many transborder issues. In the United States, numerous federal departments and agencies from the U.S. border states and from the city and county local governments initiate policies that have importance for Mexico and its border region. While the U.S. State Department tries to monitor these actions, it does not attempt to enforce absolute control. However, in Mexico actions with international implications are more tightly controlled by the Ministry of Foreign Relations. These differences in the political and administrative structures often make local transborder cooperation difficult. Direct administrative counterparts often do not exist in each of the twin cities. Usually, local government agencies in the United States are able to initiate projects independently and develop financing. Mexican local agencies usually are constrained not only by restricted mandates for independent action, but have extremely limited financial and technical resources.[14]

The border region typically has been a pawn in the relations between the two countries. Often, federal decisions that affected the border region were made for reasons unrelated to the border. For example, at various times, the U.S. government has ordered increased inspections of incoming pedestrians and vehicles at the ports of entry on the U.S.-Mexican border to discourage the southward movement of tourists, causing great economic hardship in the tourist-dependent Mexican border communities. The real purpose of these actions was to pressure the Mexican government to improve its cooperation on drug-trafficking matters. Typically, policies and decisions made in the national capitals had a significant impact on the border yet border residents had little input in these decisions.

Another difference in the political and public administration systems of the two countries that has important implications for local border relations is the nature of public service and office-holding. In the United States, the majority of local, state, and federal government employees fall under various sorts of civil-service systems. This assures that the professional staffs most responsible for the day-to-day running of agencies will remain in place even when there is a change in the elected officials. In Mexico, the situation is quite different. There, with the change of administrations, whether federal, state, or local, government employees at all levels are replaced by new political appointments. Hence, continuity and institutional memory are much more fragmented in public administration on the Mexican side of the border. This is an important bottleneck for effective binational governmental cooperation.[15]

Economic Asymmetries

A key characteristic of the economic relationship between the two neighbors, and one that is especially apparent in the border region, is economic asymmetry. The 1994 Gross Domestic Product (GDP) of the United States was 6,600 billion dollars, approximately 18 times that of Mexico's GDP of 373 billion dollars. The Gross Regional Product (GRP) of the greater Los Angeles area exceeds the GDP of Mexico, but with one-tenth the population. At the border-regional level, the County of San Diego had a 1996 GRP of over 70 billion dollars, whereas that of the Municipality of Tijuana was around three billion dollars. The combined annual governmental budgets of the County of San Diego and the City of San Diego exceed the GRP of the Municipality of Tijuana.[16] Although such marked asymmetry is less elsewhere along the border, the disparities are still significant. These enormous economic asymmetries make transborder cooperation by government entities difficult due to the great differences in physical and human resources available to each side.

Demographic Features

Both U.S. and Mexican border populations are highly urbanized as seen in the more arid western end of the border, which tends to be more highly urbanized than the eastern end in the lower Rio Grande Valley where more small agricultural-based settlements exist in the areas outside the urban cores. The Municipality of Tijuana's lower level of urbanization is due to development of luxury housing along the coastal strip and emergence of outlying urbanized areas such as Rosarito. Figure 4 demonstrates the high degree of urbanization of the border population.

Figure 4. Urbanization of Border Municipalities and Counties

Municipality or County	Percent of Population in Urban Core	Municipality or County	Percent of Population in Urban Core
Tijuana, Baja California	81.0	Webb County, Texas (City of Laredo)	95.7
San Diego, California	93.2	Nuevo Laredo, Tamaulipas	98.0
Ciudad Juárez, Chihuahua	96.0	Cameron County, Texas (City of Brownsville)	74.0
El Paso, Texas	96.1	Matamoros, Tamaulipas	78.9
Santa Cruz, Arizona (City of Nogales)	76.7		
Nogales, Sonora	97.0		

Source: Data for the Mexican border municipalities are for 1970 and are from Mario Margulis and Rodolfo Turián, 1983: Cuadro C2; U.S. data are for 1980 and are from the U.S. Department of Commerce, 1983.

In addition to urban concentration, border populations have been, and continue to be, distinguished by rapid growth rates. Swift demographic expansion has brought a continuing infrastructure- and urban-services crisis in border cities, particularly in the Mexican cities that have fewer resources and ability to cope with the burgeoning demand. Figure 5 clearly demonstrates this urban dynamism.

Figure 5. Annual Growth Rates of Twin Cities by Decade

City & State	1940–50	1950–60	1960–70	1970–80	1980–90
San Diego, California	6.4	7.1	2.1	2.6	2.4
Tijuana, Baja California	13.4	9.8	6.4	4.0	5.0
Calexico, California	1.9	2.4	3.3	4.3	2.6
Mexicali, Baja California	12.8	10.4	4.4	2.5	2.5
Nogales, Arizona	2.0	1.8	2.3	7.5	2.2
Nogales, Sonora	7.7	6.3	3.4	2.7	4.9
El Paso, Texas	3.5	11.2	1.6	3.2	1.9
Ciudad Juárez, Chihuahua	9.4	7.5	5.1	3.3	3.8
Eagle Pass, Texas	1.3	6.6	2.7	3.9	-.4
Piedras Negras, Coahuila	7.6	7.6	-.04	7.2	3.6
Laredo, Texas	3.1	1.8	1.4	3.3	3.0
Nuevo Laredo, Tamaulipas	7.0	4.9	5.0	3.0	0.8
McAllen, Texas	6.9	6.3	1.5	7.6	2.4
Reynosa, Tamaulipas	3.4	8.1	6.6	3.4	3.2
Brownsville, Texas	6.1	7.5	9.1	6.2	1.5
Matamoros, Tamaulipas	11.0	7.3	4.2	3.1	3.5

Source: For the United States, Reich ed., 1983; U.S. Department of Commerce, 1983. For Mexico, Margulis and Turián. 1980–1990 growth rates calculated from Lorey ed., 1993.

Migration is the most important factor shaping the demographic picture of the binational border region. For example, Tijuana's population grew 6.9 percent between 1987 and 1988; 1.9 percent of the growth was natural increase and 5 percent was the result of immigration. During the same period, Ciudad Juárez saw a 1.8 percent natural increase and a 7.5 percent increase from migration. In 1980, 48.9 percent of the population of the border counties and municipalities consisted of migrants. Of the 48.9 percent, 8.4 percent were from a foreign country. The 1980 population of the Mexican border municipalities had 31.8 percent migrants, while the figure for the U.S. border counties was 58.2 percent.

Eleven percent of the migrants in the Mexican border municipalities were foreign born, while the figure was a much larger 20 percent for the U.S. border counties.[17]

U.S. border communities are further distinguished by considerable numbers of undocumented immigrants who are primarily from Mexico. For example, estimates indicate that there were about 96,000 undocumented aliens in San Diego County by the end of 1986. For 1993, estimates of numbers of undocumented immigrants in San Diego County were as high as 220,000.[18] Most of these individuals are Mexican. Since most undocumented aliens arrested in the San Diego region and elsewhere along the border are from Mexico, it may be assumed that most illegal aliens in the border region are Mexicans (See Figure 7).

The growing number of Spanish-speaking individuals in the United States, largely in the Southwest, and the close personal ties they have with Mexico are another factor that adds to the commonality of interests and interdependence between the two countries at the border. The Hispanic, or Latino, percentage of border cities' populations has been significant and is increasing, as illustrated by Figure 6.

Figure 6. Latino Population of U.S. Border Cities

City	1980 Percent Latino	1990 Percent Latino
Los Angeles	27.5	34.6
San Diego	14.9	20.7
El Paso	62.5	68.9
Laredo	93.0*	93.5
Brownsville	87.3*	89.8

* 1985 data.

Source: *Statistical Abstract of Latin America* 25: Figure 667; 1990 data from U.S. Department of Commerce 1991.

The combination of declining growth rates for the Anglo population, high natural rates of increase for Hispanics, and Hispanic immigration is dramatically shifting the ethnic composition of border states such as California.[19] In border cities like San Diego, this *Hispanization* process is especially apparent. The decade 1980–1990 saw an increase in the local Hispanic population from 14.9 percent to 20.7 percent of the total population. The growing Hispanic ethnic group has interesting political implications, both domestically and internationally, particularly in regions such as San Diego where the shift from Anglo to Latino has been dramatic.[20]

Border Culture

The presence of Hispanic populations on both sides of the international boundary, stimulated by important transboundary economic ties, has encouraged strong social and cultural linkages. Although difficult to quantify, these social and cultural aspects of interdependency are nonetheless real and growing. Oscar Martínez, in his recent work titled *Border People* (1994), as well as in earlier works, discusses the emergence of groups of borderlanders who participate in a vibrant border culture that is firmly linked to Mexico and to the United States. These individuals, who are able to function in both cultures and to participate in activities on both sides of the border, in some ways represent the future of the border. At the current level of interdependence, the percentage of borderlanders in the total border population is not large, but as the region moves toward more advanced integration, the number of specialists who are fully functional on either side of the border will increase.

In a number of areas along the border, binational cultural activities are prospering. Transboundary cultural events in fine arts, classical and contemporary music, and literature are ubiquitous. Transboundary linkages are also to be seen all along the border in the area of popular culture. *Corridos* and other traditional Mexican folk songs are encountered everywhere in the binational border region, as are traditions in popular literature and folk tales, humor, folk medicine, and other beliefs. Youth movements, such as that of the *cholos* from East Los Angeles, spread to U.S. and Mexican border cities and ultimately to Mexico City.[21] Sports are also a feature of the transboundary popular cultural life. Professional and intercollegiate athletic teams regularly draw fans from the other side of the boundary. Finally, everwhere along the border, television and radio stations, as well as the print media, have important impacts on the other side of the boundary.

Higher Education in the Border Region

An aspect of culture that is of great importance in the border region is higher education since these institutions train the leaders who will manage the region in the future.[22] The border has seen the slow development by Mexican and U.S. border universities of transborder cooperation on faculty research, faculty exchange, student exchange, and joint programs. The process is now moving more rapidly under the impetus of NAFTA as more students, faculty, and administrators realize that to be competitive, university graduates must be able to operate on both sides of the border, in both languages and cultures. Although there is movement in the direction of better articulation of Mexican and U.S. universities in the border region, much more change is needed adequately to serve the needs of the region, now and in the future. This contrasts strongly with Europe where joint advanced degree and research programs have been created in the Regio Basiliensis region of France, Switzerland, and Germany, and an area-wide undergraduate program for the European Economic Community has been developed. Nevertheless, U.S. and Mexican border universities have taken a leadership role on bilateral cooperation and programmatic development, reversing the traditional role of the border region. Instead of simply following national trends, the border region is providing innovation in this important area.

4. Border Issues

As the U.S.-Mexican border region has grown and developed, new areas of conflict have emerged as traditional issues have continued. Concerns that might have a relatively simple domestic solution often become quite complicated in a transborder, international framework. The next section provides an overview of the most important issues that affect border communities.

Environmental Issues

Mexico and the United States have very different traditions regarding environmental protection and policies. Mexico has been more concerned with creation of jobs and providing people with basic services, such as potable water, rather than with preventing and cleaning up industrial pollution or with providing sewage collection and treatment. Mexican officials often felt that environmental protection and rigorous standards were a luxury that developing countries could afford but were an unfair burden for Mexico. These different approaches to the environment stood out in strong contrast at the border and were, at times, a source of conflict between twin-city communities and between countries. Changing perceptions in Mexico about the environment, including development of a strong Mexican environmental movement, mean that there is more agreement across the border about environmental policies and priorities. However, the considerable economic asymmetries mean that there are still bothersome barriers to effective binational action on managing the environment. Significant bottlenecks for Mexico's efforts to upgrade environmental monitoring, enforcement, and infrastructure continue. The most cemtral areas of border environmental concern are listed below.[23]

A. Water Quality and Supply Problems.[24] The U.S.-Mexican border region is characterized by its aridity, particularly on the central and western parts of the border. Many of the regions of the border find water in short supply for the growing urban populations and agricultural enterprises. San Diego currently imports about 95 percent of its water from the Colorado River and from northern California; Tijuana increasingly depends upon water imported through an aqueduct from the Colorado River. El Paso and Ciudad Juárez rely on underground water supplies that are shared, but not regulated, and are projected to last only another 15 to 20 years. The major population centers of the border do not have a secure supply for this basic resource.

Since all surface waters in the border region are fully allocated by international treaties and since groundwater deposits are very limited, there is simply no more new water available for future growth. The two major river systems of the border region are the Colorado River and the Rio Grande. Both of the basins have, in the past, been subjected to intensive development through irrigation, storage, and flood-control projects. Those on the Colorado River include the Hoover Dam, which provides management primarily for production of hydroelectricity. Release of runoff downstream occurs according to the needs of electric power generation or when the storage system is at capacity; release of water is not timed for the benefit of downstream users, including Mexico. The water resources of the Rio Grande are also well developed. The part of the water course shared by Mexico and the United States has seen the development of a series of international dams, jointly constructed and administered by the two countries.[25]

The traditional wisdom in border communities has been that water reclamation, combined with conservation, is the only viable solution for providing an adequate long-term water supply for sustainable growth and development in the region. However, water reclamation involves significant capital costs for infrastructure and major energy costs for reclamation and pumping. Recently, attention has turned to an examination of developing water markets that would permit transfer of water from agriculture to urban uses. In the case of California, only five percent of agricultural water would have to be transferred to urban uses to assure an adequate supply for the foreseeable future. Participating in transboundary water markets might be a viable alternative for Mexican border cities in order to avoid huge infrastructure costs.

All Mexican border cities discharge significant amounts of untreated sewage into the environment, causing great concern in their American counterparts. Often the sewage contains hazardous and industrial wastes, worsening its environmental impacts and making reclamation more difficult. Human-health impacts of sewage pollution are to be seen in higher infant-mortality and gastrointestinal-disease rates in Mexican border cities and in irregular and uncontrolled settlements on the Texas side of the border in areas known as *colonias*.[26] Improving sewage-collector and processing systems everywhere along the border is a high priority.

B. Hazardous and Industrial Waste. With the growth of manufacturing and the *maquiladora* industry, there has been a great increase in industrial-waste generation in the border region. Largely because of the lack of infrastructure and regulatory and enforcement capacities in the border region, particularly in Mexico, only a small percentage of hazardous waste from border *maquilas* is being disposed of in a fashion that would meet generally accepted international standards. The rest is being stored (often improperly), dumped in municipal landfills, or discharged into the wastewater collector system. Some individuals and groups have taken advantage of the border illegally to transport and dump hazardous materials on the Mexican side. So the traditional function of border regions as a haven for lawless elements has continued in new forms. Improper disposal of industrial waste has serious implications for human populations in the region.

C. Air Pollution. As the size of border twin-city pairs increased, air quality became an important transborder problem. The most serious cases are in the El Paso-Ciudad Juárez region and in the San Diego-Tijuana region. In these areas, air pollution is generated from sources in two countries and is transported by winds to affect the entire air basin. Sources of pollutants tend to differ on each side of the border. Particular problems on the Mexican side include the uncontrolled burning of trash, industrial air pollution from cement factories in urban areas, dust raised from vehicular traffic on unpaved streets, electrical power generation with fuel oil rather than natural gas, leaded fuel, poor maintenance of vehicles, lack of pollution-control equipment on motor vehicles, and the older vehicle fleet. Enforcement of U.S. federal and state air quality regulations has brought improvement regarding pollution sources on the U.S. side—including significant reduction in industrial pollutants and motor-vehicle pollutants—but the continued growth of populations and numbers of vehicles has made improvement in quality of air difficult. At every border town, long lines of idling vehicles at the border-crossings, in part due to drug interdiction policies of the U.S. Customs Service, contribute significantly to air pollution.

Topography and other features have combined to make El Paso almost continually in noncompliance with federal United States Environmental Protection Agency standards for air quality. In large part, this is due to pollutants produced in Ciudad Juárez and to high levels of pollutants associated with the border crossing lines.[27] Consequently, until an international air basin pollution control authority is established, little can be done to alleviate the situation in this twin-city pair. The El Paso-Ciudad Juárez region is leading the way with an innovative effort to develop an air basin management authority, where both cities and countries will cooperate to protect a common resource.[28]

D. Bioresource Issues. The impressive growth and development of the borderlands over the past decades have produced significant negative impacts on the native flora and fauna and ecosystems of the region. Expansion of urban areas, destruction of native habitats through grazing activities or agriculture, lowering the water table through excessive pumping of water deposits, and impacts of recreation on fragile ecosystems have all had important consequences on the border region. While efforts have been made to protect certain endangered species, such as the masked bob-white and the white-winged dove, it has been difficult for U.S. and Mexican authorities adequately to cooperate to establish transborder biosphere reserves to protect habitats of species that live on both sides of the border.[29]

Resolution of Border Environmental Issues

The 1983 Border Environmental Agreement, signed by the presidents of Mexico and the United States, established a framework mechanism for dealing with the range of border environmental problems. Because the International Boundary and Water Commission, a Mexican-U.S. agency charged with maintaining the boundary and allocating surface waters, limited its activities to a few water contamination issues, it was felt necessary to establish a more comprehensive way of dealing with the growing number of border environmental issues. The 1983 Agreement created a number of working groups to meet regularly to deal with transboundary pollution issues and also called for participation in the process by researchers, universities, and state and local governments. These efforts produced a series of annexes dealing with specific issues, such as the smelter pollution of the Sonora-Arizona region, the binational sewage treatment plant of the San Diego-Tijuana region, expansion of the binational sewage treatment plant for Nogales, Sonora, and Nogales, Arizona, and the binational treatment plant for the Laredo-Nuevo Laredo region.

Despite some successes, the U.S. federal government has been slow to respond to transboundary pollution problems that technically are a federal responsibility but which have local impacts. However, the great debate in the United States prior to the approval of NAFTA by Congress produced a commitment by the President and Congress that border environmental concerns would be addressed. The first concerted effort to address the many border environmental issues was the development by the U.S. Environmental Protection Agency and its Mexican counterpart, the Secretaría de Desarrollo Social (SEDESOL), of the *Integrated Environmental Plan for the U.S.-Mexican Border Area (First Stage, 1992–1994)*. This plan laid out major border environmental problems and identified specific solutions, mainly in the areas of improved enforcement and infrastructure projects. A subsequent effort by the United States and Mexican environmental agencies, *U.S.-Mexico Border XXI Program Framework Document* (1996) focused on process and community participation in addressing border environmental issues. In addition, the creation through NAFTA side agreements of the BECC and the NADBank increased federal attention to transborder environmental problems.

Immigration Issues

Along with the environment, issues relating to international migration are of first priority in the border region. Migration problems are very much border issues since border communities and states are most heavily affected. Both push and pull factors, both supply and demand, are evident in this phenomenon. Mexican development and social strategies over the last half century have produced one of the most inequitable societies in the world in terms of income distribution. These policies have produced the concentration of enormous wealth in the hands of the few, with poverty and lack of adequate social investment for the masses. For decades, even during periods of sustained growth during the Mexican *economic miracle* from the 1940s into the 1970s, waves of economic refugees have fled north from Mexico. They came first from the rural near north, then from the rural south, and now increasingly from urban Mexico. The flow of undocumented Mexicans to the United States has been of significant benefit to Mexico's arcane social, political, and economic systems. Illegal migration makes available jobs and social services for its citizens that Mexico is unable or unwilling to provide.

The remittances of wages by undocumented workers in the United States are a main economic prop for entire villages and communities in Mexico. Mexican authorities, aware of the *safety-valve* value of undocumented migration to the United States, also recognize the importance of the remittances and have generally refused to cooperate with United States requests to assist with control of transborder flows of undocumented persons. In the past, the United States clearly benefited from this flow of migrants, through the incorporation of energetic and motivated workers into entry-level positions in the economy, and through the rich culture and traditions these people have brought with them. Over the past several decades, the costs and benefits of this arrangement increasingly have been critically examined in the United States and in the border region to the point where it has turned into an ongoing, acrimonious national debate. There seems to be a growing consensus against undocumented migration in the border region of the United States.

Figure 7. Arrests of Undocumented Immigrants by U.S. Border Patrol (All figures by fiscal year, October 1-September 30)

Year	U.S.-Mexican Border			San Diego Sector (Includes parts of Riverside County)		
Fiscal year, Oct-Sept	Total	Total	OTMs (Other than Mexicans)	Total	Mexicans	OTMs (Other than Mexicans)
1986	1,615,844	1,573,068	42,780	629,660	614,610	15,050
1987	1,122,067	1,099,577	22,490	500,330	492,280	8,050
1988	942,560	912,750	29,810	431,590	420,580	11,010
1989	852,506	807,930	44,570	366,760	355,140	11,620
1990	1,049,321	1,020,256	29,070	473,320	465,790	7,530
1991	1,077,876	1,058,078	19,700	530,350	535,710	4,640
1992	1,145,574	1,132,148	13,340	565,580	562,490	3,090
1993	1,212,886	1,185,951	16,940	531,690	526,850	4,840
1994	979,100	963,130	15,970	450,150	445,990	4,160

Source: Immigration and Naturalization Service, Statistics Division, Washington, D.C.

Attempts by the United States to restrain the flow of undocumented immigrants have not been successful. The 1986 Immigration Reform and Control Act combined legalization of long-term undocumented residents with improved enforcement, but with minimal results. Arrests of undocumented immigrants fell after the passage of IRCA, but the number of people detained again increased until 1993 and 1994 when augmented enforcement and border fence construction activities once again slowed the flow.[30] Figure 7 includes data from 1986 through 1994. It should be noted that these figures include multiple arrests of the same individual and that the total number of arrests varies according to the deployment of patrol agents. Border Patrol officers estimate that two or three times the number arrested successfully cross into the United States. Despite these caveats, the data clearly demonstrate the scale of the flows of undocumented workers at the border and indicate that nearly one-half the activity is concentrated in the San Diego region.

Although a number of studies have suggested that undocumented workers in the United States contribute as much or more in taxes as they use in public services, it is clear that the costs and benefits of undocumented immigration are different according to region. Studies of Los Angeles and San Diego have made the negative fiscal impacts of undocumented immigrants quite clear to policymakers and the general public, although hotly contested by some academic researchers and supporters of the rights of undocumented immigrants.[31] The states of Texas and California initiated legal actions against the federal government, requesting reimbursement for state expenditures for undocumented immigrants since the federal government failed to control the entry of persons without proper documentation. Undocumented immigration became a major theme of the November 1994 elections in California with Proposition 187 on the ballot. Basically, Proposition 187 was a grass-roots initiative designed to deny undocumented immigrants in the state access to social, nonemergency medical, and educational services. The proposition passed easily, despite strong opposition from Hispanic groups and surprisingly direct involvement by Mexican government officials and political figures. Although Proposition 187 possibly will never be implemented due to challenges in the court system, it is a strong indicator of the mood of residents in California that may presage similar movements elsewhere along the border. One positive impact of Proposition 187 is that it has encouraged thousands of Mexicans who were long-time legal residents of the United States to apply for citizenship status in order to be able to vote.

Border-Crossing Issues

Flows of documented people across the border, or legal crossings, have grown so much as to cause serious congestion at ports of entry. The long delays that often occur when crossing from Mexico into the United States are a source of constant aggravation and increased costs for border residents. Everywhere along the border, the number of people and vehicles crossing has increased significantly, which is a good indicator of growing interdependence between the two countries and of integration of the binational border region. Figure 8 provides annual crossing figures for the entire U.S.-Mexican border.

As interactions have increased between the Mexican and U.S. parts of the twin-city pairs along the border, more and more border residents have been inconvenienced by excessive delays at crossing due to saturated infrastructure, inadequate staffing of border checkpoints by U.S. Customs and the Border Patrol, and inspection policies that emphasize drug interdiction and determining the migratory status of crossers. The perception of many local people is that this is another case of a federal responsibility not being discharged properly, with local border residences forced to suffer the consequences. As more border residents are involved in activities on the other side of the boundary, they suffer delays and inconveniences because of inadequate infrastructure for vehicular, pedestrian, and commercial crossing. Although both Mexico and the United States benefit from the increased trade flows across the border, border residents suffer the negative impacts of saturated infrastructure.

Figure 8. Crossings into the United States along the Mexican Border (By fiscal year, October 1-September 30)

Year	Total Crossings	% Increase in Crossings	Alien Crossings	% Alien Crossings
1985	176,844,524		105,771,089	60
1986	193,019,856	9.1	116,978,424	61
1987	195,920,926	1.5	118,768,977	61
1988	225,970,850	15.3	138,264,511	61
1989	244,395,272	8.2	149,249,020	61
1990	253,494,906	3.7	158,294,654	62
1991	235,336,948	-7.2	151,581,043	64
1992	252,529,133	7.3	164,028,528	65
1993	269,349,987	6.7	175,472,973	65
1994	306,981,264	14.0	199,592,936	65

Source: *INS Statistical Yearbook*, various years: Immigration and Naturalization Service, Statistics Division, Washington, D.C.

Law Enforcement and Criminal Justice Issues

A continuing problem for most U.S. and Mexican communities along the border is in the area of law enforcement and criminal justice issues. Very different legal codes are juxtaposed at the border, very different administrative and law enforcement structures are present, and the traditional use of the border by criminals for illegal activities is ubiquitous. These factors make the administration of justice and maintenance of law and order in the border context problematic. The large number of local, state, and federal law enforcement agencies involved make matters more complex and difficult to coordinate. In the Imperial Valley in California, for example, there are at least 14 U.S. law enforcement agencies operating, while just across the border in Mexicali there is an equivalent number of Mexican agencies.[32]

Concerns in U.S. border communities regarding law enforcement issues focus on a number of areas. In every border city in the United States, a significant amount of the local auto theft is directly linked to organized groups operating out of Mexico.[33] Once in Mexico, the vehicles generally are registered with false documentation obtained from cooperating Mexican officials and then sold to Mexican consumers. Traditionally, Mexican border law enforcement authorities have provided little cooperation for vehicle-recovery efforts. Thefts and burglaries committed by individuals and groups from Mexico are ongoing problems for U.S. border communities. At times, organized gangs use juveniles (under age 18) so that if they are caught they will be sent back to Mexico and not prosecuted in the United States. Drug trafficking is another area of significant concern in border communities. Mexican communities cite a number of issues related to transborder criminal activities. Mexican criminals frequently avoid prosecution by fleeing to U.S. border communities. There is considerable smuggling of consumer goods into Mexico at the border, although as NAFTA is phased in, price differentials will disappear, and the incentive for smuggling these goods will be eliminated. Finally, Mexico is concerned about the illicit flow of firearms across the border from the north. While over the past five years transborder law enforcement cooperation has improved, economic asymmetry, and realities and concerns about sovereignty, as well as the very complexity of the issues, will continue to produce concerns for border residents in this area.

5. Growing Transborder Linkages

All of the above features of border life serve to link the two sides of the border and provide continuities from south to north and north to south that enable us to speak of the border as a geographical region. The two parts of this region are far from Washington, D.C., and Mexico City, and people on the border often feel neglected by the national capital when dealing with transboundary issues of local, but vital, concern. Thus, over the years, border residents have evolved a whole range of informal arrangements to deal with transborder aspects of their daily lives. Examples include the informal, but regular, cooperation of fire departments, health authorities, and police to deal with emergencies without the intervention of either federal government. At some point, these sorts of interactions will begin to bear upon the national policies of each country and will begin to redefine the nature of the relationship that exists between the United States and Mexico.[34] Transboundary linkages, both informal and formal, reflect the increasing interdependency of the two nations, particularly in the border zone. To some degree, on the micro level, interdependency offsets aspects of asymmetry, producing more collaborative, parity relationships. Growing transborder linkages and interdependence between the United States and Mexico have given U.S. border communities a much larger presence on the Mexican side. This has created a powerful lobby to temper the asymmetrical use of power by Washington, D.C., vis-à-vis Mexico.

The border region of 1996 is very different from the border region of 1980 in terms of transborder interdependence and cooperation. The great burst of activity stimulated by economic linkages between the two neighbors and NAFTA built upon slow progress made over many decades. The economic forces in the border region, first the *maquiladora* industry and then the opening of the Mexican economy that culminated with NAFTA, have driven broad changes elsewhere in the bilateral relationship, particularly as manifested at the border. NAFTA made the border a priority for both countries, particularly the United States. Beginning at the time of the discussions about NAFTA in 1993, many U.S. federal agencies began to pay greater attention to border-related issues within their areas of competency. This has had several effects. First, all this activity has raised the visibility of the border in Washington, D.C. Second, the clients and constituents of these federal agencies in the border region have participated in greater levels of border-related activity. Finally, these agencies have tended to renew relations and establish new linkages with counterpart Mexican agencies, and some part of the activities have border components.

At the regional level along the border, particularly within the framework of the twin-city pairs, transborder interactions have demonstrated a remarkable vitality and growth due to the processes and circumstances described in this essay. In the San Diego-Tijuana region, for example, the micro-regional expansion of transborder contacts and linkages has been significant over the past decade or so, particularly since 1993 and the NAFTA discussions.[35] The expansion of collaborative relations has been across the board, including local and state government agencies, higher education, nongovernmental organizations of all sorts, private businesses, chambers of commerce, and civic and cultural groups. While many of these transborder relationships go through a predictable process of initial contacts and activities, disillusionment, and decline, there is clearly an increase in solidly grounded projects and endeavors by participant groups. These usually bring measurable benefits to both sides by establishing mutually advantageous interactions. The sum of all these small efforts has been to expand significantly the number of actors in the two communities who are involved in transborder activities and to move the entire binational region farther along the path towards increased interdependence and integration.

Anecdotal information suggests that this process is ubiquitous along the border. Despite short-term setbacks associated with economic cycles and political difficulties, the level of transborder interaction is increasing over the long and medium term. The U.S.-Mexican border region is so dynamic that it is not easy to predict how far the process of integration will advance. Nevertheless, Mexican and American border communities have made much progress toward conceptualizing and managing their regions in a transborder mode.

NAFTA has been a catalyst, for it made border issues a high priority on the bilateral agenda and brought increased federal involvement and funding to border issues, particularly by the U.S. federal government. At the same time, the long standing inclination of the U.S. government and the decentralization process in the Mexican public administration have combined to facilitate greater transborder cooperation at the local level in the border region. Increasing transborder linkages in most areas and increasing interdependence economically, socially, and culturally are clear indicators of the direction of change in the U.S.-Mexican border region. This zone that is the interface between two asymmetrical partners is moving toward greater interdependence and regional integration.

Notes

1. Frederick R. Gehlbach (1981) provides an excellent description of the ecology of the border region.

2. For treatments of the historical development of the borderlands, see David J. Weber (1979 and 1988) and Paul Ganster, Bernardo García Martínez, and James Lockhart (forthcoming).

3. Richard Griswold del Castillo (1990).

4. Martínez, *Troublesome Border* (1982) details the story of these border conflicts.

5. Piñera (1995) is a study of one case in Ensenada, Baja California, that involved American and British capital.

6. See Manuel A. Machado (1982), Ovid Demaris (1971), for a journalistic view of this period on the border. T. D. Proffitt III (1994) and Oscar J. Martínez (1975) analyze the growth of Tijuana and Ciudad Juárez, respectively.

7. See Abraham Hoffman (1974) for a discussion of these repatriations.

8. For a brief overview of the *Bracero* Program, see Karl M. Schmitt (1974: 214–20); also, see Richard B. Craig (1971).

9. Ganster (1993).

10. The published literature on Mexico's *maquiladora* industry is extensive. See, for example, the trade magazine, *Twin Plant News* (El Paso, Texas).

11. Of course, the *maquila*-generated employment benefitted Mexican border cities economies as well. Salvador Mendoza Higuera (1993: 57–64)

12. U.S. Environmental Protection Agency and Secretaría de Desarrollo Social, *Integrated Environmental Plan for the Mexican-U.S. Border Area (First Stage, 1992–1994)* (Washington, D.C.: USEPA [1994]).

13. For discussions of the first year of NAFTA, see "Happy Ever NAFTA?" *The Economist*, 333:7893 (December 10, 1994); Jim Weddell, "NAFTA, One Year After," *Hispanic*, 7:10 (November 1994), pp. 52–56.

14. Administrative complexities regarding transborder environmental projects are discussed in Clifton G. Metzner, Jr. (1988).

15. Many problems of transborder government communication are discussed by Joseph Nalven (1984).

16. Rey et al. (forthcoming) details San Diego and Tijuana economic characteristics.

17. U.S. Department of Commerce, Bureau of Census (1983) and Peter L. Reich (1984).

18. Joseph Nalven (1986); Richard A. Parker and Louis M. Rea (1993).

19. *Characteristics of California Population: 1985 Update and Projections to 1990, 1995, 2000* (Palo Alto: Center for Continuing Study of the California Economy, 1986), 204; "1990 Census. Race and Hispanic Origin Population Change, 1980–1990," SANDAG, 1991.

20. The connection between the Latino population and U.S. and Mexican foreign policy is explored in Richard R. Fagen (1983), Rodolfo O. de la Garza (1983), and Juan Gómez-Quiñones and Carlos H. Zazueta (1983).

21. See José Manuel Valenzuela Arce (1988), for a discussion of *cholos*. Also see Steven Loza (1993) for a discussion of the influence of Los Angeles barrio music on Mexico

22. Paul Ganster (1992, 1994: 242–48); Judith I. Gill and Lilian Alvarez de Testa (1994).

23. Ganster and Walter, eds. (1990) provide an excellent overview of border environmental concerns; also see U.S. Environmental Protection Agency and Secretaría de Medio Ambiente, Recursos Naturales y Pesca (1996).

24. Metzner (1989) provides a discussion of water quality issues in this region, including low technology and traditional solutions to the problems.

25. See Gary D. Weatherford and F. Lee Brown (1986) for a discussion of the Colorado River and the use of its waters; Mumme (1986) treats water management.

26. U.S. Environmental Protection Agency and Secretaría de Desarrollo Social (1992), *Integrated Environmental Plan for the Mexican-U.S. Border Area* provides data on this.

27. Robert Gray, Jesús Reynoso, Conrado Díaz Q., and Howard Applegate (1989).

28. See Peter Emerson (1995a) and his "Why Not Trade Pollution, Too?" *The New York Times* (January 1, 1995).

29. Discussion of border bioresource issues is to be found in Ganster and Walter, eds. (1990).

30. "Border Fence Update," information sheet from the United States Border Patrol, San Diego Border Patrol Sector, February 1995.

31. County of San Diego, Department of Transborder Affairs Advisory Board, "Consultations in Cost and Benefits of Migration in the San Diego Region: A Local Response" (San Diego, CA: 1990); Parker and Rea, *Illegal Immigration in San Diego County* (1993).

32. See Robert L. Wilhelm (1987: 157–64).

33. Michael V. Miller (1987: 12–32).

34. Ivo B. Duchacek, "International Competence of Subnational Governments: Borderlands and Beyond," and the other essays in Oscar J. Martínez (1986).

35. Paul Ganster (1994) provides a discussion of the process and a listing of San Diego organizations with ties in Mexico.

References

Center for Continuing Study of the California Economy. 1986. *Characteristics of California Population: 1985; Update and Projections to 1990, 1995, and 2000.* Palo Alto: Center for Continuing Study of the California Economy.
County and City Data Book. 1983. 10th ed. Washington, D.C.: Government Printing Office, U.S. Department of Commerce, Bureau of Census.

County of San Diego, Department of Transborder Affairs Advisory Board. 1990. "Consultations in Cost and Benefits of Migration in the San Diego Region: A Local Response." San Diego: County of San Diego.

Craig, Richard B. 1971. *The Bracero Program: Interest Groups and Foreign Policy.* Austin: University of Texas Press.

Comisión Económica para América Latina y el Caribe. 1994. *México: La industria maquiladora.* N.P.: LC/MEX/R.495 (28 October).

de la Garza, Rodolfo O. 1983. "Chicanos and U.S. Foreign Policy: The Future of Chicano-Mexican Relations." In *Mexican-U.S. Relations: Conflict and Convergence,* Carlos Vásquez and Manuel García y Griego, eds. Los Angeles: University of California at Los Angeles, Chicano Studies Research Center and Latin American Center.

Demaris, Ovid. 1971. *Poso del Mundo.* New York: Pocket Books.

Duchacek, Ivo B. 1986. "International Competence of Subnational Governments: Borderlands and Beyond." In *Across Boundaries: Transborder Interaction in Comparative Perspective,* Oscar J. Martínez, ed. El Paso: Texas Western Press.

The Economist. 1994. "Happy Ever NAFTA?" 333: 893 (10 December).

Emerson, Peter. 1995a. "Solving Air Pollution Problems in Paso del Norte." In *Energy and the Environment in the California-Baja California Border Region,* Alan Sweedler, Paul Ganster, and Patricia Bennett, eds. San Diego: Institute for Regional Studies of the Californias, San Diego State University.

Emerson, Peter. 1995b. "Why Not Trade Pollution, Too?" *The New York Times* (1 January).

Fagen, Richard R. 1983. "The Politics of the United States-Mexico Relationship." In *U.S.-Mexico Relations: Economic and Social Aspects,* Clark W. Reynolds and Carlos Tello, eds. Stanford: Stanford University Press.

Ganster, Paul. 1993. "Affordable Housing in San Diego and Tijuana and Transborder Linkages." Unpublished manuscript.

Ganster, Paul. 1994. "Transborder Linkages in the San Diego-Tijuana Region." In *San Diego-Tijuana in Transition: A Regional Analysis,* Norris C. Clement and Eduardo Zepeda Miramontes, eds. San Diego: Institute for Regional Studies of the Californias, San Diego State University.

Ganster, Paul. 1996. *Environmental Issues of the California–Baja California Border Region.* San Diego: Institute for Regional Studies of the Californias, San Diego State University.

Ganster, Paul, and Hartmut Walter, eds. 1990. *Environmental Hazards and Bioresource Management in the United States-Mexico Borderlands.* Los Angeles: UCLA Latin American Center Publications.

Ganster, Paul, Bernardo García Martínez, and James Lockhart. 1997. "Northern New Spain." In *Historical Atlas of the U.S.-Mexican Border,* Norris Hundley, ed. Tucson: University of Arizona Press (forthcoming).

Gehlbach, Frederick R. 1981. *Mountain Islands and Desert Seas: A Natural History of the U.S.-Mexican Borderlands.* College Station: Texas A&M Press.

Gómez-Quiñones, Juan. 1983. "Notes on an Interpretation of the Relations Between the Mexican Community in the United States and Mexico." In *Mexican-U.S. Relations: Conflict and Convergence,* Carlos Vásquez and Manuel García y Griego, eds. Los Angeles: University of California at Los Angeles, Chicano Studies Research Center and Latin American Center.

Gray, Robert, Jesús Reynoso, Conrado Díaz Q., and Howard Applegate. 1989. *Vehicular Traffic and Air Pollution.* El Paso: Texas Western Press.

Griswold del Castillo, Richard. 1990. *The Treaty of Guadalupe Hidalgo: A Legacy of Conflict.* Norman: University of Oklahoma Press.

Grunwald, Joseph, and Kenneth Flamm. 1985. *The Global Factory: Foreign Assembly in International Trade.* Washington, D.C.: The Brookings Institution.

Herzog, Lawrence A. 1990. "Border Commuter Workers and Transfrontier Metropolitan Structures along the United States-Mexico Border." *Journal of Borderlands Studies* 5 (2).

Hoffman, Abraham. 1974. *Unwanted Mexican Americans in the Great Depression: Repatriation Pressures, 1929–1939.* Tucson: University of Arizona Press.

Ladman, Jerry R. 1995. "The U.S. Border Regional Economy: Interdependence, Growth and Prospects for Change." In *Views across the Border,* Stanley R. Ross and Jerry R. Ladman, eds. 2nd ed. Tempe: Latin American Center, Arizona State University.

Lorey, David E., ed. 1993. *United States-Mexico Border Statistics since 1900. 1990 Update.* Los Angeles: UCLA Latin American Center Publications.

Loza, Steven. 1993. *Barrio Rhythms: Mexican American Music in Los Angeles.* Champaign: University of Illinois Press.

Machado, Jr., Manuel A. 1982. "Booze, Broads, and the Border: Vice and U.S.-Mexican Relations, 1910–1930." In *Proceedings of the 1982 Meeting of the Rocky Mountain Council on Latin American Studies,* C. Richard Bath, ed. El Paso: Center for Inter-American and Border Studies, University of Texas.

Margulis, Mario, and Rodolfo Turián. 1983. *Nuevos patrones de crecimiento social en la frontera norte: la emigración.* México, D.F.: El Colegio de México, Centro de Estudios Demográficos y de Desarrollo Urbano.

Martínez, Oscar J. 1987. *Border Boom Town. Ciudad Juárez since 1848.* Austin: University of Texas Press.

Martínez, Oscar J. 1988. *Troublesome Border.* Tucson: University of Arizona Press.

Martínez, Oscar J. 1992. "Border People and Transnational Interaction." In *The Mexican-U.S. Border Region and the Free Trade Agreement,* Paul Ganster and Eugenio O. Valenciano, eds. San Diego: Institute for Regional Studies of the Californias, San Diego State University.

Martínez, Oscar J. 1994. *Border People: Life and Society in the U.S.-Mexico Borderlands.* Tucson: University of Arizona.

Martínez, Oscar J., ed. 1986. *Across Boundaries: Transborder Interaction in Comparative Perspective.* El Paso: Texas Western Press.

Mendoza Higuera, Salvador et al. 1993. "Tijuana: Short-Term Growth and Long-Term Development." In *San Diego-Tijuana in Transition: A Regional Analysis,* Norris C. Clement and Eduardo Zepeda Miramontes, eds. San Diego: Institute for Regional Studies of the Californias, San Diego State University.

Metzner Jr., Clifton G., ed. 1988. *Water Quality Issues of the California-Baja California Border Region.* San Diego: Institute for Regional Studies of the Californias, San Diego State University.

Miller, Michael V. 1987. "Vehicle Theft along the Texas-Mexico Border." *Journal of Borderlands Studies* 2 (2).

Mumme, Stephen P. 1986. "Engineering Diplomacy: The Evolving Role of the International Boundary and Water Commission in U.S.-Mexico Water Management." *Journal of Borderlands Studies* 1 (1).

Nalven, Joseph. 1984. "A Cooperation Paradox and an 'Airy' Tale Along the Border." *New Scholar* 9 (1–2):171–200.

Nalven, Joseph. 1986. *Impacts and Undocumented Persons: The Quest for Usable Data in San Diego County, 1974–1986.* San Diego: Institute for Regional Studies of the Californias, San Diego State University.

Parker, Richard A., and Louis M. Rea. 1993. *Illegal Immigration in San Diego County: An Analysis of Costs and Revenues.* Sacramento: California Legislation, Senate Special Committee on Border Issues.

Piñera, David. 1995. *American and English Influence on the Early Development of Ensenada, Baja California, Mexico.* San Diego: Institute for Regional Studies of the Californias, San Diego State University.

Proffitt III, T. D. 1994. *Tijuana: The History of a Mexican Metropolis.* San Diego: San Diego State University Press.

Reich, Peter L. 1984. *Statistical Abstract of the United States-Mexico Borderlands,* Los Angeles: UCLA Latin American Center Publications.

Rey, Serge, Paul Ganster, Gustavo del Castillo, Juan Alvarez, Ken Shellhammer, Alan Sweedler, and Norris Clement, "The San Diego-Tijuana Region." In *Integrating Cities and Regions: NAFTA and the Caribbean Face Globalization,* James W. Wilkie and Clint E. Smith, eds. Publisher to be determined, forthcoming.

SANDAG (San Diego Association of Governments). 1991. *1990 Census. Race and Hispanic Origin Population Change, 1980–1990.* San Diego: SANDAG.

Schmitt, Karl M. 1974. *Mexico and the United States, 1821–1973. Conflict and Coexistence.* New York: John Wiley & Sons.

Spicer, Edward H. 1981. *Cycles of Conquest. The Impact of Spain, Mexico, and the United States on the Indians of the Southwest, 1533–1960.* Tucson: University of Arizona Press.

Statistical Abstract of Latin America 25. 1987. Los Angeles: UCLA Latin American Center Publications.

U.S. Department of Commerce, Bureau of Census. 1991. *1990 Census of Population and Housing.* Washington, D.C.: U.S. Department of Commerce, Bureau of Census.

U.S. Department of Commerce, Bureau of Census. 1983. *County and City Data Book.* 10th edition. Washington, D.C.: U.S. Government Printing Office.

U.S. Department of Justice. Immigration and Naturalization Service. *INS Statistical Yearbook.* Washington, D.C.: U.S. Department of Justice, Immigration and Naturalization Service.

U.S. Environmental Protection Agency and Secretaría de Desarrollo Social. 1992. *Integrated Environmental Plan for the Mexican-U.S. Border Area (First Stage, 1992-1994).* Washington, D.C.: USEPA.

U.S. Environmental Protection Agency and Secretaría de Medio Ambiente, Recursos Naturales y Pesca. 1996. *U.S.-Mexico Border XXI Program. Framework Document. October 1996.* Washington, D.C.: USEPA.

U.S. Embassy, Mexico City. 1994. "Mexico. Foreign Investment Report. Winter 1994/1995." México, D.F.: U.S. Embassy.

U.S. Immigration and Naturalization Service. Various years. *INS Statistical Yearbook.* Washington, D.C.: Immigration and Naturalization Service, Statistics Division.

United States Border Patrol. 1995. "Border Fence Update." Information sheet from the San Diego Border Patrol Sector (February).

Valenzuela Arce, José Manuel. 1988. *A la brave ése.* Tijuana: El Colegio de la Frontera Norte.

Weber, David J., ed. 1979. *New Spain's Far Northern Frontier. Essays on the American West, 1540–1821.* Albuquerque: University of New Mexico Press.

Weber, David J., ed. 1988. *Myth and the History of the Hispanic Southwest.* Albuquerque: University of New Mexico Press.

Weddell, Jim. 1994. "NAFTA, One Year After." *Hispanic* 7 (10).

Wilhelm, Robert L. 1987. "The Transnational Relations of United States Law Enforcement Agencies with Mexico." *Change and Continuity. Pacific Coast Council on Latin American Studies Proceedings* 14 (2).

Zazueta, Carlos H. 1983. "Mexican Political Actors in the United States and Mexico: Historical and Political Contexts of a Dialogue Renewed." In *Mexican-U.S. Relations: Conflict and Convergence,* Carlos Vásquez and Manuel García y Griego, eds. Los Angeles: University of California at Los Angeles, Chicano Studies Research Center and Latin American Center.

Immigration, Race, and Security on the California-Mexico Border

Randy Willoughby[1]

1. Introduction

> *Contradictions are everywhere in the world. Without contradictions there would be no world*—Mao in Schram 1974: 62

Contemporary immigration policies in the western world contain so much irony, paradox, and contradiction that we might consider exonerating the Great Helmsman if only for his judicious insistence on the dialectic. Immigration contradictions have been identified across the analytical and literary spectrum. A political scientist discusses the "boomerang politics" of an important Mexican political party (the PRD of Cárdenas), which campaigns in Los Angeles for influence in Mexico because "internal politics are no longer internal" (Dresser 1993: 96–97). A sociologist discusses the *Catch-22* between immigration ideology and economics in the aftermath of the 1986 reforms on United States immigration policy (Calavita 1989: 164, 176). An economist refers to the "liberal paradox—the notion that industrial democracies push nations to embrace free trade and investment, and ... complain that now open developing economies are sending workers over industrial country borders" (Martin and Miller 1994: 592). A novelist begins his story with the "angelic-devilish fall" of two Indians over the English Channel, one a prim and proper assimilationist, and the other an irreverent actor who intends to *tropicalize* London; the former then sprouts devilish hoofs and horns and the latter an angelic halo (Rushdie 1988).

This essay tries to drive home the argument that contradiction is central to U.S. immigration history, that Oxford-style debates and *opposing viewpoint* presentations on the subject obscure the interactive quality of immigration dynamics, and that the November 1994 referendum in California on a measure to deny illegal immigrants a variety of public services (Proposition 187) is a particularly illustrative case in point. Consider, for example, the family-unification emphasis of U.S. immigration policy since 1965, resulting in three times the number of admissions for family relations (482,000 in fiscal year [hereafter: FY] 1993) than for desired economic skills (147,000) or for political refugees (127,000), compared with the country's reputation as the most individualistic and capitalistic in the world and its founding myth as "an asylum for human kind" (in the words of Thomas Paine). Or consider the 1994 campaign by Michael Huffington for a California seat to the U.S. Senate, one of the most costly in U.S. history, which focused on the problem of illegal immigration, and which concluded with the revelation that the candidate (like two Clinton nominees for Attorney General and his campaign opponent) had employed an undocumented immigrant. Consider how a Mexican *corrido* (folk ballad), "Viva Los Mojados," counters prejudice (and the law) with betrayal (and fraud): "the law doesn't like wetbacks because they're illegal and don't speak English, but the problem can be fixed by marrying a *gringita*, getting documentation, and getting divorced."[2] Finally, consider the construction of the steel barrier along the border between San Diego and Tijuana in the same year (1989) as the destruction of the Berlin iron curtain, or the passage of NAFTA by the U.S. House of Representatives with the same percentage as the passage of Proposition 187 by the voters of California (further evidence of the Martin-Miller "liberal paradox").

Adopting not only the motif but the format of Mao's famous 1956 speech "On the Ten Great Relationships," this essay constructs a multidimensional framework that includes historical, definitional, economic, political, racial, international, and security perspectives on immigration. Special emphasis is placed on questions of race and security, or more to the thematic point, what Gunnar Myrdal called the "American dilemma" with reference to "the Negro problem and modern democracy" and what the international relations-profession calls the "security dilemma," by which the effort to enhance one's sense of protection ultimately reinforces the threat instead. At the risk of some overstatement, these two dynamics in particular give the contemporary immigration debate in the United States (and possibly elsewhere) a special, passionate quality. Ideologies of race and security have driven the most important mobilizations of U.S. history—the Civil War of the nineteenth century and the hot and cold wars of the twentieth century. In the post-Cold-War scheme of things, they contribute simultaneously to the immigration debate, commingled not only with professional and academic rhetoric, but super-enhanced by successful Hollywood images of cultural pandemonium in Los Angeles (one need only think of the film

Bladerunner, depicting Los Angeles in the year 2019, and the nuclear jihad in the Florida Keys that takes place in Schwarzenegger's *True Lies*).

Certainly the racial element in the story is far from determinant and more implicit than explicit; the security aspect is more internal than external, and the specters play out differently for different countries and immigrant groups. Still, the campaign against illegal immigration in Proposition 187 on California's 1994 ballot has arguably metamorphosed too smoothly into the "California Civil Rights Initiative" to constitute mere haphazard momentum. The perception of linkages between the new-world-disorder motifs of organized crime, drug trafficking, terrorism, and illegal immigration, critically labeled a "security continuum" by Didier Bigo (1994: 164), has been reinforced in the United States over the past two years by the violent developments in Mexico and especially by the New York World Trade Center bombing. U.S. immigration policy, in sum, normally the undisturbed preserve of agribusiness and union lobbies, political economists, immigration lawyers, and the curators of Ellis Island, has shifted, at least for the moment, from the normal and pragmatic politics of pork barrel and regulation to the more ideologically charged politics of redistribution and war.

2. History

> *Good riddance to bad rubbish*—Hedda Hopper on
> Charlie Chaplin in Robinson 1985: 579

As amended, the 1952 Immigration and Nationality Act provides the foundation for immigration law in effect today. Although these amendments would ultimately and dramatically liberalize immigration opportunities across the board, by abolishing national quotas in 1965, by broadening the definition of refugees in 1980, by providing for a generous amnesty program for illegal-alien workers in 1986, and by expanding the overall numerical limits to immigration in 1990, one of the immediate effects of the new legislation was to provide the legal foundation for the U.S. Attorney General to rescind the reentry papers of Charlie Chaplin (in London for the world premiere of *Limelight*) on moral and communist grounds. After the Statue of Liberty, it would be hard to think of a more powerful image for the "nation of immigrants" than Chaplin's 1917 short film *The Emigrant*, poignantly replayed by Louis Malle's *Au Revoir les Enfants*, a movie about the Gestapo search for Jewish children in occupied France.

Chaplin's progression from welcome immigrant to denigrated troublemaker is a single symbolic illustration of the most obvious contradiction in American immigration history, the cyclical shift from embrace to exclusion. A California variation on the theme is personified by Denis Kearney, "by 1878 the most feared single individual on the Pacific Coast" (Dillon 1970: 190). Born in Ireland in

1847, settled in San Francisco in 1872, secretary of the Workingman's Party in 1877, Kearney went from helping the police counter anti-coolie riots as a member of the "Pickhandle Brigade" to giving inflammatory speeches declaring "the Chinese must go" (Hart 1987: 151). According to Bill Ong Hing, Kearney's change of heart was far from exceptional. Although Californians greeted the Burlingame Treaty between the United States and China in 1868 with fanfare and delight because China agreed to end its strict control over emigration, a state referendum against Chinese immigrants in 1879 passed with 94 percent of the vote (150,000 to 900), setting the stage for the national Chinese Exclusion Act (Ong Hing 1993: 23). Voting on Proposition 187 revealed an element of the Kearney spirit and inverted golden rule: according to a *Los Angeles Times* exit poll, 54 percent of the first-generation immigrants who voted (10 percent of the turnout) cast "yes" votes.

This open-and-shut ambivalence has produced dramatic fluctuations in immigration flows to the United States over the past century and a somewhat intermediate position today. Between 1870 and 1930, immigration levels ran consistently between 2.8 and 8.8 million per decade, averaging over five million per decade, compared with levels between 0.5 and 3.3 million per decade between 1930 and 1970, averaging under two million per decade (Williams 1992: 15). More recent immigration levels are returning to historic highs (counting in absolute numbers) or historic averages (counting in terms of population percentages). Counting only legal immigrants, the numbers were around one million total for the 1940s, 2.5 million for the 1950s, 3.5 million for the 1960s, 4.5 million for the 1970s, 7.5 million for the 1980s, and 13.5 million for the 1990s (extrapolating from the 1990–1993 four-year total of 5.5 million). Counting with a different metric, 15 percent of the population was foreign-born in the period 1870–1920 versus 8 percent in 1990 (Passel and Fix 1994: 153). Today, the pendulum seems to have traversed the vertical and to be moving decisively in the direction of reinforced restrictions. Public preference for reduced immigration levels has moved over the past three decades from 33 percent supporting reductions in 1965, to 42 percent in 1977, to 49 percent in 1986, and to 61 percent in 1993 (*New York Times* 26 June 1993).

Still, what is striking in the U.S. dialectic may be not the sentiment and rhetoric for restriction, which Livi-Bacci argues is relatively uniform in rhetoric and inspiration in affluent western countries, but the existence and resilience of a positivist ideology that associates immigration with American success (1994: 665). In other words, at least at the level of mythology, most countries in the world have no pendulum but simply a presumption against immigration. Indeed, in 1993, roughly the same time *Newsweek* featured a cover sketch of the Statue of Liberty drowning in a sea of boat people, *Time* featured a special issue with an attractive, somewhat exotic feminine "new face of America," a computer-generated "preview" of "how immigrants are shaping the world's first multicultural society" (Fall 1993: 2).

In case the image—mathematically controlled at 35 percent southern European, 15 percent Anglo-Saxon, 17.5 percent Middle Eastern, 17.5 percent African, 7.5 percent Asian, and 7.5 percent Hispanic—and the subtext were insufficiently romantic, the managing editor delivered the message in an introductory note: "As onlookers watched the image of our new Eve begin to appear on the computer screen, several staff members promptly fell in love." The *New York Times* editorial page visited Tijuana and conjured up a less esthetic but no less effective counter-image to the illegal-alien campaign, first placing four prominent east-coast politicos (Kemp, Cuomo, Giuliani, and Bennett) into the trunk of a car on the Tijuana side of the border and then pulling them out because "they had said things that were once taken for granted in America but had become terribly unfashionable and, for politicians, even dangerous" (Rosenthal 1995: A19). Even the resolutely conservative *San Diego Union-Tribune* not only endorsed the opposition to Proposition 187 in 1994 but began the new year with a special five-page business perspective defending legal immigration; the series of articles was titled "Still Room to GROW: Determined Immigrants are Proving the American Dream is Alive and Well" (Shaughnessy 1995: C1-5).

3. Definition

> *1908: San Andrés de Sotavento ... The governor,*
> *General Miguel Marino Torralvo, issues the order*
> *for the oil companies operating on the Colombian*
> *coast. The Indians do not exist ... If the Indians*
> *existed, they would be illegal*—Galeano 1988: 14

Discussions of illegal immigration typically include numbers but rarely identify underlying assumptions and definitions. President Clinton, in an effort to mobilize support for a financial-rescue package for Mexico, projected that further degeneration of Mexico's financial situation would push around half a million additional illegal immigrants into Texas and California during 1995. Days later, a Treasury Department official conceded that the net increase would likely be closer to 40,000, because the original figure included people on brief shopping trips, and that the estimate did not consider the impact of enhanced Border Patrol operations like Gatekeeper and Hold the Line (Stern 1995a: A14). Even the gross numbers were problematic in that the figure reportedly assumed that every one-percent decline in the value of the peso would translate to a one-percent increase in illegal immigration, a relationship that would have predicted the emigration of the entire country in the period 1976 to 1994, when the peso depreciated from 12.5 to 1 to over 3,000 to 1.

The United States Immigration and Naturalization Service (INS) estimated that there were around four million unauthorized immigrants in the United States in 1994, that the average annual net growth in the illegal population is around 300,000, that about forty percent of the population is in California, and that some sixty percent of the illegal population originated in Mexico (Warren 1994: 30). The breakdown between illegal immigrants who crossed borders without inspection and those who overstayed visas is roughly fifty-fifty. Of course, all of these numbers are estimates that are fraught with methodological complexities and somewhat arbitrary judgements. The 1980 census counted around two million illegal immigrants and guessed that around six million were in the country, for example. Varying assumptions can produce substantially different estimates given the enormous volume of people traversing U.S. ports of entry every year, the widespread availability of fraudulent identification, the considerable length and opportunities of the U.S.-Mexican border, and the relative openness of the U.S.-Canadian border.

Customs and INS process 56 million legal crossings per year at the San Diego ports of entry alone (the busiest in the country and indeed in the world, of which 38 million are aliens and 18 million citizens). Altogether, the San Diego District INS processed 91 million entries in 1994, with 177,000 or .02 percent referrals (Murillo 1995). Outside the ports of entry, the Border Patrol apprehended in 1994 over one million persons trying to cross the border, and (at least until recent border blockades in El Paso and San Diego) used the rule of thumb that it apprehended half of those who tried to cross. In the New York District, the INS oversees around 22 million visitors per year and estimates that fewer than one percent overstay their visas (Dunn 1995: A5).

The Urban Institute considers the INS estimates for the national illegal population to be the best of the various estimates (Clark et al. 1994: 4). Unfortunately, the INS estimates by state are less useful because they are based on information that is associated with the IRCA regularizations and, thus, are several years old. Hence, the estimates for California continue to vary considerably; for example, the Urban Institute's own estimate for the undocumented children in California schools is 307,000, while the California state government's estimate is 392,000, a difference of around 25 percent. Remarkably, the estimates vary even for the illegal-alien population arrested for felonies and incarcerated in state prisons, where privacy laws presumably have little standing. A recent California Assembly-commissioned report argued that illegal aliens constituted 22 percent of San Diego County's felony-arrest population in 1993, ranging from 3 percent of the arrests in Coronado to 35 percent of those in Escondido (Parker and Rea

1993: 71); the estimate contained a 33 percent fraudulent-document adjustment factor and carried over from the felony-arrest population to the state-prison population. These estimates were disputed in subsequent testimony before an Assembly panel as being systematically and dramatically overstated, with the evidence that the proper proportion has not changed since a more methodologically rigorous SANDAG study in 1989 produced a 12–15 percent estimate (Wolf 1993: 3).

These inherent methodological difficulties, not to mention the political machinations that further compromise some of the results, may in the end be less significant for the discussion of illegal immigration, from Mexico, in particular, than definitional guidelines. Passel and Fix are substantially correct when they argue that "U.S. immigration policy needs to be viewed as not one, but three fundamentally different sets of rules: those that govern legal immigration ... those that govern humanitarian admissions ... and those that control illegal entry. The distinction is important because each category is governed by different legislation, involves different networks of bureaucracies, is guided by different goals, and results in immigrants with largely different characteristics" (Passel and Fix 1994: 152). This caution is particularly appropriate given the popular misconception that the majority of immigrants to the United States are illegal (the INS estimate is around 30 percent), that the majority of incoming illegals are Mexican (the estimate is around 40 percent), and that refugees are simply seeking promising economic alternatives. These popular impressions are reinforced by the polemic that "leaders who work only to halt illegal entries would, if successful, ensure merely that future immigration will take four years to create the burdens on America that today occur in three years" (Beck 1994: 27). Legislatures in several states and on Capitol Hill are considering resolutions that go beyond the illegal-alien scope of Proposition 187 and seek to deny health-care and welfare benefits to legal as well as illegal immigrants (*San Diego Union-Tribune* 9 November1994).

Those favoring strong restrictions on all types of immigration are not the only ones who muddy the definitional waters surrounding legal, illegal, and other forms of migration. Some, especially militants in the Chicano/Mexican American community, resist the immigration label for the north-south movement of Latinos, so that the Texan migrant in a Tomás Rivera novel and Mexican immigrant in a Jack Nicholson movie are not only birds of passage but birds of a feather; the "Corrido Pensilvanio" speaks of Mexican migrants who go to Pennsylvania and West Virginia and say they are from Fort Worth; and the novelist Arturo Islas complains of those reviewers who "tripped all over themselves not wanting to understand the very clear distinction I make between migrant and immigrant" (Islas 1988).

The definitional dialectic, thus, consists of diametrically opposed political agendas engaged in a common campaign of definitional blurring. Both challenges have analytical and historical merit. Mexican immigration to the United States developed its initial momentum in the late nineteenth century, late enough to diminish the militant quip that Mexicans did not cross the border, the border crossed them, but early enough to support the argument that legislative and administrative creations around the turn of the century had the effect in turn of creating "the category of illegal immigrant out of a preexisting, established flow" (Portes 1985: 77). Up to the turn of the century, Portes points out that Mexicans traveled freely across the U.S. border, paying only for transportation across the Rio Bravo: "after 1917, they needed: two birth certificates, a certificate of good conduct, another of good health, proof that they would not be a public charge, a fee of ten dollars for the visa and another eight for entry tax" (77). García y Griego documents a variation on the theme of administrative over demographic determination of the illegal-immigrant flow in his discussion of the Bracero Program, particularly the middle years. The precipitous decline in illegal apprehensions during the mid-1950s, from 1.1 million in FY54 to .25 million in FY55 to .07 million in FY56, was a straightforward function of government-assisted *bracero* contracting at the border, which rose from around .2 million per year before 1954 to .3 million in 1954 to .4 million in 1955 and for the balance of the 1950s. Indeed, during Operation Wetback in 1954, it was not uncommon for Mexican workers to be expelled from the United States and then to return the same day as U.S.-contracted workers (García y Griego 1993: 102).

The more recent track record of the U.S. legislative and administrative machine, however, has been remarkably permissive with regard to regularization of illegal immigrants, and their promotion has not been to *bracero* but to permanent resident/citizen status. The 1982 Supreme Court decision on *Plyler v. Doe* refers to the note by the 1978 District Court that "under current laws and practices, 'the illegal alien of today may well be the legal alien of tomorrow'" and to the testimony in the earlier trial by one of the plaintiffs' experts that "fifty to sixty percent … of current legal alien workers were formerly illegal aliens" (*Plyler v. Doe*: 6). In 1986, IRCA legalized the status of roughly three million illegal immigrants over a three-year period. Over a more recent four-year period, another quarter-million visitors to the U.S. who overstayed their visas became legal residents by way of marriage, work, or the visa lottery (Dunn 1995: A5). Also recently, following the announcement by the Clinton administration that it would end the temporary-protection status for Salvadoran refugees in January 1995, the INS Commissioner conceded that their right to stay and work will be extended automatically at least nine months, that they will be apprised of their right to file for asylum status, and that many will be eligible to adjust to permanent-resident status by virtue of having been in the country for more than seven years (Stern 1994b: A21).

4. Economics

> *One fanatical quantifier in the sixteenth century …*
> *figured the weight of a 10 ¾ inch ball as 61 lb, 1 oz,*
> *2 drams, 1 scruple, and 15 685644/1414944*
> *grains*—Fischer 1970: 61

Cost-benefit analyses invariably seem to contain a notorious discrepancy between the precision of the individual assessments and the extreme variance of the collective outcomes. The Pennell et al. (1989) and Parker and Rea (1993) estimates for the annual criminal-justice-system costs in California for undocumented immigrants were respectively $15,227,435 and $151,220,101. The disparity between these particular estimates could be a simple reflection of change over time, and in fact the number of illegal aliens in state prisons has reportedly increased from 5,600 (or 7 percent of the prison population) in 1988 to 20,147 (16 percent) in 1994 (Nuñez 1994); still, a threefold change in numbers should not drive a tenfold change in expenses. To give another and more substantial example, regarding the national fiscal impact of all immigrants, Donald Huddle of Rice University reportedly found that they cost the American government 40 billion dollars annually (Borjas 1994: 46). By contrast, Passel and Fix suggest a 25–30 billion-dollar net gain annually, arguing that "the best recent research using a variety of data sources and modes of inquiry estimates that all immigrants arriving after 1970 pay a total of 70 billion dollars in taxes … generating 25 to 30 billion dollars more than they use in public services" (Passel and Fix 1994: 158).

These discrepancies, as discussed earlier, reflect the broad range of methodological possibilities and judgements. Whether or not marginal or average costs should be calculated, for example, is not only a reasonable judgement call but one that could introduce different biases for different calculations (one cannot reasonably assume that marginal costs are zero, however). More dubious assumptions include the one by Huddle that for every six immigrants who enter the country, one native is displaced from his job and joins the welfare rolls (Borjas 1994: 46), and the one by Cornelius and Martin (1993: 27) that the absence of accelerated immigration from southern to northern Europe following the expansion of the European Community may be one of the reasons for only a limited increase in immigration from Mexico to the United States following NAFTA.

None of this is meant to suggest that all of the economic information on immigration is indeterminant. Borjas (1994: 43) presents persuasive evidence that over the period from 1970 to 1990, immigrant households shifted from being slightly underrepresented in the distribution of welfare benefits (constituting 6.8 percent of all households and receiving 6.7 percent of public-assistance income) to substantially overrepresented (8.4 percent of all households and receiving 13.1 percent of public-assistance income). We still have a mystery in the final political analysis, because it is not clear how this collection of economic arguments ultimately plays out in the electorate. Some observers argue that the intensity of the current immigration debate is clearly linked to broader dissatisfaction with the welfare state. Several unions abandoned their long-standing crusade against illegal immigration and opposed Proposition 187. Indeed, California voters on 187 did not express strong feelings about the merits of the economic arguments one way or another, with only 32 percent of those voting in favor saying they agreed that it would save the state millions of dollars, and only 15 percent of those voting against saying they agreed that it would cost the state billions in federal funds (Mendel 1994a).

5. Parties, Interest Groups, and Bureaucracies

> *Explained the Cleveland Plain Dealer in 1854:*
> *When one Know Nothing wishes to recognize*
> *another, he closes one eye, makes an O with his*
> *thumb and forefinger and places his nose through it,*
> *which interpreted reads eye-nose-O—I know*
> *nothing*—Safire 1978: 360

In 1994, the Republican Party gained control of both chambers of Congress for the first time since 1954. The surge of Republican strength clearly contributed to the victory of Proposition 187 in California, where 78 percent of Republican but only 36 percent of Democratic voters cast ballots in favor of the initiative (with 62 percent of independents). The partisan contradiction, nevertheless, lies not between but within the parties, and particularly within the new majority, which seems to be divided over a whole range of immigration-related issues. On issues of scope, for example, members of the party swing from Know Nothing to Libertarian extremes. While the new chair of the House Ways and Means Committee argued, "philosophically, I have no problem saying that it is not our responsibility to take care of people who have not become citizens" (Kirschten 1995: 150), New York Mayor Rudolph Giuliani stated on television, "if you come here and you work hard and you happen to be in an undocumented status, you're one of the people who we want in this city" (Beck 1994: 32). In between, California's Governor Pete Wilson, more than anyone else, promoted illegal immigration as a premier problem and linked his gubernatorial reelection campaign to that of Proposition 187, but he generally distinguished welcome legal immigrants from unwelcome illegal ones. Senator Alan Simpson, along with Jack Kemp and William Bennett, emphatically disassociated themselves from the 187 campaign. Kemp and Bennet declared the proposition "politically unwise and fundamentally at odds with the best tradition and spirit of our party," and Simpson commented, "I have a little trouble with saying that someone 7- or 8-years-old is ... 'deportable,' when we don't even have the resources to deport criminal aliens who are in jail" (Kirschten 1995: 151).

To complicate matters further, Simpson is determined to push the development of a secure identification system for verification of employment and welfare-benefit eligibility (*Interpreter Releases* 7 March 1994: 314). But other conservatives, including William Kristol, described as a GOP strategic guru, have categorically denounced the much less intrusive recommendation by the bipartisan U.S. Commission for Immigration Reform for a computerized registry, calling it "another leap forward in the ever encroaching police powers of the federal government" (Kirschten 1995: 154). Last but not least, there is a fundamental, although still relatively latent, contradiction among Republicans about the mesh between immigration and culture. On the one hand, there is a "conservative proposition...that the U.S. is not an ideological abstraction but a nation" with a culture that can be traced "predominantly from the British Isles" (Beck 1994: 30). Francis Fukuyama, however, goes straight to the heart of the argument that immigrants from countries other than northern Europe are the source of a multicultural problem in America; in his words, "Paul Gigot may or may not be right that a million Zulus would work harder than a million English, but a million Taiwanese certainly would, and would bring with them much stronger family structures and entrepreneurship to boot" (1993: 31). Put differently, Murphy Brown and Ice-T, not hard-working, divorce-averse immigrants, are responsible for the degeneration of the American family and culture.

Should the Republican Party find a formula that survives the various cleavages within the party, the Democratic Party will probably deliver reinforcements. President Clinton proclaimed illegal immigration to be a major problem within a month of his inauguration and will undoubtedly continue to keep a count on the 167 electoral votes (60 percent of the magic number needed for election) in the six states that are engaged in legal or diplomatic wrangling with the federal government to gain reimbursement for expenditures associated with illegal immigrants.[3] The Vice President has promoted a demographic and environmental agenda whose spirit is not inconsistent with a campaign to limit immigration to the United States, especially in light of the exorbitant per-capita consumption of this country. One of the Democratic Senators from California, Diane Feinstein, became a frequent visitor to the San Diego border this past year and initiated the campaign for a border-crossing fee that was briefly endorsed by the President.

Finally, the Secretary of Labor has a long track record of emphasizing the expansion of high-skilled jobs in the manufacturing sector and of downplaying the significance of low-wage jobs in the services sector, a position that effectively associates illegal immigration with industrial stagnation and comparative disadvantage. Although the California Hispanic community is heavily Democratic and was the constituency that voiced the firmest opposition to Proposition 187 (Hispanic voters opposed the initiative by 77 percent to 23 percent), their political clout was diminished by youth and low turnout, seen in the huge discrepancy between its share of the California population (27 percent) and its share of the Proposition 187 vote (10 percent).

A final duality in national immigration politics involves the disparity between legislative hyperactivity and bureaucratic paralysis. Efrem Zimbalist, Jr., Tom Clancey, *Top Gun*, and *The Untouchables* have all presumably taken some of the popular bite out of being associated with bureaucracies in the FBI, Pentagon, Treasury, and CIA, notwithstanding Aldrich Ames, Waco, Texas, and other public-relations nightmares. The INS has only *The Coneheads* and *Green Card*, the former a "Saturday Night Live" lampoon about personable extraterrestrials unsuccessfully pursued by an INS District Director, the latter a French-American marriage arrangement whose romantic development is thwarted by an intrusive INS agent. More substantially, the *New York Times* ran a week-long series of articles under the headline "Chaos at the Gates" in which it assaulted the agency across the board for incompetence (inability to answer the phones), corruption (clerks taking bribes for green cards), callousness (endless lines for document processing), criminal neglect (deporting a tiny percentage of eligible criminal aliens) (Brinkley 1994: A1). Altogether, the first-day front-page article announced, "the INS is broadly dysfunctional." Other experts refer to the INS as a "bureaucratic Siberia" that has neither the budget nor reputation to attract the talent that other agencies can.

To be fair, particularly in a country without a strong state and high-level administrative-corps tradition, the agency is in the unenviable position of taking punches for historical neglect by its political supervisors. Congress has consistently underfunded the agency, initially providing the Border Patrol in 1924 with 45 agents to guard 8,000 miles of border, for example. The INS currently has 284 deportation officers to cover an estimated 200,000 or more criminal aliens, often scattered in a variety of state facilities. Elected in November 1992, Clinton did not nominate an INS Commissioner until June 1993, the Senate did not conduct hearings until September, so that the agency was leaderless for nearly a year. When Commissioner Meissner suspended the transfer of fingerprint cards to the FBI because of a budgetary shortfall, the Congressional oversight committee chairman reminded her that "There are some things not within your discretion to do. This is one of them" (*Interpreter Releases* 2 May 1994: 589). Congress substantially increased the INS budget for fiscal year 1995, from roughly 1.5 to 2.1 billion dollars, directing a good portion of the increase in funds to the Border Patrol to reinforce the new operations of *forward defense* along the El Paso and San Diego borders. Altogether, the Border Patrol has deployed 1,000 additional agents at the border, around 500 of whom are new agents and 500 are reassigned (Interpreter Releases 29 August 1994: 1141-42) Journalists continue to report that "budgetary bungling by the INS has left the agency understaffed, underequipped, and struggling in its fight against illegal immigration," especially in the field offices (Stern 1995: A1). Short shrift is given by agency officials to the defense that it is not easy to digest a large, sudden, and uncharacteristic infusion of money while simultaneously undergoing a major reorganization. Little attention is devoted to the difficulty of enforcing employer sanctions given agribusiness-lobbied legislation that earlier distinguished illegal "harboring" from acceptable employing (the Texas proviso of 1952) or that currently combines the absence of tamper-resistant documentation and a perfunctory requirement on employers to make document checks (the IRCA legacy of 1986).

6. Federalism and the Courts

> *Scarcely any political issue arises that is not resolved sooner or later into a judicial question*—De Tocqueville

Because an estimated 40 percent of the illegal-immigrant population resides in California and most of the balance in five other states, this issue has been wrung through the federal mechanism of U.S politics. The relationship between Washington, D.C., and the states has pendulum qualities of its own, ranging from a smooth synergy to open confrontation. In the former category, consider the one-two punch by which restrictions were placed on Asians around the turn of the century. In 1870, Congress modified the 1790 U.S. law governing citizenship in order to extend naturalization rights to those of African descent, but at the same time it denied such rights to Asians (including those from India after the Supreme Court ruled in 1923 in *U.S. v. Bhagat Singh Thind* that Indians would no longer be considered white persons) (Ong Hing 1993: 30). Unauthorized to regulate immigration directly, California enacted an Alien Land Law in 1913, which barred aliens ineligible for citizenship from owning land. Karen Leonard describes how some Punjabis in the Imperial Valley responded by entrusting their land to Anglos banks, one of which became known as the Hindu bank, or occasionally by transferring ownership to their Mexican spouses (1992: 56).

In other respects, the federal government exercises its immigration prerogatives in such a way as to keep the states either subordinate or entirely excluded. Although the Supreme Court held in *Decanas v. Bica* in 1976 that "the court has never held that every state enactment is regulation of immigration and thus per se preempted," and specifically upheld a California statute prohibiting employers from hiring aliens not entitled to legal residence if an adverse impact on legal-resident workers would ensue, subsequent legislation by Congress in 1986 and 1990 may have extended the range of preemptible state actions, particularly state laws on employment (Weissbrodt 1992: 59–60). More emphatically, the preliminary court injunctions on the enforcement of Proposition 187 have relied not only on the 1982 *Plyer v. Doe* ruling, which overturned a Texas law excluding illegal-immigrant children from the public educational system because the risk of creating a permanent underclass and punishing children for the acts of their parents outweighed the state interest in the case (Egelko 1994: A3–4), but also on the presumption that the propositions directives could not be made consistent with national law, even with carefully written agency regulations. According to the U.S. District Court Judge in Los Angeles, Mariana Pfaelzer, "You would have to stitch up each section of 187 with regulations, and I am sure it can't be done" (Noble 1994: A18). Her written decision referred to the possibility that Proposition 187 represented a "scheme to regulate immigration," invading the exclusive authority of the federal government (*San Diego Union Tribune* 20 January 1995: A1).

Likewise, California's attempt to sue the government for reimbursement for various expenses associated with educating, incarcerating, and providing health care to illegal immigrants has been struck down by the U.S. District Court in San Diego in part because the federal government is immune from lawsuits seeking monetary damages (Cleeland 1995: A1). Although the President and Congress appear prepared to begin providing reimbursement moneys to heavily affected states, this responsibility has been on the legal books since 1986 with respect to incarcerating illegal aliens but has never been funded. In the meantime, the reported result of Governor Wilson's trip to Capitol Hill seeking Congressional redress in January 1995, with a much more favorable Republican majority and much smaller request (.6 million in 1995, 2.3 in 1994, and 1.5 in 1993), was "sympathy, no cash" (Barabak 1995: A1). Finally, California Republican Dana Rohrbacher did not even get sympathy when he introduced an amendment to a House education bill to require schools to report undocumented students to the INS; it was defeated by a vote of 329–78 (*Interpreter Releases* 14 March 1994).

The political maneuvering and legal proceedings surrounding Proposition 187 remain as substantial, if at a lower public profile, as during the fall campaign. The *Plyler v. Doe* case was originally decided five to four, two of the slender majority votes have been replaced by new justices on the Supreme Court, and even constitutional-law scholars sympathetic with the original decision have indicated that there is nothing automatic about a reaffirmation of the principle. Lawyers supportive of Proposition 187 recognize that the initiative contains some potentially problematic language but are particularly confident that a substantial state interest can be demonstrated, especially now that the GAO and Urban Institute show estimated costs to California to be in the billions of dollars.

7. Race

> *Hindus Too Brunette to Vote Here*—1923 Headline
> in the *Literary Digest*, from Leonard 1992: 55

Gunnar Myrdal's classic study of the "Negro problem" begins with the argument that racial discrimination is an integral part of "the whole complex of problems in the American civilization. It cannot be treated in isolation" (1962: lxxv). That being said, race and immigration have at least in some cases enjoyed a certain independence from one another. The Know Nothing Party was fanatically opposed to European Catholic (especially German and Irish) immigration, and although the party did not survive the fallout from the Civil War, its objectives were largely fulfilled in the National Quota laws of the 1920s that used 1890 flows as the baseline for future immigration to minimize southern and eastern European immigration (i.e., before the 1890–1910 surges in immigration from that part of Europe.) In this case, xenophobia was at least partially color-blind. The 1965 modifications to the immigration laws, which were passed at the peak of the civil rights campaign in 1965 (i.e., the same year as the Voting Rights Act that would allow the Justice Department to draw majority-minority congressional districts in seven southern states), and which would profoundly change the ethnic mix of immigrants to the United States, were not expected to have any substantial ethnic and racial impact. In this case, immigration liberalization was at least partially color-blind.

By contrast, the histories of the American Black and Asian communities demonstrate virtually complete racial and immigration linkage. Blacks were obviously a kind of reverse refugee, abducted into a situation of well-founded fear of persecution, beginning in the seventeenth century. Asians began arriving in California around the mid-nineteenth century, and the same national civil-rights law that outlawed racial discrimination against blacks in 1870 permitted continued discrimination against Asians. The Chinese Exclusion Act was upheld by the Supreme Court, even though the basis for exclusion was race, on the ground that "over no conceivable subject is the legislative power of the Congress more complete"—that is, over even the Constitution (Weissbrodt 1992: 55). The subsequent Geary Act of 1892, which placed a registration requirement on Chinese already in the United States in order to enforce the exclusion on new Chinese, was also upheld by the Supreme Court. Immigrants from India, and later from the Phillippines, were subsequently judged by the Supreme Court to fall under the Asian regime in the 1920s; the spirit of the headline "Hindus Too Brunette To Vote Here" was racially apt, especially since so many of the Indians in California were Sikhs and Moslems, not Hindu. Anti-miscegenation laws remained on the California books until after the Second World War.

Mexicans and Mexican Americans have also been the victims of discrimination, although arguably not as systematically as Blacks and Asians. They were victimized in the nineteenth century by court rulings like *Botiller v. Domínguez*, in which "the protection of private property ostensibly guaranteed by the Treaty of Guadalupe Hidalgo was essentially invalidated" (Griswold del Castillo 1990: 76–77), and in the twentieth century by popular violence like the Zoot Suit rioting, by Jim Crow-type arrangements, and by exploitative labor practices. Yet, at the same time, Mexicans in the annexed territories were at least in principle invited to take U.S. citizenship following the Mexican American War, unlike the Chinese coolies, and were not subjected to the Alien Land Laws that applied to other "brunettes." For the past 30 years, Cubans have enjoyed a very permissive refugee status, codified in 1966 legislation that uniquely exempts them from the burden of proving an individual fear of persecution and provides them with permanent-resident status after one year and one day in the United States. The fortified Black Caucus of the 1993–1994 Congress has been quick to contrast that arrangement with the summary repatriation by the Bush and Clinton administrations of 30,000 Haitians and the denial of 94 percent of the roughly 60,000 Haitian applications for asylum filed between 1992 and mid-1994 (*Economist* 16 July 1994: 23); indeed, the *New Yorker* labelled Clinton's retreat from a campaign promise to discontinue summary repatriation of Haitians the "most shameful single feature of the Clinton administration's first year" (10 January 1994: 5). The status of the Hispanic community is, thus, somewhere intermediate between the racist temptation and the commitment to equal opportunity that together formed the "American dilemma."

The mixed messages of Proposition 187, hence, should come as no surprise. The Black and Asian communities split almost evenly on the proposition (47 percent "yes" votes for each), in spite of the sentiment expressed by Bill Ong Hing, Asian-immigration expert at Stanford University that "for most, economics is a diversion. Underneath it's about race" (Guskind 1994: 1298). The Hispanic community voted overwhelmingly against the initiative, even though their history is less marred by the "Negro problem" and even though the results of the Latino National Political Survey contained dramatic indications of Latino opposition to further widespread immigration from Latin America and "pride in America" (*Economist* 8 January 1993: 32). Although exit polls indicated that 39 percent of those voting against the initiative considered it racist/anti-Hispanic, the single most cited basis for opposition was that the measure was "poorly written/wouldn't solve the problem" (*San Diego Union Tribune* 9 November 1994: A3). All in all, Myrdal's observation for the United States in the 1960s that "prejudice as an attitude was still common, but racism as a comprehensive ideology was maintained only by a few" (1962: xliii) might apply equally well to California in the 1990s.

Unfortunately, the nexus between prejudice or racism and immigration may not only endure but become fortified as America moves into the next century. Numbers and images make California the cutting-edge case. Demographic projections show the state becoming majority non-White by the year 2002, with cities like Monterey Park already 57 percent Asian, up from 3 percent 30 years ago. In fact and fiction, the Los Angeles riots of 1992, and the *Bladerunner* depiction of the city in 2019, have laid an inauspicious foundation for the transition. Articles on immigration that ostensibly adopt a balanced perspective already contain arguments that descend consciously or unconsciously into a racial mode. For example, "Anglos who ask why should I learn Spanish may ride into the next century on the back of the bus" (Canlen 1993: 119). The attack on Affirmative Action, already provocatively dubbed the son of 187, has moved race front and center. If the attack is a function of a variety of both simple and complicated factors, including a dominant culture whose collective unconscious and sense of history are awakened only on presidential holidays, it is still guaranteed to reignite the most problematic issue in this country's history. Already, as the University of California at Berkeley Chancellor noted in response to a law-school incident stemming from insidious fliers in support of the new "Civil Rights" initiative, "the older I get, the more convinced I become of the centrality of the issue of race in American society. The issues surrounding it never go away ... Inevitably, it seems the melting pot boils over" (Ayres 1995: A22).

8. International

> *I am clear of red tape and I know of no Rio Grande*—Major Langhorne, 1917, in Nadelman 1993: 75

The international dynamics surrounding immigration and other issues linking Mexico to California are sufficiently complicated that a theorist of the California-Mexico connection concluded that it "may never achieve greater integration, but nothing in the foregoing exploration suggests that it will disintegrate .... Its components are too numerous, too tenuously connected, and too linked into diverse decision centers ..."(Rosenau 1993: 30). This political diversity is reflected in Mexican lobbyists on Capitol Hill, Mexican-government sensitivity to the political pulse of the Mexican American community in Los Angeles, California's development of a Pacific-Rim foreign policy, and San Diego's establishment of a special twin-city relationship with Tijuana. Simultaneous conflict and cooperation, from the close cooperation between American and Mexican agents enforcing neutrality laws in the early twentieth century to the brinksmanship and virtual closure of the border following the murder in Mexico of Drug Enforcement Agency Enrique Camarena in 1985, are the result.

Immigration politics are pushed and pulled by these cross-border "intermestic" dynamics. One of the Mexican results is a mixed package of incentives and disincentives for cooperation with the United States in limiting the flow of workers to the other side. A clear benefit of noncooperation is a substantial flow of remittances to Mexico, estimated at 3.2 billion dollars in 1990, falling just short of tourist income at 3.4 billion dollars and ahead of foreign direct investment in Mexico at 2.6 billion dollars (Lozano 1993: 64). A more cooperative attitude, at least nominally, became associated with the Salinas campaign for the North American Free Trade Agreement Association and has become an outright price to be paid by Zedillo for U.S. support for the stability of the Mexican currency. Mexico has already taken the relatively painless steps of increased vigilance against third-country passage through Mexico to the United States, with interceptions at Mexican airports (against potential illegal immigration to the United States from the Middle East), along Mexico's southern border (reducing Central American flows), and off the Pacific Coast (most famously, turning back boats of Chinese, for which the United States subsequently paid nearly half a million dollars). In addition, Mexico is now expanding its special police force (Grupo Beta) along the U.S.-Mexican border, created to reduce criminal activity associated with immigration, and has pledged to work to suppress the production of fraudulent identification cards in Mexico and to increase efforts to break up immigrant-smuggling rings (Stern 1995: A12). The Zedillo initiatives included a high profile, public pledge of cooperation with the United States. This was perhaps the most striking part of the package given the sensitivity of a border first taken and then ignored (*a la* Major Langhorne) by the U.S. military.

9. Security

Opium smoking, along with morphine and cocaine addiction, is spreading very rapidly among the white American population not only in California, but throughout the territory of the States ... For this

reason alone, the Chinese immigration should be
stopped and an effort should be made to remove the
coolies already here—Emmons 1991: 42, writing
about California in 1891

The effort to reconceptualize security for the post-Cold-War era has moved into high gear. Unfortunately, if scholars and officials labored under an overly restrictive definition of threats for the past half century, obsessed with nuclear bolts out of the blue, the new experience is a virtual feeding frenzy of perceived dangers, running from classical military rogues to environmental problems, mafia and other transnational criminal operations, drug trafficking, agricultural trade wars, terrorism, and, most relevant for our purpose, illegal immigration. Illegal immigration has been depicted as a new and potentially significant threat because of the size of the feared flows (typically measured in water flows like floods or tidal waves), because of reevaluations of the importance of society and culture in international security (societal security, civilization conflict), and because of links with the other dangers (narcotics trafficking and fifth-column terrorism in particular).

Each component in this threat package is problematic, however, at least for the United States. So far, this country has not been confronted with refugee flows from a new-world disorder; the U.S. Committee for Refugees Survey of 1993 shows only 100,000 refugees and asylum seekers in need of protection and/or assistance in the United States, compared with 5.7 million in Africa, 5.6 million in the Middle East, 3.3 million in Europe, and 2.7 million in Asia (Meissner et al. 1993: 99). Articles that warn of over 100,000 Chinese illegally entering the United States per year (the 1994 INS estimate of illegal aliens from China and Hong Kong in the United States as of October 1992, was 27,000) sound vaguely like earlier ones that grossly inflated the number of Warsaw-Pact divisions facing NATO (Smith 1994: 60). As for new or resurrected paradigms in international security that emphasize society and civilization over state, the Huntington dia-tribe against Islam's "bloody borders" and against the weapons transfers from its sinister "Confucian connection" is particularly superficial. Among other short-comings, it completely denies the significance of the remarkable cross-fertiliza-tion of contemporary societies, utterly fails to account for the remarkable political coalition formed by the United States in the Gulf War, and omits the thoroughly dominant position of the United States in the global arms bazaar.

Those analyses that associate illegal immigration with far more sinister dangers in a "continuum of threats" are less preposterous, but the connections generally seem meager or incidental, and the broader ramifications for social harmony are especially harmful. It is true that the Mexican connection has graduated from a "marijuana border" in the 1970s—in the words of Elaine

Shannon (1988: 42)—to a major purveyor of a whole variety of drugs (e.g., Colombian cocaine redirected from the Caribbean) in the 1990s, and that NAFTA will make interdiction even more difficult as border traffic is expedited to accommodate the growth in trade volume. But the only major connection between illegal immigration from Mexico and drug shipments from Mexico is that they cross the same border and have similar destinations; the immigrants themselves neither carry nor consume substantial quantities of drugs. In FY 1994, the Border Patrol in the San Diego sector apprehended a total of 450,000 illegal aliens, of which a mere 95 (.02 percent) were arrested for drug possession (U.S. Border Patrol 1995). As for the connection between criminal organizations and the smuggling of illegal immigrants, the suggestion that the latter is the security threat is to confuse the tail with the dog.

Finally, as for the terrorist connection with illegal immigration, the World Trade Center bombing in New York City and follow-up trials have clearly demonstrated a connection between immigration irregularities and national-security risks. Mahmud Abouhalima, for example, became a key participant in the World Trade Center bombing after overstaying a tourist visa and regularizing his status through a fraudulent amnesty application, claiming to have worked on a South Carolina farm when he was driving a cab in New York (Behar 1993: 59). Unfortunately, the association between Islam and terror seems to have moved from an exceptional marriage of ruthless convenience to a generalized identity for persons from the Middle East. We see the simplification particularly in labels like "Islamic fundamentalist" and "Arab terrorist," in which all four terms become effectively synonymous; Saddam Hussein and the Ayatollah Khomeini seemed for many Americans to have a kissing-cousin relationship, and the fanatical Arab terrorists in the very popular movie *True Lies* quite naturally transport their smuggled nuclear warheads in large Persian artifacts.

Government efforts to develop more effective counterterrorism techniques may be necessary, but the specter of a fifth-column network must be addressed in a way that recognizes the danger of allowing a generalized post-Cold-War equivalent to the indiscriminate internment of Japanese Americans in World War II and the response to the Plan of San Diego in World War I. The latter, lesser known case, involved a genuine Mexican plan (named after a small Texan town and designed by Carranza) calling for Mexican American rebellion within the United States and the slaying of all adult Anglo males, and produced about a dozen incursions into U.S. territory around 1915–1916. According to Ethan Nadelmann (1993: 74), however, the "principal victims were the hundreds of Mexican Americans lynched by the Texas Rangers and local vigilantes."

In the end, perhaps the most convincing relationship between security and immigration remains the historical one in which European and American empires and spheres of influence, inspired by geopolitical competition, generated or accommodated immigrant flows from the Third World. Guest worker programs have invariably reflected "neocolonial" relations, whether Algerians to France or Mexicans to the United States. Refugee flows have also reflected specific global pretensions, such as Cubans in Florida and Vietnamese in California. Most recently, the network that planned the New York City bombings may have been trained, funded, and otherwise assisted (in getting admitted to the United States) by U.S. agencies involved in the campaign against the Soviet Union in Afghanistan. Ironically, immigration from the empire became the most effective instrument of Third-World independence. In the United States, for example, "exclusion and independence were tied together" for Filipinos during the 1930s debate that led to the Tydings McDuffie Act of 1934 (Ong Hing 1993: 35). In France, the integral quality of French Algeria was arguably "finished" long before the end of the war by simple virtue of the demographic realities of nine million Muslims reproducing at a much higher rate than 50 million Europeans. In Britain, immigration became the trump card in the postwar "decolonization" of the Tory Party in the 1960s; Enoch Powell's infamous "Rivers of Blood" speech represented an emphatic finish to imperial nostalgia (Kahler 1984: 133).

10. Conclusion

> *The two men, Gibreelsaladin Farishtachamcha,*
> *condemned to this endless but also ending angelic*
> *devilish fall, did not become aware of the moment at*
> *which the processes of their transmutation*
> *began*—Rushdie 1988: 5

Proposition 187 may very well mark the beginning of a transmutation in U.S. immigration policy, but which voting bloc grows halos (like the vulgar exhibitionist Farishta) and which bloc grows hoofs and horns (like Chamcha, who as a boy in Bombay already anticipated the Tebbit rule and cheered for the English cricket team) remains to be seen. What is clear is that there are no revolutionary syntheses; indeed, there are not even any running-dog compromises in the making. Illegal immigration is a problem by definition, because to modify Churchill's formula slightly, the rule of law is the worst form of authority except for all the others. César Chávez called it a "severe problem" in the 1970s and routinely reported undocumented farm workers to federal authorities. The high level of fraud in the 1986 SAW (Seasonal Agricultural Worker) legalization program, when 250,000 to 350,000 applications were expected and 1,275,000 applications were received, added insult to injury (Cornelius 1993: 167). The estimate that 15 percent of the population in the country is foreign-born but that

30 percent of the additional annual flow into the country is illegal (Passel and Fix 1994: 152–53) does not suggest the problem is being resolved.

On the other hand, illegal immigration is a problem screaming for a sense of proportion, a sense of history, and a bit of nuance. "Severe" is an overstatement, particularly with respect to the overall economics. At $600 million, the California governor's bill to the federal government for reimbursement for spending on illegal immigrants in 1995 is equal to $20 per California resident, one percent of the state budget, or 50 percent of the Air Force's marginal cost for another B-2 bomber (without fuel or payload). The severe danger is that the rhetoric on both sides of the issue will transform a very complex issue into a demagogic one with a racial fillip. The "save our state" slogan certainly does not depart from the typical standards of campaign simplification, but statements like that by one of Proposition 187's authors, Harold Ezell, that "we can't afford to educate, medicate, incarcerate, and compensate all the illegals of the world" (Guskind 1994: 1299) and the suggestion by California State Senator William Craven that Latinos would be required to carry identification cards should the proposition pass, do move the measure into the demagogic and racial realms, respectively. California demographics have been heavily multiracial and multiethnic since the establishment of the state in the mid-nineteenth century, as reflected in the names of the early mining towns and camps of Sonora Bar, Chili Camp, Dutch Flat, Irishtown, Italian Gulch, Portuguese Flat, Norwegian Mine, Swiss Bar, and Chinese Camp (Hart 1987: 151). This diversity has been reinforced both by the push and pull of international economics, the linkages established by Manifest Destiny on the continent, and the campaign against Communism all over the world. Residents of the United States do not have to celebrate diversity, but they do need to tolerate it. The alternative would be the national equivalent to Khomeini's response to Rushdie's dialectic, a nation in hiding from intolerance and its own founding mythology.

Notes

1. Special thanks to Al Sweedler, Didier Bigo, Dan Wolf, Peter Nuñez, Del Dickson, Michele Magnin, Doug Payne, Gail Perez, Manuel García y Griego, George Borjas, Vali Nasr, Orlando Espin, Jon Sandy, Rudy Marillo, and Polin Soth for thoughtful guidance and frequent disagreement. Thanks also to the financial support from the James Irvine Foundation and the University of San Diego. Finally, thanks to Ana Evans de Carvalho, Anthony Moreno, and Ivani Vassoler for research help.

2. Verse from *corrido* "Viva Los Mojados," presented by the Alma y Corazón Latino group, San Diego, March 1994:

Por que somos mojados / No le gusta a la ley / Por que somos ilegales / Y no hablamos el inglés / El gringo nos viene a sacar / Pero el problema se puede arreglar / Hay que conseguir una gringuita para poder casarse / Y cuando tengas los papeles / Ya te puedes divorciar... Viva todos los mojados / Los que van a inmigrar / Los que van a pasar / Y viva los que se van a casar / Para poder arreglar.

Because we are wetbacks / The law doesn't like us / Because we are illegal / And we don't speak English / The gringo comes to expel us / But the problem can be fixed / You find and marry a *gringuita* / And when you have the papers / You can get divorced ... Long live the wetbacks / Those who immigrate / Those who cross the border / Long live those who get married / To get their papers.

3. The vote breakdown was: California 54, New York 33, Texas 32, Florida 25, New Jersey 15, and Arizona 8.

References

Ayres, B. Drummond. 1995. "Conservatives Forge New Strategy to Challenge Affirmative Action." *New York Times* (16 February).

Barabak, Mark Z. 1995. "Wilson Gets Sympathy, No Cash Commitment from U.S." *San Diego Union-Tribune* (2 February).

Beck, Roy. 1994. "Right of Silence? The GOP and Immigration." *National Review* (11 July).

Behar, Richard. 1993. "Mahmud the Red." *Time* (4 October).

Bigo, Didier. 1994. "The European Internal Security Field." In *Policing Across National Boundaries*, Malcolm Anderson and Monica den Boer, eds. London: Pinter.

Borjas, George. 1994. "The Economics of Immigration." unpublished manuscript.

Brackman, Harold, and Steven Erie. 1993. "The Once-and-Future Majority." In *The California-Mexican Connection*, Abraham Lowenthal and Katrina Burgess, eds. Stanford: Stanford University Press.

Brinkley, Joel. 1994. "At Immigration, Disarray and Defeat." *New York Times* (11 September).

Calavita, Kitty. 1989. "The Immigration Policy Debate." In *Mexican Migration to the United States*, Wayne Cornelius and Jorge Bustamante, eds. San Diego: Center for U.S.-Mexican Studies, University of California at San Diego.

Canlen, Brae. 1993. "San Diego Burning." *California Lawyer* (August): 44–119.

Canlen, Brae. 1994. "Who Gets In?" *California Lawyer* (August).

Chavez, Lydia. 1994. "More Mexicans, More Profit." *New York Times* (9 December).

Clark, Rebecca L., Jeffry S. Passel, Webdy N. Zimmermann, and Michael E. Fix. 1994 "Fiscal Impacts of Undocumented Aliens: Selected Estimates for Seven States." Washington D.C.: The Urban Institute.

Clad, James C. 1994. "Slowing the Wave." *Foreign Policy* (Summer).

Cleeland, Nancy. 1994. "U.S. Court Decision Blocks Prop. 187." *San Diego Union-Tribune* (15 December).

Cleeland, Nancy. 1995. "State's Suit Over Illegal Immigrants Dismissed." *San Diego Union-Tribune* (14 February).

Collinson, Sarah. 1993. *Beyond Borders*. London: Royal Institute of International Affairs.

Cornelius, Wayne. 1993. "From Sojourners to Settlers." In *U.S.-Mexico Relations: Labor Market Interdependence*, Jorge A. Bustamante, Clark W. Reynolds, and Raul A. Hinojosa Ojeda, eds. Stanford: Stanford University Press.

Cornelius, Wayne, and Philip Martin. 1993. *The Uncertain Connection: Free Trade and Rural Mexican Migration to the United States*. San Diego: Center for U.S.-Mexican Studies, University of California at San Diego.

De Tocqueville, Alexis. 1945. *Democracy in America*. New York: Random House.

Dillon, Richard. 1970. *Humbugs and Heroes: A Gallery of California Pioneers*. New York: Doubleday and Company.

Dresser, Denise. 1993. "Exporting Conflict: Transboundary Consequences of Mexican Politics." In *The California-Mexican Connection*, Abraham Lowenthal and Katrina Burgess, eds. Stanford: Stanford University Press.

Drummond, Tammerlin. 1994. "Experts Weigh Ballot Measure's Possible Impact." *New York Times* (4 September).

Dunn, Ashley. 1995. "Greeted at Nation's Front Door, Many Visitors Stay On Illegally." *New York Times* (3 January).

Economist. 1992. "The Mexican-American Border—Hi Amigo." (12 December).

Economist. 1992–1993. "Columbus's Children." (26 December–8 January).

Economist. 1993. "Fencing." (5 June).

Economist. 1993. "A Giant Sucking Sound." (5 June).

Economist. 1994. "They Shall Not Pass." (9 July).

Economist. 1994. "Walking Round It." (9 July).

Economist. 1994. "America's Least Wanted." (16 July).

Egelko, Bob. 1994. "Prop. 187 Doesn't Violate Due Process, State Says." *San Diego Union-Tribune* (8 December).

Emmons, Terence. 1991. *Around California in 1891*. Stanford: Portable Stanford Book Series.

Engelberg, Stephen. 1994. "GOP's Voice on Aliens Roars Challenge to Party." *New York Times* (8 December): A14.

Fischer, David Hackett. 1970. *Historians' Fallacies*. New York: Harper and Row.

Fukuyama, Francis. 1993. "Immigrants and Family Values." Commentary (May).

Galeano, Eduardo H. 1988. *Century of the Wind*. New York: Pantheon.

Ganster, Paul, and Alan Sweedler. 1990. "The United States-Mexican Border Region: Security and Interdependence." In *U.S.-Mexico Border Statistics Since 1900*, David Lorey, ed. Los Angeles: UCLA Latin American Center Publications.

García y Griego, Manuel. 1993. "Policy-Making at the Apex: International Migration, State Autonomy, and Societal Constraints." In *U.S.-Mexico Relations: Labor Market Interdependence*, Jorge A. Bustamante, Clark W. Reynolds, and Raul A. Hinojosa Ojeda, eds. Stanford: Stanford University Press.

Griswold del Castillo, Richard. 1990. *The Treaty of Guadalupe Hidalgo*. Norman: University of Oklahoma Press.

Gross, Gregory. 1995. "Border Entry Fee Proposal Stuns Many." *San Diego Union-Tribune* (7 February): B1.

Gross, Gregory. 1995. "Tough Trail Leads New DEA Boss Here." *San Diego Union-Tribune* (5 February): A1, B5.

Guskind, Robert. 1994. "Border Backlash." *National Journal* (6 June).

Hart, James. 1987. *A Companion to California*. Berkeley and Los Angeles: University of California Press.

Interpreter Releases. 1994. "Senator Simpson Introduces Major Immigration Reform Bill." (7 March).

Interpreter Releases. 1994. "House Considers More Immigration Restrictions in Emotional Debate." Vol. 71, no. 10 (14 March).

Interpreter Releases. 1994. "Clinton Policy on Haitian Boat People Appears Lost at Sea." (11 July).

Islas, Arturo. 1988. Ernesto Garlarza lecture series. Palo Alto: Stanford University.

Kahler, Miles. 1984. *Decolonization in Britain and France*. Princeton, NJ: Princeton University Press.

Kirkpatrick, Jeane. 1995. "The Consequences of Immigration." *San Diego Union-Tribune* (13 January).

Kirschten, Dick. 1994. "Immigration and Rancor are Soaring." *National Journal* (18 June).

Kirschten, Dick. 1995. "Second Thoughts." *National Journal* (21 January).

Leonard, Karen. 1992. *Making Ethnic Choices*. Philadelphia: Temple University Press.

Livi-Bacci, Massimo. 1994. "Nous et eux: l'Europe et les Etats Unis face a l'immigration." *Politique Etrangere* 59 (3).

Lozano Ascencio, Fernando. 1993. *Bringing It Back Home.* San Diego: Center for U.S. Mexican Studies, University of California at San Diego.

Martin, Phillip. 1994. "Immigration and Agriculture: An Endless Debate." *National Forum* 74 (3).

Martin, Phillip, and Mark Miller. 1994. "European-American Immigration Convergence." *International Migration Review* XXVIII (3) .

Meissner, Doris M., Robert D. Hormats, Antonio Garrigues Walker, and Shijuro Ogata. 1993. *International Migration Challenges in a New Era.* New York: The Trilateral Commission.

Mendel, Ed. 1994a. "Immigrant Initiative's Foes Ready Lawsuits." *San Diego Union-Tribune* (9 November).

Mendel, Ed. 1994b. "Measure Slips in Poll, Could Face Close Vote." *Los Angeles Times* (19 November).

Morrison, David. 1994. "Robocops." *National Journal* (16 April).

Morgan, Neil. 1993. "Mexico Boosts Role in Fighting Border Crimes." *San Diego Union-Tribune* (28 December).

Murillo, Rudy. 1994. INS briefing, San Ysidro Port of Entry (13 September).

Myrdal, Gunnar. 1962. *An American Dilemma.* New York: Pantheon.

Nadelmann, Ethan A. 1993. *Cops Across Borders.* University Park: Pennsylvania State University Press.

National Journal. 1994. (18 June).

Newland, Kathleen. 1993. "Ethnic Conflict and Refugees." *Survival* (Spring): 81–101.

New Yorker. 1994. "The Same Boat?" (10 January).

New Yorker. 1994. "A Visit with Sheikh Omar." (10 January).

New York Times. 1993. (26 June).

Noble, Kenneth B. 1994. "Court Deals Another Blow to Backers of Proposition 187." *New York Times* (15 December).

Nuñez, Peter. 1994. Presentation to the San Diego World Affairs Council (19 October).

Ong Hing, Bill. 1993. *Making and Remaking Asian America through Immigration Policy.* Stanford: Stanford University Press.

Parker, Richard, and Louis Rea. 1993. *Illegal Immigration in San Diego County: An Analysis of Costs and Revenues.* Prepared for Senator William A. Craven, California State Senate, Special Committee on Border Issues.

Passel, Jeffrey S., and Michael Fix. 1994. "Myths About Immigrants." *Foreign Policy* (Summer).

Pennell, Susan, Christine Curtis, and Jeff Tayman. 1989. *Impact of Illegal Immigration on the Criminal Justice System.* San Diego: San Diego Association of Governments.

Plyler v. Doe. 1982. Supreme Court of the United States, No. 80–1538 (15 June).

Portes, Alejandro, and Robert Bach, 1985. *Latin Journeys.* Berkeley: University of California Press.

Portes, Alejandro, and Ruben Rumbaut. 1990. *Immigrant America.* Berkeley: University of California Press.

Robinson, David. 1985. *Chaplin, His Life and Art.* New York: McGraw-Hill.

Rosenau, James. 1993. "Coherent Connection or Commonplace Contiguity?" In *The California-Mexican Connection,* Abraham Lowenthal and Katrina Burgess, eds. Stanford: Stanford University Press.

Rosenthal, A. M. 1995. "Working in Tijuana." *New York Times* (21 February).

Rushdie, Salmon. 1988. *Satanic Verses.* Dover: The Consortium.

Safire, William. 1978. *Safire's Political Dictionary.* New York: Ballantine.

San Diego Union-Tribune. 1994. (9 November).

San Diego Union-Tribune. 1994. "In Sharp Backlash, N.Y. County Stops Protecting Latin Refugees." (19 December).

San Diego Union-Tribune. 1995. "Judge Bars State from Enforcing Prop. 187." (20 January).

Schain, Martin, and Sophie Body-Gendrot. 1992. "National and Local Politics and the Development of Immigration Policy in the US and France." In *Immigrants in Two Democracies: French and American Experience*, Donald Horowitz and Gerard Noiriel, eds. New York: New York University Press.

Schram, Stuart. 1974. *Chairman Mao Talks to the People.* New York: Pantheon.

Shannon, Elaine. 1988. *Desperados.* New York: Viking.

Shaughnessy, Rick. 1995. "Many Immigrants Demonstrate Flair for Creating Jobs." *San Diego Union-Tribune* (31 January).

Smith, Paul J. 1994. "The Strategic Implications of Chinese Emigration." *Survival* 36 (2).

Stern, Marcus. 1994a. "State Taxpayers' Tab for Illegal Immigrants in '94." *San Diego Union-Tribune* (1 December).

Stern, Marcus. 1994b. "Sanctuary Status Ends for Refugees from El Salvador." *San Diego Union-Tribune* (3 December).

Stern, Marcus. 1995a. "White House Inflated Data on Migrants." *San Diego Union-Tribune* (28 January).

Stern, Marcus. 1995b. "Foul-Ups Keep Cash from INS in Field." *San Diego Union-Tribune* (5 February).

Stern, Marcus. 1995c. "Mexico to Boost Border Controls." *San Diego Union-Tribune* (16 February).

Time. 1993. "The New Face of America." Special issue (Fall).

U.S. Border Patrol, San Diego Sector. 1995. Telephone interview (February).

Walker, Lynne. 1994. "Along the Border, California is No Texas." *San Diego Union-Tribune* (9 December): A2.

Warren, Robert. 1994. "Estimates of the Unauthorized Immigrant Population Residing in the United States, by country of Origin and State of Residence: October 1992." Washington D.C.: INS Statistics Division.

Weiner, Myron. 1992. "Security, Stability and International Migration." *International Security* (Winter).

Weissbrodt, David. 1992. *Immigration Law and Procedure.* St. Paul: West Publishing Co.

Williams, Jim. 1992. *Ellis Island and Statue of Liberty.* San Francisco: American Park Network.

Wolf, Daniel. 1993. "The Rea-Parker Study of Undocumented Alien Fiscal Impacts: How Accurate?" Testimony to the Immigration Hearing and Public Forum of Assemblyman Bill Morrow, Oceanside, CA (9 December).

Wright, Lawrence. 1994. "One Drop of Blood." *New Yorker* (25 July).

Border People and Their Cultural Roles: The Case of the U.S.-Mexican Borderlands[1]

Oscar J. Martínez

1. Introduction

Isolation, underdevelopment, and neglect characterized border regions around the world in the nineteenth century and the first half of the twentieth century. Above all, an unstable international climate kept borderlands generally underpopulated and economically backward, as central governments hesitated to develop areas where the likelihood of fighting in time of war was the highest. After World War II, however, changes began to occur in the world that would profoundly affect many border regions, particularly in Western Europe and North America. Territorial disputes declined appreciably, allowing formerly tense borderlands to attain stability and to turn former locational disadvantages into assets for achieving growth and development. This turn of events reflected larger global transformations. Advances in air warfare diminished the importance of land-based combat, thus rendering borderlands much less significant as buffer zones to keep real and potential enemies at a secure distance from nations' heartlands. At the same time, the global economic system became highly internationalized, and many countries drew closer together through interdependent networks that arose from greatly increased trade.

As front-line zones of contact, borderlands encountered opportunities previously unavailable to them. Their functions underwent substantial redefinition, from frequently ignored wastelands to dynamic centers of trade, commerce, and even industrialization. Many closed borders became open, allowing capital, people, and products to move from country to country in search of new opportunities. Borderlands that were enmeshed in this process developed economic

293

activity sufficient to spur the growth of existing population centers and the emergence of new ones. Borderlanders affected by such trends, especially borderlanders from developed nations, found a new place in the world, playing roles long denied them by an international system previously driven by global tensions and the ideology of rigid national sovereignty.

In North America, the U.S.-Mexican borderlands provide striking evidence of the trend toward closer ties among the world's nations and societies. The intense economic interaction between Americans and Mexicans has spawned unique forms of interdependence with profound social and cultural consequences. In a functional sense, two systems have combined to produce one order that is quite distinct from those of the two parent societies, and a population whose lifestyles differ considerably from what is found in heartland zones.

Out of economic necessity as well as personal desire to venture into "other worlds," border Mexicans, Mexican Americans, and Anglo Americans intermingle at close range, borrowing from and contributing to one another's way of life. That three-way association, ranging from superficial contact to intimate relations, has produced unique patterns that comprise key components of what is commonly referred to as *border culture*.

Fundamentally, border culture, or the border *way of life*, is rooted in the influences that the boundary exerts on *fronterizos*. First, borderlanders are surrounded by internationality; they go from one nation to the other frequently on shopping trips, on business, or for leisure. Transnational interaction is normal and routine. Second, they are accustomed to dealing with conflicts spawned by the border itself or by larger international controversies. *Fronterizos* know the border is a flashpoint, and they are used to putting out fires. Third, border people are adept at ethnic interaction; over several generations they have learned how to transcend group differences. These experiences, then, are central elements in the values, thinking, and behavior of border people.

But other factors play a significant role as well. Regionalism, an important variable in the configuration of the borderlands, is evidenced in the expression of U.S. southwestern and Mexican *norteño* cultural styles. Distinct subregions are identifiable, each with its own characteristics shaped by local environmental factors and contact with the outside world. Above all, the singularity of the border population rests on the many traits that derive from its subgroups, including cross-borrowing of such things as language, religion, customs, traditions, holidays, foods, clothing, and architecture. In short, U.S.-Mexican border culture may be said to be the sum product of forces and influences generated by the boundary itself, by regional phenomena, and by the transculturation shared by Mexicans, Mexican Americans, and Anglo Americans.

Border culture is most vibrant in the core zone of the borderlands, or the strip of territory where the border cities are situated. Beyond the border area there is a secondary domain where border culture is strongly felt; important cities in the Texas-Mexico region include San Antonio, Houston, Monterrey, and Saltillo. Each of these centers feels the import of the other side of the border through constant migration flows. The impact of the border diminishes in the interior of each nation, but selected spheres of influence are readily apparent. For example, in the United States, places like Denver and Chicago have large Mexican American populations that maintain direct links with the borderlands. An important part of that contact is carried on by migrants who constantly travel between Mexico and the interior United States. Within Mexico, cities with cultural connections with the border include Guadalajara and Mexico City, to name two large cities, and hundreds of towns and villages that send migrants to the borderlands or the greater United States.

Significantly, the vastness of the borderlands assures subregional variation in the manifestation of border culture. Hence, while fundamental commonalities characterize the lifestyles of borderlanders regardless of their location, local peculiarities shape the cultures of different places in distinct ways. For example, the New Mexico/West Texas-Chihuahua borderlands exhibit patterns characteristic of an isolated high desert zone and a population heavily dependent on the major rivers in the region, i.e., the Rio Grande, Pecos River, and Río Conchos. Cultural strains from Chihuahua and New Mexico are strong here, but mainstream Mexican and U.S. cultural influences have made their presence felt in recent years with the arrival of many immigrants. For example, several generations of newcomers have modified traditional folkways characteristic of the region. Migration is of particular importance because this zone has served as a major corridor between central Mexico and the U.S. Southwest for centuries.

East along the Rio Grande, the South Texas-Northeast Mexico borderlands manifest influences arising from a subtropical climate, a large agricultural and ranching society, and a strong mix of Texas Anglo culture with Mexican *norteño* culture, that is the *Tex-Mex* culture. The mix of these strains is illustrated in *Tex-Mex* music, which combines instruments and sounds from both nations. As in other border locales, deep and widespread poverty constitute an important variable in the shaping of the culture of this zone.

Few who reside on the Mexican side of the border are able to escape the overwhelming influence of the United States, and consequently most Mexican borderlanders have direct or indirect ties to Americans. Such links have resulted in heavy consumption of U.S. products and popular culture, but that does not necessarily imply a corresponding loss of national identity; Mexicanness as a rule remains strongly embedded among all Mexican *fronterizos* regardless of their external orientations.

On the U.S. side, vast numbers of Mexican Americans maintain substantial bonds with Mexico. They live bicultural and transnational lifestyles to a far greater degree than any other sector of the borderlands population. Out of economic necessity and by the sheer force of the U.S. *melting pot* phenomenon, most Mexican American borderlanders, including many first-generation immigrants, have learned the English language and have absorbed large doses of American culture. At the same time, the proximity to Mexico has assured strong adherence to the Spanish language and Mexican culture. Generally speaking, then, with some exceptions Mexican American borderlanders are transnational in outlook and behavior.

By contrast, relatively few Anglo American borderlanders manifest transnational characteristics, although some do interact in a substantive way with Mexicans and Mexican Americans. The low incidence of transboundary interaction and biculturalism among Anglos is principally explained by the lack of a compelling economic need to cross the border, learn Spanish, or become familiar with Mexican culture. Those who do have such a need are generally the ones who speak Spanish and function comfortably in Mexican American and Mexican circles. But there are Anglos who have become bilingual and bicultural, and who participate in transnational activities for personal reasons rather than economic self-interest.

Based on the level of transboundary contact, the border population may be divided into two general types: (1) national borderlanders and (2) transnational borderlanders. National borderlanders are people who, while subject to foreign economic and cultural influences, have minimal or superficial contact with the opposite side of the border owing to their indifference to their next-door neighbors or their unwillingness or inability to function in any substantive way in another society. Transnational borderlanders, on the other hand, are individuals who maintain significant ties with the neighboring nation; they seek to overcome obstacles that impede such contact and take advantage of every opportunity to visit, shop, work, study, or even live on the "other side." Thus their lifestyles strongly reflect foreign influences. For some transnational borderlanders such influences are modest, but for those who are seriously immersed in transborder interaction, foreign links govern central parts of their lives. Ambivalence over national identity and loyalty certainly exists among some individuals heavily immersed in transnational interaction, but for most, that appears not to be a major problem. The fact that Mexico and the United States maintain a relatively friendly relationship tends to mitigate self-doubt or guilt stemming from intimate contact with the "other side."

Varying factors determine whether borderlanders are *national* or *transnational*, including length of residence in the borderlands, ties with interior areas, occupation, sources of income, level of education, family networks, and social relationships. It must also be kept in mind that the border population includes both permanent and semi-permanent residents, plus large numbers of transients who spend little time in the border communities. Population fluidity and turnover are especially strong on the Mexican side. The longer a person lives at the border, the greater the chances that she/he will be caught up in transnational processes. Consequently, long-term border residents are more likely to reflect transnational characteristics than newcomers.

At one end of the border-population spectrum are people who by circumstance or choice are largely unaffected by the border milieu, while on the other are individuals whose lives revolve around it. Many who adhere to a strictly national and unicultural perspective have surrounded themselves with walls to keep out the hybridizing influences of the border. By contrast, those with a transnational orientation have built bridges that enhance and promote binational and bicultural symbiosis. That is the essence of core borderlanders, those transnationals who most exemplify the fusion of the two societies.

Core borderlanders have successfully adjusted to the innate instability generated by a boundary born of extreme territorial and cultural animosity and sustained in more recent times by great economic disparity between the two nations. They have found ways of making the border permeable and different cultural worlds accessible. They have developed attitudes, values, and behavioral strategies that allow them to move swiftly between two nations and from one cultural group to another.

In day-to-day relations, core borderlanders have collaborated to keep the channels of international communication open and to hold border-related disagreements to manageable levels. Those with a high degree of cultural versatility have provided leadership in the networks that bind the area's major groups to one another. Constant movement in and out of different cultural milieus has allowed core borderlanders to develop expertise about the ways of others and sensitivity to their concerns. Aware of the perspectives of people from both sides of the border, many core borderlanders have been prompted to look beyond their own national interest, to examine problems in broad context, and to take into consideration the implications of parochial policies and actions.

In pursuing transnational interaction and multiculturalism, they have overcome long-standing rivalries between the two countries and the sting of racial and cultural biases. Living in an environment of uncertainty and unpredictability, they have developed a high tolerance for ambiguity and mechanisms for coping

with it. In short, core borderlanders have discarded fears, inhibitions, and prejudices that afflict people with a national or ethnic-specific orientation.

The patterns of behavior among borderlanders, both positive and negative,
are a product of powerful forces that have long been reshaping two societies and
molding a social structure in which people of different cultural strands have
learned to cope and to thrive. The institutional underpinnings of the system are
so deep and so strong that attempts to diminish transnational or transcultural
interaction are exercises in futility. The convergence of groups at the border is in
concert with the *natural order* of human relationships and, viewed from an
internationalist perspective, actually represents a significant improvement in the
way people from different countries and cultures interact with one another.

What is transpiring on the U.S.-Mexican border at the present time yields
insights into what is in store in the future on a grander scale. As free trade forges
a closer relationship between the two nations, the intensity of binational people-
to-people contact is expected to rise dramatically. Borderlanders will feel the
effect of that increased interaction most acutely, but fewer and fewer people who
reside in central areas in both nations will be left untouched as the force of
transnationalism radiates beyond the frontier.

The border experience has great significance for instructing us on how
international cooperation and cross-cultural accommodation can be accomplished, and how individuals can draw strength from within themselves successfully to overcome problems that arise from living on the periphery, in an
environment that is neither mainstream U.S.A. or mainstream Mexico, but a
variation of each. At a time when national disintegration and extreme ethnic
polarization trouble other parts of the world, the U.S.-Mexican borderlands stand
out as a place that has succeeded in transforming a once predominantly conflictual
human environment into a predominantly peaceful and cooperative one.

Note

1. This paper is based primarily on original research conducted by the author and
represents concepts elaborated in: Oscar Martínez. 1994. *Border People: Life and Society in
the U.S.-Mexico Borderland.* Tucson: University of Arizona Press.

Stereotypes, Culture, and Cooperation in the U.S.-Mexican Borderlands

Samuel Schmidt

> *The phrase "melting pot" used to mean the United States of America. Now it means you put the wrong container in the microwave*—Robert Orben, *Wall Street Journal*

1. Introduction

For many people, life on the U.S.-Mexican border is rather pleasant; understanding between both societies is well developed, and the only thing people desire is the removal of border controls because they enjoy living close to one another. But when in 1993 the U.S. Border Patrol sealed the border between El Paso, Texas, and Ciudad Juárez, Chihuahua, it took little effort to manipulate El Paso society—itself 70 percent Hispanic—to accept discriminatory arguments in favor of stopping migration. The Border Patrol's arguments included the charge that Mexicans are criminals and abuse the welfare system. Neither allegation has been proved since the so-called border blockade was initiated.

A governmental policy such as the border blockade supported by a discriminatory rationale was possible, among other things, because of the existence of stereotypes that differentiate societies, creating an image of superiority and discrimination. This essay will describe the existing stereotypes between the United States and Mexico and will analyze how cultural differences obstruct binational collaboration, especially binational planning, which is an instrument to facilitate working jointly toward a common future.

2. About Stereotypes

Perceptions that different social groups have with regard to other social groups, ethnic or otherwise, generally derive from stereotypes constructed over the years. The stereotype is a contrast where the archetypal group, aided by biased images, differentiates itself from the stereotyped group. Stereotypes result from a serious lack of understanding of the other's values (Haddox 1981: 7), are based on the archetypal group's self image, and are superimposed over the stereotyped group's image to make evident the negative aspects of the stereotyped.

Stereotypes develop from misunderstandings about concepts, symbols, myths, beliefs, and cultural attitudes central to other peoples and nations. While they may contain some elements of truth, they also provoke discrimination and promote the exclusion of the group being stereotyped—considered, in most cases, to be inferior to national *charter* groups. The U.S.-Mexican case is no exception. Stereotypes about both countries are the result of mutual perceptions and history and usually are a distortion of reality. Furthermore, these stereotypes are partially related to the border and border interactions.

3. The Border and Definition of the Other

One concept shared by both governments is that of the border as an empty area. This idea originated with Spanish and British colonization. For the Spaniards with a *rentista*[1] mentality, tribute and labor were scarce and not plentiful enough to motivate migration to the region. For the settlers of the early colonies, land was open for expansion. From an early time, the border region was an ecosystem for violence as a consequence of being removed from direct governmental supervision and a lack of law enforcement by the centers of power. Border people had the feeling that the region had its own morals and values. For the English colonizers, the frontier's wild west was an area for adventure and expansion. "Until the late 1800s the borderlands were regarded as badlands or *malpaís*—the realm of rattlesnakes, *bandidos*, and desert rats" (Barry and Sims 1993: 19).[2]

The arid desert climate helped perpetuate the perception of the area as empty space and "wastelands without beauty or life" (Barry and Sims 1993: 19). This image has been prevalent in the border policies of both countries, although the United States' expansion in the nineteenth century—which cost Mexico half its territory—was the main event defining the border relationship. For the United States, the border region has since been seen as a national-security issue; for Mexico the border has been a vulnerable part of the motherland. In other words, the United States views Mexico as its backyard with the the border representing a protective fence (however, while backyards are often in disarray and even "trashed," it is imperative to maintain a beautiful front yard). At the same time, the United States does not allow "strangers illegally" to jump over the fence; to intrude, as it were, onto their private property. It should be remembered that U.S. law protects homeowners who kill trespassers.

For U.S. authorities, Mexican migrants are intruders jumping over the fence; thus, they are considered criminals and must be subject to the strongest punishment. For many police officers who feel they are protecting the fence, their abuse of Mexicans is a natural consequence.[3] Even if they kill an undocumented migrant, the law will protect them.[4] Incarcerating Mexicans who cross the border without documents or with forged papers helps support the stereotype that Mexicans are criminals.

For Mexicans, the United States is a colossus against whom they cannot fight and with whom they must be careful in dealing. There are benefits of working with the United States but also potential dangers, such as an invasion. This paranoia has motivated a purportedly ambiguous and nonactive border policy. Under the typical liberal laissez-faire policy many things could happen in a militarily unprotected border region where different policy forces interact. This, together with the loss of territory and a history of U.S. military invasions in the continent, also supports the Mexican stereotype of Americans as abusive.

Stereotypes Regarding Mexico

Most of the U.S. stereotyped perceptions of Mexico have a foundation in health issues and basically are related to water. For many years, Mexican potable water in big cities was considered by the United States as nondrinkable. Consequently, Americans are always warned to be careful in Mexico because it is not safe to drink the water. Many Americans carry purified water along with medicines for diarrhea and stomachache when they visit Mexico. There were rumors that former U.S. ambassador to Mexico John Gavin had water transported to Mexico via air. Mexico, then, is associated with sickness and dirt, and Mexicans are stereotyped as dirty people. Recent sociological research in El Paso-Ciudad Juárez shows that Americans associate dirt with Mexico even if they see a photograph of their own backyard. They said that if the backyard was dirty it must be Ciudad Juárez (Vila in Schmidt and Lorey 1994).

Although it is possible to get sick in Mexico, the same is true for anybody going to another country and experiencing a substantial change in diet. For example, in the summer of 1992 a group of Mexican teachers enrolled in a program at the University of Texas at El Paso, and some of them started getting sick at the beginning of the second week. The reason was that the university cafeteria had changed the menu.

The perception of lack of cleanliness leads to association of Mexicans with backwardness. This image is applied to the entire country. It is hard for travelers to find precise information about regional differences in Mexico. The assumption is that all areas of the country are equally bad with respect to cleanliness. The degree of modernization of different regions seems to effect very little those negative perceptions.

There is not much difference in the stereotypes recorded by various scholars (see Figure 1). Johnson (1980) applied a questionnaire to a group of experts in order to record the existing stereotypes about Latin Americans. O'Connor and Nystrom (1985: 4) analyzed biases in U.S. history books to determine if stereotypes about Latin America were transmitted to U.S. students. They concluded that U.S. history texts "influence the perpetuation of unidimensional-dimensional world views" (1985: 4). They added that U.S. students read history books, unaware of manipulated images in textbooks. A Spanish-language political-science book used in the United States flatly ignored the nineteenth-century Latin American wars of independence (Woodford and Schmitt 1993, Chapter 15), which took place a decade earlier than the Greek independence that was mentioned in the book. O'Connor and Nystrom concluded that "in the process of filtering relevant information about Latin America, textbook creators promote certain cultural stereotypes and lead students of American history to gauge the value of Latin American life according to some United States' standards" (O'Connor and Nystrom 1985: 3).

This is not something reserved for history books. In fact, most U.S. analysts use U.S. culture as the paradigm for understanding any society and especially Latin America (Busey 1985). Beezley (1991) analyzed U.S. popular perceptions and recorded Mexican stereotypes very similar to Johnson's and those of O'Connor and Nystrom. Johnson documented the stereotype but did not explain its origin. O'Connor and Nystrom explored the creation of the stereotype, implying that scholars played an important role in its creation and reproduction. Thus, we find a cycle where the experts transmit their stereotyped image of Latin America to their students and the students, reproduce it everywhere.

Among the elements that helped create and reproduce the Mexican stereotype in the United States is what is called the *Walt Disney effect*. According to one Latin American analysis (Dorfman and Mattelart 1973), in Disney's comic books the Latin American is portrayed as lazy, foolish, ignorant, and easy to cheat. The Mexican image falls into the same categories. A novel useful to illustrate the influence of this perception is James Michener's *Texas* (1985). Among the "flowers" that can be picked from Michener's "garden of prose" are the following excerpts from the dialogue of his many characters:

Figure 1. Stereotypes of Latin Americans and Mexicans

Beezley	O'Connor/Nystrom	Johnson
lazy	lazy	lazy
poor with technology	technological inferiority	emotional
dirty	emphasis on climatic features	religious
thieving	low educational level	backward
devious	lack of cultural sophistication	suspicious
sexually hyperactive	lack of economic sophistication	friendly
overly fond of alcohol	volatile character of emotions	dirty
carefree	Latin America backward rural	proud
romantic	U.S. as protector of the region	imaginative
poetic by nature	U.S. mighty and Latin America weak	dark-skinned
debonair	U.S. as helper of Latin America	shrewd
charming		intelligent
women tempestuous		honest
women sultry		brave
women sexually tempting		generous
venal		progressive
sexually promiscuous		efficient

It's Mexico, remember, and from what we hear up here, that's a most unstable country. It's not like Prussia, even England ... and God knows it's not like the United States (345–46).

It's a Mexican wilderness, and who wants to live in a country that can't govern itself (369).

They'll never be able to govern it by themselves (534).

With Mexicans, nothing is ever allowed to be simple (373).

Why can't Mexico ever do anything right? (378)

Mexican men can never settle upon one course of action and follow it for a generation; even the slightest mishap diverts them (406).

Mexican law doesn't count, because the richest man can always buy the judge (410).

Mexicans and Indians, you can't tell the difference ... In Texas there ain't no place for a Cherokee or a Mexican (549).

An analysis of U.S. Ambassador to Mexico John Gavin's opinion about Mexico in the 1980s (Morris 1991), gives the impression that the diplomat was following Michener's script: "All of the many problems of Mexico, from the economy, to drugs, to mass migration, to the lack of democracy, are the results of a system that is corrupt" (120); "The total corruption made popular by Santa Anna was going to become a way of life in Mexico, contaminating government for the next century and a half" (599).

Another question relates to the elements helping to create the stereotype. The books analyzed by O'Connor and Nystrom (1985: 3) create a "Hispanophobic fallacy that has permeated the United States' propaganda and perceptions about Spain and Latin America over the years." We can assume, to a certain extent, that teachers who use the books share these biases and reinforce them with students. It may also be that some of these scholars were influenced by Mexican books. Three books are important in this regard. Ramos (1938) concludes that Mexicans have an inferiority complex. Paz (1986), perhaps one of the most widely read Mexican authors in the United States, even before he received the Nobel prize, reinforces Ramos's conclusion. Fuentes (1970) demolished the image of the Mexican Revolution through his narrative that portrayed it as a source of corruption and abuse of power, even while Mexican leadership heralded the Revolution as the first social revolution of the twentieth century and the major political achievement of the new political elite. The Mexican stereotype has been reinforced by the negative and pessimistic description of Mexican authors of their own people. When Mexicans analyze themselves, usually they reach negative conclusions.[5]

It can be expected that closeness between societies would eliminate stereotypes because constant interaction will reveal a more accurate image of people. However, this is not the case of the U.S.-Mexican border where nationals from both countries meet on a regular basis. In an exercise to measure stereotypes regarding Mexico that San Diego State University students and the author conducted in 1989, a questionnaire listing Johnson's stereotypes was applied to a group of U.S. students. The answers were very similar to the responses Johnson received. Closeness between San Diego and Tijuana, which can be considered sister cities, not only did not change the stereotype but confirmed the biases that U.S. students who go to Mexico for recreational purposes have toward Mexicans. This observation suggests that the stereotype is deeply rooted, and daily interaction reinforces it.

Stereotyping is also reflected in language. Some of the concepts used in the United States referring to Mexicans or Mexico reflect the images and perceptions Americans have. Some words taken from Chapman (1989), referring to Mexicans are:

Aztec two-step, Montezuma's revenge, or turista = diarrhea

Big enchilada = boss or leader

Chili, greaser, or taco = a person of Mexican origin

El Cheapo = a cheap product

Mexican breakfast = a cigarette and glass of water

Mexican red = high-quality marijuana

Mexican promotion or Mexican raise = promotion without salary increase

4. Mexican Stereotypes Regarding the United States

The stereotypes that Mexicans have about the United States vary depending on the social class, which itself is an interesting problem, because different social classes have different contacts with the United States. Herrera-Sobek (1979) shows how the people's (folk) perceptions can be diametrically opposed to those of the elite. When she analyzed the perceptions about the Bracero Program (a system for temporarily contracting Mexican workers in the United States that was abolished in 1964), she discovered that migrant workers regarded the program as a positive and fruitful experience. The elite, however, viewed the same program in negative terms because it exploited Mexicans. This dichotomy is well presented in the Héctor Suárez film, *El Mil Usos*.

For a portion of the upper and middle classes in Mexico, the United States represents success and grandeur. These social strata copy U.S. habits and "success" models, very well portrayed on Mexican television advertisements and duplicated by social behavior of Mexican youth as seen in their entertainment preferences and expectations. During the interviews for a scholarship competition in Mexico City (August 29, 1991), the majority of the social-sciences candidates wanted to study for a Ph.D. in the United States as an avenue to success. Two public-administration candidates openly said that their chosen universities were those attended by the current president and the secretary of the treasury.

In 1992, the author had the opportunity to talk to four Mexican graduate students at Columbia University. The four said they were studying there to prepare their political careers. They even mentioned that other students were preparing to be able to participate in the 1994 Mexican electoral campaign. What is relevant is their belief that attending graduate school in the United States was a requisite for success in Mexican politics.

The lower classes do not have money or education to follow U.S. consumption patterns. Nevertheless, they also share the perception of the United States as a powerful, dominant, and exploiting country and of Americans as people who take advantage of Mexicans.

Figure 2. U.S. and Mexican Stereotypes

Americans about Mexicans	Mexicans about Americans
Backward	Dominator
Ignorant	Invader
Lazy	Dunce
Lacks Initiative	Easily Deceived
Dark-Skinned	Blond
Nonperforming	Abusive
Untrustworthy	

In their stereotypes about the United States, Mexicans scorn Americans with epithets such as *gringo* or *bolillo*. This is reflected in the behavior of a youth gang in Matamoros, a border city of the state of Tamaulipas on the border with Texas, where the initiation into the gang includes fooling or evading U.S. police officers (Zúñiga 1991). The Mexican also makes the American the victim of humor, portraying the American male as a fool and easy to cheat, and the U.S. female as an easy sexual catch, as seen in the following joke:

> Una gringa viajando por el norte de México sufre una ponchadura en una llanta. Un indio le ayuda a cambiarla y cuando termina, ella abre el monedero y él responde: "No, ni lo saque. Yo no acepto dinero de una vieja." Ella medita sobre que es lo que él quiere y entonces empieza a desnudarse. Cuando llega a las pantaletas él dice: "Ni se los quite, no me van a quedar."

> A *gringa*[6] driving in the north of Mexico has a flat tire. An Indian helps her replace the tire, and when he finishes she opens her purse but he says, "Don't even think about it; I take no money from women." She thinks about what he wants and then begins to undress. When she gets to her panties he says, "Don't even take them off; they're not my size."

Even more interesting are jokes portraying the United States as a country with no freedom:

> A Mexican dog and a U.S. dog meet at the border. As they talk, the American dog says, "In my country, we have plenty of food and wonderful female dogs." The Mexican dog answers, "Then what are you doing here?" "I came to bark," responded the American dog.

4. Perceptions and Culture

Stereotypes develop, ignoring the other's symbols, myths, beliefs, and cultural attitudes. Sometimes a superficial observation might give credence to what becomes a stereotype. Taking a *siesta* (afternoon nap) is perceived by the

Anglo-Saxon culture as laziness. In fact, the custom of the *siesta* makes sense in a country with extremely high afternoon temperatures when people are forced to stop working. The *siesta* does not mean that these people are lazy. A superficial analysis by people who do not live in these types of climates might lead the observer to conclude he or she is witnessing lazy people.

There are innumerable examples of how perceptions of advancement or backwardness of societies are based on the observer's standard of living. This, combined with discrimination, will extend a negative perception to the rest of the country without recognizing differences.

With respect to the U.S. perception that Mexicans are dirty, Vila (in Schmidt and Lorey 1994) discovered that people on the U.S. side of the borderline refuse to recognize their own garbage, saying that if a house was dirty it must be in Mexico. The same happens with the perception of undocumented Mexican migrants. If they have to jump a fence or swim the river they cannot be expected to be squeaky clean, but many Americans will assume all Mexicans are dirty. A similar picture exists regarding work. Mexican undocumented migrants work hard but most often in agriculture or menial jobs that carry almost no prestige. Yet, they are stereotyped as lazy. The same happens with the perceptions of Americans. Not all Americans are invaders or are willing to exploit Mexicans. Of course, not all women go to Mexico looking for a Latin lover. However, a few experiences contribute to these perceptions.

Language, while an expression of culture and of political culture, also separates people. In this way, there are diametrically opposed meanings in language. The same word, phrase, or concept can have very different meanings for two societies (Figure 3). In the United States, "narc" means drug agent while in Mexico it means drug dealer.

Figure 3. Same Words with Different Meanings

Concept or Word	U.S. Meaning	Mexican Meaning
narc	drug agent	drug dealer
potable water	water safe to drink	piped water regardless of safety
public denial of charge of misconduct	necessary to avoid tacit admissions of guilt	providing unnecessary excuses is tacit admission of guilt
public demand of problem resolution	is considered to be a sign of weakness	is considered to be a sign of strength
request for new government funding	is legislature	are central and decentralized agencies
bite (Mexican term for bribe that usually buys a service)	bribe	user tax

Regional and social origins may significantly influence understanding of words or concepts. This is true not only along the border, but within each country. For example, the Mexican attitude may differ by region or social class from the American attitude with regard to justice, government, or truth. In Mexico a narc may be regarded as a Robin Hood-type person who successfully challenges and defeats government; the narc as a police agent might be regarded as the arm of a corrupt justice system that has abused society for a long time. The following joke touches on the theme of police abuse in Mexico:

> A group of police agents go into a police station, pick up a drunkard, take him to a barrel full of excrement, and ask him, "Where are the jewels?" The drunkard says, "I don't know." They submerge him in the barrel, take him out, and ask again, "Where are the jewels?" "I don't know." So after a few times the drunkard says, "Look, I can't find the jewels; please get another diver."

Perception of government and an individual's position with respect to political power are a strong determinant for culture and language. Political culture (Almond and Verba 1963) is important for language, but it also reinforces stereotypes since people transfer their values to their interpretation of other societies. Under the influence of stereotypes, both cultures collide. Acculturation is also influenced by the social, economic, political, and cultural environment. When migration was criminalized (García y Griego and Verea 1988: 55), legal experiences produced outcomes apparently funny but also tragic. One example of the latter is a bilingual sign at a seafood stand on the Santa Monica Pier in Los Angeles, California, that reads: "deep fried, extra charge." The Spanish translation was: *"hondo freir, extraordinaria acusación"* (deep fried, extraordinary criminal complaint). "Charge," in this case, should be translated as *cargo* or *costo*. Extra charge should be *cargo adicional*. The legal term "charge" can be translated into Spanish as *acusación*.

5. About Changing Stereotypes

Multiple contacts between societies can be expected to change stereotypes. This can be a conscious effort, as exemplified by former Governor Ann Richards of Texas, who saw "opportunities from free trade as a chance for Texas and Mexico to free themselves of stereotypes—nothing but cowboys and cattle for Texas and Pancho Villa and revolutionaries for Mexico" (Scharrer 1991: 2A).

In other cases, increasing contacts generated by economic development have modified mutual perceptions (Ganster 1991). Although, as Ganster points out, the *maquiladora* industry modified the perceptions of Mexicans as lazy among some sectors in the border zone, it is doubtful that this has fully permeated popular perceptions. Various racist groups in the San Diego-Tijuana region refuse to accept the change, as reflected in persistent cases of violence against undocumented immigrants.

Even though closeness can reveal an accurate image of people, it can also show defects that are magnified due to ideological distortions. Stereotypes are not independent of ideology and politics, which make it difficult to correct perceptions. Ideology and governmental decisions might help prevent the correction of inaccurate stereotypes. This is particularly problematic with racist groups. One case in point is U.S. immigration administration and law that, since the last century, has been trying to deny access to undesirable foreigners, principally based on the assumption that illiterate migrants or those with mental illnesses and social problems might become public burdens.

The mere concept of *alien*, as used by U.S. immigration law, is intended to show that the migrant is different from the local citizen. In September 1993, following this policy, the Border Patrol started a border blockade between El Paso and Ciudad Juárez with the argument that Mexicans are criminals and abuse the U.S. welfare system. In fact, after almost a year of blockade, pickpocketing diminished only in a six-block downtown area of El Paso. Violent crime increased in the rest of the city, and crime did not increase in Ciudad Juárez. None of the schools reported child absenteeism, and food-stamp use did not increase because only legal residents have access to this program. Finally, Thompson General Hospital in El Paso reported an increase in use of its services right after the blockade started. Even with all this evidence, it is difficult to convince the Border Patrol to understand that the arguments used to support the operation were wrong and biased. In addition, many complaints supported the evidence of discrimination against Mexicans during the blockade (Koulish et al. 1994).

Manuel García y Griego (García y Griego and Verea 1988: 126) claims that U.S. officials have manipulated public opinion by exaggerating numbers and attributing to Mexicans all kinds of evil actions. This often motivates hostile attitudes toward Mexicans. García y Griego also addresses the contradiction of the INS characterization of Mexicans being willing to take jobs and accept low wages and simultaneously being lazy and a burden for the U.S. welfare system. He also highlights the INS argument that Mexican migration in fact means a silent invasion (1988: 137).

For Mexicans, closeness to the United States does not eliminate the perception that the northern neighbor is unfriendly or has bad intentions. Once at a binational conference in a resort in the state of Colorado, one of the Mexican participants asked, "What is it that they want? Why do they treat us so nice?"

The U.S. and Mexican governments signed a Free Trade Agreement (NAFTA), which is perceived by many as the beginning of new opportunities, by others as the beginning of an integration process, and by yet others as a risky business with possible negative consequences. Almost none will perceive the process as two partners working together building a common future.

6. Planning in a Transboundary Metropolis

Urban planning is not only a need, but it also shows an effort to organize the urban space and work for a better future urban environment. In the U.S.-Mexican border region, urban planning can help avoid conflict (Graizbord in Herzog 1986: 20) and plan for a better use for scarce resources since most of the cities are poor and located in the desert (Schmidt 1994). The El Paso-Ciudad Juárez region is considered by many as a single region divided by a river (Martínez 1994). Although this is a romantic idea, it is far from reality because authorities from the two cities hardly communicate with each other. In fact, it is surprising when city employees do communicate with each other and, frequently, when this happens it is because external actors, such as academics, facilitate the interaction. However, cooperation between city officials is more a matter of personal interest than a result of institutional priorities and willingness to work together. City planners from El Paso, Sunland Park, Las Cruces, Doña Ana County, El Paso County, and Ciudad Juárez created the Regional Planning and Development Committee (Goodman Corporation 1992),[7] which practically disappeared when both El Paso and Ciudad Juárez administrations changed in 1993, and the priorities for the new mayors also changed. A believable hypothesis is that lack of communication is due to stereotypes and cultural differences. Arreola and Curtis (1993: 3) assert that:

> the popular perception of the Mexican border towns still conjures two persistent images. First, border towns are seen as tawdry yet convenient and accommodating tourist outlets, albeit for short term visits. Second, they are viewed as small places, not really large enough to be considered cities.

In other words, Mexican border cities are not considered reliable partners. This perception, added to a lack of communication systems and good data,[8] prevents joint decision making. The following examples, taken from interviews conducted during 1992–1993, show the differences in the definition of priorities between city administrators in El Paso and Ciudad Juárez.[9]

Health Services

Ciudad Juárez: Allocation of resources is based on criteria set by the previous administration.[10] Budget is not assigned by specific areas, and it is allocated according to specific needs.

El Paso: Most pressing concerns are to increase the number of food inspectors to meet federal guidelines. Water and sewage improvement, especially in the Lower Valley (highest concentration of *colonias*), and immunization-outreach programs are also priorities.

Planning

Ciudad Juárez: Priorities are supported by technical studies. Among the criteria is the highway plan, which supports the city's structure. Design of new transportation routes sets the criteria for paving streets.

El Paso: Priority projects are those for which money is available and that meet the most objectives. Development of jobs, especially for youth, for elimination of crime is important. Education needs to be considered to develop employable youth. Transportation has become a priority because that is where the money is, and it creates jobs.

Public Works

Ciudad Juárez: Priorities are set based on the city's master plan for urban development. The public works department also bases its decisions on requests from individuals and groups. Street paving is decided through preliminary studies of main streets, the need to improve public transportation, and restructuring conflicting intersections due to traffic problems or flooding. Paving of *colonias* is based on requests from people. Another interviewee said that when it comes to public works for the community, the planning department intervenes to determine which tasks have priority and in what part of the city.

El Paso: The Public Service Bureau's priority is to provide a safe and adequate supply of water within the city limits and to insure an adequate supply of water in the future. The quality and quantity of water available are a priority.

The El Paso Transportation Department's priority is the safe and free flow of people and goods through the city. Air quality is a priority because the United States Environmental Protection Agency now has to approve every single project. No project will be approved unless the Department of Transportation can prove that it will improve air quality.

Social Development

Ciudad Juárez: Operation is based on the Solidarity[11] programs. They also base their budget on those of previous administrations and respond to social demands.

El Paso: (Chief Financial Officer) Priorities are fairly standard for every city: Fire stations within three miles of each house, general welfare, water, utilities, transportation, and so forth. Top priority is law enforcement in the broadest sense, including education and prevention. Second-level priority is economic development that does not require a great deal of money and is a slow, long-range process. Third-level priorities are public libraries and transportation. The public's priority is "no more taxes." The city must determine if this means that potholes and present quality of libraries are all right in their present condition.

Water Authority

Ciudad Juárez: Priorities are determined by demographic growth. Eight percent of the budget is used to provide water and sewage in the periphery, and 16 percent is for repairs to the system.

In Ciudad Juárez, the departments of Planning, Public Works, and Social Development guide their budgets by the federal allocation through the Solidarity program. Once the money is allocated, state and municipal governments match the funds for specific projects. These departments also raise funds with the local treasurer and have loans from the World Bank and BANOBRAS (the Mexican development bank, which funds public works at the municipal level).

7. Conclusion

Cultural differences between U.S. and Mexican borderland people are strongly influenced by cultural and historical developments including a difficult border relationship in the nineteenth century that resulted in the United States taking half of Mexico's territory. This event created images of weakness in Mexico and strength in the United States and might be the main component of the stereotypes people share.

Although family ties transcend the international boundary and there is, on the part of many, the desire to work jointly with the other side, a lack of institutional support for cooperation persists, and both societies continue to work separately. There is no visible sign of solid and sustainable collaboration for the future, and many people have not realized that the work neglected today might create conditions that cannot be resolved in the future. Proximity has created mistrust, exacerbating biases and prejudices.

The positive side is that with an integration process started by the U.S., Mexican, and Canadian governments via NAFTA, new opportunities and challenges will force reluctant politicians to embrace actions that otherwise they would not. Hopefully, this will be the beginning of the decline of stereotypes and prejudice.

Notes

1. To receive rent for land without necessarily working it.

2. In Sonnichen's (1943:41) description of the legendary Texas judge Bean's move to Mesilla, New Mexico: "The Bean brothers always headed for a frontier community on the make where pushy Americans could get theirs without too much regulation and interference."

3. Koulish et al. (1994a) maintain that most victims of mistreatment by immigration authorities are Hispanic U.S. citizens and legal residents.

4. Apparently, a code of honor between police officers protects them even if they abuse civilians. This, of course, is extended to their abuse of migrants.

5. This is my conclusion in a recently finished book-length manuscript on political humor.

6. Mexican slang for Anglo American women. The term generally has a negative connotation.

7. I wish to express my appreciation to Nat Campos, Director of Planning for the City of El Paso, who provided a copy of this report and who answered various questions.

8. In the framework of a conference on urban services in El Paso-Ciudad Juárez, one expert pointed out the fact that water is measured with different units of measurement.

9. For the understanding of differences between administrators of both cities, see Saint Germain (1944).

10. In 1992, the opposition party, Partido Acción Nacional (PAN), won the governorship of Chihuahua, the majority in the state legislature, and the mayorship in various cities, including Ciudad Juárez. The previous administration was controlled by the ruling party, Partido Revolucionario Institucional (PRI), which has been in power in the country since 1929. It is surprising to see an opposition party ruling under the previous government priorities.

11. *Solidaridad* is a federal program intended to fight poverty. Solidarity funds are transferred to the states and cities in addition to the Convenio Unico de Desarrollo Social. Cities and states use *Solidaridad* funds for paving streets, remodeling schools, scholarships, and other projects.

References

Almond, Gabriel A., and Sidney Verba. 1963. *The Civic Culture; Political Attitudes in Five Nations: An Analytic Study*. Princeton: Princeton University Press.

Arreola, Daniel D., and J.R. Curtis. 1993. *The Mexican Border Cities. Landscape Anatomy and Place Personality*. Tucson: University of Arizona Press.

Barry, Tom, and Beth Sims. 1993. *The Challenge of Cross-Border Environmentalism, The U.S.-Mexico Case*. Albuquerque: Resource Center Press.

Beezley, William H. 1991. "Sons and Daughters of the Cisco Kid: Images of Mexicans in American Popular Culture." In *Reciprocal Images. Education in U.S.-Mexican Relations*, Paul Ganster and Mario Miranda, eds. México, D.F.: Universidad Autónoma Metropolitana-Azcapotzalco.

Busey, James L. 1985. *Latin American Political Guide*. New York: Robert Schalkenbach Foundation.

Chapman, Robert L. 1989. *Thesaurus of American Slang*. New York: Harper and Row.

Dorfman, Ariel, and Armand Mattelart. 1973. *Para leer al Pato Donald*. México, D.F.: Siglo XXI.

Fuentes, Carlos. 1970. *La muerte de Artemio Cruz.* México, D.F.: Fondo de Cultura Económica.
Ganster, Paul. 1991. "Percepciones sobre los costos y beneficios de la migración mexicana en el condado de San Diego." *Revista Mexicana de Sociología* LIII: 3 (julio-septiembre).
García y Griego, Manuel, and Mónica Verea. 1988. *México y Estados Unidos frente a la migración de indocumentados.* México, D.F.: UNAM, Coordinación de Humanidades y Miguel Angel Porrúa.
Goodman Corporation. 1992. *El Paso-Juarez Mobility Improvement Program.* El Paso. Mimeograph.
Haddox, John H. 1981. "The Mexico-U.S. Border: Some Ethical Considerations." *Latin American Digest* 15 (2).
Herrera-Sobek, María. 1979. *The Bracero Experience: Elitelore versus Folklore.* Los Angeles: Latin American Studies Publications, University of California at Los Angeles.
Herzog, Lawrence A. 1986. *Planning the International Border Metropolis.* Monograph Series, No. 19. San Diego: Center for U.S.-Mexican Studies, University of California at San Diego,.
Johnson, John J. 1980. *Latin America in Caricature.* Austin: University of Texas Press.
Koulish, Robert et al. 1994. "Immigration Authorities and Victims of Human and Civil Rights Abuses in Two Border Communities. The Border Interaction Project Study of South Tucson, Arizona and South Texas." *Working Paper Series* No. 20. Tucson: Mexican American Studies and Research Center, University of Arizona.
Koulish, Robert et al. 1994a. *Final Report of the Border Interaction Project: A Comparative Study of U.S. Immigration Authorities and Border Communities in South Tucson, Arizona and South Texas.* Houston: American Friends Service Committee.
Martínez, Oscar. 1994. "Human Interactions along the U.S.-Mexico Border." Paper presented at the conference "Border and Border Regions: New Roles in a Changing Global Context." Berlin (28–30 June).
Michener, James A. 1985. *Texas.* New York: Fawcett Crest.
Morris, Stephen D. 1991. *Corruption and Politics in Contemporary Mexico.* Tuscaloosa: The University of Alabama Press.
O'Connor, Patricia, and Nancy J. Nystrom. 1985. *Siestas and Fiestas. Images of Latin America in the United States History Textbooks.* New Orleans: Roger Thayer Stone Center for Latin American Studies, Tulane University.
Paz, Octavio. 1986. *El laberinto de la soledad.* México, D.F.: Fondo de Cultura Económica.
Ramos, Samuel. 1938. *The Profile of Man and Culture in Mexico.* Austin: University of Texas Press.
Roberts, Scott A., and Suzanne Holl. 1988. *Bloodlore.* Minneapolis: Bent Nail Publications.
Scharrer, Gary Richards. 1991. "Fix Border Problems Before Free Trade." *El Paso Times* (24 November).
Schmidt, Samuel. 1994. *Planning a U.S.-Mexico Bi-National Metropolis: El Paso, Texas-Ciudad Juárez, Chihuahua.* Mimeograph.
Schmidt, Samuel, and David Lorey. 1994. *Policy Recommendations for the Metropolitan Area of El Paso-Ciudad Juárez.* El Paso: El Paso Community Foundation and Center for Inter-American and Border Studies at UTEP.
Woodford, Protase E., and Conrad J. Schmitt. 1993. *Ciencias políticas y relaciones internacionales.* New York: McGraw Hill, Inc.
Zúñiga, Víctor. 1991. "Los locos del barrio: O la ostentación del estigma social y fronterizo en la pandilla de Matamoros, Tamaulipas." *Río Bravo* 1 (1).

Meaning and Significance of the Canadian-American Border

Roger Gibbins

1. Introduction

In any comparative study, there is a risk in stressing the idiosyncratic features of one's own case. To argue, for example, that the Canadian-American borderlands is unique could diminish its comparative appeal. Therefore, in the following analysis, an attempt will be made to identify a number of features that the Canadian-American experience shares with the more general phenomena being addressed in this volume. At the same time, it may be the very distinctive aspects of this particular North American experience that best characterize the Canadian-American borderlands and that have the greatest impact on the interplay between the international border and transnational regional integration.

This paper has a straightforward architecture. The first section examines the nature of the Canadian-American border and identifies some of its unique characteristics. The second section briefly discusses a number of ways in which the border has been eroded in recent years, ways which in most respects are not peculiar to the Canadian-American experience but which instead reflect more global patterns. The third section explores the complexity and asymmetry of the border region, and shows how the American border region differs quite dramatically from its Canadian counterpart. The fourth discusses the interplay of the international border with the dynamics of transnational regional integration. In conclusion, a tentative examination of the extent to which the Canadian-American experience sheds useful light on the more general comparative experience with borders, borderlands, and transnational regional integration will be offered.

2. The Canadian-American Border

The Canadian-American border stretches almost 8,000 kilometers from the Atlantic Ocean to the Pacific Ocean, and then runs along the northern boundary between Alaska and both British Columbia and the Yukon Territories. Its very length has given the border a mythological significance, at least within Canada, where it is lauded as the world's longest undefended border.[1] This phrase reflects the lack of significant geographical, racial, linguistic (except in the case of Québec), or religious barriers between the American and Canadian populations, barriers which a political boundary might reinforce under less fortunate circumstances. It also reflects the fact that there has never been a need for Americans to defend themselves against Canada, and that Canadians would be unable to defend themselves against an American invasion.[2] At the same time, Canadians have made a concerted effort to defend the border through political and economic means, a defense that does not take place along the border as such but that extends backwards into the national community to incorporate a variety of barriers to American economic and cultural intrusions. For example, the tariff wall between the two countries provided the foundation of the national economic policy for more than 100 years, and there have been multitudinous restrictions on foreign investment and American content on Canadian radio and television. Indeed, debates over the need to protect Canada from American intrusions have formed one of the fundamental axes of Canadian political life (Smiley 1980). In short, the border has been of great significance to the historical unfolding of Canadian politics, a significance *not* shared in the American experience.[3]

The national asymmetry with respect to the historical importance of the border is more generally characteristic of the Canadian-American experience. The American population, which is approximately ten times that of Canada,[4] is relatively evenly dispersed throughout the country whereas three-quarters of the Canadian population live in a narrow band within 150 kilometers of the international border. Unlike the situation in Canada, where major cities—Fredericton, Québec, Montreal, Toronto, Winnipeg, Regina, Vancouver, Victoria—are strung out in close proximity to the border, few major American cities are located near the border. Those that are, owe their location to the proximity of important geographical features, such as the Great Lakes, rather than to the magnetism of the border itself. While the Mexican-U.S. border may have been "a line that attracted people" (Hansen 1981: 34), this has not been the case with the Canadian-American border. As a result of all of these factors, the border has a much more limited impact on American life than it has on Canadian life; even its impact on American communities physically proximate to the border is slight.

For Canadians, however, the border looms large because the United States has been such a pervasive factor in virtually all aspects of Canadian life. As previously noted, the bulk of the Canadian population lives in close proximity to the international border, although this demographic distribution may stem from a desire to move as far south as possible rather from the pull of the border per se. The border itself is very porous; it is spanned by extensive family and friendship ties, corporate structures, media networks, trade unions, social and religious organizations, and professional sports leagues.[5] Although it would be an exaggeration to say that the northern two-thirds of North America is seamless, the seam created by the international border is all but invisible in many respects. In the words of McKinsey and Konrad (1989: 1), "the border acts more like a sieve than a shield."

The influence of the United States is felt not only in communities proximate to the border but throughout Canada. In this sense, the border penetrates the Canadian consciousness, identity, economy, and polity to a degree unknown and unimaginable in the United States. Thus, although Canadians and Americans may share the same international border,[6] they share it in very different ways. Only Canada can be described as a "borderlands society" (Gibbins 1989). If we think of the "borderlands" as a region in which the international boundary is blurred at the same time that its saliency is heightened, then the term fits Canada remarkably well. Despite a persistent Canadian search for national differences, "things American" are so extensively woven into Canadian life that the national boundary all but evaporates. As a consequence, Canadian-American comparisons, slights both real and imagined, and undercurrents of anti-Americanism play prominent roles in the Canadian political culture and broader social fabric.

Finally, it is worth noting here that the Canadian-American border is Canada's only border of any significance, whereas the Mexican-American border has been far more important to Americans, and to the American culture and media, than has the international border to the north. (Just try to find an American restaurant specializing in "Canadian food"!) The Arctic border has not been a significant part of the Canadian public consciousness, except perhaps during the 1950s and 1960s when there was a possibility of Soviet bomber attacks.[7] Thus, Canada stands in sharp contrast to a country such as Germany, which borders on nine different nation states. Canada has but a single point of national comparison, and that happens to be the wealthiest and most powerful country in the world. As novelist Margaret Atwood (1982: 380) points out: "One of Canada's problems is that it's always comparing itself to the wrong thing. If you stand beside a giant, of course you tend to feel a little stunted."

3. The Erosion of the International Border

The Canadian-American border, like international borders everywhere, is under pressure from a variety of continental and global forces that are eroding the "lines on maps" demarcating the international state system (Gibbins 1991). These forces include economic globalization, borderless financial markets, technological change with respect to the mass media, and transnational social movements such as environmentalism and feminism, which challenge nationally-idiosyncratic approaches to social values and public policies. This pattern of change was both symbolized and reinforced in the North American context by the 1990 Free Trade Agreement (FTA) between Canada and the United States, and by the 1993 North American Free Trade Agreement (NAFTA) among Canada, Mexico, and the United States.[8] While neither the FTA nor NAFTA fully replicates the corrosive impact of the European Union on international borders, both move North America down the same road.

The erosion of the border has often been cast in normative terms by Canadian scholars who see it as a threat to Canadian cultural values, to social programs such as national health insurance, to the remnants of domestic control within the national economy and, more recently, to environmental standards. In short, the erosion of the border has been seen as a threat to Canadian sovereignty, and to the distinctive national values sheltered by that sovereignty.[9] American scholars, however, have not identified a reciprocal threat to American sovereignty or values stemming from the erosion of the international border between Canada and the United States. Although the NAFTA debate evoked some faint undertones of the Canadian debate in the United States, the American fear was directed toward Mexico rather than Canada, and toward an economic rather than cultural threat. This difference in national perspectives is rooted in the reality that should the erosion of the border lead to the convergence of cultural values or social policy, it is Canadians rather than Americans who will do the converging. As Smiley observed (1988: 442) in the context of the FTA debate:

> The thrust of any free trade agreement between Canada and the United States will be towards the harmonization of the public policies of the two countries. It is overwhelmingly likely that the direction of the harmonization will be to bring Canadian policies into harmony with U.S. norms rather than the reverse.

It is also worth noting that debates over national sovereignty are a more pressing and immediate concern in Canada than they are in the United States, a difference that again makes Canadians more sensitive to the international border. This comes only in part from the fact that Canada is the smaller and weaker partner in the continental relationship. It also reflects greater internal instability in the Canadian case. The chronic national-unity crisis, and the continued uncertainty about Québec's future within the federal state, have made Canadians more alert to threats to sovereignty and national survival. In addition, the internal-unity debates have been explicitly linked to the evolution of the Canadian-American relationship. It has been argued, for example, that continental free trade may make the sovereignty option more attractive for Québec by diminishing the importance of the Canadian economic union. For the same reason, it has been argued that free trade may increase the inherently centrifugal forces of regionalism by increasing north-south trade while at the time reducing east-west trade within Canada.

For better or worse, there is little doubt that both international borders and the internal borders of federalism in North America are being eroded, as they are being eroded elsewhere in the world. But what does this mean for the immediate Canadian-American borderlands and for transnational patterns of regional integration? To address such questions, we must begin with a closer look at the border regions.

4. The Border Regions

It might seem reasonable to expect that the border regions of Canada and the United States would be a rich and extensively exploited area of comparative research. As previously mentioned, the border has been of central importance in the evolution of Canadian political life, and the bulk of the Canadian population lives reasonably close to the border. Moreover, there have been numerous border disputes between the two countries involving such things as acid rain, fishing rights, tanker traffic, and water pollution, disputes which could provide, and in a few cases (Lemco 1991) have provided, the fodder for academic discourse.

In general, however, the borderlands region has not generated a great deal of research,[10] nor has it played a significant role in the comparative literature on borders and borderlands.[11] Certainly there has been a marked indifference among American scholars, whose research has focused almost exclusively on the Mexican-American border. Canadian scholars, for their part, have focused on the more general penetration of American business, culture, and politics into Canada; the borderlands, per se, have been of little interest. (Of course, given that such a large proportion of the Canadian population lives so near the border, this distinction can get blurred.) There have certainly been comparative studies of Canada and the United States,[12] and there have even been a few comparative studies of regionalism in Canada and the United States (Gibbins 1982). However, there have been very few comparative studies of contiguous regions in the two countries.[13]

Regional contiguity is important because the Canadian-American borderlands are a collection of very different regional communities that reflect the sheer length of the border and the geographical complexity of the two transcontinental societies. On the eastern side of the continent, the border cuts through the forests and hills of New England and the upper Gaspé before hitting the St. Lawrence River just southwest of Montreal. It follows the St. Lawrence to Lake Ontario, and then threads for almost 1,600 kilometers through the Great Lakes before running aground on the western shore of Lake Superior. (At its southernmost extension, near Windsor, Ontario, and Detroit, Michigan, the border dips below the latitude of the state border between Oregon and California.) From the Ontario-Manitoba boundary, the international border follows the 49th parallel west across the Great Plains, the Rocky, Selkirk, and Cascade mountain ranges, and into the Pacific just south of Vancouver. At that point, it dips south to follow the Strait of Juan de Fuca around the tip of Vancouver Island.

The international border follows geographical boundaries for some of its length. Thus, the St. Lawrence River and Great Lakes provide a natural boundary of sorts between the two national communities. However, there is no natural logic to the international border west of the Great Lakes; it is a political line sketched across unbroken prairie and mountain terrains. As has been so frequently noted in the Canadian literature, the natural lines of the continent run north and south rather than east and west, as the border runs. The border, therefore, tends to sever natural geographical regions and communities such as the prairies and the west coast. At the same time, we must be careful not to exaggerate the integrity of those severed communities, or hypothetically severed communities. While it is true, for example, that Vancouver has had a good deal in common with Pacific Coast communities stretching south to San Francisco, the sense of an integrated coastal community has not penetrated very far into the British Columbia interior.

Niles Hansen (1981: 19) defines border regions as "subnational areas whose economic and social life is directly and significantly affected by proximity to an international boundary." Within this context, the American border region is both thin and insignificant. The relatively few substantial American communities in the region stand with their back to Canada; their economic, social, and cultural lifelines all flow south into the American heartland (Gibbins 1974). By comparison, the Canadian border region is thicker and more significant; the Canadian communities stand with their faces to the United States and their backs to the wilderness stretching northwards to the pole. However, it is not clear that the Canadian communities form a border region in the terms that Hansen suggests, for the most important impact comes not from the proximity of the international boundary itself, but from the more general proximity of the United States.

This difference is not just one of semantics, but is fundamental to an understanding of the North American border experience. Canadian values, culture, and economic activity may wash across the international boundary to a degree, but they do so with limited impact on the immediate border region and with negligible impact on the larger American society. By contrast, American values, culture, and economic activity wash across Canadian communities irrespective of their proximity to the border. American magazines, television, products, and services are as much a feature of life in Edmonton or Saskatoon as they are in communities closer to the border. Even environmental issues seem to follow this pattern. The problems of acid rain, for example, are asymmetrical: the United States is the major contributor to a problem whose effects are disproportionately felt in Canada (Menz 1992: 48–49), and the effects are by no means limited to the immediate border region but are carried deep into the Canadian countryside. It is for these reasons that Canada at large can be seen as a borderlands society.

The vitality of the immediate borderlands is limited by the fact that there are relatively few incentives for Canadians or Americans to cross just over the border. When Canadians go south, they are likely to go deep into the United States, to Miami, Palm Springs, Phoenix, San Diego, and Los Angeles rather than to Detroit or the small border communities in Montana, Idaho, or Maine. Canadians travel in large part to flee the weather, and this cannot be accomplished by slipping across the border. There was, admittedly, a brief flare-up of cross-border shopping when the federal government imposed the seven percent Goods and Services Tax (GST) in 1990, but this has not persisted and has not left much of a mark on the borderlands. There have also been few incentives for Americans to slip north across the border where prices are generally higher, the climate is just as harsh, and standards of public and private morality, at least in the past, have been even stricter. (For most Americans, a "weekend of sin" in Canada was an oxymoron.) In short, there has been little to support a flourishing borderlands economy. Whether the falling value of the Canadian dollar and recent provincial initiatives to build gambling casinos in locations easily accessible to American visitors will change this picture remains to be seen.[14]

It is useful, in the context of the borderlands economy, to compare briefly the immediate Canadian-American borderlands with the Mexican-American borderlands to the south. The latter are remote from the American and Mexican heartlands (Hansen 1981: 156), whereas the Canadian border region in many respects *is* the Canadian heartland. (Neither border, however, is close to the American heartland, which is dispersed across the continent.) Until recently, the Mexican-American borderlands were a relatively unpopulated region. As Hansen notes (1981: 159): "... the great westward surge of population following the Civil War tended to bypass the borderlands," and until quite recently the Mexican government actively discouraged settlement in its northern states. By contrast, the center of gravity of Canadian settlement has always been very close to the international border although, and as noted earlier, there is little reason to believe that the border itself served as a population magnet. The pattern of urbanization along the Mexican-American border is characterized by paired cities straddling the border: San Diego and Tijuana, El Paso and Ciudad Juárez, and Brownsville and Matamoros come to mind. There is little evidence of any similar pattern in the Canadian case and, to the extent that contiguous border communities such as Detroit and Windsor do exist, there is little evidence that they were created in response to the border itself. The Mexican border communities have been and remain economically dependent upon the United States, whereas the border communities in Canada, to the extent that they can be distinguished from other Canadian communities, are no more dependent than the national norm. Hispanics are increasingly important players in the politics of the American borderlands and border states (Ganster and Sweedler 1990: 423; Fernandez 1989: 2), a role that has no parallel among Americans living in Canada or Canadians living in the United States.

For all of these reasons, then, the Mexican-American borderlands constitutes a distinctive and relatively integrated cultural environment with transborder cultural institutions. As Ganster and Sweedler (1990: 423) explain:

> The presence of Hispanic populations on both sides of the international boundary, stimulated by important transboundary economic linkages, has encouraged strong social and cultural linkages. Although difficult to quantify, these social and cultural aspects of interdependence are nonetheless real and growing. In a number of areas along the border, binational cultural events are prospering. Transboundary cultural events in the fine arts, classical and contemporary music, and literature are ubiquitous.

By contrast, the Canadian-American border regions do not form a distinctive cultural environment; there is nothing in the linguistic or ethnic mix, cultural traditions, or even cuisine to set the regions apart from their neighboring national communities.[15] McKinsey and Konrad (1989: 4) maintain that "borderlands can be said to exist when shared characteristics within the region set it apart from the country that contains it: residents share properties of the region, and this gives them more in common with each other than with members of their respective dominant cultures." Once again, this description does not seem characteristic of the Canadian-American border regions.

Ganster and Sweedler (1990: 419) also note that the Mexican-American border region is "where the asymmetries between the two countries are most apparent," but also where "interdependence and integration between the two nations are most visible." Neither condition holds in the case of the immediate Canadian-American borderlands where asymmetrical examples of American wealth are relatively rare and where the economic interdependence of the two countries departs little from the national norms. In short, the international boundary does not demarcate significantly different economic spheres. Certainly it does not mark "a significant division between the First World and the Third World, between the developed world and the developing world," as does the boundary between Mexico and the United States (Ganster and Sweedler 1990: 440). In most respects, then, the Canadian-American and Mexican-American borderlands have little in common, and thus it is perhaps not surprising that the extensive research enterprise that has grown up around the latter borderlands has not prompted parallel lines of enquiry with respect to the former. The two borderlands share the United States, but not much else.

It should also be noted that the complexity of the borderlands is reinforced by the fact that the international boundary is between two federal states. Thus, for example, the border between Canada and the United States is also the border between Alberta and Montana, and between Maine and New Brunswick. Seven of the ten Canadian provinces abut the international border, as do 14 of the 50 American states. (Four American and six Mexican states are strung out along the Mexican-American border.) As will be discussed below, it is in the federal character of the international border that we find some potential for cross-boundary regional integration and collaboration.

One unique feature of the Canadian-American borderlands is the number of First Nation, or Native American Indian, reserves that straddle the border or lie in close proximity to it. The best example is the Akwesasne reserve that spans five political jurisdictions: Canada and the United States, Ontario and Québec, and New York state. Approximately 8,000 aboriginal persons live on the Canadian side of the international boundary, while another 5,000 Mohawks live on the American side. There are no longer immigration or custom controls on border crossings within the reserve, but a host of jurisdictional problems remain. It is not clear, for instance, which residents are entitled to Canadian health-care coverage, or where motor vehicles should be registered. As has been seen in recent years, effective law enforcement is virtually impossible when the jurisdictional confusion is coupled with the constraints imposed by the recognition of aboriginal sovereignty.

These borderland reserves are of considerable contemporary importance as a point of entry for goods smuggled from the United States to Canada.[16] It has been estimated that by late 1993 more than 60 percent of the cigarettes purchased in Québec were bought on the black market, and most of those entered Canada through reserves.[17] Because the Canadian governments were unwilling to risk confrontations with the reserves by moving to block smuggling, the cigarette black market created intense pressure on federal and provincial taxes. High taxes led to greater consumer demand for black-market products, and the demand led to more smuggling. Finally, in February 1994, the federal government and four provincial governments—Ontario, Québec, New Brunswick, and Prince Edward Island—substantially reduced the level of taxation on cigarettes in order to reduce black-market demand; the price of a carton of cigarettes in Québec, for example, dropped from 47 to 23 dollars. Thus, this peculiar feature of the Canadian-American border led to a direct reversal of decades of high-tax policy with respect to smoking, much to the horror of the anti-smoking lobby. It also led to an estimated loss of 450 million dollars in federal tax revenues at a time when the government was battling a 45 billion-dollar deficit. This was a significant impact indeed, and there is some indication that reserve-based smuggling of alcohol may have the same impact on federal and provincial taxation policy.[18]

In many ways, the reserve communities are the most interesting aspect of the contemporary borderlands, at least in the Canadian context. Part of this interest, however, arises from the fact that economic barriers still exist between Canada and the United States, barriers that can be circumvented through the reserves and thereby provide the principal economic impetus for smuggling. It is interesting to ask, then, what impact continental free trade might have not only on the reserve communities but on the more general borderlands. In all likelihood the FTA and NAFTA should further diminish the importance of the border regions as the international boundary becomes progressively less relevant for the movement of goods and services, and less important as a factor in determining where businesses locate. In short, proximity to the border should be of reduced economic importance. If there is indeed free trade, then there is little reason for American entrepreneurs to try to develop the border market. Why should Canadians be lured across the border when Walmart will come to them? At the same time, there has never been much incentive for Americans to cross the border to shop in Canada, and there is nothing in the FTA or NAFTA that will increase the incentive.

If the economic relevance of the Canadian-American borderlands is in decline, and if the borderlands are not a distinctive cultural region, then we might be tempted to conclude that the borderlands will remain of limited research interest. Before reaching such a conclusion, however, we should consider the potential impact of the border and borderlands on patterns of transnational regional integration.

5. Transnational Regional Integration and the Border Regions

In their work on the Mexican-U.S. border, Ganster and Sweedler (1990) identified a number of factors that can be expected to promote transational regional cooperation:

- a shared "security community"[19]
- economic interdependence
- relatively easy transboundary labor flows
- a shared cultural environment
- a shared remoteness of the border regions from the centers of economic and political power in their respective national communities.

The existence of all five factors in the case of the Mexican-U.S. borderlands has created an extensive and growing network of regional arrangements that span the border, and that have developed independently from the national relationship between Mexico and the United States. Regional integration in the Mexican-American borderlands, Ganster and Sweedler argue, has followed dynamics that, until recently, have had little to do with the larger international and binational relationship. While the dynamics of regional integration may be accelerated by larger developments such as NAFTA, they are likely to retain a significant measure of autonomy.

However, the situation with respect to the Canadian-American borderlands is quite different. While both borderlands are part of a continental security community, three of the remaining four factors promoting regional integration are relatively absent in the Canadian-American case. Although economic inter-dependence characterizes the larger national relationship between Canada and the United States, interdependence is not brought into bold relief within the borderlands. There is not, in other words, a robust borderlands economy that is a direct consequence of the international border. Labor flows between the two countries in general, and between the border regions in particular, are relatively constricted. The labor mobility often characteristic of border regions (Hansen 1981: 28) does not apply in this case. It is uncommon, for example, to find Canadian day workers in the United States, or American day workers in Canada, and there are no American plants built along the border to capture a mobile Canadian work force. As previously noted, there is little indication that the Canadian and American borderlands share a distinctive cultural environment. To the extent that they have a common culture, it is because they are both thoroughly enmeshed in a continental culture that sweeps across the border. The residents of the neighboring communities of Coutts, Alberta, and Sweetgrass, Montana, may indeed have a common cultural environment, but it is not an environment that is distinct from that shared by most of their respective national compatriots.

The situation with respect to the fifth factor—a common remoteness of the border regions from the centers of economic and political power in their respective national communities—is somewhat more complex. In their discussion of the Mexican-American borderlands, Ganster and Sweedler state (1990: 424) that "the two parts of this region are far from Washington, D.C., and Mexico City, and people on the border often feel neglected by the national capital when dealing with transboundary issues of local, but vital, concern." For the most part, this observation has little applicability to the Canadian-American case. The Canadian borderlands lying to the east of Manitoba are by no means remote from the national centers of economic and political power and, if the corresponding American borderlands are somewhat more remote from Washington, D.C., this remoteness has seldom been linked to the presence of the international boundary or to the neglect of transboundary issues.

Where the observation by Ganster and Sweedler rings a more responsive chord is in the western provinces and northwest states, where perceived neglect by the national governments has been a persistent theme in regional alienation. Certainly *western alienation* has been a characteristic feature of the political culture in the prairie provinces and British Columbia, and it can be detected, albeit in a much less virulent form, in the northwest states. It is interesting to note in this context that the tariff defense of the international border by the Canadian government was one of the historical mainstays of regional discontent among western Canadians. Western Canadians believed that the benefits from the *national policy* of tariff protection accrued for central Canadians while the agricultural community in the West carried a disproportionate share of the costs. It would seem, therefore, that the fifth factor is present to a degree on the western edge of the continent.

However, Ganster and Sweedler go on to note (1990: 424) some important consequences stemming from the remoteness of the Mexican-U.S. borderlands:

> Thus, over the years, border residents have evolved a whole range of informal arrangements to deal with transborder aspects of their daily lives. Examples that come to mind are seen in the informal, but regular, cooperation of fire departments, health authorities, and police to deal with emergencies without the intervention of either federal government.

While the border between Canada and the United States would not preclude such community cooperation in an emergency situation, there is no evidence that it is more generally characteristic of even the western borderlands. Hostility toward the central authorities has seldom been linked to transborder issues, and has not promoted the evolution of transborder institutional collaboration. The absence of paired cities straddling the international boundary has also removed both the necessity of and opportunity for such collaboration. The importance of such paired cities in the Mexican-American case is stressed by Hansen (1981: 156): "Economic, social, and cultural relations between the twin-cities have been more marked by increasing symbiosis than by the confrontation of differing systems. On both sides, formal and, perhaps even more influential, informal institutions have supported a permeable boundary." To the extent that the

Canadian-American boundary is permeable, it has little to do with the twin-city phenomenon.

The general pattern, then, is clear: There has not been a great deal of transnational regional integration across the Canadian-American border. Even in the West, where the condition of remoteness from national centers of power is best met, there have been few concrete manifestations of regional integration. At the same time, the door for such integration has been held open by the fact that both Canada and the United States are federal states. This means, in turn, the existence of provincial and state governments with the capacity to pursue autonomous initiatives of regional integration, autonomous, that is, from the actions or predispositions of the respective national governments. Indeed, there is some evidence of such initiatives. The Pacific Northwest Economic Region (PNWER), headquartered in Seattle, has been formed to bring together public- and private-sector leaders from Alaska, Alberta, British Columbia, Idaho, Montana, Oregon, and Washington, and to explore opportunities for economic cooperation.[20] PNWER has a population base of more than 16 million people—six million Canadians and ten million Americans—and its organizers claim a GNP that would place it tenth among the nations of the world. While the PNWER initiative has yet to generate formal intergovernmental institutions, it appears to enjoy broad and growing governmental support across the region.

PNWER may also reflect what can best be described as the subterranean "Cascadia" movement for regional integration. The movement taps a nascent regional consciousness, a history of regional alienation, and a common perception that the key to regional prosperity is to be found in the Pacific rim rather than in the continental economy. It is a response to globalization, to the diminished importance of national communities signaled by FTA and NAFTA, and to continued unease with the federal governments in Ottawa and Washington, D.C. However, it is not yet a movement with any institutional coherence or leadership, or with much public recognition or political support. It is more likely to find expression, and even then only occasional expression, in talk shows and pubs than it is in formal political arenas.

If interest in the Canadian-American borderlands is to grow in the years ahead, it will likely be in response to developments like Cascadia. If regional communities in the United States, and particularly those in the Northwest, feel estranged from the national community, then movements such as Cascadia may gain some momentum. If the American experience begins to replicate the Canadian experience with respect to territorial alienation, then the ground may be laid for the more extensive development of a transnational, regional community in the West. This could also happen if globalization makes national economic communities less important while enhancing the importance of regional trading links. Finally, support for a transnational regional community could grow in the face of renewed constitutional conflict and deadlock in Canada. However, while one can see glimmers of developments such as Cascadia, they are not yet a significant factor in either country.

6. The Canadian-American Border in Comparative Perspective

For those interested in borders and borderlands, the international boundary between Canada and the Unites States should have a natural appeal. The sheer length of the border, its historical continuity, and its importance to the unfolding of Canadian if not American political life all suggest that it should provide a rich research venue. It should also provide an opportunity to explore the corrosive impact of trade liberalization and new social movements such as environmentalism and feminism on international boundaries. In these latter respects, the Canadian-American experience could offer some useful comparative insight into recent European developments.

At the same time, however, it is difficult not to be struck by the unique features of the Canadian-American borderlands. The region is asymmetrical in a critically important sense: It is shallow and of relative insignificance on the American side of the international boundary, and deep and of great significance on the Canadian side. The underlying similarities of the Canadian and American societies have rendered the border of little importance in the United States, and of great importance in Canada. As the larger society, Americans have little to fear from the absence of a significant boundary between the two countries, whereas Canadians, as the smaller society, have much more to fear from cultural homogenization and economic domination. This asymmetry suggests that the real comparative value of the Canadian-American borderlands will be greatest with respect to other asymmetrical situations. Yet even here, the lack of significant parallels between the Canadian-American and Mexican-American borderlands suggests that asymmetry alone does not ensure comparative value. In the final analysis, the Canadian-American border and its regional communities may indeed be a unique case.

Notes

1. By comparison, the Mexican-American border is approximately 3,200 kilometers long.

2. The thought of an American invasion may seem bizarre in contemporary times. It is worth noting, however, that the United States is the only country to have invaded Canadian soil—at the time of the American Revolutionary War, during the War of 1812, and briefly at the end of the American Civil War—and that fear of invasion played a decisive role in the confederation of the British North American colonies into the single colony of Canada in 1867.

3. To the extent that the border has registered in the recent American political experience, it has been with respect to debates in the American Congress over tariff and nontariff trade protection.

4. The Canadian-American comparison in this respect is somewhat analogous to that between Finland and Russia, or between Denmark and Germany.

5. Eighteen of the 26 National Hockey League franchises in Canada's "national sport" are located in the United States.

6. As I have argued elsewhere (Gibbins 1989: 11), the Canadian-American border is "international" only in a formal sense. There is little feeling on either side that one's *neighbours* (or *neighbors*) are "foreign" in any significant way. The relationship between the two countries is more familial than international; the international environment begins offshore.

7. However, the defense of the Arctic border has been a major preoccupation of Canadian military policy. The defense of Canadian sovereignty in the area has also led to significant diplomatic tension between Canada and the United States.

8. NAFTA was signed in 1993 and entered into force on January 1, 1994.

9. Somewhat ironically, those who bemoan the erosion of the international border often bemoan the strength of jurisdictional boundaries within the Canadian federal state.

10. The most notable exception here is the Borderlands Project orchestrated by Lauren McKinsey and Victor Konrad, and anchored by the Canadian-American Center at the University of Maine. The project initially involved more than 100 scholars on both sides of the border. For a selection of the published research, see Lecker (1991). For an earlier study of the Windsor border region, see Lajeunesse (1960).

11. Duchacek (1986), for example , dismisses the applicability of the general borderlands literature to the Canadian-American case.

12. Duchacek (1986).

13. An important exception is Stephen J. Hornsby, Victor A. Konrad, and James J. Herlan, eds. (1989). For a more recent exception, see George Melnyk (1993).

14. In May 1994, Ontario's first gambling casino opened in Windsor, which is Canada's busiest point of entry with 42,000 border crossings a day. It is anticipated that 80 percent of the casino's 12,000 daily visitors will come from the United States. Jane Coutts, "Windsor Feeling Pretty Lucky these Days," *Globe and Mail*, April 28, 1994.

15. Perhaps the closest the Canadian-American borderlands come to having a distinctive cultural character is in the appeal by American PBS television stations for pledges from Canadian viewers who receive PBS programming through cable television. Thus, for example, Calgary and Edmonton are two of the most important funding sources for the PBS station in Spokane, Washington. However, the two Canadian cities, which respectively lie 300 and 600 kilometers north of the international boundary, can be considered part of the *borderlands* only if, as suggested above, we think of Canada as a whole as a borderlands society.

16. In the case of cigarette smuggling, it should be pointed out that the cigarettes are almost entirely *Canadian* products that are exported to the United States and then smuggled back into Canada in order to avoid Canadian taxes. American cigarettes have not been smuggled in any significant quantity.

17. Royal Canadian Mounted Police Commissioner Norman Inkster asserted that 70 percent of all contraband cigarettes entered Canada through the Akwesasne reserve (*Macleans*, February 21, 1994, p. 11). The Jay's Treaty, signed in 1794 by Great Britain and the United

States, allowed Indians to cross the international border with "their own proper goods and effects."

18. It has been estimated that almost half of the hard liquor bought in Québec comes from the black market. Lysiane Gagnon, "A Perfectly Sensible Solution to Smuggling by Indian Reserves," *Globe and Mail*, March 12, 1994, p. D3.

19. A security community exists when policymakers and the public in adjoining countries do not contemplate the possibility of mutual warfare, and when no significant resources are devoted to defensive capabilities against one another. As Holsti explains (1983: 441), Canada and the United States constitute a security community, as do Mexico and the United States.

20. PNWER's formal mandate is to bring together "legislative, government, and private sector leaders to work toward the development of public policies that promote the economies of the Pacific Northwest region and respond to the challenges of the global marketplace."

References

Atwood, Margaret. 1982. *Second Words: Selected Critical Prose*. Toronto: Avanti.

Duchacek, Ivo D. 1986. *The Territorial Dimension of Politics: Within, Among, and Across Nations*. Boulder: Westview Press.

Fernandez, Raul A. 1989. *The Mexican-American Border Region: Issues and Trends*. Notre Dame: University of Notre Dame Press.

Ganster, Paul, and Alan Sweedler. 1990. "The United States-Mexican Border Region: Security and Interdependence." In *United States-Mexico Border Statistics Since 1900*, David Lorey, ed. Los Angeles: UCLA Latin American Center Publications, University of California at Los Angeles.

Gibbins, Roger. 1974. "Nationalism: Community Studies of Political Belief." (Ph.D. diss., Stanford University).

Gibbins, Roger. 1982. *Regionalism: Territorial Politics in Canada and the United States*. Toronto: Butterworths.

Gibbins, Roger 1989. *Canada as a Borderlands Society*. Borderlands Monograph Series #2. Orono: The Canadian-American Center, The University of Maine.

Gibbins, Roger. 1991. "Ideological Change as a Federal Solvent: Impact of the New Political Agenda on Continental Integration." In *The Nation-State Versus Continental Integration: Canada in North America, Germany in Europe*, Leslie A. Pal and Rainer-Olaf Schultze, eds. Bochum: Universitatsverlag Dr. N. Brockmeyera.

Hansen, Niles. 1981. *The Border Economy: Regional Development in the Southwest*. Austin: University of Texas Press.

Holsti, K. J. 1983. *International Politics: A Framework for Analysis*. 4th edition, Englewood Cliffs: Prentice-Hall.

Hornsby, Stephen J., Victor A. Konrad, and James J. Herlan, eds. 1989. *The Northeastern Borderlands: Four Centuries of Interaction*. Fredericton, NB: Acadiensis Press.

Lajeunesse, Ernest J., ed. 1960. *The Windsor Border Region: Canada's Southernmost Frontier*. Toronto: University of Toronto Press.

Lecker, Robert, ed. 1991. *Borderlands: Essays in Canadian-American Relations*. Toronto: ECW Press.

Lemco, Jonathan, ed. 1992. *Tensions at the Border: Energy and Environmental Concerns in Canada and the United States*. New York: Praeger.

McKinsey, Lauren, and Victor Konrad. 1989. *Borderlands Reflections: The United States and Canada*, Borderlands Monograph Series #1. Orono: The Canadian-American Center, The University of Maine.

Melnyk, George. 1993. "Magpie and Tortoise: Regionalism in the Two Wests." In *Beyond Alienation: Essays on the West*, George Melnyk, ed. Calgary: Detselig.

Menz, Fredric C. 1992, "Transboundary Acid Rain: A Canadian-U.S. Problem Requires a Joint Solution." In *Tensions at the Border: Energy and Environmental Concerns in Canada and the United States*, Jonathan Lemco, ed. New York: Praeger.

Smiley, Donald V. 1980. *Canada in Question: Federalism in the Eighties*. Toronto: McGraw-Hill Ryerson.

Smiley, Donald V. 1988. "A Note on Canadian-American Free Trade and Canadian Policy Autonomy." In *Trade-Offs On Free Trade: The Canada-U.S. Free Trade Agreement*, Marc Golden and David Leyton-Brown, eds. Toronto: Carswell.

Border Regions, Integration, and Transborder Conservation Initiatives in Central America

Pascal O. Girot

1. Introduction

After undergoing a decade of war, disintegration, and impoverishment during the 1980s, Central America is witnessing a resurgence of innovative regional initiatives. A trend that began in 1987 with the Central American Peace Plan, earning the Nobel Peace Prize for the then President of Costa Rica, Oscar Arias Sánchez, produced in the early nineties in an unprecedented flurry of integration initiatives. During 1994 alone, the presidents of the Central American region (Guatemala, El Salvador, Honduras, Nicaragua, Costa Rica, Panama, and Belize) held no less than five summit meetings, culminating in the signing in November of the Alliance for Sustainable Development in Central America (see Appendix for this chapter).

Such a process of intense regional consultations, in an area at war only a few years before, is in itself noteworthy. However, questions remain as to how these sweeping regional agreements will result in tangible improvements in a zone plagued with abysmal levels of poverty, health, and economic growth (with notable exceptions). The emphasis on sustainable development as the new paradigm for regional integration comes as an innovative departure from previous regional initiatives. While the Central American Common Market experiment of the 1960s centered on fostering early industrialization through protective trade barriers and the opening of national borders to regional commerce, the present-day integration model aspires to join the North American Free Trade Agreement (NAFTA), and is centered on free trade and open borders.

Questions obviously arise. How well does sustainable development fare in a Central America open to free trade? How will the Central American economies compete by opening their borders to far more powerful partners to the north? What role will border regions play in such a scenario? Sustainable development as the paradigm of the nineties provides a challenging framework in which to analyze the effect of free trade on the environment, territories, and societies of the Central American isthmus. In this article, we will address critically some of the crucial issues facing Central America at the close of the century. Sustainable development as a very broad concept forces us to think ahead: What will Central America have to offer to its future generations in the next century? How can the integrity of their cultures, landscapes, economies, and peoples be preserved while participating in the structural overhaul underway at a hemispheric level?

A pivotal point of convergence of these regional initiatives has been, and will be, border regions. Whether closed to foreign trade through tariffs, or open to the free flow of goods, peoples, and services, borders will continue to operate as the safety valve for Central American economies. However, these regions are among the most destitute, socially marginalized and politically peripheral. But they are also the richest in natural resources, with unique cultural and biological diversity. Border regions have historically played a particular function in the formation of the territorial state in Central America. As refuge for marginalized populations, indigenous people, and *ladinos* (people of mixed racial heritage), border regions have traditionally been marked by contraband, political intrigue, armed conflict, and transboundary networks of all manner, including more recently drug trafficking. Border regions have functioned throughout the 1980s as the main receptors and assimilators of massive flows of refugees, mostly from El Salvador, Nicaragua, and Guatemala.

How can states undergoing processes of structural adjustment, with ever-shrinking national budgets and drastic reductions in government services, face the growing challenge of integrating, policing, developing, and protecting the margins of their national territories? Faced with a shrinking central government, local authorities, NGOs (nongovernmental organizations), and grassroots organizations are called on to play a more important role in territorial administration. Local governments in border regions are ill-prepared for assuming new tasks such as environmental protection, road building, sanitary and land use planning, and so forth. However, there have been some notable transboundary initiatives that, when combined, provide a promising alternative. The thrust of this article is to suggest that integration begins and ends with border regions. Strengthening local governments and fostering transboundary initiatives may help solve problems of isolation, insecurity, and environmental degradation. One of the main testing grounds of the Alliance for Sustainable Development will be, without a doubt, the border regions of Central America.

2. The Historical Role of Border Regions in Central America

The history of territorial formation in Central America provides a useful backdrop for understanding the role assigned to border regions. As in many other countries of Latin America, the process of national integration was late in coming and subject to the ebb and flow of political and economic events. In several countries, vast regions, particularly the Caribbean lowlands of the Mosquito Coast, still remain isolated from their respective national economies because of lack of access. The famous dichotomy between the Pacific heartland and the Caribbean rimland formulated three decades ago by West and Augelli (1966, 1989) still applies in much of the area. The dominant national cultures are generally based in Pacific and intermontane regions, while much of the Caribbean rim is still considered peripheral, both culturally and economically.

The contrast between densely populated highlands and sparsely inhabited Caribbean lowlands is evolving fast, and the process of agricultural colonization that began in the 1960s is reaching some of the most remote corners of national territories. While the agricultural frontier in El Salvador is estimated to have reached the political boundaries of the country in the 1930s, in Costa Rica the contraction of the agricultural frontier drew to a close in the 1980s (Augelli 1987). In Panama, Honduras, and Nicaragua, the agricultural frontier is alive and well and constitutes a key safety valve for agrarian conflicts as in many other Latin American nations.

The territories undergoing processes of agricultural colonization coincide in many cases with peripheral border regions. These regions, long neglected due to difficult access, inhospitable climate, and rough terrain, have functioned for centuries as refuges for displaced populations fleeing war, political persecution, economic indigence, and land dispossession. Their function as regions of refuge has fostered a unique combination of cultural and biological diversity. The co-existence between indigenous people and tropical forests in Central America coincides often with border regions, as illustrated by the Chapin (1992) map by *National Geographic*'s Research and Exploration. As we shall see further along, these remote regions constitute the setting for border parks and indigenous territories that are under increasing encroachment by *ladino* settlers. The refuge functions of border regions was most convincingly illustrated during the war-torn decade of the 1980s. As a reception and processing platform for internally displaced and refugee populations, border regions played a crucial role in the dramatic events of the last decade. Frontier societies have by definition a greater capacity to absorb and assimilate foreign elements than do most of their respective national societies (Girot and Granados 1993). A notable exception to this rule is Belize, in which the massive influx of Salvadorean and Guatemalan refugees over the past decade has signified a dramatic demographic transformation of its entire society. One could almost argue that Belize as a whole has functioned as a border region in terms of its capacity to absorb foreign elements.

Finally, Central America's border regions have also been marked historically by a limited effective control by central governments. The presence of transboundary plantation enclaves, established as early as the 1890s, across the borders between Costa Rica, Panama, Honduras, and Guatemala illustrate the scant control by nation states of these remote regions until the second half of the twentieth century. Despite being converted into some of the most intensive agricultural-production areas, few if any of these banana enclaves have resulted in the integrated development of border regions. Today, lax government control over these remote border regions makes them prime targets for drug traffickers and contraband operations.The impact of these activities on border societies and economies remains to be determined. However, the destabilizing effect of money-laundering through land speculation, not only in border regions but in most of Central America's urban centers today, can already be seen.

3. Regional and National Territorial Integration

The political history of Central America has been marked by the swing of the pendulum between unionism and nationalism, and initiatives for regional integration and the safeguarding of national sovereignties through protectionism (Pérez Brignoli 1989: Salisbury 1984). While the object of this article is not to document the history of regional integration initiatives per se, several elements are important to point out in order to understand the formation of the territorial state in Central America and its relation to larger polities.

Overall, an important distinction must be made between the political discourse regarding integration, and the territorial setting in which these policies are, or are not, put into practice. At the end of the colonial era, Central America was characterized by scattered nuclei of densely settled population, essentially in the volcanic highlands and the pacific seaboard. Although the colonial administration had regrouped the isthmus under the Captaincy General of Guatemala, the countries were poorly interconnected, and lived essentially in a state of local autarky. The experiment of the Central American Federation (1821–1842) foundered precisely because of the lack of any real territorial, economic, and social integration among isolated provincial polities. As a result, warring factions set the conditions for the emergence of nation-states, based on the territorial divisions of provincial boundaries (Girot and Granados 1993).

The use of colonial administrative limits as the political boundaries between emerging nation-states provided a fertile terrain for litigious and conflictual interpretations of colonial texts by jurists from neighboring countries. Until the mid-twentieth century most of the border regions were remote peripheral domains, and conflict over use and occupation emerged as in most of Latin America. A notable exception to this has been the boundary between Costa Rica and Nicaragua, which closely follows a potential route for an inter-oceanic canal, and was the object of intense rivalry and legal analysis throughout the second half of the nineteenth century. The dialectics between projected canal ventures and boundary litigation between Costa Rica and Nicaragua has been well documented (Girot 1994). In most other border regions, isolation and remoteness relegated them to a very marginal role in national affairs, even up to the present.

Following the break-up of the Central American Federation in 1842, there have been recurrent attempts at reviving the unionist spirit. Between 1842 and 1863 alone, there were no less than eight initiatives directed at reconstructing the Central American Union (Karnes 1982: 156). Discrete differences existed between Unionists, who sought the creation of a unitary Central American state, and the Federalists, who vouched for the creation of a Federation of Autonomous Nation-States. All these integration forces have emerged and subsided throughout Central American history, without ever really going beyond the rhetoric stage of political discourse. Several factors contribute to explain the failure of unionism in Central America. In the first place, scant attention was paid to the economic and social fabric of which to weave a regionally integrated whole. In this sense, the attempts at political fusion were constructed on very weak foundations. The opening up of Central America to the export trade during the second half of the nineteenth century, under successive liberal governments, confirmed the consolidation of national economies. The construction of export-oriented trade networks, essentially geared to the coffee trade, signified the consolidation of a road infrastructure that linked the coffee growing highlands to coastal ports, especially on the Pacific. The linkages between Central American states remained extremely weak until the second half of the twentieth century (Girot and Granados 1993: 9).

The giddy growth of export economies of Central America consecrated the model of the liberal nation-state and provided further incentives for expanding cultivated areas, predominantly for the coffee trade. By the end of the nineteenth century, the opening up of new lands for incorporation into the export economy had occupied most of the best volcanic soils of the highlands. The expansion of the agricultural frontier was bolstered at the turn of the century by the installation of banana plantation enclaves in Caribbean lowlands of Costa Rica, Panama, and Honduras (Boza 1994). These enclaves contributed to the construction of the export empire of the United Fruit Company, which dominated the region during the first half of the twentieth century. Several of these enclaves were clearly transborder operations, particularly between Costa Rica and Panama, in which Standard Fruit and United Fruit banana plantations literally straddled the boundary. To this day, these border enclaves constitute an illustrative example of how transnational corporation transcend political boundaries in practice.

By the mid-twentieth century, the process of national territorial integration was culminating in several countries of Central America. In El Salvador, for instance, the agricultural frontier has reached the political boundaries of this small country (21,000 km^2, as well as the limits of lands favorable to coffee production. In most other countries of the region, agricultural colonization has continued as a fundamental mechanism, not only of conversion of tropical forests into agriculture or pastures, but of integration of remote regions into the national economy. In the case of Costa Rica, the agricultural frontier reached its limits by the end of the 1970s. In Panama, Honduras, Nicaragua, and Guatemala the process continues to this day with varying intensity from one country to the next.

What was considered a century ago remote and inaccessible is today part of a peripheral but increasingly integrated region of the national territory. Perhaps one of the factors that accelerated the process of national integration was, paradoxically, the creation of the Central American Common Market during the 1960s.

The integration principle differs in many ways from the unionist doctrine of the nineteenth century. First and foremost, it takes as its starting point the existence of sovereign states and precludes any notion of political fusion or union. It places a crucial emphasis on economics as the main motor behind regional integration. The Central American Common Market (CACM) was designed during the 1950s and put into practice in the 1960s. The principal thrust of the CACM was to create a larger single market, eliminating trade and tariff barriers within the region and creating a single unified trade policy for the region. The creation of a regional market was the basis on which to build a regional industry aimed at substituting costly imports of manufactured consumer goods.

The integration experiment of the 1960s had a profound impact on intraregional trade networks and fostered incipient industrialization processes in several Central American countries. By 1980, intra-regional trade reached a total value of one billion U.S. dollars, and represented a fifth of the total trade value of the region (Lizano 1989: 285). The growth of national industries was significant, but regionally skewed. The main beneficiaries of the experiment were El Salvador and Guatemala, bolstered by a cheaper and more abundant labor supply compared to their southern neighbors. The principal losers in the regional venture were Honduras and Nicaragua, left behind in the race to control markets and secure an industrial base. Costa Rica, favored by a more up-to-date infrastructure and qualified labor supply, managed to remain afloat.

Many works have discussed the demise of the Central American Common Market (Cáceres 1980; Lizano 1989), and this article does not aim to address them. However, it is necessary to point out that one of the most important shortcomings of the integration effort was to have placed excessive attention on economic growth and commerce, neglecting the processes that affect the territories and societies and, between them, the border regions of Central America. Perhaps the best illustration of this was the famed Soccer War of 1969, which set Honduras against El Salvador in a short but intense armed conflict. The war was first and foremost a border conflict and had roots imbedded in the history of the two countries. With a land-poor and densely populated El Salvador neighboring a larger, less densely populated Honduras, the law of communicating vessels applied and exacerbated the historic migration of land-hungry Salvadoreans into Honduras during the 1960s. This process culminated in armed conflict over control of the *bolsones,* prized alluvial strips on either side of the meandering Lempa River, which separates the two countries.

The Soccer War of 1969 dealt a lethal blow to the integration effort, and by the mid-1970s the process had ground to a halt. The oil crisis of the 1970s, and the impact of the global recession that followed set the scene for a deepening social and political crises that culminated in the war-torn decade of the 1980s. Perhaps the greatest losers of the eighties were the border regions of the isthmus. Ignored by the process of industrialization and excluded from the benefits of commercial integration, border regions played a relatively marginal role, with few exceptions, in the economic articulation of the isthmus. There were only a few more border crossings in 1980 than had been at the close of the 1950s. Nevertheless, border regions acted as the main recipients of the increased flow of migrants and refugees fleeing war and economic collapse. The civil war of Guatemala and the revolutionary and counterrevolutionary wars of El Salvador and Nicaragua used border regions as stages for transboundary operations and bases. The Sandinista revolution in Nicaragua of 1979 was made possible in many respects by a solid, transboundary, logistical supply system. The Nicaraguan revolution closed a decade of deepening crisis in Central America with short-lived period of hope.

4. The Lost Decade of the 1980s

The decade of the 1980s comes as a stark reminder of the intrinsic vulner-ability of the Central American isthmus in world affairs, particularly in terms of geopolitics and macro-economic policies (Girot and Granados 1993). All of a sudden, Central America was the main focus of U.S. foreign policy under the Reagan administration. The crux of the policy was geared to the containment of the Sandinista revolution, in order to avoid the contagious effect such a movement could have on neighboring countries, especially Mexico. In practice, U.S. policy toward Central America included a trade embargo against Nicaragua, massive military aid to the Honduran and Salvadorean armies, and the use of Costa Rica as model of democracy and development. These policies were combined with deep structural problems of the region (such as distorted patterns of land tenure, *latifundios/minifundios*, and the social division of labor that accompany them), and a particularly aggravating wider economic setting (world energy crisis, recession, political polarization between the superpowers).

Paradoxically, the two countries most affected by war, El Salvador and Nicaragua, can be placed on opposite extremes of the population-land ratio. The largest and smallest of Central American countries underwent widely differing consequences of the integration experiment of the 1960s. While land tenure, access to land, and greater distribution of economic power was at the heart of the Salvadorean civil war, land shortage has hardly been a crucial issue in Nicaragua (the largest country of the region with 130,000 km^2). While El Salvador boasts a greater rate of urbanization and industrialization, and a far greater percentage of its economy is in the secondary and tertiary sectors, Nicaragua has one of the lowest population densities in the region, vast tracks of state-owned lands, autonomous indigenous regions, and the longest borders of the Central American states.

The impact of the war differed widely from one country to the next. While the most devastating in terms of human impact were the revolutionary wars of Nicaragua and Salvador, every single country in the region was affected directly or indirectly by displaced populations, either internally or across borders. Esti-mates are that between 1.8 and 2.8 million persons were displaced in Central America during the 1980s (Aguayo 1989: 21). Over a quarter of El Salvador's population was displaced during that period, with over 400,000 internally dis-placed, and another 350,000 refugees in neighboring countries (See Figure 1). The brunt of the movement of the refugee population passed through, and settled in, border regions.

The environmental impacts of a decade of war are more difficult to ascertain. While some authors have suggested that armed conflict was a violent form of conservation by stopping and repelling the advance of the agricultural frontier, much of the remaining forested areas of Nicaragua, for instance, are former combat zones (Nietschmann 1990), others argue that the massive displacement of populations triggered by armed conflict concentrated environmental problems in receptor areas, such as urban centers, border posts, and transit zones (*Epoca* 1985; OAS/DRD 1983).

The 1980s truly brought about heightened tensions at a regional level. Aside from the fratricidal wars of El Salvador and Nicaragua, Panama was undergoing a geopolitical upheaval that culminated in December 1989 with the U.S. invasion of Panama to capture General Manuel Antonio Noriega. A long and protracted civil war in Guatemala, and a latent confrontation between the Guatemalan government and nascent Belize, which became independent from Britain in 1981, also had great impacts. Overall, one can summarize the geographical consequences of the war years as follows:

1. The intensification of the armed conflict between El Salvador's regular army and FMLN (Frente Farabundo Martí para la Liberación Nacional) guerrillas had several effects. The war culminated in the occupation and creation of liberated territories in the departments of Chalatenango and Morazán (Lungo 1990). At its height, this armed conflict meant the displacement and emigration of almost one out of four Salvadoreans.

2. Staged in a larger territorial context, the revolutionary wars of Nicaragua (1977–1979 and 1981–1988) displaced far more population internally than they created international refugees. Nevertheless, with the intensification in 1983–1984 of the Contra-revolutionary warfare, border regions were the principal theater for armed conflict. The northern front of the Segovias, Río Bocay, and Río Coco, bordering on the Honduran border provinces of Danlí, Río Patuca, Olancho, and the Mosquito Coast, was the setting for the most violent armed conflicts of the 1980s in Central America. The southern front, which encompasses the middle and lower sections of the San Juan River drainage basin between Nicaragua and Costa Rica, was another transboundary battlefield. The 1983 campaign brought about the evacuation, as in the case of the Río Coco Misquito Indians, of the *campesino* population on the agricultural frontier (Girot and Nietschmann 1992). Much of the evacuated populations was then resettled in FSLN (Frente Sandanista de Liberación Nacional)-organized communities, thereby increasing the flow of migrants and refugees, principally into Costa Rica. By the mid-1980s, over 300,000 illegal Nicaraguan immigrants were reported (OAS/DRD 1993).

3. In Guatemala, a war of attrition between the army and the guerilla from the early 1970s escalated by 1978–1980 into total war along the border regions with Mexico. In particular, the areas of the Río San Pedro and Río La Pasión, all

tributaries of the transboundary Usumacinta watershed, were theaters of intense armed conflict during the early 1980s. Hundreds of thousands of Guatemalan refugees sought protection north of the border in Mexico and in Belize, transforming the demographic and social composition of the neighboring regions. Chiapas was among the states most affected by Guatemalan migrants during the 1980s. Belize's population literally doubled during the 1980s, due in great part to the flow of Salvadorean and Guatemalan refugees.

4. Although Costa Rica did not undergo any internal warfare during this period, it did lend its territory as a logistical support base for the Contra-revolutionary war during the first half of the 1980s. The increased militarization of Costa Rica's northern border was object of serious concern in a country that had abolished its army in 1948 (Granados and Quesada 1986). One of President Oscar Arias' achievements was to defuse this dangerous escalation, and disengage Costa Rica from the Nicaraguan war (Fernández 1989).

5. In practically all countries, armed warfare was essentially waged in, or supplied through, border regions. These border regions became the focus of international attention, and projects were quickly implemented to attend to refugee populations and the dire needs of border populations. As war vanished from the border regions, and from Central America as a whole in the 1990s, it also disappear from television screens. Unfortunately, Central America only makes the news when its is plagued by war, natural disasters, or some other calamity.

5. The 1990s and New Regional Initiatives

Neo-Integrationism and Its Limitations

The decade of the 1990s inaugurated a new era in Central America and was hailed by many as a period of peace, reconciliation, and reconstruction of national societies torn apart by war (Arias and Nations 1993). Several momentous political shifts occurred at the onset of the decade that have marked developments since. Two discrete processes came to a head in 1990. First was the Nicaraguan presidential elections in which Violeta Chamorro came to power leading a loose coalition of parties opposed to the Sandinista regime. The transition went smoothly. By the end of 1990, another major event occurred with the United Nations-mediated settlement of El Salvador's bloody civil war. Thus, by the end of 1990, the two deadliest wars of the past decade were settled through peaceful reconciliation between warring parties, both participating in and respecting the outcome of the electoral game. Settlements included concessions concerning the role of the armies, both the United States-backed Salvadorean and the Sandinista Popular Armies. An accent on mutually conducted, verified, and UN/OEA-su-

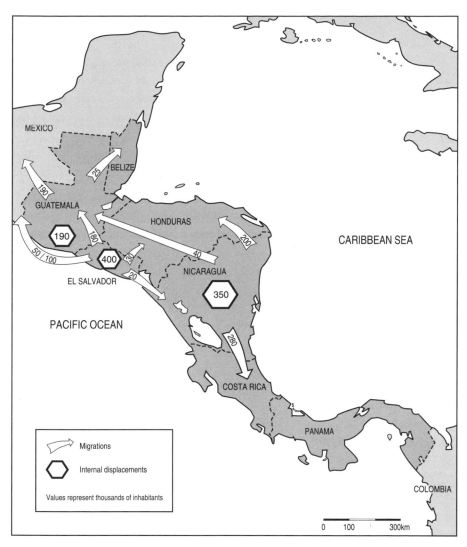

Figure1. Migratory Movements in Central America, 1980-1989

pervised demilitarization of society characterized both El Salvador's reforms and Nicaragua's political direction.

The year 1990 brought newly elected governments in practically every country of Central America. In August 1990, the presidents of Central America and Panama signed the Declaration of Antigua. This constituted a clear transition from the peace-seeking efforts of the Contadora and the Arias Peace Plan of the eighties. This time, the theme of regional integration was constructed through a series of summits and ministerial missions, resulting in the creation of the Central American Integration System (SICA). While it contains the usual dose of rhetoric and defines an extremely ambitious series of objectives, the latest version of the integration model differs from the previous in many respects:

1. It centers on economic issues essentially fixing regional economic union as a goal.

2. The integration process proposed by the SICA is driven by a free regional market, framed by a single tariff policy, with a major difference in its openness to the northern partners in NAFTA.

3. During the 1960s, emphasis was put on the protection of national industries and competition limited to regional partners. The SICA initiative implies joining forces to compete within a hemispheric free-trade bloc.

4. The economic bias of the system attributes social and environmental problems to economic policy and structural adjustments.

5. The opening up of economies weakened by ten years of war, as in the case of Nicaragua, to a free-market arena pitting Mexican, American, and Canadian businesses against each other, is bound to have dire repercussions, and affect their reconstruction effort.

6. The intra-regional disparities, already apparent in the 1960s, have increased. There is, on the one hand, an ever widening gap in living standards between Costa Rica and Panama. Costa Rica's GDP (gross domestic product) per capita is US$2,180 and that of Panama is US$1,930. On the other hand, there are ever deepening social and economic crises in Nicaragua, Honduras, and Guatemala. The 1991 GDP per capita figure was, in U.S. dollars, for Nicaragua $340, for Honduras $570, and for Guatemala $930 (OAS/DRD 1993: 14). Nicaragua is still the only country experiencing negative GDP growth, some fifteen percent for the period 1988–1993 (OAS/DRD 1993: 15).

7. The import substitution model has been replaced by one centered on commerce, import-export trade, and off shore services. The Panamanian example illustrates the model, with an extremely dynamic corridor linked to site-specific advantages of the Canal zone and a poorly articulated hinterland.

8. The model of integration proposed by SICA favors more the transisthmic, free-trade zone, and investment corridors as in the case of Panama, and increasingly Costa Rica, more than north-south regional integration through the Pan-American highway.

9. Needless to say, the proposal ignores completely the role of border regions, but the summit meeting declarations are replete with references to redoubling joint efforts in fighting poverty, corruption, crime, drug trafficking, and terrorism. These are precisely the ills that have been plaguing border regions in Central America for decades.

Still, one must make a clear distinction between the integration process proposed by SICA (which is still very tentative), and the initiatives derived from the regular summit meetings that have brought Central American presidents together several times a year since 1990. Despite its shortcomings, the new integration process has produced a flurry of parallel initiatives by civil groups, NGOS, local governments, and chambers of commerce. Both the private sector (FEDEPRICAP) and the local communities and *campesinos* (ASOCODE) have their regional institutional structures to participate in regional summits. However, the integration process is still very much centered on the executive powers of the presidential summits. Although the legislatures have their regional body (Comisión Interparlamentaria Centroamericana), the key parts of these regional initiatives are decided at a presidential level, after consultations with private and public sectors.

Sustainable Development: Risks and Opportunities

The culmination of the renewed integration efforts of the early 1990s came in November 1994 with the signing of the Central American Alliance for Sustainable Development. Framed in similar language as the SICA, the alliance does, however, introduce a strong environmental dimension to regional integration initiatives, which so far had been notoriously absent.

The Alliance is organized according to seven guiding principles (See Appendix for entire text), which include:

1. Respect for life in all its forms

2. An improved quality of life

3. Respect for, and sustainable use of, the land

4. Peace and democracy as basic forms of coexistence

5. The ethnic and cultural diversity of the Central American region

6. A greater degree of integration within countries of the region and others around the world

7. Intergenerational responsibility, which is one of the basic tenets of the doctrine of sustainable development.

The text of the Alliance then fixes four fundamental axes around which sustainable development will be organized. These are: *(a)* democracy, *(b)* socio-cultural development, *(c)* sustainable economic development, and *(d)* sustainable management of natural resources and improvement of environmental quality. Two new institutions have been created: the National Councils for Sustainable Development which, together, form the Central American Council for Sustainable Development. The creation of a permanent council designed to monitor the carrying out of these accords adds to the already long list of international conventions (including Agenda 21 of the Rio Summit in 1992), which require regular follow-up by the region's governments.

While the Alliance constitutes a clear departure from the traditional economic integration initiatives centered on markets, industries, and commerce, it remains extremely general in its scope. It places a new emphasis on the environmental and social dimension of development and, as such, provides a sort of guiding charter creating an overarching institutional framework within which many existing initiatives can be channeled. Although the text of the Alliance makes no mention of border regions, it is sufficiently broad in scope to incorporate a vision integrating local development and the conservation of natural resources.

It is too soon to judge the effects of the Alliance for Sustainable Development in Central America. However, new actors are emerging in the region. The insistence on reinforcing the full participation of local populations in matters of sustainability has fostered a number of forums that bring together government agencies, NGOs, and civil society over issues relating to local development, conservation, and production. For instance, in recent months there has been a number of regional entities, like the Central American Council for Forests (Consejo Centroamericano de Bosques), in which government officials in charge of the forestry sector, representatives of indigenous communities, *campesino* organizations, and environmental NGOs participate. A similar initiative is underway that is integrating the national parks systems of Central America.

Project Oriented Border Region Development

Although practically all of the official texts marking the new integration movement in Central America skirted the issue of border regions, the matter was discussed during several summit meetings held in the early 1990s. In the December 1992 meeting in Panama, the presidents decided to back an action plan involving the SIECA, the Organization for American States (OAS), and the Interamerican Institute for Cooperation in Agriculture (IICA), focusing on the development and integration of border regions in Central America. The emphasis of the initiative is captured by the phrase "integration through projects" (OAS/DRD 1993: 4). An argument in favor of project-oriented integration is that it avoids delicate issues like boundaries, sovereignty, and macro-economic policies. Moreover, this approach posits achieving tangible results in shorter periods of time. The border projects proposed during the Forum of Central American Vice-Presidents held in Washington, D.C., in November 1993 were geared around three interrelated objectives: (1) regional development of areas that extend over international boundary lines; (2) reversal of ecological degradation and implementation of programs of environmental management; and (3) combating poverty in areas of retarded development (OAS/DRD 1993: 20).

The project-focused border region development policy designed by the OAS is one of the official initiatives that underlines regional disparities, voicing concern about the contrast between free trade and deepening poverty levels in border regions. Specifically, OAS maintains that: "the extent and depth of poverty in Central America is incompatible with the Process of peace and democratization that the governments have embraced and could eventually undermine the model of openness and modernization now being pursued" (OAS/DRD 1993: 17). Central Americans are without a doubt poorer today than they were 30 years ago. The proportion of the total population of the region living in poverty went from 60 percent in 1980 to 68 percent in 1990, and the portion in extreme poverty increased from 38 percent to 46 percent in the same period. In some countries such as Honduras and Nicaragua, the 1990 poverty figures exceed 75 percent of the population while over half the population of El Salvador, Guatemala, and Honduras live in extreme poverty (OAS/DRD 1993: 18). Border regions are among the hardest hit by rural poverty and all the symptoms of underdevelopment, abandonment, and marginalization. The events in Chiapas and the economic slump of 1995 and 1996 in Mexico should serve as a sobering reminder that border regions can trigger change at an unsuspected scale.

Of the 18 border development projects listed by the OAS, practically all have a strong environmental component targeted at the last remaining pristine ecosystems of the region (see Figures 2 and 3). Among the two oldest initiatives, the Trifinio (the international park at the junction between the boundaries of Guatemala, Honduras, and El Salvador) and La Amistad international park between Costa Rica and Panama centered on a protected nucleus and geared actions around the preservation of these biosphere reserves. The Talamanca mountain range between Costa Rica and Panama was declared a World Heritage Site by UNESCO in 1990.

The above list of border region development projects reflects, on the one hand, a growing concern by central governments over the last remaining frontiers

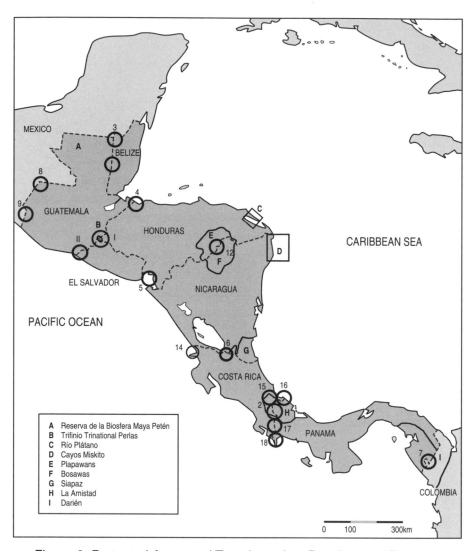

Figure 2. Protected Areas and Transboundary Development Projects
in Border Regions of Central America

Figure 3. Border Development Projects of the Early 1990s

Name of Project	Countries	Area, km^2	Population
2. La Amistad	Costa Rica, Panama	12,000	1,160,000
3. Trinational Maya Biosphere Reserve	Guatemala, Belize, Mexico	15,700	4,300*
4. Gulf of Honduras	Honduras, Guatemala	9,460	720,000
5. Gulf of Fonseca	El Salvador, Honduras, Nicaragua	8,000	390,000
6. San Juan River Basin (SIAPAZ)	Nicaragua, Costa Rica	12,000	190,000
7. Darien-Katios Biosphere Reserve	Panama, Colombia	38,500	250,000
8. Nenton River Watershed	Guatemala, Mexico	1,451	139,000
9. Suchiate River Watershed	Guatemala, Mexico	1,404	300,000
10. Upper Belize River Watershed Management	Belize, Guatemala	13,620	80,000
11. Paz River Basin Integrated Development	El Salvador, Guatemala	2,500	40,000
12. Bosawas-Plapawans Biosphere Reserves Management Plan	Honduras, Nicaragua	13,750	20,000
13. Bismuna-Pahara Lagoon and Miskito Keys Marine Park	Honduras, Nicaragua	8,000	200,000
14. Rivas-Guanacaste Ecotourism Circuit Development Plan	Nicaragua, Costa Rica	3,800	95,000
15. Talamanca Biological Corridor	Costa Rica, Panama	120	8,000
16. Lower Talamanca Coastal Ecotourism Development	Costa Rica, Panama	5,000	50,000
17. Chiriqui Viejo-Coto Brus Watershed Development Plan	Panama, Costa Rica	3,500	120,000
18. Chiriqui Viejo-Coto Brus Ecotourism Development Plan	Panama, Costa Rica	2,630	100,000
Total		151,435	3,866,300

* In Guatemala.

Source: OAS/DRD 1993: 22–37.

of their own territory. Even though the figures are approximate, these border regions projects involve about 10 percent of Central America's population and almost a third of the land surface of the isthmus. This indicates the importance of the territories at stake. On the other hand, these proposed projects are, for the most part, at an early stage of formulation and have involved scant participation by local communities and border region governments.

Mario Boza (1994), in a recent document, outlines a strategy from biodiversity and development in Mesoamerica, an area ranging from the Yucatan Peninsula to the Darien Gap. The major strategy coincides with the OAS development proposals in that it recommends the creation of a Mesoamerican Biological Corridor uniting 17 major biodiversity sites, all of which are located in or near border areas. This would enable preservation of some of the region's most extraordinary biological heritage.

Much of the remaining tropical forests of Central America have been under the custody and stewardship of indigenous peoples. At least 12 of the 18 projects outlined by the OAS involve regions predominantly populated by indigenous groups. Historically assigned a minor role in development planning, for generations most of these indigenous communities have fostered transboundary trade, kinship ties, and networks. They are by definition transborder cultures, as in the case of the Emberá and Kuna between Panama and Colombia, the Bribri and Ngobe between Costa Rica and Panama, and the Misquito between Honduras and Nicaragua. The degree of decentralization, true regional autonomy, and self determination varies enormously from one context to the next. Panama boasts perhaps the most progressive indigenous legislation in Latin America, some of it dating back to the 1920s with the creation of the Kuna Yala Comarca in San Blas. In Nicaragua, the historical struggle by the Misquito people to secure regional autonomy has been marked by distrust, intrigue, and, most recently, war. Any border development project that ignores the cultural and ecological intricacies of these marginalized regions is bound to fail.

The willingness by the region's governments to sacrifice centralized control of remote border regions and to share the responsibility for the long-term management of natural resources with people who have co-existed for centuries with tropical ecosystems is still tenuous, if not unacceptable, in most countries. However, it is becoming increasingly clear that the preservation of Central America's extraordinary biological endowment will not be made possible by the work of central governments alone (Boza 1994). Many border regions encompass ecological- and cultural-heritage sites that have been preserved for centuries through the presence of thriving indigenous communities. New mechanisms for involving local communities and regional governments in joint-management ventures are being timidly developed, while serious challenges, such as claims for regional autonomy and self-rule by border populations, remain. These create serious geopolitical tensions within and between Central American states. Furthermore, increased incursions by *ladino* farmers and ranchers are common and reckless timber and mining concessions continue to be granted in indigenous territories with little or no previous consultations in the regions affected. The 1990s will probably witness an increase in conflict between nation states and indigenous communities along border regions.

6. Conclusions

Bringing Central American integration down from the realm of political discourse to the stark reality of border regions is a necessary step, but one full of unpredictable liabilities. One can forcefully argue that integration begins and ends with border regions. For generations, they have witnessed the praxis of integration in their daily lives. Border residents have been the primary victims of the wars of the 1980s, as well as their main actors. Transboundary networks through kinship systems, commercial alliances, and contraband partnerships are activated or deactivated according to complex mechanisms. These are yet to be carefully documented for Central America. However, it is plausible to argue that therein lies one of the major potentials for consolidating long-lasting border development. Populations on both sides of political borders in Central America often differ in their appreciation of fiscal policy, migration, customs regulations, and trade restrictions. They often work around them, against them, or with them, according to their particular interests.

The historical role of border regions as refuges for displaced populations makes them particularly adaptable to the influx of outside populations. Their capacity for absorption was clearly demonstrated during the war-torn decade of the 1980s. However, the prerogatives of national sovereignty and the centralizing character of Central American states make for a difficult dialogue between center and periphery, between the capital and border regions. The economic development produced by earlier integration experiments was circumscribed to urban areas and adjacent commercial thoroughfares. Trade liberalization, and the creation of a Central American appendix to NAFTA (which is foremost in the political agenda of the region's politicians) will probably benefit most those areas involved in export/import activities, both in urban zones and across the inter-oceanic corridors present in most countries. One can wonder whether much of the prosperity promised by the proponents of these liberalization schemes will ever reach border populations.

The renewed interest in regional integration, particularly under the new paradigm of sustainable development, is occurring in a region profoundly impoverished by war and national disintegration. While the official language of integration is analogous to similiar earlier experiments, the broad orientations of the present-day initiatives differ significantly from the integration process of the 1960s. There is a clear emergence of a new set of actors, drawn from civil society in the political arena, originating from both the private/entrepreneurial and local/grassroots sectors of society. In a context of structural adjustment, ever-shrinking government entities face ever-increasing tasks. The transfer of responsibilities to civil society is a process fraught with imponderable outcomes in Central America. Local governments, peasant and indigenous organizations, chambers of commerce, and other nongovernmental organizations are assuming progressively a more important role in territorial administration.While in many countries, matters of national sovereignty and national security are still theexclusive preserve of the armed forces, there is a progressive transfer of responsibilities to local governments over natural resources, land tenure issues, water supply, and other locally managed systems.

The transfer of responsibilities from central governments to civil society will inevitably affect border regions. Although most local border region governments are ill-prepared for assuming these new requirements, many interesting initiatives are taking place. The project-centered approach for border regions' development can be easily criticized. It is still in the hands of technocrats and experts, and the very nature of these projects is seldom discussed and decided at a local level. The greatest merit of the approach forged by the OAS in the region is to provide the inventory of transboundary projects and point out the very critical environmental and social conditions prevailing in border regions. Whether these conditions will be reversed or preserved through projects remains to be seen. One would argue more in favor of processes that include the conduct of transboundary initiatives geared to resolve the problems many of the border regions have in common. These are often very basic and linked to immediate tangible results such as the access to markets, schooling, and medical care across political boundaries. The few ongoing experiments, such as in La Amistad between Panama and Costa Rica, have proven quite effective. Grand transborder development schemes seldom work, especially if they have been conceived in San José or Washington, D.C.

In conclusion, Central America as a whole is undergoing momentous change in the 1990s, and border regions are not immune to these transformations. Perhaps the most significant development of recent years is the greater role assumed by civil society in matters traditionally reserved for the political class. The reform and reduction of the state creates a vacuum that is being filled by a contrasting but vigorous series of local and national initiatives. The Alliance for Sustainable

Development in Central America reinforces this trend. It is too soon to judge its merits or limitations. These regional initiatives open, without a doubt, a new page in Central American history. Whether they will provide answers to such pressing needs is an open question. Surely, the border regions of Central America will provide a key testing ground.

References

Arias, Oscar, and James Nations. 1992. "A Call for Central American Peace Parks." In *Poverty, Natural Resources and Public Policy in Central America,* Annis Sheldon, ed. New Brunswick: Transaction Publishers, ODC, U.S.-Third World Policy Perspectives.

Aguayo, Sergio. 1989. "Las poblaciones desplazadas y la recuperación y el desarrollo centroamericano." In *Recuperación y desarrollo en Centroamérica,* William Ascher and Ann Hubbard, eds. San José: Trejos Hnos.

Ascher, William, and Ann Hubbard, eds. 1989. *Recuperación y desarrollo en Centroamérica.* San José: Trejos Hnos.

Augelli, John 1987. "Costa Rica's Frontier Legacy." *The Geographical Review* 77 (1).

Boza, Mario. 1994. *Biodiversidad y desarrollo en Mesoamérica.* San José: CCC-WCS/COSE-FORMA GTZ.

Cáceres, René Luis. 1980. *Integración económica y subdesarrollo en Centroamérica.* México, D.F.: Fondo de Cultura Económica.

Chapin, Mac. 1992. "The Coexistence of Indigenous Peoples and the Natural Environment in Central America*." National Geographic Society Research and Exploration* (special map supplement). Spring.

Epoca. 1985. "Militarization in Central America: The Environmental Impact." San Francisco: Epoca.

Fernández, Guido. 1989. *El desafío de la paz en Centroamérica.* San José: Editorial Costa Rica.

Girot, Pascal Olivier. 1991a. "Origen y estructuración de una frontera viva: El caso de la región norte de Costa Rica." *Geoistmo* 3 (2).

Girot, Pascal Olivier. 1991b. "Perspectiva canaleras en Centroamérica." In *La política exterior de Estados Unidos hacia Centroamérica,* José Luis Barros and Mónica Verea, eds. México, D.F.: Editorial Miguel Angel Porrúa.

Girot, Pascal Olivier, and Bernard Q. Nietschmann. 1992. "Geopolitics and Ecopolitics of the Río San Juan." *National Geographic Society Research and Exploration* 1.

Girot, Pascal Olivier, and Carlos Granados. 1993. "La integración centroamericana y las regiones fronterizas ¿Competir o compartir?" *Presencia* 5 (19).

Girot, Pascal Olivier. 1994. "The Interoceanic Canal and Boundaries in Central America: The Case of the San Juan River." In *The Americas: World Boundaries,* Vol. 4, Pascal O. Girot, ed. London: Routledge.

Granados, Carlos, and Liliana Quesada. 1986. "Los intereses geopolíticos y el desarrollo de la zona nor-atlantica costarricense." *Estudios Sociales Centroamericanos* 40 (Enero-Abril).

Kames, T. 1982. *Los fracasos de la Unión. San José: ICAP.*

Lizano, Eduardo. 1989. "Perspectivas de la integración regional." In *Recuperación y desarrollo en Centroamérica,* William Ascher and Ann Hubbard , eds. Durham and San José.

Lungo, Mario. 1990. *El Salvador en los 80: contrainsurgencia y revolución*. San José: Facultad de Ciencias Sociales, Editorial Universitaria Centroamericana.

Menjívar, Rafael, and Juan Diego Trejos. 1992. *La pobreza en América Central*. San José: FLACSO.

Nietschmann, Bernard Q. 1990. "Conservation by Conflict." *Natural History* (November).

Organization of American States, Department of Regional Development and Environment. 1993. *The Development of Border Regions in Central America*. Washington, D.C.: OAS/DRD

Pérez Brignoli, Héctor. 1989. *Breve historia de Centroamérica*. Madrid: Alianza Editorial.

Salisbury, Richard V. 1984. *Costa Rica y el Istmo 1900–1934*. San José: Editorial Costa Rica.

Segura, Olman, ed. 1992. *Desarrollo sostenible y políticas económicas en América Latina*. San José: DEI.

West, Robert, and John Augelli. 1966/1989. *Middle America: Its Lands and Peoples*. Englewood Cliffs: Prentice-Hall.

Appendix: Central American Alliance for Sustainable Development

Introduction

The Presidents of Costa Rica, El Salvador, Guatemala, Honduras, Nicaragua, and Panama, and the representative of the Prime Minister of Belize, meeting during the Central American Ecological Summit for Sustainable Development, in Managua, Nicaragua, agree that the circumstances prevailing in the region require a new approach and we have therefore agreed to adopt a comprehensive strategy for sustainable development in the region.

As indicated in the Declaration of Guacimo, we hereby set down our ideas in a national and regional strategy we have called the "Alliance for Sustainable Development," a comprehensive Central American initiative that addresses political, moral, economic, social, and ecological issues, which we have translated into a program of immediate actions through which we hope to become a model for other regions.

The Alliance for Sustainable Development is a complex of short-, medium-, and long-term policies, programs and actions that aim to bring about changes in the current development model, as well as in our individual and collective attitudes and in local, national, and regional policies and actions, in pursuit of the political, economic, social, cultural, and environmental sustainability of our societies.

The Alliance is a regional strategy to coordinate and build consensus on interests, development initiatives, responsibilities, and the harmonization of rights. The Alliance will be implemented through the existing institutional framework; it will not replace existing regional integration mechanisms or instruments, but rather complement, support, and strengthen them within and outside the region, especially in the process to make sustainable development the key strategy and policy of the countries and the region as a whole. The Alliance will strengthen and renew commitments that have already been assumed by the countries vis-a-vis the new pursuit of sustainable development in the Isthmus.

In this effort and commitment to sustainable development, as it applies to the Central American community, we pledge to make better and more efficient use of the resources of our region.

We believe that the international community can and should contribute to the sustainable development of Central America by changing its own attitudes, policies, and actions in the region. This will totally redefine the relationship between the international community and the countries of the Isthmus to make it mutually beneficial.

The Central American Council for Sustainable Development, which is promoting the Alliance, will promote and negotiate with individual countries, blocs of countries, and regions, as well as with regional and international cooperation agencies, through mutual agreement and with the support of the pertinent national and regional institutions, the signing of agreements that contribute to sustainable development in Central America.

Central America will define rights and responsibilities under Agenda 21, approved in Rio de Janeiro, with a view to becoming a model of sustainable development for all countries. The principles that guide us in the future will be respect for all life forms; steady improvement in the quality of life; respect for the vitality and diversity of our land; peace; participatory democracy; respect for, promotion, and protection of human rights, as well as respect for the cultural plurality and ethnic diversity of our peoples; economic integration in the region and with the rest of the world, and an intergenerational commitment to sustainable development.

The Concept of Sustainable Development

Based on the peculiarities and unique characteristics of the Central American region, we have adopted the following concept of sustainable development:

Sustainable development is a process that pursues progressive change in the quality of human life and which targets human beings as the central and primary target of development. It is achieved through economic growth with social equity and changes in production and consumption patterns, based on ecological equilibrium and the support of the region. This implies respect for regional, national, and local ethnic and cultural diversity, and the enhanced and full participation of all citizens, living together in peace and harmony with nature, not jeopardizing but rather guaranteeing the quality of life of future generations.

Principles of the Alliance for Sustainable Development

The following are the seven fundamental principles that we, the citizens of Central America, have adopted in our pursuit of sustainable development. They will be reflected in all the policies, programs, and activities promoted by our countries, individually or collectively, and by civil society, inasmuch as they are the basis of objectives and commitments of common interest.

1. Respect for All Life Forms

Life involves a system of ethics and a scale of moral values based on respect, personal responsibility, and consideration for all other living things and the Earth. Sustainable development cannot be achieved at the expense of other groups or future generations, nor can it threaten the survival of other species.

2. Improvement of the Quality of Human Life

The goal of sustainable development is to improve and guarantee the quality of human life. This will enable people to develop their potential and lead a full and dignified life. To this end, it is imperative that they be given security through human development, which will enable them to fully develop and participate in democratic processes, respect cultural plurality and ethnic diversity, and have access to education and technical and professional training that contributes to economic growth with equity.

3. Respect for and the Sustainable Use of the Vitality and Diversity of the Earth

Local, national, and regional development will be based on the sustainable use and management of the Earth's resources, as well as the protection of the structure, functions, and diversity of natural systems, on which all living things depend. Therefore, actions will be taken to:

- conserve life-sustaining systems and ecological processes that affect the climate and the quality of air and water, regulate the water supply, recycle essential elements, create and generate soils, and enable ecosystems to regenerate themselves;

- protect and conserve the biodiversity of all plant and animal species and other organisms, as well as the different genetic populations of each species and the variety of ecosystems; and

- ensure the sustainable use of natural resources, particularly of soils, wild and domesticated species, forests, cultivated lands, and marine and fresh water ecosystems.

4. The Promotion of Peace and Democracy as the Basic Forms of Human Coexistence

The following are essential for promoting peace and democracy as the basic forms of human coexistence: political freedom; the respect for, protection, and promotion of human rights; the struggle against violence, corruption, and impunity; and respect for duly formalized international agreements.

Peace and democracy are strengthened by citizen participation. Hence, sustainable development must include the strengthening of democratic institutions, mechanisms for participation, and the rule of law.

5. Respect for Cultural Plurality and Ethnic Diversity

To different degrees, the countries of Central America are ethnically arid, culturally diverse societies that constitute a great wealth that must be preserved. Conditions must be such that, within a framework of freedom, all expressions of culture can be developed, particularly the cultures of indigenous people who have descended from cultures that were subjugated during the conquest and colonization periods. The right to a cultural identity is a basic human right and the key to coexistence and national unity.

Indigenous peoples generally live in areas of great biological diversity, and their lifestyles are frequently in harmony with the natural environment. Their world view is compatible with the objective of sustainable development in that it perceives nature as inseparable from human beings.

Therefore, respect for ethnic diversity and the development of indigenous cultures, an objective in itself, is synonymous with respect for the environment. Nevertheless, if respect for the environment is to translate into an effective practice, people must have access not only to ideas, but also to possibilities for self-sustaining development.

Respect for ethnic diversity can only be achieved within a framework of peace and democracy, and by promoting access to opportunities for sustainable development.

6. Achieving Greater Degrees of Economic Integration among the Countries of the Region and Between The and the Rest of the World

Within the framework of globalization, the benefits of free trade must be accessible to the entire region, particularly through the promotion and implementation, by the more developed countries, of policies that will make it possible to establish, in the short term, a large free-trade zone and economic integration that involve the countries of Central America under suitable terms and that take into account the level of development of each.

7. Intergenerational Responsibility Vis-à-Vis
Sustainable Development

The strategies, policies and programs of the countries will foster sustainable development and the well-being of present and future generations, promoting human development in a variety of areas: political, economic, social, cultural, and environmental.

Bases of the Alliance for Sustainable Development

Sustainable development is a comprehensive approach to development that calls for parallel efforts in four key areas of this Alliance, as well as well-balanced progress in all four areas.

Democracy, characterized by the population's participation in decisions that affect society, requires that public policies, the patterns of production, and the ways in which citizens coexist be expanded and made participatory. Likewise, in order to successfully combat poverty, there must be economic growth. This means using social policies to upgrade human resource capabilities and improve economic opportunities for the most disadvantaged sectors.

Democracy and economic and social development will not be sustainable if they do not preserve the environment and natural resources. For this reason, the thrust of this approach to sustainable development depends on simultaneous efforts to strengthen democracy, promote economic growth with equity, foster social development and the sustainable management of natural resources, and improve the quality of the environment.

1. Democracy

There is a very close relationship between democracy, as the basic form of human coexistence, and sustainable development. Well-being and justice will be attained in Central America only in a democratic and participatory society where the rule of law prevails.

Support for the consolidation of democratic processes and the protection and absolute guarantee of human rights are expressions of respect for human dignity and, therefore, one of the main pillars of sustainable development.

The decentralization and deconcentration of the state's political, economic, and administrative activities will contribute to the viability of the process, as will the strengthening and consolidation of democratic institutions and local and municipal governments. It is also important to upgrade nongovernmental and community organizations.

Through this type of human coexistence, strong and lasting peace will make it possible to achieve sustainable development, which calls for harmonious relations among all human beings and between them and the environment.

2. Social and Cultural Development

The major social challenge is to overcome extreme poverty in the countries. Poverty is not only a manifestation of serious backwardness but also one of inequality, which is an obstacle to harmonious conciliation and national integration and is a potential threat to democratic coexistence and firm and lasting peace.

Social development as part of sustainable development in Central America is based on the criteria of assistance, solidarity, shared responsibility, self-management, and meeting the basic needs of the population; it is also based on training for and participation of the communities.

The communities and their organizations, intermediate-level organizations and local governments will have principal responsibility in these efforts. The success of sustainable development in the region will depend on the establishment and strengthening of the municipal structures responsible for community organization and participation, as well as on decentralized social services that involve broad participation of beneficiaries.

Efforts will focus on the following:

a) Investments in human resources. Here, priority will be given to basic education, preventive health, environmental protection, and training.

b) Execution of programs that support the family and high-risk groups, with a view to fostering integrated development of minors, adolescents, women, and the elderly;

c) Greater access to social services and social and economic infrastructure for lower-income groups.

d) More job opportunities. The aim is to establish the necessary conditions for generating production activities by providing more credit to micro- and small businesses, as well as technical assistance and other actions that improve economic opportunities for the needier sectors of the population.

Considerable emphasis will be placed on raising the awareness of the public as to the importance of promoting sustainable development.

Respect for all life forms and the resource on which they all depend—land—requires a value system that champions a national identity that values cultural plurality and ethnic diversity. Sustainable development also requires a set of attitudes, habits, and lifestyles that strengthen solidarity among peoples and, as a result, their sense of identity. Our historical, cultural, and natural heritage will be duly analyzed and appropriately used to promote sustainable economic and social activities, and creativity in the arts, sciences, and technology.

3. Sustainable Economic Development

Sustainable economic development in Central America will be based on freedom, dignity, justice, social equity, and economic productivity.

The sound and efficient administration of macroeconomic and sectoral policies, as well as the establishment of clear and consistent rules, are indispensable for achieving and maintaining economic and social stability. Our future socioeconomic organization will bring together everything that is necessary for peaceful coexistence of all members of society and the humanization of the economy; cost benefit values, environmental degradation and natural resource management will also be important considerations.

Economic infrastructure, especially electricity, telecommunications, and transportation, must be improved not only for boosting the region's economic productivity, but also for stimulating overall economic activity.

The economics of our region still depend overly on the exportation of a limited number of raw materials; this is reflected in the persistence of a substantial external debt. For this reason, our products must have better access to industrialized economies.

Our foreign debt and the cost of servicing it have seriously limited our countries' ability to accelerate growth and eradicate poverty. In order to reactivate development, an immediate solution must be found to the problems associated with the foreign debt.

Financial strategies will be developed for securing resources for sustainable development from both internal and external sources, and mechanisms will be contemplated for canceling, converting, and rescheduling bilateral and multilateral debts in accordance with the situation in each country. Other mechanisms could include the establishment of revolving or trust funds, as well as restructuring and reallocating national budgets to give appropriate priority to the objectives of sustainable development, and readjusting security and defense expenditures to bring them into line with circumstances in the countries and the climate of peace that is being consolidated in the region.

The sustainable development model pursued in the region will promote greater participation by the private sector and the full development of its creative capabilities. It will encourage direct investments to provide services to the most disadvantaged groups, as this will be a means of boosting productivity and competitiveness, and of mitigating poverty.

Initiatives will be developed to make sound use of renewable energy sources. expand trade and increase sustainable investments in production, encourage savings and the de-bureaucratization of public administration, provide support for research and the development of clean technologies through research centers that facilitate the development of technical-environmental standards for Central America, and initiate environmental certification of our exports. This will contribute to the industrial reconversion process currently under way in the region, and will make use of sustainable production processes that use preventive measures, such as ongoing environmental impact assessments, rather than ones that attempt to remedy a faulty situation.

Human resource development is both a basic requirement for improving productivity and an important vehicle for establishing greater social equity. Special emphasis must be placed on investments in education and health, especially for the most disadvantaged groups, as a way to boost productivity, enhance competitiveness, and reduce poverty in the region.

Growing tourist activity in the region requires that steps be taken to ensure that a balance be established between environmental protection and conservation and the development of tourist activity, taking into account the natural and cultural wealth of our peoples.

A strengthening and consolidation of Central America's commitments to integration will result in improved standards of living in the region, greater intraregional trade, the development of new markets, and a better position for Central America in the world economy.

To this end, all the countries must meet their commitments to halt protectionism and provide greater access to markets, particularly for those sectors of greatest interest to developing countries. Better access must be obtained for raw materials through a gradual dismantling of barriers that restrict the importation of raw and processed products from Central American countries, with a steady and substantial reduction in the different types of support that reduce competitiveness, such as production and export subsidies.

4. Sustainable Natural Resource Management and Improved Environmental Management

A major obstacle to Central American development is the depletion and deterioration of the region's renewable natural resource base. Water, air, and land pollution have grown at an alarming rate and, unless current development and industrial processes are reoriented, they are likely to continue. The most serious threats to the environment are deforestation and deteriorating water supply and quality which, in turn, are among the principal causes of disease and death among the poor.

Sustainable natural resource management and improved environmental quality provide protection for ecological processes and genetic diversity, both of which are essential for maintaining life. They also contribute to efforts under way to preserve biological diversity, conserve protected areas, control and prevent water, air, and soil pollution, make sustainable use of ecosystems, and rehabilitate those that have been degraded.

In order to ensure that environmental conservation is used as an instrument for implementing and promoting sustainable development, the countries of Central America pledge to design policies that are based on internal and external legal frameworks and that address land-use planning, energy, transportation, human settlements and population, forests and biological diversity, and measures for controlling water, air, and soil pollution, among others.

In view of the serious situation faced in Central America, it is imperative to formulate a policy and a master plan for the generation, marketing, and consumption of energy, promoting the use of renewable and alternative energy sources and energy efficiency programs, and for linking the electrical services of the Central American countries.

Objectives of the Alliance for Sustainable Development

General Objectives

1. To make the Isthmus a region of peace, freedom, democracy, and development, by promoting a change in personal and social values for building a model of sustainable political, economic, social, cultural, and environmental development, within the framework of Agenda 21.

2. To manage the territory in a sustainable and integrated manner in order to ensure the conservation of the region's biodiversity, for our benefit, and for the benefit of all humanity.

3. To inform the international community of the Alliance for Sustainable Development, and of the importance and reciprocal benefits of supporting this sustainable Central American model.

4. To foster conditions that will contribute to improving, on an ongoing basis, the capabilities and participation of society in improving the quality of life now and in the future.

These objectives are described in greater detail in the appendix, which is an integral and inseparable part of this Alliance for Sustainable Development.

Instruments of the Alliance for Sustainable Development

1. National Councils for Sustainable Development

The Governments have agreed to establish National Councils for Sustainable Development, to be made up of representatives from the public sector and civil society.

The areas of action and responsibilities of the National Councils for Sustainable Development in each country will be to ensure that national policies, programs, and projects are consistent with the sustainable development strategy.

2. Central American Council for Sustainable Development

The Central American Council for Sustainable Development will be made up of the Presidents of the Central American countries and the Prime Minister of Belize, who may be represented by their delegates.

The Council shall adopt and execute its decisions, commitments, and other agreements related to sustainable development through Central American organizations and institutions. The Council of Ministers of Foreign Relations, with the Minister of Foreign Affairs of Belize, will coordinate the implementation of presidential decisions, with the support of the General Secretariat of the Central American Integration System (SG-SIC), which will work in close coordination with the technical secretariats of regional subsystems and entities.

The Central American Council for Sustainable Development will establish mechanisms to ensure the participation of civil society throughout the sustainable development process, particularly the Advisory Committee, which is mentioned in the Tegucigalpa Protocol. We hereby adopt this Alliance for Sustainable Development, in the city of Managua, Republic of Nicaragua, on the twelfth day of October of nineteen hundred and ninety-four.

José María Figueres Olsen President Republic of Costa Rica	**Armando Calderón Sol** President Republic of El Salvador
Ramiro de León Carpio President Republic of Guatemala	**Carlos Roberto Reina Idiaquez** President Republic of Honduras
Violeta Barrios de Chamorro President Republic of Nicaragua	**Ernesto Pérez Balladares** President Republic of Panama
Representative of the Prime Minister of Belize	

Index

Index